The Blossoming of the Soul
Devotionals from the Heart of a Christian Counselor

Mark Graham, Ed.D., LPC

The Blossoming of the Soul
Devotionals from the Heart of a Christian Counselor

Copyright 2007, 2011, 2013 by Mark Graham, Ed.D.

Unless otherwise noted, all scripture quotations are from the The Holy Bible, Revised Standard Version.

All rights reserved under International Copyright Law. Contents and/or cover may not be reproduced in any form, except for brief quotation in reviews, without the written permission of the publisher.

Third Printing, revised 2013
Printed in the United States of America
Mark Graham, Ed.D.
Covington, LA

Graham, Mark
    The Blossoming of the Soul
    1. Devotional 2. Counseling, 3. Psychology, 4. Christianity

ISBN: 978-0-9779689-9-2

PREFACE

It's amazing how many times I have opened the Bible or a devotional book and read something that felt like a personal message from God to me, based on my current situation and need. And I have heard the same from countless brothers and sisters in Christ. [Perhaps I shouldn't be amazed at this, knowing that God is very present and personal.] Years ago I developed the habit of reading a devotional and praying with my clients at the outset of every counseling session. One lady glowingly responded at the end of our reading and prayer, "OK. I can go now. That's all I needed!" Devotional reading has been an immeasurable aid to my spiritual growth; and writing them even more so.

Devotional reading is one way of disciplining or taming our minds. For a few minutes, while we are reading and meditating, we think about God—what He has spoken to us; what He desires for us; His love for each of us; His marvelous, liberating Truth. When we prayerfully open the pages of a devotional book, we are drawing near to God, and He has promised to respond by drawing near to us [Jam 4:8]. When we seek sincerely, we discover the truth of this promise, over and over again.

Devotional reading is one way to cultivate the garden of our soul. We recognize many seeds in our thought life—good and evil. Thoughts don't tend to "drift" in good directions. Mine tend to drift toward vain fantasies. Devotional reading sows good seeds into our soul, and replaces those that can lead to destruction. *For as he thinketh in his heart, so is he* [Prv 23:7]. Our thought life shapes our character. God wants our character to be shaped by thoughts that are *true, honest, just, pure, lovely, reputable, virtuous, and praiseworthy* [Phil 4:8].

Devotional reading is also a means by which God may convict us regarding our areas of needed growth. All of us need to be confronted at times. Conviction might be described as loving confrontation that leads to a temporary sense of contrition, then to gratitude and peace. If we are not experiencing some occasional conviction, it means one of two things: We have attained perfection, or we are in denial. The willingness or unwillingness to suffer godly conviction separates the men from the boys as far as spiritual growth is concerned. But remember, God does not want us to live in perpetual guilt because of our imperfections. He loves us! He wants us to be mature enough to face the truth about ourselves; cooperate with Him in working on our areas of needed growth [using accountability partners as needed]; take responsibility for our problems; protect others from what is not yet sanctified in us, and then continue onward in the love, joy, and peace of Christ. Remember, Christ died to cover you in those areas in which, despite your best efforts, you continue to fall short. We do not presume upon His grace, but we are *so thankful* for it! We realize that God does not want us to wait until we are perfect to experience His peace and joy. If any of these writings cause you to suffer conviction or a sense of failure, press on until you get to the joy. It's right around the corner of forgiveness and grace!

My deepest and most sincere prayer is that God will use the words in this book to encourage, confront, heal, restore, awaken, enlighten, and liberate in all ways that are pleasing to Him and that bring forth more of His goodness within us. May these readings assist you in appropriating into yourself all that God has given us to experience abundant and eternal life and to live in the love, peace, and joy of Christ our Lord. May these writings be to your soul as the sun is to the bud—an encouragement to blossom into full bloom.

I am deeply thankful to more people than I can acknowledge here, but I must acknowledge some of them. My parents, Burk and Travis Graham, for giving me the unspeakable gift of a stable, nurturing, and reverent childhood. My wife for her faithful, steadfast love. She, more than any human, has suffered due to my character defects. And she loves me! God's grace and forgiveness abound in her and I am truly thankful. My sons, Marty, Brad [deceased] and John David, for teaching so much about God's love and inspiring me to become a better man. I pray that they will go further along the wonderful pathway of Christ than I have gone. Brad's death in December, 2011 confirmed the reality of the "Foundation" [devotional 252] in a profound and personal way. To my wonderful friends in Christ, Lynn and Phyllis Harrington, who have been such encouragers and fellow adventurers. To Chuck Schof, DDS, who is personally responsible for this book being in the hands of over a hundred souls. Roy Jenkins, who wrote the "Forward," has been a faithful friend, and in him beats as sincere a heart for Christ as I have seen in any quarter. And finally to my dear client-friends, who have blessed me by sharing their deepest struggles. The fruit of those struggles constitutes the fabric of these devotionals.

FOREWORD

I have called Mark friend for almost 18 years having learned with him in Seminary, taught with him in Bible studies, sat with him in church, raised a family with him, served in a mission church with him and shared adventures in canoes, sailboats and motorcycles. We have played guitar and sang together, sailed through storms together, walked through life-storms together, and sowed the Word of God together. We have talked about many things as we have shared everything from pulpits to campfires. Now we are reaching the stage in life where we are re-packaging what God has taught us to sow godly seeds into the lives of those coming along behind us. Mark is the real deal, and he drinks deeply from the living water. He serves it back in a pure form to anyone who thirsts. If you hunger for this living water, you'll want to read this book. He has been sending me his devotions in e-mails for the last two years, and I have been reading and saving them, being blessed by them.

As you will find out, Mark is a gifted healer, a spiritual doctor. He listens like Jesus did—past the words, and to the heart. As a pastoral counselor he uses his gifts from the Holy Spirit wisely, discerning the cause of the pain, and then gently applying the Word of God for instruction, correction and training in the right path to take. He works in partnership with God, praying, teaching and encouraging, always tied to the truth. He is a student of human nature and world events. He has taken what he has learned from the world of psychology, philosophy, theology and "real-worldology" to present a divinely inspired and directed medicine of hope for his fellow strugglers in this life, but always, always with his eyes fixed on the author and perfector of our faith, our Lord and Savior Jesus Christ, who healed him from his wounds.

Get a cup of coffee, take a seat, open this book and visit with my friend. Drink deeply from God's Word and you'll hear God speak to you.

Roy Jenkins, M.Div., New Orleans Baptist Seminary
Motocross Racing Chaplain, public school tutor, Bible teacher and author of two devotion books: "Devotions for Racers," "Racing Fuel for the Spirit;" along with the "Dirt Bike Ike" fictional series--A dirt bike racing adventure that helps young people see how to overcome adversity, find their purpose and achieve their dreams.

The Blossoming of the Soul

In Memory of
Brad Graham
1976-2011
Your laughter and love
still brighten our hearts.
Thanks for the
"Rainbow Perspective" [#189]
2Sam. 12:23

Marty
Thanks for being a wonderful son, big brother,
husband, soldier and father. Your discipline,
perseverance and compassion are inspirational.

John David
Thanks for your great humor and heart for helping
people; and for being able to hang out with your Mom
and I. Never doubt that you brighten our lives.

My most fervent and perpetual prayer is that you will know
Christ, and the infinite depth and riches of His Love, Peace and
Joy.

TABLE OF CONTENTS

TITLE	Page
Drawing Near To God	14
The Need for Solitude	15
The Kingdom of Heaven	16
Boyhood, Manhood	17
True Freedom	18
Kingdom Suffering	19
"And Peter": God's Amazing Forgiveness	21
His Holiness and Love	22
Sowing Seeds of Life	23
The Heresy of Jesus	24
The Focus of Life	25
Avoiding the Obvious	26
What We Have Inherited	27
The Hatred of Christianity	29
Trusting His Love	30
We Live What We Really Believe	31
Minding the Mind	32
The Importance of Our Sanctification	33
They Caught Nothing	34
Decadence and Decay	35
Victorious Acceptance	36
Stay With Us	38
The Source of Confidence	39
What We Owe	40
Life Changing Decision: A True Story	41
Joy Embracing Sorrow	43
Christianity for Dummies	44
The Futility and Sadness of Envy	45
The Bleak Darkness of Evil	46
Peaceful Warriors	47
Don't Get Choked	49
Who is Jesus?	50
Take Warning	52
The Most Dreadful Words You Could Ever Hear	53
The Daily Buffet	54

"I Rule Hammond"	55
How Bad Can It Get?	56
Pleasure and Power	58
Security In The Elder Years	59
Discernment and Setting Boundaries	60
The Body of Christ	61
Glorious Lucidity	62
Jesus Knows Your Stuff	63
Letting Go	64
Asleep In the Storm	66
Becoming A Family	67
Alive and Awake	68
You Can't Judge a Book By Its Cover	69
Full, Fat, and Forgetful	70
It's Not That Bad	71
Getting Free From Relationship Entanglements	72
Glorious Servanthood	74
What Does God Owe Us?	75
God Sets Limits	76
"Good! Now You Know How It Feels!"	77
Contrition Or Condemnation	78
Blaming the Sufferer	79
Healing Dissension	80
Please Don't Take Your Life For Granted	82
Living on Tips	83
My Son	84
The Wonderful Power of Jesus	85
Please Don't Take Jesus For Granted	87
Swallow The Frog	88
Loving Beyond the Comfort Zone	89
Obedience Leads To Healing	90
Are You A Good Person?	92
We Are So Blessed	93
Love Your Enemies	94
Love as Confrontation	96
Who Are You?	97
You Are The "Righteousness of God"	99
The Narrow Gate Into Eternal Life	100
The Blessedness of Mourning	101
Dullness of Heart	102
I'm So Overwhelmed!	103
Self-Control: Pathway To Fuller Life	104

Freedom Together In Marriage	105
Seeing More Clearly	106
Victory Beyond The Circumstances	107
How To Do What We Do	108
Abundant Life	109
The Most Important Thing In The World	111
How Alive Are You?	112
Freedom	113
A Clean Heart	114
Keep First Things First	115
Thoughts & Actions	116
Choosing Gratitude	117
Salvation Is Not Automatic	118
Do You Feel Free?	119
The Dark Side of Christmas	121
Loving or Impressing People	122
You Can Change Your Life	123
Housetop Living	124
It's Not Good To Complain	126
You Don't Have To Be Religious To Please Jesus	127
People Need The Lord	129
Don't Get Sidetracked	130
Feelings Do not Determine Reality	131
Power and Control vs. Servant Leadership	133
Death	134
God Is Not "Nice"	135
The Little Things of Today Are Important	137
Idolatry Lives	138
Joy	139
Variations On A Theme	140
The Solution	141
Keep Following Christ. Don't Look Back.	142
Be Prepared	143
The Dangerous "Rational" Mind of Man	145
Living Beyond Ego	146
Mysterious But Not Secret	147
Abundant Life and Joy	148
God In what Can Be Seen	149
Are You A Murmurer?	151
Jesus Doesn't Answer All Questions	152
Where do I Get My Needs Met	153
It's About Becoming	154

Abide In Christ	155
The Golden Rule	157
Be Proactive Spiritually	158
Whose Church Is It?	159
Be Still and Know	160
On Eagle's Wings?	162
Even the "Lone Ranger" Had Tonto	163
The Importance of Christian Fellowship	164
Approach God Reverently	165
Under God's Wing	167
Right Understanding; Courageous Living	168
The Kingdom In Our Midst	169
Because of Jesus	171
What Determines You?	172
Jesus Teaches Us How To Be Happy	173
The Problem is Theological	174
Dying To Live	175
Love: The Mood Stabilizer	177
Choose Your Suffering	178
The Importance of Evil and Death	179
Who Determines Truth?	180
The Judgment Seat	181
God Upholds The Righteous	183
Morning In the Heart	184
The Ongoing Warfare	185
The Power of Fellowship	186
You and Your Shadow	188
Dying Daily	189
Freedom	190
From Generation to Generation	191
Walking The Talk	193
Some Get It. Some Don't.	194
Where To Turn	195
The Faith Factor	197
My Cat Doesn't Need Me Too Much	198
The Nation's Immune System	199
New Beginnings	200
Thank God For Mockingbirds	201
Christians Are Responsible Servants	203
Peace On Earth, Good Will To Men	204
Are You Among the "Few"?	205
Godly Versus Worldly Sorrow	207

Momma (& Jesus) Said There'd Be Days Like This	208
Living For The Future	210
Manhood and Womanhood	211
God Speaks Through His Creatures	213
The Wisdom of Collaboration	214
Be Thankful In All Situations	215
We Are Not Victims!	216
Surprised By God	218
Sorrow and Joy	219
Our Life's Work	220
For God's Sake Don't Stop Loving!	222
Jesus Is In You	223
Thank God For Ruby Bridges	224
True Religion	226
Shield of Faith	227
Your Word Is Your Bond	228
The Creator Has Spoken	230
Coming Into Focus	231
The Light of The World	233
Martha & Mary	234
Beyond Salvation	235
The Fruit of Our Faith	237
Unflappable	239
Reality	240
Jesus Offers Us a Wonderful Opportunity	241
Ashes and Dust	242
Glorious, Liberating Detachment	243
Rainbow Perspective	245
Alienation	246
Clear Thinking; Soft Heart	248
Help My Unbelief!	249
Are You Getting Your Needs Met?	250
Friendship Is Very Important	252
Anger	253
Joyful Conviction	255
The Solution Can Become the Problem	256
What Is Truth?	257
Be Generous	258
Living the Faith	259
Living Peacefully	261
Our Divided World	262
Is It About You, or Is It About Us?	263

The Gift of Peace	265
Come and See!	266
Overcoming	268
The End	269
New Year; New Life	270
Don't Worry. Be Happy.	272
Get a Life!	273
Satan's Hatred	274
To Get Clean, Come Clean	276
Amazing Grace	278
Life Is Difficult	279
Don't Lose the Blessing	281
Are You Having Tribulation?	282
Relational Responsibility	283
You are Responsible for You	285
Know Your Enemy	286
All We Have Is Jesus	287
Sorrow	289
Conviction and Encouragement	290
The Discipline of Power	291
Three Healthy Responses	293
God and Politics	294
Staying Active	295
E Pluribus Unum	297
Staying Fresh	298
Rebuilding	300
Rivers of Living Water	301
The Evidence of God	302
People Who Love People	303
Pouting	305
Life Is Not What We Want It to Be	306
Greed	307
We Have All Failed	308
Good Friday	310
The Power of the Resurrection	311
True Success	313
What Do You Expect?	314
Beyond Romance	316
Civility	317
Refuge	319
How Much Truth Do You Love?	320
Thank God for Grace!	321

Drifting Into the Darkness	322
America's Hope	324
Politics, Power and Peace	325
Christ and the Law	326
I Don't Care	328
Shine His Light. Stay Safe.	329
The Big Picture	330
The Foundation	332
Jesus Resolves Division	333
Metamorphosis	335
Passion or Principle	336
Snake Bit	338
Guilt: Getting Free	339
The Purpose of Problems	341
Servant Leadership	342
The Joy and Light of Christmas	344
Do Your Part	345
The Final Word	347
Alphabetical Index	349
Readers' Comments	357
A Final Word from the Author	360

1

DRAWING NEAR TO GOD

Draw near to God and he will draw near to you [Jam 4:8a].

  Why do we have devotionals? I hope, when you read these devotionals, you are motivated by one thing alone: drawing near to God so that you will be practicing a deeper mindfulness of His presence, love, goodness, and grace.

  A little cat has taken up residence in our yard. She is not an independent cat. Every time I go into the yard, she wants to be near me. If I sit down, she looks at me in a way that lets me know she wants to sit in my lap. Most of the time, I invite her to sit in my lap, and we both have some pleasure as I stroke her soft fur. She draws near to me, and I draw near to her. It is good for both of us.

  Devotionals are one of the ways we practice our faith. We expose ourselves to God's revealed Word. The Truth of it resonates within us, and our personality is shaped in a wonderful way. We become more loving and lovable. We grow stronger in our areas of weakness. Our soul blossoms, like a flower in the sun. We discover deeper levels of peace and joy. Our heart smiles with the knowledge of God's wonderful promises: to work all things together for good; to be with us always, even to the end of the age; to never leave or forsake us; to give us the desires of our heart; to prosper us, and give us a future and a hope that will not be cut off; to enable us to grow through all our tribulation; and to give us victory over death. We are delivered from fear and the worries and cares of the world. We become mindful of the true priorities of life: trusting God, loving people, and being happy. We are mindful that millions of people all over the world are also drawing near to God. They are all our brothers and sisters. We are very thankful for them and for what God is doing through them. We pray for God's continuing blessings upon them, and upon us all. We pray for His will to be done on earth as it is in heaven. Through our devotionals and the practicing of our faith, we have communion with God and with all those through all the ages who have entered into His Holy Spirit through Christ our Lord. We are the body of Christ [1Cor 12:27] and the light of the world [Mt 5:14]. This is an unspeakably joyful Reality!

Oh Lord, my God, in this very moment, I am drawing near to You. Thank You so much for always responding by drawing near to me. Teach me more of Your wonderful Way. May Your Holy Spirit dwell more evidently in me today than ever before. Give me grace to love people with Christ's love more and more each day that I may know the joy that He promised. And I pray this for all my brothers and sisters everywhere.

2

THE NEED FOR SOLITUDE

For Herod had seized John and bound him and put him in prison, for the sake of Herodias, his brother Philip's wife; because John said to him, "It is not lawful for you to have her." He sent and had John beheaded in the prison. Now when Jesus heard this, he withdrew from there in a boat to a lonely place apart [Mt 14:3-4,10,13].

This was undoubtedly a very difficult time for Our Lord. John was his cousin. He had leapt in his mother's womb when the pregnant Mary came into her presence. He was the first to recognize Jesus as "the Lamb of God, who takes away the sin of the world" [John 1:29]. Perhaps most devastatingly, his death brought into sharp focus the dark and sinister power of evil and its hatred of the truth. John the Baptist had been beheaded because he spoke the truth—for no other reason. And Jesus was Truth incarnate. He was the Truth in human form [John 14:7].

He needed solitude. He needed to commune with His Father. And so do we. We are living in the same fallen world that Jesus inhabited. We fight our battles in daily living. We come under attack of the evil one. Hatred, greed, lust, fear, and selfishness still prevail in the world of our daily relations—and within ourselves. It is wise to stay in touch with our inner selves and with God. It is necessary to do so. Without solitude and communion with God, we cannot expect to live successfully. The world will overtake us, little by little, day by day—unless we abide in the Spirit that has overcome the world [John 16:33].

What a wonderful opportunity God has given us through Christ to have communion with Him! In Christ we have access to the Spirit by which the entire universe has come into being. We have access to infinite power, wisdom, and love. Nothing can defeat us in Christ—not even death, which is our final victory—the last enemy to be destroyed [1Cor 15:26].

Please do not neglect the wisdom of Christ, Who "withdrew…to a lonely place apart."

Lord, thank You for opening the door of heaven for me. Heavenly Father, thank You for communing with me in Spirit and Truth. You are all I need for freedom, peace, joy, and prosperity of soul. Today, may I love as You have commanded me.

3

THE KINGDOM OF HEAVEN

The kingdom of heaven is like treasure hidden in a field, which a man found and covered up; then in his joy he goes and sells all that he has and buys that field [Mt 13:44].

The two phrases that stand out to me in this statement of our Lord are: "in his joy" and "all that he has." I underline them in my mind.

When we get a taste of the Kingdom of Heaven, we realize that it is better than anything we have ever known. Why should this surprise us, knowing that God is infinitely powerful, creative, and loving? What He has done for us, and what He is doing for us is beyond imagination. And yet we can experience it. We can experience the Kingdom of God! And when we do, there is joy beyond anything we have ever known. And we know that nothing else on earth, nothing within the realm of our possessions can come close to it in value. And so we *joyfully* go and sell *everything we have* to purchase this one Thing.

This "joyfully selling everything we have" is a lifelong process. All through our lives we may find that we are holding on to something of this world. Perhaps we are attached to our money, our marriage, youth, prestige, certain pleasures, or our life. Whatever we are attached to will deter us in the onward march of the Kingdom and in the unequaled freedom, peace, and joy that are exclusively discovered there. Like Abraham we must put our Isaac on the altar in order to know the blessings of God [Gn 22]. We are called to be willing to joyfully give up everything for the Kingdom of God. This is not only a reasonable thing to do; when we taste the goodness of the Kingdom—when we begin to see the Truth of Christ, we *desire* the Kingdom more than anything. We want to live always in the peace, joy, and freedom of Christ. We run as fast as we can. We sell everything. We have a big smile on our face and in our heart. We run joyfully into the arms of Christ, leaving everything behind. We find everything in Him. We want everyone—even our enemies—to know this great freedom and joy. He is the only Life that truly exists. Everything else has been a delusion and is passing away. We are like the blind man who has been given sight. We want to tell everyone.

Lord, thank You for giving me sight. Thank You for Your willingness to make a horrific sacrifice to open Heaven and the Kingdom of God to me. I will sell all that I have, and I will follow You, my gentle Master and Friend for You are the Way, the Truth and the Life.

4

BOYHOOD, MANHOOD

When I was a child, I spoke as a child, I understood as a child, I thought as a child: but when I became a man, I put away childish things [1Cor 13:11].

There is therefore now no condemnation for those who are in Christ Jesus [Rom 8:1].

I think I have been more of a boy trying to be a man than I have been a man. The crosses of manhood are difficult to bear. You must learn to love and be faithful to—and even be thankful for—one imperfect woman. You must put the needs of your children above your own. You must come to accept that your vocation is not the most important thing in your world. You must cultivate humility. You must be willing to work on others' behalf and get nothing—in this life—in return. These are tough crosses to bear. I will frequently pick up one of them and start up the hill only to notice a beautiful flower blooming by the path with a honeybee; or an assassin bug waiting to ambush a honeybee. How can I not stop and look deeply into this beauty? Deep in my soul I am saying, "Thank You, God, for such a magnificent creation." Meanwhile, something is not getting done.

When I come to myself, I feel a little guilty. I resume up the hill. I am so profoundly thankful that Jesus went the whole distance for me without faltering so that I can enjoy salvation and freedom from condemnation even though I am an imperfect boy/man. And in some mysterious way that in no way gets me off the hook of being a responsible man, I sense my Heavenly Father's delight in me as I delight in His beautiful creation, my cross lying temporarily on the side of the road.

Thank You, Lord. Thank You. May I be eternally thankful to You.

5

TRUE FREEDOM

"The Spirit of the Lord is upon me, because he has anointed me to preach good news to the poor. He has sent me to proclaim release to the captives and recovering of sight to the blind, to set at liberty those who are oppressed, to proclaim the acceptable year of the Lord" [Lk 4:18-19].

Jesus read from the Scripture in the synagogue. He read from what is now designated as Isaiah 61, and then stated that this prophecy was being fulfilled before their very eyes. He had come to deliver the captives and set at liberty those who were oppressed. This message was not well received. They knew him, and they knew where he had grown up. It was just too much to believe that this son of Joseph and Mary could be the Messiah. So they angrily drove Him out of the synagogue. This persecution would continue and culminate in His crucifixion.

We have a strange tendency to defend our familiar ways of seeing things even when they do not bring us happiness and freedom. When we defend our little egoistic ways of seeing things, we create a very small world for ourselves.

We can become trapped in the world of our small egos. The Pharisees were defending their power and control. Jesus was threatening their familiar way of seeing things—and their power and control. He spoke with true authority and therefore infringed upon the world on which they had staked an exclusive claim. Jesus sets us free. He is the door to life in the Spirit—a life that is eternal and as big as the universe. But we have to let go of our little egos, and this is not so easy to do. Some people, like some of the Pharisees, are never able to do it, and they condemn themselves to life in the prison cell of egoistic blindness.

The Pharisees loved the respect of people. They loved to teach, to be in the place of authority, and to be envied. They had God—so they believed—in a neat, little, well-defined box, and they could take Him out and display Him to the people at will. Everything was under control. Much religion is like this today. Pharisaism is alive and well. There are still blind leaders of the blind [Mt 15:14], but Jesus will set us free—completely free—even from religious enslavement.

But we must be willing to completely submit to His compassionate, wise, and benevolent authority. He is God, and we are not. He is the Lord. When we bow to Him, we discover the freedom for which we were born. We discover our rightful place in the universe. We discover our true selves. We are free from the prison cell of self—free to own and explore the universe that belongs to our Father, Who owns all and gives liberally all good gifts to His children. But from Whom we can take nothing.

Lord, thank You for setting me free with an ever-growing liberty. May all come to know this freedom.

6

KINGDOM SUFFERING

More than that, we rejoice in our sufferings, knowing that suffering produces endurance, and endurance produces character, and character produces hope, and hope does not disappoint us, because God's love has been poured into our hearts through the Holy Spirit which has been given to us [Rom 5:3-5].

We rejoice in our sufferings. In fact, there is no living without suffering. We are born in a suffering way, and we are born into a suffering way. No matter how hard we try, how good we get, how smart, rich or healthy—<u>we will suffer</u>. We cannot avoid it. We and our loved ones suffer illness, injury, injustice, crime, accidents, routine responsibilities, life in an imperfect world, and eventually, without fail, death—maybe quick, maybe lingering.

In faith we are able to sincerely rejoice in our sufferings because we know a loving, attentive God, whose ways and thoughts are beyond ours, allows them. We accept that we cannot understand everything about an infinite, loving God, but we never let go of our faith in Him *as* a loving God Who knows what He is doing.

And we can see with our eyes some of the goodness of suffering. We see the principle of "no pain, no gain" in many arenas of life. Everything truly valuable involves something of difficulty and hardship—and the harder or more skillful the work, usually the greater the gain. The suffering of psycho-spiritual growth (confession, repentance, forgiveness, obedience, service, etc.) produces the fruit of the Spirit (patience, peace, joy, faith, etc.). Diligence in the suffering of exercise yields a healthier body and its associated blessings.

But there is suffering that seems useless, unnecessary, and non-productive. We must continue in faith and use our <u>wills</u> to make this suffering count for growth—perseverance in faith, growth in character, and hope for a better day. In this way, no suffering is useless. It all becomes very valuable to us. We do not resent it. We do not dread it. We do not fear it. We know it will come. We accept it and by the Holy Spirit turn it to our and the world's advantage, following the example of Christ. We see, in the Spirit that it is all very necessary and helpful, and we rejoice in our newfound freedom from the <u>drudgery</u> of suffering—which is the dreading, resenting, and fearing of it. We rejoice in the whole of life—and how suffering fits perfectly into the whole wonderful scheme of things. We are free! Life is better than we have ever known. God is good beyond our comprehension. All is well.

Please awaken me, Lord, in my times of suffering. Awaken me to the reality of 'all is well.'

7

"AND PETER": GOD'S AMAZING FORGIVENESS

And he said to them, "Do not be amazed; you seek Jesus of Nazareth, who was crucified. He has risen, he is not here; see the place where they laid him. But go, tell his disciples and Peter that he is going before you to Galilee; there you will see him, as he told you" [Mk 16:6-7].

The phrase in verse 7, "and Peter," carries a tremendous load of meaning. Remember, Peter had totally wimped out. On three occasions, while Jesus was going through the dreadful ordeal leading up to His crucifixion, Peter had denied that he knew His Lord—the one who had healed his mother-in-law; enabled him to walk on water; raised Lazarus from the dead in his presence; been transformed before his eyes into His glorious heavenly appearance; and performed many miracles. But when the chips were down and Peter's life was on the line, he—well he did what many of us would probably do—he preserved his own life by denying the Truth. Afterwards, he "wept bitterly" [Mt 26:75] remembering that Jesus had told him that he would deny Him.

And now the women, Mary Magdalene, Mary the mother of James, and Salome had discovered that He had arisen, and the Angel told them to go and tell the disciples **and Peter**, that hope was not lost; Jesus was still at work; they were going to meet with Him. And Peter was not only *not excluded* but also was specifically *included* in those with whom Jesus would commune.

How many times have you failed in following Him in His loving, compassionate, and courageous Way? How many times have you "wimped out" in loving people in His name? It doesn't matter. He forgives. You're still included. No need to cower in the corner weeping tears of failure. Arise. Let us go and meet Him where He has summoned us. We have work to do for His glorious Kingdom.

Lord, Your forgiveness is most amazing to us. Please help us not to take Your mercy for granted. Help us to love more because we are forgiven for so much.

8

HIS HOLINESS AND LOVE

But when Simon Peter saw it, he fell down at Jesus' knees, saying, "Depart from me, for I am a sinful man, O Lord." And Jesus said to Simon, "Do not be afraid; henceforth you will be catching men" [Lk 5:8,10].

Peter's reaction when he saw deeply into Who Jesus is, calls us to mindfulness of His Holiness and of our unworthiness. As far as we know, Peter was not a murderer, spouse-abuser, alcoholic, adulterer, or thief. He was a faithful Jew [Act 10:14]—a fisherman trying to support his family. Yet he did not feel worthy to stand in Christ's presence. He did not think of himself as a good man worthy to be a disciple.

Peter had a good understanding; the same understanding that all of us should have if we really see Jesus as He is. If Jesus were to appear today in the flesh, I can imagine some people walking up to Him, reaching out to shake His hand, and thanking Him for being such a wonderful teacher and helper of the human family. This would be a very inadequate response. It would represent a great lack of insight. Peter had been given insight; therefore he fell at Jesus' knees and asked Him to depart because of his unworthiness. Because Peter had a good understanding, Jesus could say to him, "Don't be afraid; now you will be catching men." Jesus delivered Peter from a mundane, day-to-day existence and gave him the same eternally significant mission and purpose that He gives to all who bow in reverence to Him: to go out in His love and compassion for all people and to shine His Light into their hearts so that they too can be free and know the true joy of life.

But we cannot give that which we do not possess. First, we must see Jesus as He is. We must bow to Him in Spirit and Truth. Then we will know His Love in our hearts, and it will shine out of us into the world. Then we will know why we are alive. This is an ongoing, ever-deepening process.

Lord, please forgive me for my lostness and blindness. I have failed to see You as You are. I bow before you, but unlike Peter, I do not want You to depart from me, and I never want to depart from You. You have the Words of eternal life, freedom, joy, and peace. I want to abide in You forever. And in obedience to You, I will open my heart to Your love for all people, and maybe You will "catch" some of them.

9

SOWING SEEDS OF LIFE

For he who sows to his own flesh will from the flesh reap corruption; but he who sows to the Spirit will from the Spirit reap eternal life [Gal 6:8].

Everything that can be seen with the eyes or touched with the hands is in a state of transition. It will not be the same tomorrow or next year. Every living creature dies. Its body goes back into the earth to become nourishment for other forms of life. Every physical thing decays. If our thoughts and energies are totally consumed by things in the physical world, even our own bodies, we are sowing into corruption. In this verse God is encouraging us to think carefully about what kind of seeds we are sowing into our life and world. We sow by investing life-energy in the form of thoughts and actions. It might be helpful to think about how much of your thought life and actions are focused on corruptible things. How much thought and other life-energies do you invest in things like food and eating; buying and selling of merchandise; earning money; pleasure and entertainment; and sexuality and fantasies? These things may not be evil in and of themselves, but they all fall within the category of things that are transient, temporary, and corruptible. The Bible encourages us to set our mind on things above rather than things on earth [Col 3:2]. These things are eternal. If I set my mind on the things of God—if I cultivate a deep communion with Jesus—love, joy, peace, patience, kindness, goodness, compassion, and generosity blossom within me. I am sowing into eternal life. Only then do I begin to find true contentment that can never be supplied by temporary things, for the soul can only be fed by that which is of its own nature.

Today, Lord, may I be a little more careful to invest my life-energies into those things that have eternal significance—those things that are valuable to You. I thank You for the physical world and my physical body, but please help me not to get lost in the physical, since it is passing away.

10

THE "HERESY" OF JESUS

The Son of man has come eating and drinking; and you say," Behold, a glutton and a drunkard, a friend of tax collectors and sinners!" [Lk 7:34]

    The walls of the church have never excluded evil. Religion has never built a strong enough fortress to hold out every strain of unrighteousness. In fact, some of the most heinous and destructive manifestations of evil have been carried like a virus within religious contexts. When Satan finds a foothold in religious doctrine, he does some of his most devastating work. One of the most wonderful and important things about Jesus is that He delivers us from false and destructive religious doctrine. He exposes it. Any religion that does not acknowledge the truth of Christ is heretical. But the doctrine of that religion will, in the characteristically convoluted manner of evil, accuse Christ of heresy just as the religious Pharisees of His day—or else it will insidiously, slowly, over time, carry its followers farther and farther away from Christ and the truth of His teachings. Christ anchors us in Eternal Reality. He is our Lifeline to heaven.
    False religion is scornfully enslaving. Cults are populated with joyless, self-righteous, condescending fear and hate-mongers. Jesus is free within the true righteousness of God—within the context of love-for-all. And His freedom is an affront to Satan and all who have fallen into his zombie-like bewitchment. Jesus calls and invites all into this joyful, compassionate freedom, which willingly embraces righteous suffering with a cheerful heart. He continues to confront and pray for those who, even to this day, point accusing fingers at what He has propagated upon the earth. But what He has propagated is what will be left standing when all the delusionary dust of the universe has finally settled, and when all the voices screaming lies and half-truths have finally been silenced.

Lord, I pray that I may never submit to the pressures and enslavements of legalism and false religious doctrines. But I pray that I may bow perpetually in submission to Your Holy Spirit in the infinite freedom and joy and love of Christ.

11

THE FOCUS OF LIFE

Be ye therefore perfect, even as your Father which is in heaven is perfect—Jesus [Mt 5:48].KJV

In large measure life is about becoming better at those things that are valued and regarded as "good." In the Christian faith, this process is called "sanctification," and we look to Christ—His life and teachings—for the definition of "good." The Bible says that Jesus "went about doing good" [Acts 10:38]. In this same verse it says that He was anointed with the Holy Spirit and that God was with Him. Jesus promises that the Holy Spirit will be with His followers also [John 14:16]. And He made the astounding statement that we [His followers] would do even greater things than Him [John 14:12]. We can only do this good if we remain prayerfully submitted to the Holy Spirit just as Jesus was totally submissive to His [and our] Heavenly Father. As we remain so submitted, as we continue to abide in Christ, we are moving—or more precisely *being moved*—toward true perfection. Our lives are coming into focus in the most wonderful way. We realize that we are here to fulfill our Creator's purpose and will, and that by so doing, we become the true person that we were meant to be and that we have always desired to be. We do not lose our freedom in this process of sanctification; we discover the only true freedom that exists. We are free to love each other in spirit and truth—and we realize that this is true perfection.

Without this submission to God in Christ, Who loves all people equally, individually and perfectly, we can never overcome our selfish egos. We will always lose out to this powerful force within us. We will always be primarily for the *self;* others will be pushed to the background, and the "good" that we do will be to impress people with how "good" we are. Only a more powerful force of

Love originating *outside* the self can deliver us from this powerful force *within* us. So Jesus says that He stands at the door and knocks, and that if we open to Him, He will come in and commune with us [Rev 3:20]. He comes in by invitation only. And He comes in with everything we will ever need to be truly successful in the ultimate sense.

Lord Jesus, I open the door to You anew today. Come in and redeem everything about me and focus my life on the things of the Kingdom. Perfect me.

12

AVOIDING THE OBVIOUS

For what can be known about God is plain to them, because God has shown it to them. Ever since the creation of the world his invisible nature, namely, his eternal power and deity, has been clearly perceived in the things that have been made. So they are without excuse [Rom 1:19-20].

"Have not my hands made all these things and so they came into being?" declares the Lord [Is 66:2].

Because of the fear of the authority of God, or perhaps because of the fear of having to submit to someone's concept of Him, many people push away the Reality of God. They choose not to believe. This leaves a tremendous and very obvious question hanging in the air: Where did everything come from? Scientifically speaking, nothing has ever come from nothing. Everything has always come from something. Grass comes from grass. Trees come from trees. People come from people. It is unscientific to believe that the universe came from nothing. And it takes a giant leap of something akin to faith to believe that *inorganic* material – dust and gasses – can bump together randomly over any number of millennia until they accidentally form a living cell. But a single cell wouldn't survive alone; somehow a whole organism would have to randomly come together. But it would also have to *accidentally* have reproductive capabilities. Or else, somehow, *accidentally*, during the exact same time period, both male and female organisms of the same species would have to emerge from the *inorganic* material floating around. And by the way, where did this material come from? Multiple life forms would have to appear suddenly, at the same time, because life needs other life in order to survive. Even a single living cell is a complicated complex of various forms of organic material. The various forms of the cell would have to have formed independently and come together. Do you begin to see how far-fetched this is? Somehow, by *chance*, we have frogs, crickets, herons, alligators, and sea horses? Somehow, by *chance*, we have an earth with a protective atmosphere, which provides us with everything we need for life and also with more beauty than we can ever comprehend?

If we look deeply enough into the created world, we begin to see that there is a creative Force, infinitely powerful [the sun], infinitely creative [variety of life], and infinitely beneficent [the gift of life and consciousness]. We begin to see God. We are without excuse. We no longer want an excuse. God is so good to us, how can we not be thankful to Him.

Lord, please help those who are in the darkness of unbelief. Please help those who are blind to Your beneficence and love. May they come to know the joy and freedom of faith. And please protect Your faithful ones from doubt spawned by blind intellectualism.

13

WHAT WE HAVE INHERITED

And when the LORD your God brings you into the land which he swore to your fathers, to Abraham, to Isaac, and to Jacob, to give you, with great and goodly cities, which you did not build, and houses full of all good things, which you did not fill, and cisterns hewn out, which you did not hew, and vineyards and olive trees, which you did not plant, and when you eat and are full, then take heed lest you forget the LORD, who brought you out of the land of Egypt, out of the house of bondage [Dt 6:10-12].

The truth of these verses applies to all people who live in prosperity. If you think of it, we all are living in houses that we did not build, drinking water that we did not pump from the ground, eating much food that we did not grow, process, or even prepare; using electricity that we did not generate, driving on roads that we did not build, using services of all sorts that are provided by others and have been refined in terms of quality through many generations of trial and error and research performed by many hard-working people, going far back into antiquity.

Our government has been forged in the crucible of human error and suffering. Our religious principles have been refined through history as our ancestors have weeded out erroneous interpretations of Scripture and allowed that which is true to slowly rise to the top. The study of history is the study of the ongoing development of our world into something that sustains progressively higher qualities of life. Wars have been fought, and an untold amount of human blood has been shed in order to protect and defend those principles and ways of life that were deemed best for the human family—those qualities that you and I enjoy today.

I recently took a 1000-mile road trip. I was able to stop and enjoy rest areas that I did not build. I ate at restaurants in which people had gone to some degree of work and effort to provide tasty and nourishing food. I had no trouble crossing state lines because of well-maintained laws in all states. The roads were good. I was able to fill my car with clean gasoline whenever it was running low—and have a cup of coffee in the process.

And yet, in spite of this, it is so easy to lapse, like a spoiled child, into a complaining and entitled mindset in which we are unthankful and unhappy, feeling deprived of something that we do not have, and blaming someone for the fact that we don't have it.

God warns us to remember where we have come from. Our ancestors would be amazed at the technology and amenities we have at our disposal. And on a deeper level, our life and everything we experience is a gift from God. He did not have to bring us into existence. He did not have to create a world that we could develop in this way. He did not have to create us in His image, giving us creative abilities in the likeness of His own.

We should be careful to be thankful. And we should be careful to live in ways that not only maintain what we have been given, but further refine it for the next generation. We are failing if we do not offer the next generation a better world than we inherited. And we are failing if we do not pass along to them the deep spiritual truths of Christ so that they will not squander or ignore what they have been given.

Lord, please forgive us for taking the blessings of life for granted. Help us to be mindful of what You have done for us in Christ and the sacrifices of our ancestors

14

THE HATRED OF CHRISTIANITY

If the world hates you, know that it has hated me before it hated you.... He who hates me hates my Father also [John 15:18,23].

Jesus predicted the hatred of His followers. Any true disciple of Christ must be prepared for the hatred of the "world." We do not desire to be disliked, but we can never let the acceptance of man become more important to us than obedience to God as He has revealed Himself to us in Christ. Jesus has commanded us to let His light shine through us [Mat 5:16]. If the world wants us to keep quiet about our faith, the Lord, and the Truth of His Word, we have to decide whom we are going to obey. The hatred of Christianity is a manifestation of evil. It is Satan's way of keeping the Truth suppressed and obscured. To discredit Christianity for its failure to live up to the precepts of Christ is in no way a discredit to Christ Himself; though I fear that in many quarters it is unconsciously taken that way. It would be much wiser for the world [presuming that the world could be wise] to encourage Christians to be *more* Christlike rather than to discredit Christianity for the failures of its followers. This would be a way to create a better world, even for non-Christians, since they and their children would be living with more gracious, honest, and compassionate neighbors. I have recently heard of one Jewish author who wants America to continue to be a "Christian" nation because he believes that Judaism is safer within Christianity than it could be in any other philosophic orientation. Anyone who thinks the world would be better without Christianity should look carefully at what he would be excluding from the world. Which of Christ's teachings does he object to? Can he find anything in all of Christ's teachings that is selfish, cruel, mean-spirited, or that would in any way be harmful to anyone in the human family?

And if not, then he should carefully examine his own objections to the faith. He may be liberatingly horrified at what he discovers it to be rooted in.

Lord, thank You for preparing me for the hatred of the world. And thank You for Your courage and perseverance in the face of this hatred. May Your Spirit in me and all Your followers be similarly victorious. And please, oh Lord, keep us from the evil of returning hatred for hatred.

15

TRUSTING HIS LOVE

He who did not spare his own Son but gave him up for us all, will he not also give us all things with him? [Rom 8:32]

The Bible is an amazing love story. The more we know about God as He has been revealed through His Word, His Son, and by His Spirit, the happier we are. Our doubts and fears are progressively dissolved as we grow in Christ. God is good, powerful, wise, and loving. The created world speaks of His goodness and love. The song of the mockingbird and the aroma of the honeysuckle are lying to us if God is not good. The amazing way that we are made—man and woman, child and parent, brother and sister; and the fact that we live as families; our creative abilities; our capacity to imagine and dream; the beauty and bounty of the earth with all its lovely creatures and features—speak with a resounding, clear and perpetual voice, "God loves us!" And if God loves us, what do we really have to fear? Nothing. Nothing. Nothing—nothing in life, and nothing in death. The same loving Lord Who has brought us into life in this beautiful world, and Who has given us His Holy Word, His Spirit, His own beloved Son to sustain and protect us through all that we will experience in this world, will also most assuredly hold us in His loving arms as we are ushered through death's door into the life to come, more glorious and free, with new adventures awaiting, and a greater comprehension of His Love.

Lord, all I can say just now is: Thank You! Thank You! Thank You! May Your name be praised forever and ever!

16

WE LIVE WHAT WE REALLY BELIEVE

So faith by itself, if it has no works, is dead [Jam 2:17].

There is no true belief that does not manifest in some form of outward action. Jesus said that what is in the heart comes out the mouth. [Mt 12:34]. And He said that every tree is known by its fruit [Lk 6:44]. The inner essence of the tree is known by the outer manifestation of what the tree produces. If I truly believe in Christ—if He is my Lord—my life will have certain manifestations that are different from someone who does not believe in Christ. Recently someone told a friend of mine, "When I heard your voice on the phone, I knew you were a Christian." The Bible teaches that the Holy Spirit enters into us when we receive Christ [John 14:16,17], and the Holy Spirit is a discernable Reality to sensitive people. Even though we have the Holy Spirit in us, we still must use our consciousness; we must focus our attention on our lives and pray for discernment regarding our daily actions. We must ask God, "Am I living in accordance with the Truth of Christ? Am I living in the Love of Christ for all people? Am I using the resources at my disposal to further the Kingdom of God? Am I growing in the peace [John 14:27] and joy [John 15:11] that Christ promised His followers?" And we must listen carefully to God's reply.

Lord, thank You for delivering me from vanity and meaninglessness. Today, may my life be a true manifestation of Your love into the world. May I be the salt, light, and leaven that You have ordained me to be. And may I celebrate with all the saints of all time this wonderful, victorious Life in the Kingdom.

17

MINDING THE MIND

Finally brethren, whatever is true, whatever is honorable, whatever is just, whatever is pure, whatever is lovely, whatever is gracious, if there is any excellence, if there is anything worthy of praise, think about these things [Phil 4:8].

    This verse from God's Holy Word to the human family teaches us to be mindful of our minds and to be conscious of our thoughts. As a counselor I have been blessed with access to the inner thought life of many people. And I have come to realize that the kindest, most gracious people can have thoughts that are startlingly sinister, morbid, perverted, and evil [I include myself in this category]. These thoughts are like seeds or young plants—if they are watered and fertilized, they can grow into destructive behaviors. If we pull them up or ignore them and replace them with thoughts that are true, honorable, just, pure, lovely, gracious, excellent, and praiseworthy; these seeds will grow into the godly formation of our very character. This is one way of describing our sanctification process—our spiritual growth. We should not be fearful of our evil thoughts; we should simply ignore them. In Christ, we have no intention of acting on them.

    Having a *devotional life* is a very good way of sowing the good seeds into our mind on a regular basis. Devotional passages are prayerfully designed to bring God's truth into focus—to uncover the diamonds and nuggets and treasures of the Kingdom and hold them up for clarity and appreciation—and most importantly, for *assimilation* into our character. A morning devotion is to the spirit what a very healthy breakfast is for the body. It gives us something to refer to throughout the day and shapes our character in the most wonderful way imaginable. I hope that you will resolve to feed your mind very good food that will refresh and renew your spirit, and help you become the person that God created you to become: joyful, loving, peaceful, and free.

Lord, thank You for Your Holy Word and for Your Spirit in me, drawing me to Your Word and helping me to understand it. Today and always may I be careful to focus my attention on those things that are true, good, pure and worthy. And may my life be transformed into something beautiful and holy in Your sight.

18

THE IMPORTANCE OF OUR SANCTIFICATION

For the time has come for judgment to begin with the household of God, and if it begins with us, what will be the end of those who do not obey the gospel of God? And "If the righteous man is scarcely saved, where will the impious and sinner appear?" [1Pet 4:17-18]

We have come to understand that when we received Christ, we were delivered from condemnation and ushered into the Kingdom of God and into eternal life. But we did not attain perfection at that time; rather we began a process called 'sanctification' in which God, with our cooperation, is clearing away our character defects day by day. This is, of course, a very important process for us to be seriously engaged in. This devotional reading is a means of sanctification. We participate in devotionals to enhance our sanctification—to move from being "scarcely saved," toward the very center of the Kingdom of God. We want to draw near to God, and to understand more about Him, ourselves, life, good, and evil so that we will be progressively more joyful, loving, peaceful, and free servants of God and man. This has never been an easy process. Satan and the world of evil work diligently to prevent or retard it. How else can we explain the fact that God, in the flesh, has walked upon the earth, teaching us to love our enemies, to bless those who curse us, to pray for those who despitefully use and persecute us, demonstrating His validity by praying for His tormentors and arising from the dead before hundreds of reliable witnesses; and yet we still, two thousand years later, murder, steal, cheat, deceive, abuse, and use each other? Yes, evil is real, and we are all—within and outside the Kingdom—affected by it. It is in the cultural water we drink and air we breathe.

And that is why it is very important for those of us who call ourselves "Christians" to be serious, diligent, and thankful followers of Christ. We must be very careful to have a personal relationship with Christ Himself through the Holy Spirit, Who is with us always "even to the end of the world" [Mt 28:20]. We must be mindful of His teachings and His Way, and we must walk in it. The Truth of Christ—His Holy Spirit within us—is our only protection from the persistent, insidious corruption and deceptions of the world. History is full of examples of whole cultures or nations that have drifted into destructive philosophies or religious ideas. The people in those cultures believed they were justified in their beliefs and behaviors, perhaps primarily because of intelligent and influential [but spiritually blind] leaders. In the Christian faith, no leader can ever take precedence over Christ Himself, Who has revealed our God and Creator as One Who loves and desires the best for all people, and will judge all people based on what He has revealed in Christ. We understand that it is better to die in Christ than to live in heresy. We entrust ourselves to Him Who determines the final destination of the eternal *soul*, rather than to anyone who might have the power to simply destroy the physical body.

Lord, I am thankful for this work that You are doing within and through me. I renew my devotion to You and to Your wonderful Way of life, Your Love, goodness and grace. I choose to abide in You always.

19

THEY CAUGHT NOTHING

Simon Peter said to them, "I am going fishing." They said to him, "We will go with you." They went out and got into the boat; but that night they caught nothing [John 21:3].

The Lord was gone. He had appeared to them after the crucifixion, but they had no idea that He might do so again. Maybe there was a sense of relief. Discipleship had been tough. They had left their old, more comfortable ways, but now, maybe they would return to them.

"I'm going fishing." This does not seem to be a prayerful decision on Peter's part. Was he being led of the Spirit? Or was he taking a break? Or *making* a break?

How many times have we felt the impulse to "go fishing"? How easy it would be to go back to the old dispensation—B.C.—before Christ. There are many versions of "going fishing."

But where would it lead? "They caught nothing." Life without Christ is futile, void—empty as those nets. But when we walk with Him, when we "feed

His sheep," when we become "fishers of men," then life is so abundant and full—the nets are strained and you can't even get all the fish into the boat!

Lord, please help me to never look back. I know, deep in my soul, that You are Life and all else is futility or death. You are all I will ever need to be all that I have been created to be. In You, everything else about life becomes beautiful, useful, and good. Without You everything eventually dries up and loses its vitality. I am so thankful that You have given me a meaningful mission.

20

DECADENCE AND DECAY

Wherever there is a carcass, there the vultures will gather [Jesus, Mt 24:28 RSV].

The day after Thanksgiving the mall was so crowded, a woman was standing in a vacant parking space, reserving it for her party, who was enroute in the car. I walked around outside while my mom, sister, and wife shopped. If we worship the god of materialism, the mall is his temple. So much activity, anticipation, all combinations of people, hustling and bustling in the vast, varied, glittering, alluring, and jangled world of stuff for sale.

I was looking at faces. There wasn't much joy—mostly fatigue, frustration, or blank stares. Some children were crying—maybe they wanted something they couldn't have, or maybe they had engendered wrath by encumbering the shopping endeavor. I saw a young woman angrily confront another young woman who, while backing up to get to a soon-to-be-vacant parking space, almost ran over her. I saw a teenage girl make an obscene gesture toward a teenage boy. I heard an obese, young, black woman talking about "gittin' up in that nigger's face." I saw a rat run across an opening in the foliage near the place where a restaurant had dumped a bag of garbage—brown fluid running out of the bag onto the street. In their haste, no one seemed to notice the few flowers that were blooming in the unkempt, narrow band of foliage around the outside edge of the building. Much garbage had been windblown or dropped in the tangled landscape. The police had initiated a new security measure—the "skywatch"—which was an elevated, small cubicle from within which security guards could observe parking lot activity through one-way windows to curb the anticipated increase of theft in this season. I noticed a disproportionately high number of attractive people, as compared to most other social gatherings—a football game, grocery store, or church, for instance.

The materialism god seems to attract attractive people. And they want to be *more* attractive, judging from much of the stuff that is offered for sale. I thought of Jesus' statement "Where there is carrion, the vultures will gather." And two other words kept coming to mind: "Decadence" and "Decay."

Lord, in these "end times," please keep me close to You, where I am eternally safe no matter what happens.

21

VICTORIOUS ACCEPTANCE

In the world you have tribulation; but be of good cheer, I have overcome the world [Jesus, John 16:33].

I in them and thou in me, that they may become perfectly one, so that the world may know that thou hast sent me and hast loved them even as thou hast loved me [Jesus, John 17:23].

For me, these have been some of the most wonderfully liberating of all Christ's teachings. Jesus tells us that in the world we will have tribulation. As long as we live in this world—no matter how intelligent, rich, affluent, hard-working, responsible, successful, righteous, obedient, spiritually mature, well-connected or loved—we will have tribulation. Tribulation means: problems, trials, difficulties, snags, blocks, things not working the way we want them to work, things working the way we *don't* want them to work, people not treating us fairly, sickness, bad moods, etc. And we don't get to *choose* which tribulation we will have.

I recognize within myself [and in others also] a tendency to be waiting or straining for the time when all the tribulation finally stops; when I will finally reap the harvest of all my hard work and diligent effort, prayer and Bible study, service and obedience. The bad stuff will fade away into the background, and I can "retire" in the place of perpetual peace and smooth sailing. Until then I just have to grit my teeth, clench my fists, and press on through one frustrating battle after another.

Jesus teaches me that this is a painful and unnecessary delusion. It ain't gonna happen in *this world*! At first this is a bitter pill to swallow. It's depressing to hear that we are not going to arrive in the land of "no tribulation." But as we choke it on down, it becomes very good medicine. It delivers us from being in a strain or a holding pattern. It puts us in a posture in which we can begin to understand what He was talking about when He said, "Nevertheless, be of good cheer."

It seems paradoxical that Jesus would tell us that the tribulation would keep happening, but we can be of good cheer because He has "overcome the world." We might respond, "Well, that's great, Lord, but how does that help *me*. You've done *Your* great work and are seated at the right hand of Our Father, but *I'm* still groveling around down here." But if we press further into the truth of this matter, we say, "Oh, I see, I am *one with You*! You are *in me*! I'm starting to get the picture. Your victory over the world is *my* victory also. I don't have to fight these battles. I have overcome in You. I am free at last, free at last, thank God almighty; I'm free at last!"

Lord, thank You for Your wonderful work and teachings that liberate us. I accept deeply that I am going to have tribulation in this world. I choose to be a cheerful servant anyway! May we abide always in Your victory over the world, and in freedom, peace, and love.

22

STAY WITH US

So they drew near to the village to which they were going. He appeared to be going further, but they constrained him, saying, "Stay with us, for it is toward evening and the day is now far spent." So he went in to stay with them. When he was at table with them, he took the bread and blessed, and broke it, and gave it to them. And their eyes were opened and they recognized him; and he vanished out of their sight [Lk 24:28-31].

This event happens after the resurrection on the road to Emmaus. Jesus had walked with them a way, and taught them, and "appeared to be going further." But they urged Him to "stay with us." In this we see the glorious reality of God bending His will toward the good desires of man. Here is some reassurance for the heart that doubts His attentive and intervening actions in our affairs. Jesus was "going further," but when they asked Him, He stayed with them awhile longer.

But what if they had not asked Him to stay with them? Would their eyes have been opened? What if we do not seek? Will we find? Jesus and all of Truth and Life are marching onward. He does His part. He offers Himself. He walks with us. He is available. He loves us. He invites us.

But He does not force Himself upon us or compel us to follow Him or seek Him. Eternity depends upon our will—our choice—our willingness to respond to the burning hunger in our hearts and to say, "Stay with us." And if we do, He will open our eyes also, and we will recognize Him in His mysterious reality—the Messiah. We will realize the foolishness of our petty doubts and fears. We will be delivered, and we will soon hear Him say, "Follow me," or "Go and teach, love and serve." And in this going, teaching, loving, and serving, we find our rightful place in the universe. We come home. We realize and take part in the "enduring revolution."

Lord, now and always: Stay with us.

23

THE SOURCE OF CONFIDENCE

He said, "Come." So Peter got out of the boat and walked on the water and came to Jesus, but when he saw the wind, he was afraid, and beginning to sink he cried out, "Lord, save me." Jesus immediately reached out his hand and caught him, saying to him, "O man of little faith, why did you doubt?" [Mt 14:29-31]

Peter was doing fine until he "saw the wind." Fear overcame him, and he began to sink. In His fear he "cried out" to the Lord, Who "immediately reached out His hand and caught him." How many times have we gone through this cycle? We start out faithfully toward the Lord, shift our focus to our problems, start sinking in them, fearfully cry out to Him, and He lifts us back up where we belong. It seems to be a principle that if we focus fretfully on our problems, we sink down into them. But if we focus on Jesus, we walk right on over the troubled waters.

Let's continue to grow in faith. Today, let's keep our eyes faithfully on Christ. Don't worry about the wind and storm. Remember, Christ has authority over all. And He loves us. And He is with us always, "even to the end of the age." Of all the things in this world that men put their faith in, nothing is more reliable than Christ. We who have trusted Him should, of all people, be confident.

Lord, thank You for encouraging me to walk across the troubled waters of my life faithfully and peacefully. You have never let me down. Today, I will trust You more deeply than ever.

24

WHAT WE OWE

Making melody to the Lord with all your heart, always and for everything giving thanks in the name of our Lord Jesus Christ to God the Father.... For we are his workmanship, created in Christ Jesus for good works, which God prepared beforehand, that we should walk in them [Eph 5:20; 2:10].

We are indebted. We're indebted to God for life and every good thing: our bodies, minds, sensitivity, creativity, a beautiful world, manhood, womanhood, children, etc. We're indebted to our parents for the work they did to keep us alive when we could not take care of ourselves. And we are indebted to our ancestors who have worked to develop the world into what we have inherited.

We are indebted to the Founding Fathers of this great nation for forging out of the crucible of human experience a government for and by the people—a government that provides freedom, including the freedom of religion, and a system of checks and balances to prevent corruptive power. We are indebted to hundreds of thousands of soldiers who have fought, and especially those who have given their lives for the high principles that provide for those qualities of life that we enjoy each day. We are indebted to the saints of history; those who have fought the great spiritual battles for truth, justice, compassion, and freedom from tyranny of the human soul; those who have been willing to expose evil at the peril of their own or their families' lives.

What do we owe God and these people? Primarily two things: First, we owe happiness in the form of gratitude. We really ought to be thankful. This means that we are careful not to complain. God did not bestow these tremendous blessings upon us; Jesus did not suffer the crucifixion; soldiers did not bleed to death in the trenches in foreign countries, so that we could complain about how long it takes to get the cable TV repaired or the long lines at Wal-Mart checkout. We owe God and our saintly ancestors' *gratitude*.

Second, we also owe the next generation a better world than we inherited. We are created for "good works"—not just to enjoy what we have.

This means that today [and every day] we peacefully work to make the world a little better for others and ourselves.

God, in His infinite love for us, rightly commands us to be thankful in all situations, and He reminds us that we are created for "good works" to help and serve others.

Lord, thank You for every good gift. Help me to have a growing mindfulness of the goodness of the life You have given me in Christ. Please forgive me for complaining about anything, ever. Set my feet on the firm ground of willingness to do the good works that You have exemplified in Christ, Who "went about doing good."

25

LIFE CHANGING DECISION: A TRUE STORY

Choose you this day whom you will serve,...as for me and my house, we will serve the Lord [Jos 24:15].

He told them another parable. "The kingdom of heaven is like leaven which a woman took and hid in three measures of flour, till it was all leavened" [Mt 13:33].

Two brothers grew up with a father who had a tragic accident leaving him partially paralyzed at a relatively young age. The father fought a colossal spiritual battle against despair and frustration. In his better times, he offered his sons a noble example of survival and perseverance. In his worst times, he was abusive and struck terror into their hearts. The boys grew up with wounded hearts and suffered in ways that they did not know were related to the fear and anger that had tormented them as children. They brought this suffering into their marriages and families.

One of the brothers made a conscious decision to receive Christ as his Lord and Savior, and he took this decision seriously. He began drawing near to God in spirit and truth. He studied the Bible—especially the life and teachings of Christ. He began to examine his life in light of the Scriptures. The Truth of God's Word began to work in him like yeast in moist flour. He recognized his mistakes with his wife and children, sought forgiveness, and began changing his way of handling his frustrations. He prayed for God to make him a better husband and father. He sought help from other men in Christ whom he respected. His relations with his wife and children became much more harmonious and fulfilling. Though he was not blind to the difficulties of his childhood, he was able to benefit from his father's wisdom and strength, and he had many pleasant memories of his childhood, including his relations with his dad.

The other brother, however, became bitter through the years. He could not understand his brother's "soft" attitude toward their father. He thought his brother was in denial or must have blocked out the painful memories. He did not choose to forgive his father for the cruelty of the early years. He felt justified in his ongoing anger. When his brother tried to talk with him about the Lord and the importance of forgiveness, he felt that his brother was being critical and taking a "holier than thou attitude." The Christian brother finally stopped bringing up their father in their conversations since it felt like rubbing salt in an open wound. There was a silent rift in their relationship. He continued to pray that his brother might allow Jesus to help him forgive their father and find peace.

Lord, through spirit eyes, we see the reality of Your word. If we choose to receive Christ and walk in the Light, our lives begin to blossom. We are transformed. I choose You again today.

Note: Since the writing of this devotional, the unforgiving brother discovered that he had cancer, and subsequently drew near to God as never before. He was able to forgive his father and be restored to a deep peace. He maintained this peace and even joy [evidenced by a great sense of humor] until his death.

26

JOY EMBRACING SORROW

(In Gethsemane) Then he (Jesus) said to them, "My soul is very sorrowful, even to death; remain here, and watch with me" [Mt 26:38].

These things I (Jesus) have spoken to you, that my joy may be in you, and that your joy may be full [John 15:11].

The difference between worldly happiness and Godly joy is *sorrow*. If we are to be authentic human beings living in the light of Truth, we must acknowledge the reality of evil and its devastating effects in our world. We must acknowledge the vast, abysmal, unnecessary, and perpetual suffering caused by our failure to hear and heed what God, through the prophets, and especially through Christ, has communicated to us. So much life wasted! So many children abused, abandoned, or ignored! So many opportunities to love untaken! So much life unlived! So much blind passion wreaking havoc in peoples' lives! How we have "stoned the prophets and killed them that were sent to us!"(Mt 23:37).

The stench of all the blood and psychological damage from all the wars and murders, and all the cries from those who have been raped, abused, and maliciously deceived reaches the ears and nostrils of God in a way that calls for repentance and healing—or judgment. Yes, sorrow is legitimate.

But if it motivates us to do the work of love—the work for which we were created—then a wonderful thing begins to happen in our souls. Joy begins to blossom! Joy that is not in denial about the suffering but realizes that sorrow is being swallowed up—consumed in the fires of loving service. I do not think it coincidental that one of the most joyful people in recent history—Mother Teresa—lived and served in one of the most impoverished populations on earth.

In the aftermath of Hurricane Katrina, one of the most significant observances was the obvious *joy* in the people who were helping those in need. Joy arises out of the fires of sorrowful human experience being consumed in loving service. And faith is involved (of course) because we know, in a growing and deep way, that God is mysteriously working *all things*—even those things that seem so wasteful and destructive—together for *good* for those who love Him and are called into the work of His wonderful, redemptive purposes (Rom 8:28). Sorrow is real. But in the Kingdom of God, joy not only has the final word but is also our constant, sustaining companion! Jesus has said that He wants our joy to be *full*!—Even while we continue to live in this world that has come under the domain of its dark prince.

Lord Jesus, we are deeply thankful to You for what You have done, for what You have taught, and for what You are continuing to do through Your Holy Spirit in us and in our world. May Your joy fill our hearts as we lovingly serve those whom You place in our pathway today.

27

CHRISTIANITY FOR DUMMIES

But these are written that you may believe that Jesus is the Christ, the Son of God, and that believing you may have life in his name [John 20:31].

"This is my commandment, that you love one another as I have loved you" [John 15:12].

Therefore, since we are justified by faith, we have peace with God through our Lord Jesus Christ [Rom 5:1].

One of the most popular series of books in recent history is the (*Any Subject*) *For Dummies* series. People love them because they are concise and very student-friendly. I am a fan of brevity and succinctness also. I like to boil things down to the very basics. I realize that we have to be careful in doing this with any slice of reality, especially so with our doctrines of faith. Nevertheless, I think it is helpful to have a foundational, structural understanding of Christianity from which we can launch into the infinite reaches of life and understanding. So here goes.

Christianity may be boiled down to three basic foundations: Faith, Love and Peace. Jesus repeatedly encouraged His followers to believe in Him, and to have faith in God. He indicated that the miracles were to confirm their faith in Him as the Messiah. God spoke in an audible voice from heaven on more than one occasion confirming the Sonship and Lordship of Jesus the Christ. Christians are known as "believers."

If we believe, then what? Well the main thing, according to Him in Whom we believe, is to *love*. His primary commandment is for us to love God and each other above all other motivations and endeavors. This is a lifelong process that none of us ever master. We must always consider ourselves beginning students in the practice of love.

But if we are sincere in our faith and in the practice of Christ's love, *peace* will begin to arise in our souls like mercury in a thermometer on a warm summer day. We will begin to find our rightful place in the universe. We will have so much joy at times that tears will flow from our eyes. Our "cup will overflow." Our soul will "mount up with wings as eagles" and soar into places that we never knew existed. Rivers of living water will flow out of us into our loved ones, washing away everything that oppresses them and us. These are the things that God promises. And these experiences have been confirmed in millions of Christians through history.

Lord Jesus, increase my faith. I choose to believe that You are the Messiah. Everything that You taught and everything You did and everything that was done through You confirms Your Messiahship. Your impact on the human family and on history also confirms You as the Chosen One. I will love as You commanded and gave example. And I gladly receive the gift of peace—Your peace.

28

THE FUTILITY AND SADNESS OF ENVY

So when they had gathered, Pilate said to them, "Whom do you want me to release for you, Barnabas or Jesus who is called Christ?" For he knew that it was out of envy that they had delivered him up [Mt 27:17-18].

Webster defines envy as "a feeling of resentment and jealousy over the possessions, achievements, etc. of another." In the above passage, we see the terrible fruit of it in its worst and full-blown form. Envy brought Jesus to Pilate, and to the Cross.

Most of us never experience that level of envy, but what we do experience can rob us of much joy in life. Imagine two men standing on a hilltop overlooking a beautiful landscape during a spectacular sunset. One of the men is thinking, "I could have owned a place like this if my business dealings had gone better. The guy that owns this place is no smarter or better than me, in fact, I know he inherited all this from his wife's side of the family—lucky jerk. And he doesn't keep it up very well at all—look at the condition of that barn. Etc." His envy causes him to feel deprived and depressed.

The other man is thinking, "God! How beautiful! How incredibly beautiful! God, You have blessed us with so much beauty! My soul cannot contain it. Thank You, God. Thank You so much." He feels a sense of awe and wonder and gratitude. In a very real sense, he owns the landscape.

Lord, please deliver us from envy. Help us to be mindful of it when it arises within us, and to quickly turn away from it, and into the life and freedom of Christ.

29

THE BLEAK DARKNESS OF EVIL

But when the Pharisees heard it they said, "It is only by Beelzebul, the prince of demons, that this man [Jesus] casts out demons" [Mt 12:24].

The Pharisees—very religious people—could not recognize the Son of God. Even when Jesus did His wonderful miracles, healing people and delivering them from long-term suffering, the Pharisees in their astounding blindness and envy accused Him of operating in the power of Satan. This is a unique and very devastating technique of the Evil One. When Truth exposes evil as evil, evil has its sinister response: It counters by labeling Goodness and Truth "evil."

In a time when the prevailing philosophy is post-modern relativism, this can be a very powerful tool of Satan. Let's say that I believe that it is a good thing for adults to have sex with children [as, I understand, some people do]. If you tell me that this is evil because it wounds the spirits of the children, I will counter that you are trying to deprive me of my "freedom of choice." "You are an evil, religious, deluded zealot," I might say, "blindly depriving people of harmless pleasure."

If we do not believe that God has revealed the Truth in the Scriptures and most concisely in the life of Jesus, then what is our standard of truth? In the confusion of uncertainty, the evil one can wreak havoc because the human mind, unrestrained by a standard of truth and the Holy Spirit, has infinite capacity for delusions and rationalizations. And selfishness and the desire for pleasure and power are the most powerful forces in the unredeemed human psyche.

But when we look deeply into the life and teachings of Jesus, we begin to see the God of creation, Who loves all and desires the best for all. The Way of Jesus has stood the test of time. Jesus has set countless millions of people free to love and serve God and their fellow man. How blessed we are when our inner spirit resonates with the Truth of Christ! In Him we enter into abundant and eternal life.

Lord, thank You that we do not have to wonder what is true for the human family. You have revealed Yourself as the Truth that sets us free!

30

PEACEFUL WARRIORS

Put on the whole armor of God, that you may be able to stand against the wiles of the devil. For we are not contending against flesh and blood, but against the principalities, against the powers, against the world rulers of this present darkness, against the spiritual hosts of wickedness in the heavenly places [Eph 6:11-12].

And the harvest of righteousness is sown in peace by those who make peace [Jam 3:18].

We are in warfare. And we are *peaceful* warriors, walking in the victory that has been secured by Christ our Lord.

The Church is called, among other things, the "Body of Christ." The Kingdom of God is, in some ways, like a physical body. Recently I discovered a tick on my shin. The place where it was attached was surrounded by a dime-sized, bright, red circle with a dark spot in the middle. I discovered on the Internet that I had been bitten by a black-legged tick—the species that transmits Lyme disease—and that the infectious markings on my shin were indicative of that disease. I read about the debilitating and long-term effects of this infection with growing alarm. I am currently taking a round of powerful antibiotics to hopefully destroy the bacteria before it gains an irreversible foothold in my body.

    Our bodies are constantly under attack. If we are healthy and have strong immune systems, we are comfortable and don't even know that our bodies are fighting for us all the time. If we have a major infection or illness, we may have to concentrate the major portion of our life-energy upon surviving. As with the physical body, so with the Body of Christ. Always, false doctrine threatens to invade, take hold, and insidiously destroy the quality of life quietly provided by the Truth and Love of Christ. If we become apathetic—if we grow lax in discipline and adherence to Truth—we are like couch potatoes, cigarette smokers, excessive drinkers, and junk-food junkies. We will eventually weaken our immune system or the health of some vital organ, and suffer a major setback or death. If we remain devoted to the Truth; if we stand against false doctrine; if we compare our way of living to what God has revealed in His Holy Word and prophetically expose evil; then we will not only maintain, but prosper in all that is valuable to the human family. Evil, like a virus, deceives, and then destroys its host. None of us, cut off from sincere devotion to the revealed Word of God, is beyond the deceptive powers of evil. Those who are most deceived are those who arrogantly proclaim their independence and disdain for the authority of God. They look condescendingly down upon the humble, contrite, and peaceful warriors of God, every one of whom, like the cells in a healthy immune system, are quietly protecting all that is valuable in the organism of the human family. It is through these peaceful warriors of Christ that Life is being preserved.

Lord God, You are God and I am not! Thank You for revealing to us the Truth that sets us free. Please deliver us from the delusions of arrogance and pride. May we always remember that it is Your Way that works, ultimately, for the human family and that no doctrine that is contrary to Your Holy Word will lead us in a good direction.

31

DON'T GET CHOKED

But the cares of the world, and the delight in riches, and the desire for other things, enter in and choke the word, and it proves unfruitful [Mk 4:19].

They are not of the world, even as I am not of the world [John 17:16].

Jesus helps us stay emotionally clear. As a counselor, the concept of emotional clarity has become very important to me. People seek counseling because, among other things, they are unhappy—in emotional pain—frustrated, angry, hurt, afraid, etc. In other words, they are not clear—transparent—free—open—at peace with God, self, and others. One of the major manifestations of emotional turmoil (unclarity) is *worry*. Worry is a powerful destroyer of the peace and happiness that results from loving people the way Jesus wants us to love. It chokes out one's capacity to love, and therefore robs him of the joy of life. Worry is delusional. By that I mean it is based on unreality. If the Bible is true, and if I have received Christ as my personal Lord and Savior, then there is nothing in the universe of human experience that I need to worry about. The Truth of the Bible and of Christ includes, among other wonderful revelations: My sins are totally forgiven and God is holding nothing against me (Rom 8:1); Jesus is with me always, even to the end of the age (Mt 28:20); greater is the Holy Spirit in me, than the evil one of this world (1Jn 4:4); no spiritual weapon will prevail against me (Is 54:17); I am more than a conqueror over all of life's difficulties and tribulations (Rom 8:37); the Creator of this universe loves me enough to sacrifice His only Son for me (John 3:16); and death will be my final victory (1Cor 15:54). I have been promised abundant life (John 10:10), peace (John 14:27), joy (John 15:11), freedom (Is 61:1), and eternal life (John 11:25).

In spite of these wonderful, historically validated, and eternally secure promises, I frequently find myself worrying about some triviality as if my life and well-being depended on it. But the Holy Spirit awakens me, again and again, ever more quickly, from my daytime nightmares and delusions. I am released from the chokehold of anxiety. My heart smiles with the reality of God's Word. I am free to love again. I am not of this world. My life is hidden with Christ, who sits at the right hand of God. I am already living in the eternal Kingdom of God. And if Christ is your Lord, so are you.

Lord, please deliver me from the worries and cares of this world. Today may I walk in the clarity and freedom, peace and love of Christ.

32

WHO IS JESUS?

He was in the beginning with God; all things were made through him, and without him was not anything made that was made [John 1:2-3].

This is a very profound statement in the Holy Scriptures. If you read the whole first chapter of John, you see very clearly that the "He" and "Him" in these verses refer to Jesus. Jesus "was in the beginning with God," and everything that was made, was "made through Him." That means everything in the universe. Everything that we have ever observed, studied, wondered about, or been stricken with awe about, was made through Jesus the Christ. And everything that is outside the realm of our knowledge and understanding was made through Him. He was with God in the beginning. He, himself, said to the Pharisees, "Before Abraham was, I am" (John 8:58). If we are Christians, and if we believe the Bible, we must understand that Jesus is not just one among many great teachers, prophets, or rabbis. If we have any doubts about who Christ is in this regard, we should clear them up so that we know where we stand.

We are being asked by our current culture to be "tolerant" of other faiths and other doctrines. Christians have always been tolerant of other faiths and doctrines, because we realize and accept that God has given people the freedom to choose their own pathway in life. God does not take this freedom away, and He does not allow us to take it away. Whatever we might say about the Truth of Christ, we can never say that it is something that can be forced upon anyone. No true Christian became one because he was forced, intimidated or brainwashed. This is an impossibility, and the world has no need to fear it. Jesus "stands at the door and knocks" (Rev 3:20), but He never beats down the door. He invites us into abundant and eternal life, but He does not drag us in, kicking and screaming. He teaches us to love our enemies (Mt 5:44). What safer and more wonderful doctrine could there ever be?

There is a serious problem however with some interpretations of "tolerance." Some people in our culture are asking Christians to stop believing or saying that Christ is "*the* way, *the* truth and *the* life." But Christ said this Himself (John 14:6). Others are asking Christians to agree that some lifestyles that are not ordained by the Holy Scriptures are acceptable and equal to God-ordained lifestyles. Or they are asking that, if we do not agree with them, we should at least keep our beliefs private so as not to "offend" them (see Mt 11:6). But Jesus Himself said that we are to let His light shine among people (Mt 5:16). Just as He has not given us the option of hating our enemies, He has not given us the option of being quiet about what He has taught and given to the human family. To ask Christians these things is equivalent to asking them to stop being Christians, and it represents *in*tolerance for the Christian faith as it has been set forth in the Holy Scriptures. As such we recognize it to be a manifestation of evil and ultimately very dangerous for the human family. If Jesus is accurately revealed in the Holy Scriptures, then anything that oppresses the truth that He has revealed is, at root, evil. The same evil that was so clearly evident in His time, and that ultimately nailed Him to the cross. The same evil He exposed and defeated for all eternity at that time.

Lord Jesus, please give us courage to be what You have ordained us to be, even if some are offended. And deliver us from ever being deliberately offensive. Help us to love even those who hate You. But help us not to fear them.

33

TAKE WARNING

He heard the sound of the trumpet, and did not take warning; his blood shall be upon himself. But if he had taken warning, he would have saved his life [Eze 33:5].

The Bible is full of warnings. I think it is fair to say that virtually every book in the Bible contains explicit or implicit warnings. The word "insidious" is in our language because evil is real. "Insidious" is defined by *Webster* as: "Designed to entrap. Full of wiles. Doing or contriving harm. Awaiting a chance to harm. Causing harm by stealthy, usually imperceptible means." Since evil is "imperceptible" in some of its manifestations, careful discernment and ongoing, peaceful diligence is necessary for successful living. John Newton writes in the hymn *Amazing Grace*, "Twas Grace that taught my heart to *fear*." (Emphasis mine). He wisely considers it *Grace* that issued some type of *fearful* understanding. Grace *warned* him that all was not well; that his soul was in danger; that he was vulnerable in a way that he had not been aware of. Grace exposed insidious evil. This could only happen because Mr. Newton was, on some level, seeking. Jesus said that if we will seek, we will find (Mt 7:7). Then, when we heed the warning and receive the Truth of Christ, we are delivered from fear. We know that we have the discernment of the Holy Spirit. We can see in the darkness, like our military men who have infrared goggles. The Holy Spirit is like spiritual infrared goggles.

Fools do not heed warnings. Fools live in a state of reckless, false bravery. Or, they live in denial or rebellion against the Truth. They become easy prey for the Evil One. They are used in his ongoing campaign to "steal, kill, and destroy" (John 10:10). They may be "successful," "nice" people, well dressed and admired. But they do not know the Truth because they do not know Jesus, Who said, "I am the truth" (John 14:6).

When we receive Christ and bow to His glorious, compassionate, well-deserved authority, we have heeded the warning of God in the most significant and liberating manner. We have no longer any need for fear. The promises of

God become real to us. We know that we are eternally safe and secure. Life has purpose and meaning, and death is a doorway to the next great adventure with our loving Creator.

Lord, thank You for warning us of the dangers of evil. And thank You for delivering us from evil through Christ our Lord. Today may we live in His Grace and Love.

34

THE MOST DREADFUL WORDS YOU COULD EVER HEAR

On that day many will say to me, "Lord, Lord, did we not prophesy in your name, and cast out demons in your name, and do many mighty works in your name?" And then will I declare to them, "I never knew you; depart from me, you evildoers" [Mt 7:22-23].

It would be delusional to assume that I know *everything* about Lynn, my wife. Even after thirty-five years of marriage, she still surprises me at times. But I do *know* her. I know her in many settings. I know how she would respond to many circumstances. Her voice is frequently in my mind. I act in ways that honor our relationship, and I try not to hurt her. Wherever I am, in a very real sense, she is there. I *know* her.

There is a man who lives down the street. I see him when he walks his dog. He seems friendly and always speaks when he passes by. He is married and has a son who is in college. He teaches at a local school. I know *about* this man, but I do not really *know* him.

There is a distinct difference between *knowing* someone, and knowing *about* them. *Knowing* is personal, intimate, deep, and broad. Knowing *about* is distant, shallow, uninvolved.

Where are you with Jesus? Do you really *know* Him, or do you just know *about* Him? More importantly, does He know you as a friend and fellow worker in His Kingdom? When you come face to face with Him, will you be meeting a friend or stranger? What will He say to you?

Lord, I want to know You. And I want to be known by You. Search my heart and reveal the Truth to me. Come into my life and stay with me always. Teach me how to be free.

35

THE DAILY BUFFET

But I say unto you, that every idle word that men shall speak, they shall give account thereof in the day of judgment (Jesus) [Mt 12:36 KJV].

Life is in some ways like a buffet. Every day, a great variety of "food" is laid out before you. You can pick and choose. You have many options in terms of what to do with your life-energy—your thoughts and actions. Some people in our world today are thinking about how to kill and terrorize as many of their "enemies" as they possibly can. They are pouring out their life-energy into murder and terror. Some people are thinking about how to have more fun. They love to play, go on vacations, or weekend excursions. Work is an unpleasant diversion for them. They live from weekend to weekend. Some are addicted to alcohol, drugs, or sex. Their thought life is consumed with the addictive behavior. They live for the next opportunity to drink, use, or act out. Everything else feels like marking time to them. Some people are trying to eradicate certain diseases from the human family. Some are trying to find better ways of distributing the world's food and wealth—to alleviate poverty and hunger. Some are trying to convert souls—to help people become more aware of God and His love for all people, and the responsibilities they have to the human family.

All up and down the scale of usefulness and goodness, on the one hand, to utter destructiveness, on the other, we have choices in the buffet of life—each day. Jesus helps us focus our lives in the most wonderful ways. He loves us, and wants us to have joy. He loves others and wants us to treat them with compassion. He teaches us how to use our life-energy in the most compassionate and joyful ways. He teaches us how to live in ways that truly do make the world a better place, so that, at the time of our death, we will be very thankful for most of the choices we have made in the buffet of life.

Lord, thank You for delivering us from futility, idleness, and vanity, into a truly meaningful life with eternal significance. Today, may we abide in Your Love.

36

"I RULE HAMMOND"

But Jesus called them to him and said, "You know that the rulers of the Gentiles lord it over them, and their great men exercise authority over them. It shall not be so among you; but whoever would be great among you must be your servant, and whoever would be first among you must be your slave; even as the Son of man came not to be served but to serve, and to give his life as a ransom for many." [Mt 20:25-28]

In a park on the sidewalk in a nearby town, I saw these words written in chalk: "I rule Hammond." Here, from the writings of a young person no doubt, is a statement straight from the sinful nature. My sinful nature wants to *rule*. At core, my sinful nature (and yours) wants to be God. The sinful nature wants total and complete control of everything. What it cannot control or use, it ignores, and it hates anything that thwarts its control or that has legitimate authority over it. Haman hated Mordecai [and all the Jews] because Mordecai did not bow and show reverence to him (Est 3:2f). Regarding power, Satan acted in an opposite manner than Jesus. Satan did not have the power that he coveted, so he tried to seize it. Jesus had "all power in heaven and earth" (Mt 28:18), but He did not consider it something to be grasped, but rather laid it aside willingly in an awesome act of love (Phil 2:6-7). The orientation toward power, therefore, is a major means by which evil is discerned from good.

Here is why we consider a democratic form of government superior to totalitarianism. But do not be deceived; the totalitarian mindset exists within democracy. The seeds of totalitarianism are in each of us—in all families, cultures, and nations. And the Christian faith is its archenemy. Jesus teaches us humility, kindness, grace, mercy, forgiveness, and a willingness to serve. This is on the opposite end of the spectrum from power, control, the desire to *be served*, intimidation, abuse, and domination. It is important to allow ourselves to be examined deeply and completely in the light of the Holy Spirit of Christ, and to allow God to deliver us from anything in us that wants to dominate and control.

Lord Jesus, thank You for Your willingness to lay Your heavenly power aside and lay down Your life for me. Please teach me how to be a servant also. Deliver me from the miserable need to control.

37

HOW BAD CAN IT GET?

Abraham said, "I did it because I thought, There is no fear of God at all in this place, and they will kill me because of my wife" [Gn 20:11].

And among these nations you shall find no ease, and there shall be no rest for the sole of your foot; but the LORD will give you there a trembling heart, and failing eyes, and a languishing soul; your life shall hang in doubt before you; night and day you shall be in dread, and have no assurance of your life [Dt 28:65-66].

Two recent movies—*Black Hawk Down* and *Hotel Rwanda*— depict cultures that had drifted far away from the Christian ideal. During the atrocities in 1994, a priest in Rwanda made the following statement to a journalist: "There are no devils left in hell; they're all in Rwanda." True Christianity can never condone genocide, mass murder, or any form of violence other than self-defense. But in nations or cultures in which "there is no fear of God," there seems to be no limit to the depths of misery, despair, and violence. If man is not subdued by the Holy Spirit of the God Who loves all people and holds us accountable for how we treat each other, then he becomes a medium for the demons of hell to inflict devastation upon the human family. We have seen this repeated throughout history. One Christian writer has compared the fires of Christianity, burning in a culture, to the fires of the ancient cavemen, which kept the nocturnal beasts of prey at bay. There was safety as long as the fire burned brightly, but the glaring eyes of the beasts of prey pressed against the firelight, seeking an opportunity to "steal, kill, and destroy."

If God's Word, the Holy Bible, is true, then the only reason we have been blessed in America for so long is because we have been "One nation, *under God."* Our government and our people have been, at least to some degree, submitted to the God of the universe—the God Who revealed Himself to us in His Word and in His Son, Jesus Christ. Jesus teaches us to love our enemies, bless those who curse us, and do good to those who hate us (Mt 5:44). How could there ever be a safer, more peace-engendering doctrine for the human family? Isn't it obvious that this teaching is from God, Who loves all people as His children? Jesus breaks down the walls of division between people with love. When we fight for our "rights" to live in ways that are not ordained by God, we move ourselves out from under His protective care. We make ourselves vulnerable to destructive powers in the spiritual realm that we do not control, and that have power to make life on earth more miserable than we can imagine. We lose our ability to discern good from evil. Good is labeled "evil," and evil is called "good." Whole generations of children have been brought up in cultures that have gone so far astray of the Truth that there is little hope for many of them to discover it, and be set free. (Though with God, all things are possible [Mt 19:26], and we must never give up hope.) We maintain a safe culture and preserve the ongoing blessings of God by maintaining a sincere reverence for and devotion to God through Jesus Christ, our Lord. This is the old message that is new in every generation, and with every breath.

Lord God, please keep us from evil. Preserve our nation as a nation that is truly "under God," so that there can be peace, liberty and justice for all.

38

PLEASURE AND POWER

Thou dost show me the path of life; in thy presence there is fullness of joy, in thy right hand are pleasures for evermore [Ps 16:11].

And Jesus came and said to them, "All power in heaven and on earth has been given to me... I am with you always, even to the close of the age" [Mt 28:18,20].

There are pleasures and delights in the Kingdom that far surpass any earthly pleasures. And there is power in the Kingdom of God that is greater than all earthly power. These are not emphasized so much in the Faith, however, because they are not primarily what the Kingdom is all about. As Christians, we do not usually hold out pleasure or power as the carrot-on-a-stick to move people toward salvation because a predominantly power or pleasure orientation will preclude one from entering the Kingdom. Paradoxically, one has to be willing to suffer and acknowledge his/her weakness and dependence in order to discover the ultimate delight and power of life in Christ. Outside the Faith, pleasure and power become gods—and they are very ruthless ones. It is very important to examine ourselves frequently to determine, in the Spirit, to what degree we are being motivated by the desire for pleasure or power/control, as opposed to the Love of Christ for the human family.

Lord, please deliver me from the futility of excessive pleasure-seeking, and save me from the agony of needing to control. I pray that the driving force of my life will be Your Love for the people that You place in my life each day.

39

SECURITY IN THE ELDER YEARS

Even to your old age I am He, and to gray hairs I will carry you. I have made, and I will bear; I will carry and will save [Is 46:4].

    I recently returned from a visit with my eighty-two year old mom. She has just completed her first year of life without her "best friend" and husband of sixty-four years. They had known each other since elementary school in rural Alabama, married at seventeen, grew up together bringing three children into the world, and taking very good care of them in every way. Dad had Alzheimer's, and in the end, he didn't know Mom a lot of the time, but she was able to keep him at home until he went into the hospital one week before his soul peacefully departed from his body. During the last months of Dad's life, I would ask Mom if she was keeping her head and heart above water in the sometimes-grueling task of caring for him. "God is sustaining me," she said. She reminded me of the time Dad had visited her diligently when she was hospitalized for depression. He would work all day—he was a welder and pipe-fitter—go home and shower, and drive fifty miles to stay with her in the Birmingham hospital, drive back home then get up early to work the next morning. Despite Mom's objections, he kept this tough schedule until her discharge.
    She could not bring herself to put him in a nursing home, and since he had so much of Christ in him because of his lifetime of faith and devotion, he never got too ungentlemanly for Mom to handle, even when this woman that he didn't know was forbidding him to get in his truck and drive to town.
    Though Mom is still grieving, and probably will be, to some degree, the rest of her life, she trusts God to only leave her here as long as there is some life to live. We picked blackberries and blueberries—five and a half gallons in all. I have a beautiful picture in my mind. It is of Mom standing on an old pulpwood road with an orange flowered bonnet, a bouquet of purple wildflowers in one hand, and a plastic pitcher full of blackberries in the other, pointing out sassafras, black gum, poplar and maple. For the life of me, she looked like a little girl! I think she's getting closer and closer to heaven.

Lord, thank You for taking care of all Your children, even to their old age.

40

DISCERNMENT AND SETTING BOUNDARIES

From that time Jesus began to show his disciples that he must go to Jerusalem and suffer many things from the elders and chief priests and scribes, and be killed, and on the third day be raised. And Peter took him and began to rebuke him, saying, "God forbid, Lord! This shall never happen to you." But he turned and said to Peter, "Get behind me, Satan" [Mt 16:21-3]!

Peter must have been shocked! Jesus looked at him and said, "Get behind me, Satan." Was Jesus delusional, or was Satan speaking through that most honored of all disciples, who seemed to simply be concerned that Jesus would not do anything to shorten His earthly ministry? No, Jesus never spoke a delusional word. It was that evil one, subtly trying to tempt Christ away from His mission, speaking words through Peter that the human side of Jesus must have been sorely tempted to heed. "Don't offer yourself into the hands of those evil Pharisees, Lord. Stay here with us and continue to teach us long into your old age. You might even take a wife, live a normal life, and show us how to grow old gracefully." But Jesus didn't waste a moment entertaining persuasions that had nothing to do with God's plan of salvation for the human family. He immediately discerned the lies of that evil one who had tempted Him earlier in the wilderness, and He sternly rebuked him.

Was Peter evil? Certainly not in the malicious sense. He meant well. And Jesus loved him more than any of us yet know. Here is an amazing lesson for us. Satan can speak through well-intentioned but misguided people. In fact, when we bring this into focus, we realize that Satan has spoken through all of us at one time or another. Any time we have been verbally abusive, or encouraged anyone in some behavior that is contrary to God's way; if we have catered to someone's weakness vs. his or her strength, we have been used of Satan, just as Peter was unknowingly being used of him. This calls us to be mindful of two important relationship dynamics: First, we must be very careful of what we say, and of what spirit is motivating our words. Second, we must carefully discern what is coming through the words of others. We need the gift of discernment; and we need to be very careful to respond only to the truth of the Holy Spirit.

Both God and Satan speak through people. God calls us to listen to the One, and to rebuke or protect ourselves from the other. God always has our best interest at heart. Satan never does—even when his words are smooth as honey.

Lord, thank You for not allowing Yourself to be tempted away from the excruciating pathway that led to my salvation. Please help me to be discerning and strong that my life may be a manifestation of your Light in this world. Please protect us from the evil one, especially when he is speaking through our own family, friends or loved ones. Keep our hearts safe in Your Love.

41

THE BODY OF CHRIST

Now you are the body of Christ, and members in particular [1Cor 12:27].

    A couple came to me for counseling recently. He had been unfaithful on two occasions—once earlier in their marriage, and again recently, bringing a devastating blow to the marriage. They had two young children, and they had been separated, by her choice, for five months. She had discovered that, even during the separation, he had continued a phone relationship with female friends, and she said it was over—she was "done." He was "broken and humiliated," by his own definition and had completely lost hope, when, to his great surprise, she told him she was willing to try again. They both had been meeting with friends in Christ—her with women, him with men—who had been encouraging and confronting them regarding the sanctity and importance of their marriage. The women had been confronting her with the imperative to forgive and love. The men had been confronting him with the necessity to seek forgiveness and commit to faithfulness to his wife. She told me that many people in their congregation had been praying for them and encouraging them. I had a vision as I listened, and I shared it with them. "The Church is the Body of Christ. It is as if Christ Himself is holding you up, keeping you together, teaching you, and encouraging you, one of His hands underneath each of you, through His body of believers." They both immediately nodded in understanding and agreement.

This is a most amazing Reality. We are the Body of Christ, carrying on His marvelous, redemptive work. We are loving people with His love, speaking His liberating truth, being filled with the very same Spirit that lived in Him during His earthly incarnation, saving marriages and preserving families, binding up the wounded of spirit, lifting up the fallen, confronting the arrogant lost, forgiving the sins of the humble and contrite, protecting children from harm, nourishing the souls of the elderly, and spreading kindness throughout the earth. How truly blessed we are, beyond comprehension or words to say, to have been invited into such a wonderful enterprise that gives our lives eternal significance, and fills us with joy!

Lord, we bow in profound gratitude to You for ordaining us to be Your body on the earth. And we are mindful that You are the Source of all goodness and truth and the Fountainhead of the Living Water that flows through us. May we abide in You forever, and may Your love pour forth through us into this world like a mighty healing river.

42

GLORIOUS LUCIDITY

Then Elisha prayed, and said, "O LORD, I pray thee, open his eyes that he may see." So the LORD opened the eyes of the young man, and he saw; and behold, the mountain was full of horses and chariots of fire round about Elisha. [2Kngs 6:17]

Now and then, if we are seeking and following in the way of God, we have lucid moments in which we realize in a deeper and more profound manner the unspeakable goodness of God. We realize that all His promises are true, that He is infinite love, and that, as Julian of Norwich exclaimed, "All shall be well, and all shall be well, and all manner of things shall be well." And as Horatio Spafford wrote, "It is well, it is well with my soul." We realize that the night sky, the peaceful sounds of cicadas, birds, frogs, and crickets; sunrises and sunsets; and the feelings that we have for our loved ones—these are all gifts from the God that has brought *all* into existence. In Christ, we are in His loving domain—the Kingdom of God. We are safe, and have everything we will ever need. We realize that, even though there are experiences that extend beyond our ability to reconcile with a loving God, these have to do with our limited understanding—not with God's limited love. In these moments, those normal places in our mind and heart that tend to doubt and fear are totally obliterated by the Light that floods our soul with what seems to be complete understanding, love, and faith. We know that we know that "all shall ever be well."

We may not remain in these places of lucidity for very long. Like Peter, James, and John at the Transfiguration, we must come down from the mountain [Mt 17:9]. Like them, we have work to do. But we come down transformed, inwardly strengthened, more enlightened, better prepared for whatever lay ahead until we pass through our final "victory" [1Cor 15:26,54]. We do not work or strain for these moments of lucidity. They are not the goal of our walk in Christ. Our goal is to be the loving servants that He has commanded and ordained us to be, better and better each day. But we are very thankful that, as He deems necessary or good, we have these moments of clarity and revelation. And it is fitting that, like Elisha, we pray for our loved ones' eyes to be opened.

Lord, thank You for opening our eyes. Please open the eyes of our children. Let them see the unspeakable goodness of life in the Kingdom.

43

JESUS KNOWS YOUR STUFF

The woman answered him saying "I have no husband." And Jesus replied, "You are right in saying you have no husband, for you have had five husbands, and the man you are living with now is not your husband. In this you have accurately responded" [John 4:16-17].

I once heard a man give an account of a near-death experience in which his whole life was being demonstrated before him in the presence of Jesus, and he was terribly embarrassed and frightened. This experience changed his life radically and wonderfully. The Bible says "the eyes of the Lord are in every place, beholding the evil and the good" [Pr 15:3]. Jesus saw right into the life and heart of the Samaritan woman. And he sees right into yours and mine. But if you read this beautiful story in the fourth chapter of John, you see clearly that Jesus was not criticizing the woman. He was offering her the greatest gift imaginable – living water; a perpetually fulfilling inner fountain, welling up to eternal life. Her lifestyle, rather than something to be condemned, was an indication of needs and inner darkness that Jesus had come to fulfill and enlighten—if she would receive him as the "Messiah." And she apparently did. And it changed her to the degree that her community noticed, and wanted to know more. And when they experienced Jesus, they too believed. Countless millions of people have had this life-changing experience with Jesus. They have come to realize that Jesus knows their most degrading and embarrassing faults—and still loves them, and offers them unspeakable gifts of the Spirit.

Lord, today I receive anew the gift of forgiveness and overflowing life. And I am thankful for what You are doing inside me. May I love today, with Your love, and may others become interested in You because of what they see in me.

44

LETTING GO

So Moses and Aaron went in to Pharaoh, and said to him, "Thus says the LORD, the God of the Hebrews, 'How long will you refuse to humble yourself before me? Let my people go, that they may serve me. For if you refuse to let my people go, behold, tomorrow I will bring locusts into your country'" [Ex 10:3-4].

The story of the Exodus confirms God's love of freedom, and His demand that all His children be free. The plagues were God's way of getting Pharaoh to let His people go. Pharaoh had a hard time letting go. Water turning to blood, gnats, flies, frogs, hail, boils, darkness, locusts, and death of livestock didn't do it, even though his subjects were pleading with him to let them go. He tried to bargain. "You can sacrifice to your God here in Egypt" [8:25]. "I'll let the men go, but not the women and children" [10:12]. "Okay, okay. All the people can go, but not the flocks and herds" [10:24]. Not until he suffered the devastating loss of his firstborn son, destined for the throne, along with the loss of all his people's firstborn—as well as the firstborn of the livestock—did Pharaoh relinquish. Talk about holding on to control!

I've been like Pharaoh. There are some things I've held on to—against the leading of the Holy Spirit—that dragged me through some plagues of my own. In fact this seems to be a principle. I think we are all like Pharaoh in this way. A hard-hearted Pharaoh rules over certain parts of our personality, and he hangs on to his little tight-fisted control through plague after plague. God is calling all parts of our personality into freedom, and He will not stop until we are completely free. But the little hard-hearted Pharaoh in us avoids, bargains, resists, and hangs on to his addiction—control. Maybe its money that God wants us to let go of. Maybe pornography. Maybe control of our mate. Maybe anger or unforgiveness. Maybe laziness or apathy. All these things represent some form of enslavement. God seems very determined to get us free. I hope we don't have to suffer some version of the loss of our firstborn before we let it all go and get on with the journey into the Promised Land.

Lord, thank You for caring so much about the freedom of my soul that you torment everything in me that is holding on to anything that is not fit for heaven. Today— right now—I let it all go and launch out into the wilderness of Your Love and Freedom.

45

ASLEEP IN THE STORM

But he was in the stern, asleep on the cushion; and they woke him and said to him, "Lord, do you not care if we perish?" [Mk 4:38]

We've just come through Katrina, the storm of the century, here in southeast Louisiana. The devastation is incomprehensible. Imagine an F-3 tornado 200 miles wide and traveling a hundred miles. The aftermath is a storm in itself—a storm of chaos, confusion, uncertainty, separation of families, inability to communicate, disruption of the major routines and amenities of life, lasting weeks for some, permanently for others. Families were uprooted from their lifelong communities and thrust into strange living circumstances: new schools, no jobs, living doubled or tripled up with family or friends in unfamiliar surroundings, trying to find scarce workers and materials to repair damaged roofs to prevent further water damage, having to find new jobs, doctors, dentists, churches, furniture, and appliances—all while dealing with insurance agencies, FEMA, expensive and scarce gasoline, long lines and sluggish traffic everywhere, nagging uncertainty about the future, along with whatever normal family problems might arise. Katrina did not end when the wind and water subsided.

In the midst of this panic and despair, I have been strangely and wonderfully sustained by this image of Jesus asleep in the boat during a storm so severe as to cause even those seasoned fishermen to fear for their lives. I can see their panic-stricken faces as they shook Him awake: "Don't you care that we are about to die, Lord?" I envision Jesus, tired and perhaps annoyed by their lack of faith. "Peace. Be still." And it all ended. "Where is your faith?" he asked them. Somewhere, deep in my soul, during this storm, I have Jesus, asleep. I will not wake Him up. I already know what He will say. He is taking very good care of me, even while He sleeps.

Lord, thank You for the peace that goes beyond understanding – the irrational peace of God.

46

BECOMING A FAMILY

"Whoever does the will of God is my brother, and sister, and mother" [Mk.3:35].

For he himself is our peace, who has made the two one and has destroyed the barrier, the dividing wall of hostility [Eph 2:14].

In the Kingdom of God, we are all family. Jesus breaks down the dividing walls of hostility between people. He destroys enmity [Eph 2:15]. Jesus teaches us to love our enemies. In this way He turns enemies into friends. He does this between brothers and sisters, husbands and wives, mothers and daughters, fathers and sons, neighbors, denominations, nations, cultures, and races. And He does this without destroying the unique personalities of individuals, and without destroying the beautiful diversity in the various cultures of people on Earth. In fact, the Holy Spirit, entering into a person through Christ, *enhances* his unique personality—clarifies it and focuses that person's life so that he or she becomes a unique and beautiful light in the human family. The children of God are like flowers in the garden of the human family—each with its own unique colors and aroma—each contributing its unique beauty to the whole garden. And other cultures are like other gardens, with completely different species of flowers that are no less beautiful. An oriental rock garden is no less beautiful than the flower gardens in my neighborhood. I am personally very thankful for the unique beauty of African praise music and Celtic hymns. Jesus makes us one, while enhancing our uniqueness and diversity. In Christ we celebrate our differences instead of allowing them to create enmity between us.

Lord, help me to be mindful of the family that You have created on the earth—the wonderful Family of God. And help me to be a life-enhancing influence in my family today.

47

ALIVE AND AWAKE

Therefore it is said, "Awake, O sleeper, and arise from the dead, and Christ shall give you light" [Eph 5:14].

Before we came into Christ, we did not know that we were lost, blind, and on a pathway to nowhere—or worse! Our ideas about life were basically delusions—dreams destined to turn into nightmares. We did not know what life was about, and we were not thankful for the gift of life. We complained a lot because we weren't getting enough of the stuff the world promises. The promises of the world were not making us happy, and we thought we were entitled to happiness. We basically were trying to get more of the stuff that made us feel good and that helped us forget that we were going to die—and it was getting harder and harder.

Jesus encouraged us to face the whole Truth. He did not want us to be in denial. He knew that we did not need to be. He knew that the Truth would set us free. But He would not force this Truth upon us—He would only encourage us, or sternly warn us, to seek it. And He boldly stated that He was the Truth [John 14:6]. When we follow Christ, we grow in our comprehension of the Truth about life, death, God, relationships, love, and everything that is necessary for a truly successful life. We begin to awaken from our nightmares and delusions. Dawn breaks into the darkness of our understanding. We begin to discover the meaning of the word "freedom" [Lk 4:18]. Peace begins to arise in our souls like mercury in a thermometer on a warm spring morning. Our heart smiles. We say, "Good morning, God, thank You very much." And He replies, "Good morning my child, welcome to everything!"

Lord Jesus, what You have done, and what You are doing is too wonderful for words. Thank You for awakening me into the Love of God and into abundant and eternal life.

48

YOU CAN'T JUDGE A BOOK BY ITS COVER

"Woe to you, scribes and Pharisees, hypocrites! for you are like whitewashed tombs, which outwardly appear beautiful, but within they are full of dead men's bones and all uncleanness" [Jesus., Mt 23:27].

Peoples' lives have an outward appearance—a veneer—and an inner reality. The poem, *Richard Cory*, by Edwin Arlington Robinson exposes this reality. The entire poem is about how enviably admirable, well-schooled, attractive, gentlemanly, rich, and well-dressed Mr. Cory was. People "looked at him" when he came into town, and he "fluttered pulses" when he said "Good morning." The last lines hit like a load of bricks:

So on we worked, and waited for the light, and went without the meat, and cursed the bread.

And Richard Cory, one calm summer night, went home and put a bullet thru' his head.

Richard Cory's inner world, unlike his outer appearance, was nothing to be envied. The veneer disguising the enslavement and despair of spiritual blindness may be impressive. It may be composed of excitement, fun, attractiveness, happy faces, prosperity, power, and control. The outward manifestations of the Way of Christ are not impressive by worldly standards. But this Way leads into an infinite treasure of inner freedom, joy, and peace. It consists of a sincere surrender to the lordship of Christ, the responsibilities of righteousness, restraining or re-channeling of the passions, the work of love, service, humility, and simplicity of lifestyle.

In either case, we ***live with*** what is underneath the veneer, in the same way that we live with the personality, rather than the outward appearance, of our mate.

Lord, Thank You for searching and revealing the depths of the heart. And thank You for delivering us from the hollow deceptions of evil. Deepen our spiritual perceptions today. Help us to be more alive and free in Your Holy Spirit.

49

FULL, FAT, AND FORGETFUL

When thou hast eaten and art full, then thou shalt bless the LORD thy God for the good land which he hath given thee. Beware that thou forget not the LORD thy God, in not keeping his commandments, and his judgments, and his statutes, which I command thee this day [Dt. 8:10-11 KJV]

God had delivered His people from slavery in Egypt. They had wandered, complaining and faithless, in the desert. Now He was about to deliver them into a land "flowing with milk and honey." For the first time in their history, they would prosper. And in His infinite wisdom, He gave them a warning. "When you are full, beware that you do not forget."

There is a temptation that comes with wealth and prosperity. Jesus pointed it out to us also: *"And again I say unto you, It is easier for a camel to go through the eye of a needle, than for a rich man to enter into the kingdom of God"* (Mt 19:24). In America, we have been prosperous. We have been rich by world standards for decades. And we have been exposed to the temptation that God warned the Hebrews about in the above verses. Crisis, pain, and imminent need tend to drive us toward God. Prosperity tends to lull us into false security, apathy toward God, and laxity in our spiritual growth. The word "religion" is derived from Latin words meaning, *"to bind back."* God was attempting to *bind* His children to the commandments and the laws that would enable them to prosper spiritually as they prospered materially. Without spiritual growth, material blessings become curses. Prosperity without spiritual growth causes a people to become spoiled, entitled, selfish, vain, and addicted to a vast array of substances or activities: shopping, sex, drugs, alcohol, entertainment, gambling, etc.—simply because we have such easy access to these things, and they give us immediate gratification. Our physical obesity is a metaphor of the more dangerous spiritual laxity that we have allowed to descend upon us like an oppressive, stinking wet blanket.

Perhaps one of the greatest challenges for Americans is to throw off this wet blanket, rouse ourselves up from the deadly slumber of prosperity-induced spiritual apathy; to roll up our sleeves, and dig in to some serious Bible study, meditation, prayer, confession, repentance, humility, and compassionate service. Maybe we have become *full, fat and forgetful.*

Lord, please forgive me for ignoring that which is most important: my relationship with You and obedience to the Way of Christ, my Lord. Today I vow to be more awake, aware, thankful, and loving In His name.

50

IT'S NOT *THAT* BAD

These things I have spoken to you, that you might have peace. In the world you have tribulation; but be of good cheer, I have overcome the world-- Jesus [John 16:33b].

We are afflicted in every way, but not crushed; perplexed, but not driven to despair; persecuted, but not forsaken; struck down, but not destroyed-- Paul [2Cor 4:8-9].

When I was in the second grade, my dad showed up at school to tell me that my grandfather had died. This first encounter with death was a shocking and frightening event for me. I had never seen my family members and extended family in grief—so many tears; so much sadness. I had never seen so many people in our little church, all in such a solemn spirit. By the time we got into the family car to go to the gravesite, I was falling over the brink of hysteria. Something of the finality and awfulness of this loss had begun to dawn in me. I began to wail and cry. My mom, in her quiet wisdom, reached over the seat and put her hand gently but firmly on my shoulder and said, "Mark, Son, It's not *that* bad!"

There is no way that Mom could have realized what a profound and formative statement that turned out to be for me. In this first close exposure to death, I had lost touch with a foundational security that, theretofore, I did not even know I possessed. The bottom fell out from under me. Her statement brought my hysterical spirit right back down on the ground of that foundation. I could see and feel in her that everything was still fundamentally ok. Yes, we had suffered a loss, but the world wasn't coming to an end. And later, as I grew in the faith that she and my dad planted in me, I would realize that, even if the world *were* coming to an end, there would still be no need for hysteria. In a profoundly powerful way, Mom planted a seed of faith in me that is confirmed over and over again in the Scriptures and in our life in Christ. In all of life's experiences, from birth through death, however bad things may get, there is nothing to fear; nothing to dread. God is with us. And He loves us. He will sustain us. He will set limits—just as He set limits on Job's afflictions [Job 1:12]—to what He will allow us to suffer. And there will always be a redemptive, victorious response. Suffering will come to all, but for all who are in Christ, joy has the final word!

Lord, please keep me in Your perfect peace. Deliver me from the delusions of fear and dread.

51

GETTING FREE FROM RELATIONSHIP ENTANGLEMENTS

But Jesus did not trust himself to them, because he knew all men and needed no one to bear witness of man; for he himself knew what was in man [John 2:24-5].

Jesus had performed some miracles, and He was at a high point of popularity among the people. "But He did not *trust* Himself to them, because He *knew* what was *in* man." We see this as another wonderful manifestation of the infinite wisdom of Christ. If He had trusted Himself to them, later when some of them were shouting, "Crucify Him!" He would have felt let down, disappointed, hurt, wounded, victimized, angry, etc. But if He had failed to *love* them, He would have failed in His mission of redemption. A great and liberating truth is here: Loving people does NOT mean entrusting yourself to them, making yourself vulnerable to them, or allowing your inner self to be ripped apart by their failures in returning your love. As Christ protected Himself from the sinful natures of the people He loved and came to redeem, so His Spirit in us protects us from "what is in man," even those of our own household.

And what is it that He knew that was in man? He knew the blindness of Judas who betrayed Him. He knew the weakness of Peter who, despite a sincere commitment to follow Christ into death, denied Him. He knew the blind envy and arrogance of the Pharisees who would be used as Satan's pawns to ensnare Him. He knew the blood lust of the Roman soldiers who ravaged his body. And He loved them all, prayed for them, and brought them salvation—if they would receive it. And He knows the passive-aggressive anger of your husband. And He knows the disrespect and coldness of your wife. And He knows the hostility of your employer, and the critical spirits of your co-workers. He knows how they have painfully misunderstood you, betrayed you, snubbed you or simply ignored you. And He commands you to love them, but He PROTECTS YOU [if you allow Him] FROM WHAT IS IN THEM. All our tribulations, even those that are evoked by the sinful natures of others, have to do with our own personal growth and ongoing sanctification. God is not so unjust as to limit our ability to receive and experience, in ever-increasing measure, all the gifts of Christ [peace, love, joy, soul-freedom, contentment, victory, etc.] by the failures of others. In that case we would indeed all be victims of each other because all of us have sinned against each other and failed in so many ways. Our gracious and wonderful Lord has given us the example of victory over the most malicious, vicious and deceptive forms of evil as well as the simply blind and weak forms of it. And He empowers us to attain that same victory!

Lord, we open our hearts to the outpouring of Your ever-increasing inner peace, love, joy and freedom of soul that are not dependent on what others do or fail to do. Free us from life-depleting attachments to and needs from others. You supply "all our needs."

52

GLORIOUS SERVANTHOOD

Whoever would be greatest among you must be servant of all. For the Son of man also came not to be served but to serve, and to give his life as a ransom for many [Mk 10:44-45].

In the aftermath of Hurricane Katrina, people in my community were in need of basic supplies like food, water and ice. Many people came into southeast Louisiana, some from as far away as Washington State, to serve us in our time of need. Frequently, during this time, I had tears of joy when I saw and felt deeply the compassion and willingness to serve on the part of so many people. I heard countless stories of people who had lost everything, and who were carried in the arms of compassion when they could not maintain themselves. One woman, from one of the hardest hit parishes, who had lost everything, and whose parents and in-laws had also lost their homes, told me that she felt she had *gained more than she lost* because of the compassion that had been shown to her family.

I drove through a well-maintained distribution point and received some food and ice from a polite, smiling national guardsman who *thanked me*. I said, "I should be thanking *you!*" The young man said, "Our pleasure, sir." [I have seen this same spirit of polite, proud willingness to serve, in my own son, a captain in the army, and those of his fellow soldiers that I have been privileged to meet.] I was struck by the contrast between the mindset of our military [and police] and that of other totalitarian or developing nations. Our military and police consider themselves to be the *servants* of the people and of the principles that make freedom, equality, and preservation of life possible. We do not *fear* our military and police personnel, even though they carry arms. We are comforted by their presence. I don't think that this phenomenon is common in our world though we take it for granted here in the U.S. Generally, I think the military and police are fearful, belligerent, authoritative entities. I am very thankful that we are "one nation under God" and that the principle of servanthood, given to us by Christ, has permeated our ideas and principles of government. I hope we never lose our willingness to submit to this principle and to its Author.

Lord, thank You for washing the disciples' feet, and for teaching us the joy of servanthood. Today, may we be open to the opportunity to serve, and may we know the joy of serving.

53

WHAT DOES GOD OWE US?

I will not restrain my mouth; I will speak in the anguish of my spirit; I will complain in the bitterness of my soul [Jb 7:11].

I had heard of thee by the hearing of the ear, but now my eye sees thee; therefore I despise myself, and repent in dust and ashes [Jb 42:5-6].KJV

A major transformation transpired in Job's understanding between the two above verses, and it had to do with a revelation from God. Job's losses were monumental. And he was by God's own account a perfect and righteous man who feared God and shunned evil. {Job 1:8} But in the course of his prolonged sufferings, he drifted away from perfection. He began to complain, and he began to demand an explanation from God and to question His fairness {10:1-7}. When God responds to Job's lamentations {Chapters 38-41}, Job has an awakening expressed in the above verses [5,6]. Job realized that God did not owe him anything—not even an explanation.

This is a very good understanding for all of us. When we look deeply into what God owes us, we realize that He does not even owe us our *lives*. We were not somewhere before we were born doing hard labor, and performing difficult acts of righteousness, so that, at the appointed time, we could stand before God and say, "OK, God, I've worked for it; I've earned it; now you must give me my life." Our life—the most valuable thing we possess—is a *gift*. Everything we have ever experienced—the taste of food, intimacy with our mate, laughter, children, diving into a cool swimming pool on a hot day, flowers, sunsets, a good night's sleep—are all *gifts*. God has given us everything, but He owes us *nothing*—not even an explanation for the suffering that we do not understand. There is a saying I have heard frequently in Christian circles. I think it is a very good saying, indicative of at least a moderate level of spiritual maturity. It is: "Thank God that because of Christ, I don't get what I deserve!"

Lord, please deliver us from the destructive mindset of entitlement. You have given us more than we could ever have hoped for – life itself, and every blessing of life. We understand that You owe us absolutely nothing.

54

GOD SETS LIMITS

And the LORD said to Satan, "Behold, all that he has is in your power; only upon himself do not put forth your hand." So Satan went forth from the presence of the LORD [Job 1:12].

  Here is one of the most comforting verses in the Scripture. God determines what Satan can and can*not* inflict on Job—and on you and me. God says to Satan, "You can do this, but you cannot do that." I think sometimes we make the mistake of seeing God and Satan as two *equal* but opposing forces. This is false theology. Satan is a created being—one of the angels. Though he rebelled and was cast out of heaven, he remains under the authority of God, along with all creation. There is no force, personage, or power that is equal to our God. The same God Who loves us enough to sacrifice His "only begotten Son" on our behalf {Jn 3:16}, also determines what Satan can and cannot do. He sets limits on the old serpent. Greater is He that is in us, than he that is in the world {1Jn 4:4}. We need not fear evil, for He is with us {Ps 23:4}. In Christ, we are "more than conquerors" over all the evil forces of this world {Rom 8:37}. Let us therefore abide in Christ—in His love, faith and goodness—so that we can grow increasingly confident and free from the fear of evil. We are eternally safe in Christ. Even death is a victory for us—our final victory {ICor.15:26}.

Lord, thank You for securing an eternal victory over evil, and the fear of evil, for us. Thank You for revealing in Your Holy Word the Truth that sets us free.

55

"GOOD! NOW YOU KNOW HOW IT FEELS!"

Be not overcome of evil, but overcome evil with good [Rom 12:21].

Repay no one evil for evil, but take thought for what is noble in the sight of all [Rom 12:17].

Earlier in their marriage, a husband's relationship with a female co-worker had evoked feelings of insecurity in his wife to the point that she questioned his faithfulness. He was [inappropriately] indignant but assured her of his fidelity. Later, her involvement with a man stirred his feelings of insecurity, and when he shared these feelings with her, she said, "Good! Now you know how it feels!" This is an example of a common mistake in marriage. It is a violation of the "Do not return evil for evil" principle. We can never overcome evil with evil—only with good. When those we love fail to act in ways pleasing to God, we are strongly tempted to act out of our sinful nature in response. God commands us to resist this temptation. We must rise above the sinful nature manifestations of our loved ones, and live in the wonderful freedom of the Holy Spirit. Jesus, from the Cross, did not pray for His tormenters to receive their just rewards for their actions; He prayed for their forgiveness. This is our example. When we return evil for evil, or when we gloat in the sufferings of those through whom we have been hurt, we only retard our growth into the freedom of Christ. His prayer for His tormenters is the evidence of His glorious freedom from the suffering of unforgiveness and the need for revenge. The freedom into which He invites us.

Lord, thank You for this wonderful freedom from vulnerability to the failures and shortcomings of our loved ones.

56

CONTRITION OR CONDEMNATION

The sacrifice acceptable to God is a broken spirit; a broken and contrite heart, O God, thou wilt not despise [Ps 51:1].

There is therefore now no condemnation for those who are in Christ Jesus. [Rom 8:1].

There is a very important and frequently overlooked difference between contrition and condemnation. Contrition is defined as "remorseful or guilty because of one's sins or shortcomings." It is temporary, and leads ultimately to forgiveness and freedom, greater understanding, and spiritual growth. To condemn is to "hold or prove to be wrong or guilty; to declare unfit." It is chronic and debilitating for the soul. It is an unnecessary load that God does not want His children carrying. If you have children, you know the difference. When our children misbehave [sin], we want them to feel some contrition—to be sorry for their bad behavior. [It is a very bad omen if our children do not feel sorry for their disobedience, dishonesty, etc.] But we don't want them to go around with heads hanging, feeling like a miserable failure for the rest of their lives. The Bible teaches that once we come into Christ we have within us His Holy Spirit, Who convicts us when we stray from the path of life, toward death—the direction of sin. The healthy response to honest conviction is contrition [which God loves], and repentance [changing the bad behavior], leading to a new level of life in the Spirit. The evil one [Satan] loves to extend contrition into condemnation, bringing up every sin you've ever committed and piling them on top of you. He is called the "accuser of the brethren" [Rev 12:10]. Though God has forgotten our forgiven sins [Heb 8:12] and put them as far away as the East is from the West [Ps 103:12], Satan will bring them up on every occasion, and if you allow him, will drag you all the way down into chronic remorse [condemnation] with every mistake. But God has put up a glorious detour to this downward trek with Rom 8:1 [see above]. And it is very important for us to receive the gift of "no condemnation," forgiveness, and cleansing from "ALL unrighteousness" [1Jn 1:9]. Just as He said to the woman caught in the act of adultery, so He says to us when we sin: "Who condemns you?" And like her, we will always respond, "No one, Lord." And again He will say, "Neither do I condemn you. Go and sin no more" [John 8:11].

I want us to experience conviction. If we are not experiencing conviction periodically, then one of two things has happened: [1] We have attained perfection, or [2] We are in denial. We know that we have not attained perfection, and we don't want to be in denial. Therefore, let's embrace conviction as the gift of love that it truly is and the associated [short-term] contrition. That's how we know we are still growing in the sanctification process. But let's refuse to let Satan drag us into condemnation. We have been set free from that—in Christ. Joy always has the final word—in Christ.

Lord, thank You for delivering us from condemnation. Please help us to remember that we are forgiven. Help us to stay honest with You, ourselves and trusted others about our sins. And help us to stay on the pathway of life and love for all.

57

BLAMING THE SUFFERER

"And when did we see you sick or in prison and visit you?"[Mt 25:3]

And the King will answer them, "Truly, I say to you, as you did it to one of the least of these my brethren, you did it to me" [Mt 25:40].

In the amazing and enlightening story of Job, we see the interesting phenomenon of the theology of Eliphaz, Bildad ,and Zophar—Job's friends. Their belief was that Job's sufferings were directly related to his denied or hidden sins. They could not grasp that God would allow the righteous to suffer. They were obliquely critical of Job, adding to his torment. I think this is common theology.

For the past three years, I have had the opportunity to work with "homeless" families in my community: families in major transition, living with other family or friends, or in sub-standard conditions. Within myself and in many people with whom I collaborated in helping these families, I detected a tendency to judge these people as "irresponsible and shiftless" and to conveniently write them off, so to speak. I think I went into the job with this prejudicial idea about these adults, but resolving, nevertheless to try to help the innocent children involved. But when I looked more deeply into their lives, I began to see that most of these people were no less diligent and hard working than me. They had simply been hit with not one but sometimes multiple waves of crises. Before they could recover from one, another wave swept over them. And they were not looking for a handout; in fact many of them had not reached out to a single soul, but were trying to go it alone. Many of them had insufficient coping skills. Many had not been loved very well in their upbringing. But they were doing the best they could. I had to repent of my judgmental attitude. And it was disheartening to hear co-workers at times make degrading remarks about people that they really knew little about, simply because of their life situation. I think we really do have a tendency to blame sufferers for their suffering. [And this happens in the context of marriage also.] It certainly is an easy way to get ourselves off the hook of any diligent efforts to minister to them—or simply to be with them in a compassionate spirit, since, sometimes, as with Job, we can't make their suffering go away.

Lord, please help me be compassionate rather than judgmental with those in critical life conditions. May I remember that, "there, but for Your grace, go I."

58

HEALING DISSENSION

Love your enemies, bless those who curse you, do good to those who hate you, and pray for those who despitefully use and persecute you, that you may be the children of your Father which is in heaven." Jesus [Mt.5:44-45].

If we are true to our Lord, we cannot hate any human being, regardless of their political orientation, sexual behaviors, character disorders, religious beliefs, or downright meanness and cruelty. We can hate evil, but as the apostle Paul came to understand, *we wrestle not against flesh and blood, but against*

***principalities**, against **powers**, against the rulers of the darkness of this world, against spiritual wickedness in **high places** [Eph 6:12]*.

Jesus understood/understands that those who live outside the Kingdom of God don't know what they're doing [Lk 23:34]. No matter how intelligent, schooled or respected, they are pawns in Satan's ploy to steal, kill, and destroy. But if we hate these victims of the evil one, we become victims ourselves. We cannot overcome evil with evil, only with good. Evil tends to beget evil. When my wife is in a bad mood and acting badly, it is very hard for me to remain civil. My tendency is to return evil for evil. When we are hurt, our natural tendency is—like a two year old—to hurt back. When we are attacked, we want to do a little more than just defend ourselves. This tendency is evil according to Jesus. And we must not give in to it. The world is full of sad examples of people hating each other, from families to nations, lashing out at each other verbally—criticizing, condemning, killing. Evil is always winning the day when people hate each other. Christians are responsible to be peacemakers—to sow seeds of peace in areas of strife, as in the wonderful prayer of St. Francis:

> *Lord, make me an instrument of your peace,*
> *Where there is hatred, let me sow love;*
> *Where there is injury, pardon;*
> *Where there is doubt, faith;*
> *Where there is despair, hope;*
> *Where there is darkness, light;*
> *Where there is sadness, joy.*

This peacemaking process is the work of the Holy Spirit in us, and it must begin in our own hearts, marriages, families, neighborhoods and workplaces. We must guard our hearts against being critical or judgmental of people who do not believe or behave the way we do.

Lord, thank You for this wonderful commandment to love our enemies. Give us the strength of Your Holy Spirit to overcome our tendency to hate any person.

59

PLEASE DON'T TAKE YOUR LIFE FOR GRANTED

Jesus answered him, "Truly, truly, I say to you, unless one is born anew, he cannot see the kingdom of God" [John 3:3].

In a conversation in a coffee shop, a friend told me that his brother is a scientist who studies solar wind. His brother told him that without the moon, we would not be protected from the fatal effects of the sun. It is not simply the gravitational field of the earth that protects us, but rather the *combination* of the gravitational fields of the earth and moon. Therefore, without the moon we would not be. The more we learn about life, the more we realize how amazing it is. My coffee shop friend, a social worker, told me that he had recently come into a renewed faith in Christ. He had gone through a period of doubt fortified by secular education, but in the aftermath of a serious life crisis—a sort of "bottoming out"—he had come to believe in Christ. And he was discovering new life. He was examining his own life and life in general, in a new light. He said, "Even if you don't believe in God, the fact that we are here is a miracle."

I think I have taken life for granted. And I don't think I am an exception. I believe that Jesus wants us to wake up and realize how amazing and wonderful it is that we are here. I think He wants us to be "born again."—born into a greater awareness and aliveness. When we come into Christ and receive the Truth that God is offering us, we begin to truly live. We begin to discover what life is really all about. And this new life is so wonderful we want it for everyone that we love. And we love everyone. We realize that we have been reborn and that this rebirth will continue throughout eternity. We are very thankful. And we are very happy. We realize now that life is exactly what it is supposed to be, and what we have always wanted it to be. We find rest for our souls [Mt 11:28].

Lord, thank You for my new birth into abundant and eternal life. Thank You for waking me up. I offer myself as a living sacrifice, to be used by You to awaken others into this joy. Please continue to deliver me from the world of the walking dead.

60

LIVING ON TIPS

If I give away all I have, and if I deliver my body to be burned, but have not love, I gain nothing [1Cor 13:]).

For my people have committed two evils; they have forsaken me the fountain of living waters, and hewed them out cisterns, broken cisterns, that can hold no water [Jer 2:1].)

    A couple came to me for counseling because the wife was in despair and feeling unloved, even from the beginning of their marriage. The husband, by his account, was trying, but she felt that he was totally selfish. "It's always been about him," she said. "I've been giving and giving and giving and getting absolutely nothing in return, and I have given out. I can't give anymore." She was giving out of her need to be loved, and she was looking to her husband for the impossible. It struck me after the session that she was like a person living on tips. Her giving and serving were attempts to get her husband to put a few dollars in the tip jar. And whatever he happened to drop in there was her life's wages—and it was a very meager existence. Without realizing it, she had hewn out a broken cistern. She had not discovered the Fountain of Living Waters. She was doing good things, but she was not doing them in *love* but rather out of *need*. This couple, as you might imagine, had been on the sidelines as far as spiritual growth is concerned. They were peripherally religious. They saw religious life as a sideline issue—sort of important if you have an affinity for it or if you ever have time to get around to it, but meanwhile they had these practical issues of marriage problems to deal with. The husband had failed to be a spiritual leader. Their problems were God's way of knocking on the door—a little louder. I was trying to help them open the door—the door to Everything they would ever need, to the infinite love of God, and to the Fountain of Living Waters.

Lord please help us remember that if we do not keep our priorities straight, our lives will deteriorate. And Help us to remember that You are always at the door; always knocking, and willing to come in if we open it.

61

MY SON

And you shall tell your son on that day, 'It is because of what the LORD did for me when I came out of Egypt.' And when in time to come your son asks you, 'What does this mean?' you shall say to him, 'By strength of hand the LORD brought us out of Egypt, from the house of bondage [Ex 13:8,14].

God commanded the Israelites to pass on the truth about their deliverance from slavery in Egypt to their sons. He gave them this solemn responsibility, so that all generations would know that God had done this for His people. We all have this same solemn responsibility to let our children know, clearly and beyond doubt, that God has delivered us from slavery also—the slavery of guilt, remorse, feelings of inadequacy, prideful delusions, attachments to the things of this world, laziness, self-centeredness, and the weakness of lust. He has delivered us from the slavery of fear of death and fear of life, even the dreadful fear of what might happen to our children. He has progressively, wonderfully, and mercifully delivered us from the slavery of self into the glorious freedom of Christ, who plainly said, *"I have come to set at liberty those who are oppressed and to preach deliverance to the captives"* [Lk 4:18]. Just like the children of Israel, we could not deliver ourselves any more than we could pull ourselves up by our own bootstraps. God had to do it—and He did! Our deliverance is as much an act of God as was the deliverance of the Jews from Egypt—the plagues, the Passover, the pillars of fire and smoke, the parting of the sea. Jesus reached into the bleak ignorance of our lives and lifted us up just as He lifted Peter out of the waves [Mt. 14], and He began teaching us the Truth about life, love, freedom, peace, and joy. He inspired us with a hope that has grown brighter and brighter, and with a deepening security that will never end. He made life meaningful. He restored vitality. We know now, more than ever, that He has the words of eternal life. His Spirit is growing in us. We still sin, but less than ever. We seek forgiveness more quickly. On our best days, we are better than ever, and our worst days are good. We complain less than ever. We frequently cry tears of joy. We can feel His love flowing through us. We are more grateful than ever. We owe all this to Jesus. We don't want to pretend otherwise, and we will not be embarrassed to say it. In Christ we really do grow up into manhood. We love our people faithfully. We feel free and thankful. We gracefully accept our suffering, and peacefully embrace death as our final victory. God has given us life, and in Christ He has delivered us into the reborn life of His spirit—eternal life that is progressively more abundant. And at the peril of our very souls and the well-being of our children, we must never forget it. You have this torch now. We have done, and will continue to do the best we can to pass it to you. You must refine what you have received and carry it into your generation. You have to discover Jesus for yourself. My Jesus can never be adequate for you because you cannot internalize my Jesus. You must have your own personal relationship with Him as He reveals Himself to you. He will only do this if you seek with your whole heart. Jesus is not a half-hearted Lord, and He doesn't sit well on the back burner. How can we call ourselves Christians if we don't pray or have a working understanding of what Jesus taught? If you are not following in His way, I want you to be convicted because conviction is the work of the Holy Spirit. I want you to be convicted until you are free. I want you to fear for your soul until you know absolutely, beyond doubt, that there is nothing to fear. I don't want you to live in the half-life world with just enough religion to inoculate you from the reality of your need for Christ as Lord. Why? Because I love you.

Lord, thank You so much for our children! How You have blessed us so tremendously with them. Please give us grace to be for them what You would have us be. Keep us all from evil.

62

THE WONDERFUL POWER OF JESUS

They are not of the world, even as I am not of the world [John 17:16].

While driving home from a Thanksgiving visit with my family, I was thinking about a TV news segment showing security guards physically restraining a man who had broken into a long Thanksgiving shopping line to get a reduced price on a lap-top computer in a Wal-Mart store. It was a violent and disheartening scene. I told my wife that it looked like some footage of people in famine stricken nations fighting for food;

only here, they were fighting for the latest technology deal. Further on down the road, I pulled into the left lane to pass a slower vehicle, and the driver behind me flashed his lights and pulled up close behind me to express his disapproval. He was a good distance behind me, and I felt perfectly justified in the maneuver. I felt the seeds of rage beginning to sprout. I began a dialogue in my head with this "jerk." My chest tightened, and I clinched my teeth. I considered a hard brake application, or some inappropriate gesture. The Holy Spirit awakened me, and I began to call on Jesus: "Jesus, Jesus, Jesus, please help me. Please deliver me from this stupid anger." My heart softened into a smile of gratitude. Later, it occurred to me that I have the same seeds growing in me that were manifesting in the Wal-Mart shopper—the seeds of entitlement and inner demand that life and people be what it and they are supposed to be—and by my definition,. The seeds of selfishness and blindness. I realized, in a new light, that Jesus continually delivers us from futility, stupidity, and blindness. I think we would all be astounded if we knew how many acts of violence, rage, or greed were thwarted each day because someone silently called on Jesus for deliverance. Jesus, the "Prince of Peace," our "very present help" in times of trouble, Who commands us to love our enemies, and Who has delivered us out of this world, even while we continue to live in it.

Lord Jesus, thank You for the power that we have in Your name to overcome our various forms of blindness and ignorance. Please continue to awaken us into peace and gratitude, self-control, freedom and love for the unlovable. Thank You that we are not of this world.

63

PLEASE DON'T TAKE JESUS FOR GRANTED

Then turning to the disciples he said privately, "Blessed are the eyes which see what you see, for I tell you that many prophets and kings desired to see what you see, and did not see it, and to hear what you hear, and did not hear it." [Lk 10:23-24]

In Franklin Graham's book, *Rebel with a Cause*, he tells about a trip he took with Bob Pierce, founder of World Vision and Samaritan's Purse. Bob wanted Franklin to see "the poverty of pagan religions and the hopelessness and despair of the people," and to see "what it was like when people lived in total spiritual darkness." They traveled to Borneo, Bangkok, Katmandu, Nepal, and Iran among other places. Franklin relates that he sensed an "evil presence" in a village run by a witch doctor, saw Hindu priests sacrificing animals and sprinkling the blood on cheering worshippers, and witnessed the abysmal living conditions of tens of thousands of Communist refugees risking their lives for the freedom that we take for granted. We see oppression and violent tyranny in many cultures and nations on the earth. We in America are the beneficiaries of a culture that has been deeply rooted in and shaped by the wonderful, liberating teachings of Jesus Christ. We are a mixture of many cultures and races and even religions, able to live peaceably because our political system has been informed by the teachings of Christ, Who has commanded us to love our enemies, and has taught us that God has given freedom to man—even the freedom to reject Him—and that we cannot force people into the Kingdom of God. The Holy Spirit of Christ has been light and salt and leaven in our culture and has shaped the social environment in which we live. When we look at the history of the human family, and at the various forms of darkness continuing to permeate many cultures today, we realize how blessed we are, and we lift our hearts in grateful praise to God for giving us Jesus, and to Jesus for His willingness to shine His glorious light into our world. We don't know why we were chosen to inherit the Kingdom of God in which there is freedom, peace and joy, but we are very thankful for the gift of Christ, and we know that we must fulfill the mission of Christ by loving all people with His love. Because we have Christ in our hearts, we want all people to be free in His love. And so we do the best we can to further the Kingdom and minister to the needs of all people in His name. The more we grow spiritually, the more we realize how blessed we are. We do not take for granted that God has spoken to us through Jesus Christ and that what He has spoken is unspeakably wonderful!

Lord Jesus, we receive the blessings You offer. We understand that You bring abundant and eternal life, and that Your life and teachings are the very voice of God, our Creator. Please help us to live in the ever-newness of life and love.

64

SWALLOW THE FROG

Then after the morsel, Satan entered into Judas. Jesus said to him, "What you are going to do, do quickly" [John 13:27]

    Mark Twain encourages us, in his humorous way: "If you've got a frog to swaller, it's not good to look at it for too long. And if you've got two to swaller, don't start with smallest one."

    Procrastination stinks! It is an oppressive weight that we can get used to carrying and even lose awareness of the fact that we are carrying it. It retards us in our personal growth and slows down the onward march of the Kingdom. Important things, left undone, turn into lead within the soul. But as soon as they are done, they become wings, lifting us into new heights of freedom and potentiality, and we wonder why we waited so long to get it done!

    Jesus had a dreadful mission to accomplish. He knew what was coming. He had been trying to prepare His disciples for it, and He was not driving with the brakes on. "Do it quickly," was His way of sending Judas off to fulfill Satan's mission: Christ's betrayal, which would lead to the Cross, and ultimately to the salvation of the human family [for all who believe]. This was the next step for Jesus, and He did not procrastinate. All of us have some "next step" that we need to take— perhaps some bad habit that we need to shed like an outgrown shell; perhaps an accountability partner or group to get us over the hump; perhaps some issue in a relationship we need to face and talk about. Satan will distract us as long as we allow him, and he has an endless supply of excuses; but there will be no satisfaction or joy in dawdling. God wants us to enjoy life, but because of His Holy Spirit in us, we cannot enjoy it unless we are being fruitful—growing, loving, serving, sowing the seeds that have been sown in us, moving beyond the old boundaries of our soul. Whatever it is, *please*, Get It Done! Move on into the joy and new freedom! Jesus is with you, but He is also moving onward. If you hold back, He will seem farther and farther away.

Lord Jesus, thank You for accomplishing Your wonderful mission that has changed the course of human history and has set me free. Thank You for not procrastinating. Empower me through Your Holy Spirit to continue taking the steps that lead into heaven. Deliver me from the distractions that bring no joy. Whatever it is, Lord, that I most need to get done, please focus my energies in that direction with confidence in Your presence and aid. In You, I can do all things.

65

LOVING BEYOND THE COMFORT ZONE

The Lord said, "You have been concerned about this vine, though you did not tend it or make it grow. It sprang up overnight and died overnight. But Nineveh has more than a hundred and twenty thousand people who cannot tell their right hand from their left, and many cattle as well. Should I not be concerned about that great city?" [John 4: 10-11]

Jonah's story is a great example of the perennial battle of personal ego, or "flesh," and the Holy Spirit. God sent him to Nineveh, but Tarshish looked better to him, so he ended up in the belly of a fish. He was more concerned with his personal reputation and comfort than with the salvation of over a hundred thousand souls. So he ended up angry because the Ninevites didn't get punished, and his little vine died.

God has compassion for all people, and wants them to know the Truth that sets them free. He sends His people, those who have come to know the joy and peace of Christ, into every corner of humanity as light shining into the darkness. There are countless thousands of people who, like the Ninevites, still do not know their right hand from their left. They are spiritually blind. We will encounter some of them today. The condition of their souls is more important to God than whether we have ten or a hundred TV channels to choose from; or whether we upgrade to the next level of computer technology; or whether we are driving a newer model automobile; or whether we can figure how to make more money this year. Jesus did not endure Calvary, setting us free, so that we could feather our nest and become entertainment gluttons. He knows that our greatest joy is in being the light of the world that He has ordained us to be [Mt 5:14]. We rejoice with the angels in heaven with every soul that receives eternal and abundant life in Christ [Lk 15:7]. Our tendencies toward selfishness and comfort always war against the calling of God to love beyond the comfort zone.

Lord, please deliver me from the prison cell of my self, into the glorious and infinite freedom of Your love for all people. Today, may I be mindful of the "Ninevites" that You may place in my pathway, and may I be a manifestation of Your compassion and truth for them.

66

OBEDIENCE LEADS TO HEALING

Blessed is the man...whose delight is in the law of the LORD, and on his law he meditates day and night. He is like a tree planted by streams of water, that yields its fruit in its season, and its leaf does not wither. In all that he does, he prospers [Ps 1:1-3].

A middle-aged woman came into my counseling service with the expressed problem of not being able to "honor" her mother. She knew that God required this honor—it is one of His commandments—but she was uncertain as to how. She had experienced an extremely difficult history with her mother, which included [on the part of the mother] severe emotional disturbances, multiple hospitalizations, electro-convulsive therapy for anxiety and depression, resulting in general instability in the family. My client was a recovering drug addict, had suffered major bouts of anxiety, and had gone through a divorce. She had a brother who was a longtime, chronic drug user, still in denial. Her sisters had gone through a litany of severe problems, all of which seemed to be rooted in their chaotic upbringing. Recently, the mother had spent a month living with her daughter [my client]. The daughter characterized the relationship as distant, civil, cordial, and guarded. She perceived that her mother was trying to have a closer relationship, but she felt the need to keep distant. The Holy Spirit was convicting her regarding this, and she was seeking, in therapy, a solution to the conflict between the need to guard herself from her mother on the one hand, and the need to honor her, in obedience to God, on the other. As she moved more deeply into an understanding of her feelings, she was able to articulate them in this way: "It's like she's trying to be a mother to me now; but I don't need a mother now. I needed her earlier, and she wasn't there for me or my siblings. I don't think she was trying very hard to be a mother to us then, and I just can't open my heart and let her move into that role with me now as if all that terrible stuff had never happened." It began to dawn on both of us that she was still wounded, and the recent time with her mother, and especially her mother's desire to be closer to her, had brought the woundedness into a painful focus. Without Christ in her life, she could have very easily maintained a cordial distance and kept the hurt encapsulated in her soul. It would have had some negative effect on her, as we have seen repeatedly in the world of therapy, but she may have never made the connection between the negative effect and the unfinished business with her mom. But because she honored God and had come to realize the importance of obedience, she could not allow herself that option. God was not allowing her to stay in that place of mother-woundedness. He was bringing her in to a place of deeper healing through forgiveness. *And it was her desire to be obedient to God that was the tender, loving cord by which God was drawing her into this new freedom.* The painful "obligation" to honor her mother became the doorway to a deeper healing and new freedom in Christ. The more we see this wonderful way of God, the more we "delight in His law."

Lord God, all Your commandments and everything about Your Way have to do with Your love for us and Your desire for the very best for us. Please help us to delight in them, and to obey You, even when it is very difficult to do so.

67

ARE YOU A GOOD PERSON?

And as he was setting out on his journey, a man ran up and knelt before him, and asked him, "Good Teacher, what must I do to inherit eternal life?" And Jesus said to him, "Why do you call me good? No one is good but God alone..." (Mk 10:17-18).

Frequently in my counseling practice I will hear someone say, "I am a good person." They will elaborate by describing certain behaviors they do or abstain from doing. This is usually in defense of themselves when something has come up that casts a bad light on them. I always think of the above statement from Jesus when I hear that comment. Jesus clearly stated "No one is good but God alone." The Apostle Paul was chosen by God to give us more than half of the New Testament—without a doubt, the most inspirational literature on earth, to say the least. Paul did not consider himself a good man. He described himself as a "wretched man", the "chief" of sinners, who could not do the good that he knew he should do, and could not keep from doing the evil that he should not do [Rom 7:19-24]. Since he realized the truth about himself—his sinful nature and his need for redemption—God could use him in a very powerful way to help billions of people. If he had thought of himself as a good person, he would have been useless to God. He probably would have continued persecuting the early Christians and feeling justified in doing so. When we think of ourselves as "good" we do not grow. We have "arrived." The most destructive acts of evil are committed by people who are certain that they are in the right and are convinced that they are doing good. The Pharisees thought of themselves as good people. They were the religious leaders of their day. They knew the Scriptures, and they were well respected. And they crucified Christ. Peter, on the other hand, asked Jesus to depart from him, feeling unworthy to even be in His presence [Lk 5:8]. John the Baptist stated that he was not worthy to carry Jesus' shoes [Mt 3:11]. It is dangerous to think of ourselves as good. It is much safer to recognize that we have selfish tendencies and that we have hurt many people and ignored many opportunities to help the needy. When we confess this truth about ourselves, we open the door for God's forgiveness, which He has promised to us [1Jn 1:9]. Mature Christians do not think of themselves as good;

rather they are very thankful that God, for Christ's sake, loves and forgives them even though they have *not* been good. The Bible teaches that, when we receive Christ as our Lord, His righteousness is imparted to us [Phil 3:9; Rom5:17]. This is a wonderful mystery. God does not want us to feel guilty and ashamed because we are sinners. He wants us to be thankful and joyful because we are forgiven in Christ. But we first must realize that we need forgiveness. And "good" people don't need forgiveness.

Lord, thank You for reminding me that only God is good. And thank You for imparting Your righteousness to me through Your sacrifice on my behalf at Calvary. I gratefully receive Your forgiveness, and ask You to help me live more faithfully today than ever before.

68

WE ARE *SO BLESSED!*

Blessed be the God and Father of our Lord Jesus Christ, who hath blessed us with all spiritual blessings in heavenly places in Christ [Eph 1:3].

One of the results or by-products of our spiritual growth is that we begin to realize how blessed we are. We have been given the gift of life. God did not have to give us life. We did not earn it or work for it. And yet here we are, alive, aware, eating and drinking, laughing and celebrating the holidays, and working through our problems as if it were the most natural thing in the world. We have been given the gift of life! This in and of itself is enough to cause the spiritually awakened person to be perpetually joyful! If we are in Christ, God has delivered us from slavery just as surely as He delivered His children from the bondage of Egypt. We are living in the land flowing with milk and honey. We are living in the Promised Land! We have abundant and eternal life in Christ. Death is our final victory. Though evil is real, very powerful, and destructive, Christ has overcome it for us. And we are in Him, and He is in us, and He will never leave us nor forsake us. He has given us a beautiful world to live in. We will never be able to see and enjoy all the beauty that is in this world. There is more beauty in a suburban backyard than any spiritually awakened person can possibly comprehend. Even though evil is real and has done tremendous damage to our spirits, Christ has overcome; and in Him we overcome all its devastation. If we are not thankful, we are not yet awake to Reality. The angels in heaven are rejoicing, not because they are deluded, but rather because they are in touch with the Truth that we see "through a glass darkly" [1Cor. 13]. But the Holy Spirit is clearing away the fog that dims our vision, and as the Truth comes into focus, we cannot contain our joy—it overflows into every aspect of our lives and into all our relationships. And some understand and some don't. But we understand that it has always been this way. Some understood Christ. They knelt and called Him Lord. Some said that He was a heretic. They crucified Him. But He was who He is, no matter what people thought [or think] of Him. And we are who we are in Christ, no matter what people think. And who we are in Christ is beyond words to describe. We are joyful, loving, and free servants of God and man. The Gospel is too good to be true. And yet it is True!

Lord, what You have revealed to us is better than anything we could have conceived on our own. Life, the way it is in the Kingdom of God, is better than anything humans could have possibly created. Help us to be aware, alive, and appropriately thankful.

69

LOVE YOUR ENEMIES

But I say unto you, Love your enemies, bless those who curse you, do good to those who hate you, and pray for those who despitefully use you, and persecute you--Jesus [Mt 5:44]

All of us who call ourselves Christians must hear what Jesus is saying to us and, with the aid of the Holy Spirit, live according to His teachings. This wonderful teaching from the Sermon on the Mount delivers us from the dangers of heretical extremism that we have seen repeatedly in the religious world. Whenever religious ideologies clash and people hate each other across the lines of division between them, Jesus is reaching out to those on both sides saying, "Love your enemies." If you are Biblically correct in your ideology, and another is clearly in the wrong, you must still love that person by Jesus' standards. I once heard the testimony of a Satan worshipper who was converted because a young Christian woman, whom he and others had abused, expressed the love of Christ to him. If she had feared or hated him, this never would have happened. No Christian is allowed to hate any person. If we find ourselves hating or rejoicing in the death of any human, we must realize that we are not abiding in the spirit of Christ, and in that moment, our soul is in jeopardy. People are going to continue to be deceived, ensnared by evil, and used of Satan to wreak havoc in the world. And God is going to continue to bring judgment against people and nations in His own time and way. And the world is a better place because some people have been removed from it because they have allowed their souls to be devoured by the evil one. (But we must never rejoice in this.) And we must never hate those people. We must lament their loss, not from this world, but from the Kingdom of God, where there is love and peace for all. It is not God's will that any should perish [2Pet 3:9], and this must also be our desire. No matter how far away from godliness a person may be, we must not hate that person. If we hate any person, evil is already taking root in our own heart. Jesus did not hate the Pharisees. He did not hate Judas. He does not hate Muslims. He does not hate liberals or conservatives, republicans or democrats, Catholics, Jews, Protestants, or atheists. He does not hate murderers, rapists or those who molest children. He does not hate people because of their sexual perversions. He does not hate any person in your family; no matter how much pain they have caused you. He does not hate the person who drives carelessly and causes you problems on the highways. He *does* hate—and so can we—the evil that is done by any and all of these people as well as the evil that you and I have committed. He hates this evil because it is destructive to the people that He loves. And He gives us the understanding that if we allow ourselves to be absorbed into evil, we will lose our souls—something that He laments and continually warns us against. He taught us to pray, "Deliver us from evil." This includes the evil of the hatred of any person in the human family.

Lord Jesus, You are in such a wonderful place of spirit and soul. You are in Heaven, and You are in us. You teach us such wonderful, liberating Truth. Please abide with us forever, and deliver us from evil. Always convict us when we are ensnared by hatred of any person. Help us to forgive, and to overcome evil with good.

70

LOVE AS CONFRONTATION

But he turned and said to Peter, "Get behind me, Satan! You are a hindrance to me; for you are thinking as a man, and not as God." [Mt 16:23]

When we confront, we are not confronting the *person*, but rather what we perceive to be a *destructive dynamic* in his/her personality. We are striving, through confrontation, to separate the *person* from the destructive dynamic. This is an act of love for the purpose of the ongoing sanctification of the soul of that individual. Jesus frequently confronted the Pharisees—sometimes scathingly [Mt 23]. He also confronted Peter, telling him that he was thinking the thoughts of men and not of God and thereby allowing Satan to speak through him [Mt 16:23]. Another example of confrontation is the Biblical account of the prophet Nathan confronting King David about his absorption in desire for Bathsheba to the point that he set her husband up to be killed in battle [2 Sam 12]. It was for David's sake [and for others under his kingship] that Nathan confronted him. And it is for our sake that God, through His Word and Spirit, confronts us—so that we might be separated from the evil that would otherwise continue to exert a destructive force in our lives. We become an agent of God's redemptive work in the human family when we make ourselves available for this type of confrontation. And we earn the right to confront only by first opening ourselves to *being* confronted by whatever difficult truth we need to know about ourselves and also by prayerfully insuring that our *motive* in confronting is the love of Christ. Confrontation motivated by anything less than Christ's love [*agape*] is diminished in terms of its healing and liberating power. It takes courage to confront. In the above account, King David had the power to put Nathan to death. The Pharisees had the power of life and death over Jesus (though, as He stated to Pilate, they had no power other than that allowed by His Father [John 19:11]). We are not responsible for how confrontation is received. We are only responsible to make sure that we desire the best for those we confront, and that we confront in a spirit of humility, acknowledging our own failures and the need for the ongoing convictions of the Holy Spirit. We are not Christ. We have not lived a sinless life. When we pray, "Father forgive them, for they know not what they do," we must also pray, "and forgive me, for I also have been blind and sinned against God and man." When we confront, we are not coming from the up to down standpoint. We are speaking as a brother, sister or fellow struggler. We are on equal ground. Our goal and desire is not to embarrass or punish; it is to liberate. And we accept that the outcome is in the hands of the person confronted and God.

Lord Jesus, thank You for Your courageous willingness to speak difficult Truth to Your followers and to those in power. Please give me grace to be confronted with what I need to hear about my shortcomings. And give me grace to confront in ways that help others understand Your love and freedom.

71

WHO ARE YOU?

So we do not lose heart. Though our outer nature is wasting away, our inner nature is being renewed every day. For this slight momentary affliction is preparing for us an eternal weight of glory beyond all comparison, because we look not to the things that are seen but to the things that are unseen; for the things that are seen are transient, but the things that are unseen are eternal [2Cor 4:16-18].

At this writing, I'm approaching 57 years of life on this earth, and I'm beginning to experience some of the things associated with the word "elderly": certain inexplicable aches and pains; tiredness and the need for a nap occasionally; forgetting things as never before; falling behind in the worlds of technology and fashion, etc. I see my sons and grandchildren going into a world that I will not know. I am so thankful that God has delivered us from the fear and dread of growing old. I accept deeply that my body is going to deteriorate. I accept deeply that I am going to suffer various illnesses and the loss of ability to do basic activities that I have taken for granted for years. I accept deeply that I and everyone I love are going to die. But of course, I am speaking only of the body. Thank God, I am not my body! As Longfellow wrote in "Psalm of Life":

Life is real - Life is earnest -
And the grave is not its goal
Dust thou art, to dust returneth,
Was not spoken of the soul

I *have* a hand, but I am not a hand, leg, ear, foot, etc. I am something that inhabits this body; and that "something" is eternal. My "inner nature is being renewed every day." At this stage of life, I see more clearly than ever the necessity and importance of cultivating the spiritual life. I see it even more clearly in my 82-year-old Mom, who seems to be more in the Spirit now than ever and is quite OK with the fact that she will probably not be on this earth much longer. In fact she is looking forward to seeing my Dad, her "best friend," who passed from this earth a year and a half ago. We sing a hymn frequently at our church entitled "Turn Your Eyes Upon Jesus." The chorus is:

Turn your eyes upon Jesus, Look full in His wonderful face,
And the things of earth will grow strangely dim
In the light of His glory and grace.

How wonderful that, when the things of earth grow "dim," instead of darkness, there is *"light"*! The *"light"* of *Christ's glory!* The world of man is constantly changing, and we are all destined to be left behind as we get too old to keep up. But the inner man [the world of the Spirit] is being renewed eternally. Christ is in me, and he is eternally new, alive, and fresh as an artesian well springing up into eternal Life.

Lord, thank You that have provided for us throughout the course of our entire life on this earth and into eternity. Deliver us from the fear of aging and death. Teach us how to love at every stage of life.

72

YOU ARE THE "RIGHTEOUSNESS OF GOD"

Therefore, if any one is in Christ, he is a new creation; the old has passed away, behold, the new has come.... For our sake he made him to be sin who knew no sin, so that in him we might become the righteousness of God [2Cor 5:17,21].

One of the wonderful and mysterious things about Truth is that it is sometimes expressed by *paradox*. Paradox is defined as "a statement that appears to contradict itself or to be contrary to common sense, but may be true." Perhaps the most outstanding example of the paradox of our Faith is the triune, singular God. We believe that God is One. And we believe that God is three: Father, Son and Holy Spirit. Logic and common sense would tell us that God is either one or three but cannot be both. But we see that He has revealed Himself as both three and one.

Another wonderful paradox of our Faith is that in Christ we are sinners, and we are righteous. If you ask me if I am a sinner, I would have to answer, "Yes. Every day I fall short." And if you ask me if I am spiritually clean, I will gladly answer, "By the grace of God, in Christ, absolutely!" God has blessed us in a way that we will never, in our entire lives on this earth, be able to be thankful enough for. He has imparted the righteousness of Christ, His sinless Son, to us! He has given us the GIFT of salvation from the guilt and punishment of our sins against each other, and against Him! The same apostle [our dear brother Paul] who recognized himself to be the "chief" of sinners [1Tm 1:15] also recognized his entitlement in Christ to come [can you imagine it?] *boldly* to the very throne of grace! [Heb 4:16]. In Christ we are clean [1John.1:9], forgiven [Eph 4:32], set free [Rom 8:2]. We don't have to worry about ANYTHING [Phil 4:6]. We have been delivered from condemnation [Rom 8:1]. We can hold our heads up—not in pride, but in gratitude and freedom of heart. We do not have to live in shame, and we are not in denial. We know we are sinners. We admit it. But we know the greater, triumphant truth: We are forgiven! We are loved! And in grateful obedience to Him for this unspeakable gift, we love each other, better and better, day-by-day, with the same Love that has cleansed us from all unrighteousness [1John 1:9].

Lord Jesus, help us to receive, in all humility and gratitude, the gift of Your righteousness. May we receive this gift deeply, completely and eternally. And may we never take Your grace lightly, but carefully live in obedience to Your command that we love one another as You have loved us.

73

THE NARROW GATE INTO ETERNAL LIFE

Enter by the narrow gate; for the gate is wide and the way is easy, that leads to destruction, and those who enter by it are many. The gate is narrow and the way is hard, that leads to life, and those who find it are few [Mt 7:13-14].

    The world scrambles and screams for our attention. From the four corners of the earth, it screams and calls and clambers. One could spend his whole life putting out the world's brush fires. It reminds me of an arcade game I've seen: Little mechanic creatures pop their heads up out of holes and with a club you try to hit them before they retract. You hit one and another pops up, and another, and another—then two at once, faster and faster. This is the way the world occupies the precious mind-energy of so many blind souls. The world offers a broad spectrum of occupation. Jesus calls us down to one "narrow gate": Himself. The world's broad spectrum of offerings narrows down eventually to some form of narrow, regretful enslavement. The Narrow Gate of Christ leads to infinite freedom, eternal life, and a Kingdom in which every path is a path of peace.

    What is required is faith and the mental discipline to focus—with attentiveness, humility, and an open heart—upon the narrow gate, until the chaotic, distractive noises of the world begin to fade, thankfully, into the background, and the Day Star dawns and arises in our hearts and begins to shine brighter and brighter unto the full light of day. Its light is peace, love, joy, and eternal gratitude for the calling of Christ to "enter the narrow gate."

Lord, thank you for calling me into freedom, joy, peace, and love. I realize that the Way is narrow, and I am thankful that you are a trustworthy Guide who will keep me on the path that is abundant and eternal life.

74

THE BLESSEDNESS OF MOURNING

Blessed are those who mourn, for they shall be comforted [Mt 5:4].

We all suffer losses in life. And we all make mistakes that cause unnecessary suffering. We have all, at one time or another acted selfishly or maliciously and caused someone to suffer unnecessarily. Maybe it is our mother, wife, child or husband that we have hurt, abused or neglected. And we have also been hurt in many ways.

There are two basic responses to the hurts and losses that we have inflicted and that have been inflicted upon us. We can harden our hearts; press on as if nothing has happened; try to "live around" or "live beyond" the hurt and shame; or ignore it and hope it will go away.

Or, we can *mourn*.

Jesus, our Messiah and Friend, advocates the latter. And He demonstrates it in His life; lamenting, grieving the fact that we "stone the prophets" and kill those whom God sends to us with His liberating Truth [Mt 23:37]. Today, when we harden our hearts against our hurts and guilt, we reject God anew. We stone the prophets.

It is much better to let down and grieve, mourn, cry, weep, and wail. We need to mourn all that we have done that is contrary to God's way of Love. We need to mourn every selfish, hateful act in all the history of the human family. We need to mourn for all that we have done personally to make life more difficult for our loved ones. We need to mourn our unforgiveness, our hardheartedness, our blindness and our selfishness. We need to say, "God have mercy on me, a sinner." And we need to pray for the forgiveness of those who have hurt us. When we open our hearts in this way, and empty out our grief, we are blessed with a deep peace. We know that God is with us. He forgives us. We are comforted. And we offer this same comfort to others in His name.

Lord, I am sorry that I have hurt some people in my life. And I offer my hurting heart to You. Please bless, comfort and heal my heart. Please help all of us in the human family to choose to love each other with Your Love. Amen.

75

DULLNESS OF HEART

For this people's heart has grown dull, and their ears heavy of hearing, and their eyes they have closed, lest they should perceive with their eyes, and hear with their ears, and understand with their heart, and turn for me to heal them [Jesus, Mt 13:1].

We must continue to rise above these oppressive spirits that keep covering us like wet blankets, dimming the Light of Christ in us. We have the perpetual opportunity and invitation (and we are commanded) to thankfulness, victory, light, freedom, and love. We must take care of our bodies—these marvelous Holy Spirit temples. We must not give in to our weaknesses that lead to despair. We must continue to welcome the challenge of loving people. We must get better at it. We must not level off or stagnate. Too much rest, T.V., computer, food, and vain fantasy life is not good for us and will lead to despair. Devotional reading and paying attention to our loved ones with an open heart toward God will steadily brighten our path and inner life. Be careful. Be alert and awake in the Spirit. Shake off the darkness. Arise into the Light of Christ and His freedom and love.

Lord, today I gladly awaken into the joy, peace, freedom, abundant life, and love that You offer and command Your disciples to walk within. Thank You for warning me about the dullness that can insidiously creep into my heart, robbing me of vitality and life.

76

I'M SO OVERWHELMED!

Take my yoke upon you, and learn from me; for I am gentle and lowly in heart, and you will find rest for your souls. For my yoke is easy, and my burden is light [Mt 11:29-30].

For Christians, being overwhelmed is impossible.

I can almost hear hundreds of voices raising loud objections to the above statement: "What do you mean? I'm a Christian, and I live in a constant state of overwhelm-ment! I feel overwhelmed most of the time." The key word in that last sentence is "feel."

I do not say that it is impossible for a Christian to FEEL overwhelmed. What I do say is, if our Lord's words are true, then it is impossible to actually BE overwhelmed. Here is my thinking on this. God sees, knows, and reveals the Truth. We, on the other hand, "see through a glass darkly" [1Cor 13:12]. What we see and think we know is only partly correct. What God sees and knows is totally correct. If Jesus says that His yoke is easy and His burden is light, then that is eternal Truth—no matter how I see things. His yoke and His burdens are the only ones that I should concern myself with. If it is important, Jesus wants me to be concerned—not worried [Phil.4:6]—about it. If it is not, He doesn't. And everything that Jesus wants me to do, work on, or be concerned about falls within the category of a yoke that is easy, and a burden that is light. Jesus loves me too much to assign me responsibilities that would overwhelm me. He is the "Prince of Peace," not the "Overlord of Overwhelm-ment." Therefore, it is possible to do everything that Jesus wants me to do, today and every day, without being overwhelmed. Now it's up to me not to put heavy yokes and hard burdens on myself—or to allow others to do so. And I must be careful not to put those heavy burdens and hard yokes on others also.

Whenever I start feeling overwhelmed, I remind myself of the easy yoke and light burden of Christ. And I discover that I have drifted into being unnecessarily anxious about something. "I can do all things through Christ, Who strengthens me" [Phil 4:13]. I can even live productively and responsibly WITHOUT feeling overwhelmed.

Lord, today with Your help I will not feel overwhelmed. I will carry the burden that is light and wear the yoke that fits me perfectly. I will find the perfect balance between discipline and peace.

77

SELF-CONTROL: PATHWAY TO FULLER LIFE

For God did not give us a spirit of timidity but a spirit of power and love and self-control [2Tm 1:7].

Self-control is one of the fruits of the Holy Spirit. Discipline and self-control are closely related. We all want to be "in the flow"—like an agile downhill skier, mountain climber reaching the peak, or an athlete playing the best game of his life. But think about how much discipline and self-control [work and practice] have gone into each of those activities. The greatest experiences of life are reserved for those who are willing to discipline themselves—to control the lower desires of comfort and pleasure.

How much do you want to achieve for the glory of God and His Kingdom? How much good do you desire for the human family? Are you willing to allow the Holy Spirit to manifest in you as self-control? Are you willing to allow the Holy Spirit to convict you into: Getting up a little earlier in the morning? Eating a little less and exercising a little more? Having a regular quiet time with God? Volunteering for a worthy cause in Christ? Being more mindful of your family? Being more gracious and forgiving to those in your social circle? Loving people better?

Be disciplined. Don't settle for half-life.

Lord, I ask You for the gift of self-control. Today may I focus on those priorities for which I will be most thankful at the end of my life.

78

FREEDOM-TOGETHER IN MARRIAGE

Therefore a man leaves his father and his mother and cleaves to his wife, and they become one flesh [Gn 2:24].

Oneness in marriage does not eliminate individuality of personality. What does this oneness mean? Perhaps it is best described as "freedom-together." A couple in Christ are free with each other—they feel free together—free to be the individuals that they are. This freedom is often a "given" in the early stages [the "honeymoon" stage] of the relationship, but it must be earned later. The way that it is earned is through the work of psycho-spiritual growth—or abiding in Christ. Each must allow Christ to progressively remove his/her character defects—those aspects of personality that make one unloving or unlovable. These defects are unavoidably exposed in intimate relationships. There is no intimacy that does not expose character defects. This is initially painful, but can become a glorious pathway of spiritual growth if both are willing to be revealed to themselves—to acknowledge their own shortcomings, and take responsibility to progressively overcome them with God's help. As this sanctification process continues, the two people become allies in psycho-spiritual maturity, and they become more loving and loveable. They open the doorway to joy and peace with each other. They help to make the world a better place for many people. They are free-together in the oneness of Christ's Spirit.

Lord, thank You for my mate, and how you have ingeniously arranged our desire for intimacy to move us toward You. Thank You for the fact that our relationship problems bring the blessing of growth every time that we turn toward You for the solutions.

79

SEEING MORE CLEARLY

Then Elisha prayed, and said, "O LORD, I pray thee, open his eyes that he may see." So the LORD opened the eyes of the young man, and he saw; and behold, the mountain was full of horses and chariots of fire round about Elisha [2Kgs 6:17].

Sometimes the veil is pulled back and momentarily we see more deeply into the Truth or into Reality. At these times we always rejoice. The Truth is better than any of us has yet realized. Heaven is full of rejoicing—not because its inhabitants are deluded, but because they see more clearly the Truth that we see faintly.

In 2 Thessalonians, Chapter 2, God warns us solemnly to love the truth, or else we fall into terrible deception in which we believe that which is not true. We desperately need to seek the Truth—to desire it. Jesus said it sets us free. And He said "I am the…. Truth…." Be a serious truth-seeker. Ask God to help you see yourself, Him, life, and others as you and they really are. Look deeply into the life and teachings of Jesus. Find freedom and joy and peace.

Lord, thank you for perpetually releasing me from fears and all other oppressive energies. May I always look to You for the Truth that sets me free.

80

VICTORY BEYOND THE CIRCUMSTANCES

I had heard of thee by the hearing of the ear, but now my eye sees thee; therefore I despise myself, and repent in dust and ashes [Job 42:5-6].

"My grace is sufficient for you, for my power is made perfect in weakness." [God, speaking to Paul] Therefore I will all the more gladly boast of my weaknesses, that the power of Christ may rest upon me [Paul's response] [2Cor 12:9].

And going a little farther he fell on his face and prayed, "My Father, if it be possible, let this cup pass from me; nevertheless, not as I will, but as thou wilt" [Mt 26:39].

All three of these verses represent moments of victory over extremely difficult circumstances. Job's travail, Paul's "thorn of the flesh," and—most supremely—Christ's cross have this in common: They represent powerful, circumstantial tribulation resulting in consultation with God, Who did NOT remove the tribulation, but gave a mysterious spiritual victory instead. Job was still in the ashes—still scraping his scabs; Paul continued to suffer the "thorn"; Jesus was not delivered from the cross. But Job, having new insight, came to the place of peaceful acceptance; Paul rejoiced in his newfound enlightenment that God's grace was sufficient; and Jesus peacefully submitted into the fulfillment of His life's mission, even praying for His enemies: "Father, forgive them...." Here is one of the great and wonderful mysteries of the Christian faith. There is a Power that victoriously transcends the worst imaginable earthly circumstances: The Holy Spirit in us.

There seems to be at least two distinct levels of faith in those who profess to reside in the Kingdom of God. There is the "faith" represented by those who have prayed, and their prayers were answered, and they say to themselves and others, "Praise God! He is real. You see! I have evidence." The problem with those in this category is that they are just as likely to say on another occasion, "I'm not so sure about this 'god-thing.' You know I prayed and prayed and prayed for deliverance from [some difficult experience], and I never heard a thing from God. And I've been going to Church and doing everything right." This is the "little faith." It is strong as long as everything is going according to human plans and understanding. But there is the "big faith." This faith encompasses all imaginable life circumstances: those that make sense and those that don't; those that seem to be God's loving will, and those that do not; those that seem to promote the goodness of God, and those that seem to cast doubt upon His goodness. Ultimately, we have to get to the "big faith"—the faith of Job and Paul. The faith of our Lord.

Lord, thank You for perpetually inviting me into the big faith in which I know, deeply and unshakably, that You are working ALL things together for good.

81

HOW TO DO WHAT WE DO

Whatever your task, work heartily, as serving the Lord and not men [Col 3:23].

I thought of this verse as I watched a masterful musician making many people happy with his musical talent. He was "in the flow;" in his element—at one with his guitar and fellow band members. And many people in the nightclub were at one with him and the music. He had apparently spent many hours practicing, playing his guitar, and exercising his voice. And he apparently loved his work.

I think this is something of what it is like to do things "heartily," that is, full of heart. When we do things heartily, we are at home in the universe; we are making other people happy; and we are very fulfilled.

I don't know if the musician was a man of God. I don't know if he was a man of prayer and compassion. But in his music making, he was an inspiration. If he is not a man of spiritual maturity; however, he may be abusive to his wife. He may not be faithful to her. He may not take very good care of his children. If this is the case, he is not helping the forward march of the human family—he is retarding it even though he makes very pleasing music. To do one's work "heartily, as serving the Lord," one must not only be masterful at his vocation, he must also be a man of wisdom, compassion, and self-control. He must practice not only the disciplines of his vocation, but also the disciplines of our faith: prayer, service, meditation, study, self-control, and submission to the Holy Spirit. Then he becomes a musician of the soul. He becomes an instrument himself, upon which God can play the beautiful music of the universe—the music that we were born to play, and hear, and celebrate—the music of Life.

Lord, thank You for teaching me the music of life. I pray that I might do my work heartily today, serving You in all ways.

82

ABUNDANT LIFE

The thief comes only to steal and kill and destroy; I came that you may have life, and have it abundantly [John 10:10].

Day by day He awakens us into abundant life. Beauty is all around. Do you notice it? Children. Animals. Birds. Butterflies. Flowers. Green horizons. Friendly conversations. There is more of the goodness of God in a single day than we can possibly be aware of. But we can be more aware – more aware today than ever before. More alive today than ever before. We can open our hearts.

Because of "the thief," our hearts have been wounded, and we may be afraid to open ourselves to this pain. Since he is the "father of lies" (Jn.8:44), he would also have us believe that it is not wise or necessary to open our hearts to this pain; and that we can't do anything about it anyway. But Jesus says, **"Blessed are they who mourn, for they shall be comforted"** (Mt.5:4). Jesus wants us to feel our grief, pain, hurt, remorse, sadness, anger, frustration, etc.; for He knows that this is the pathway to comfort – to freedom, peace and the abundant life. Otherwise we can spend our entire lives fearfully avoiding our inner selves. We ignore the Biblical invitation to "be still, and know that He is God" at our own peril (Psm.46:10). When we open our hearts to God – when we experience the truth of our inner self and begin to understand what is there in the Light of the Holy Spirit—life becomes new again. He restores our soul. Our cup overflows. (Ps 23).

Learning to live with an open heart may be a long-term process. But it is a worthy and fruitful process; otherwise our loving Lord would not have recommended it to us. Let's trust God with everything that is within us, especially our hurt, pain and grief.

Lord, today I open my heart to You. Please teach me the Truth about what is in it. And help me to learn to keep my heart open to You, so that I can be free in the abundant life You promise.

83

THE MOST IMPORTANT THING IN THE WORLD

And one of the scribes came up and heard them disputing with one another, and seeing that he answered them well, asked him, "Which commandment is the greatest of all?" Jesus answered, "The greatest is, 'Hear, O Israel: The Lord our God, the Lord is one; and you shall love the Lord your God with all your heart, and with all your soul, and with all your mind, and with all your strength.' The second is this, 'You shall love your neighbor as yourself.' There is no other commandment greater than these" [Mk 12:28-31].

"What is the first and greatest commandment?" For a Jew in Jesus' time to ask this question is equivalent to asking, "What is the most important thing in the world for humans to be mindful of?" because a faithful Jew would believe thoroughly that God knows what is the most important thing for the human family, and His greatest commandment would direst us toward that "most important thing." Jesus answered the question, "What is the most important thing for us to be mindful of?" And He answered by talking about supreme love for the one and only God, and unselfish love for others. The most important thing in the whole universe and all eternity is for me to love God with my whole being, and to love others as I love myself. So easy to say; a lifetime's challenge and opportunity to do. I think that most people unconsciously assume that they already know everything about love. They wouldn't dare say that they did, but they live their lives as if they did. They are not putting forth any effort to grow in the most important way—in the way of love.

What about you? If we videotaped your life, would we be able to say "Oh, he is a good student! He is applying himself"? Or would we have to say, "Well, it looks as if he has already learned everything about love. He apparently needs no more growth"?

God please help me to never stop applying myself to the wonderful, life-enhancing disciplines of loving in the way of Christ. Today I will be mindful of loving You by loving others.

84

HOW ALIVE ARE YOU?

The thief comes only to steal and kill and destroy; I came that they may have life, and have it abundantly [John 10:10].

Are you alive today? "Of course!" you might reply. "I'm breathing and my heart is beating." Jesus offered—and offers—life to living beings. Some of them thought He was crazy. He was offering *zoe* to those who had *bios*. Rabbits and turtles have *bios* – as well as grass and trees. But it may be that only humans have *zoe* (though I think some animals have a form of it as they seem to experience joy and playfulness). It is life characterized by awareness, joy, freedom, peace, compassion, and gratitude. It is life that is aware of and thankful for itself and thankful to God, the Giver of all life. It is Spirit-filled life. It is life focused on and rejoicing in nourishing life in others. It is Life that is full of Love.

How can we be more alive? Christians have historically and consistently recognized the need for devotion. Devotion is defined as "religious exercise or practice other than the regular corporate worship....being ardently dedicated and loyal."(Webster's Ninth Collegiate Dictionary.) Synonyms are "piety" and "fidelity." Some may shrink from the work associated with devotion. However, when looked at in the light of the abundant life that Christ promised to those who continued in His way, that response is obviously a sad mistake.

Are you willing to work for more of the most valuable thing you possess? Then be joyfully devoted to Christ and to His Love. Be alive today!

Lord Jesus, You promised abundant life to Your followers. I want to be a sincere disciple. Please help me to be very alive in Your love today.

85

FREEDOM

The Spirit of the Lord is upon me, because he has anointed me to preach good news to the poor. He has sent me to proclaim release to the captives and recovering of sight to the blind, to set at liberty those who are oppressed [Lk 4:18].

Freedom is a concept worthy of our careful contemplation. It is not easily comprehended, attained, nor maintained. Most of us struggle inwardly for freedom from those aspects of life that we perceive to be limiting or oppressing us without knowing much about those oppressing forces or even the struggle itself. We just don't *feel free*. We strive to attain goals, imagining that they will liberate us. When we attain them, they may become bonds from which we try to get free.

What we really need (the freedom and blessedness of God), can only exist in these places in our soul that are struggling and striving in vain desire for idols that can never fulfill. When we practice the marvelous discipline of relinquishment of the desire for these idols, aided necessarily by God's grace, we vacate the space into which His grace, love and peace can now flow into us.

One of the contemporary gods of American Democracy is CHOICE—a perverted idea of freedom. We mistakenly believe that if everyone had the broadest imaginable spectrum of choices, we would all feel free. Anything that limits our *choices*—even God or righteousness, the "common good" or the Bible—is considered an enemy to freedom. Our Pledge of Allegiance alludes to the proper understanding of freedom or liberty. It states: "...One nation, *under God*, with liberty and justice for all." Out from under God, liberty is an illusion that no spectrum of choices can bring into reality. The only true freedom is the freedom to choose righteousness (as defined by God) or evil, and when we choose evil, we destroy freedom and begin to become the slaves or victims of the evil we have chosen. Our Founding Fathers knew that if we used our "freedom" to make choices contrary to the righteousness of God, we would lose freedom. The necessary evolution of our growth in the Spirit leads us ultimately to recognize and inwardly experience the freedom of Christ. His magnificent, unimpeachable freedom is gloriously evident in His prayer from the Cross. He was encompassed by the most malignant forms of evil: religious, political, and military. He had been betrayed by His own inner circle of friends, denied by His staunchest disciple, falsely accused of blasphemy and demonic possession, beaten, spat upon, mocked with a crown of thorns, and pierced with nails and spear. And what was His response? *"Father, forgive them, for they know not what they do."* He was bleeding to death on a cross, and He was freer than you or I have ever yet been. Absolutely nothing could make Him stop loving. And we are called into this same freedom from everything that can possibly dim the Light of His Love shining through us. The power of this freedom resides in all who have received Him. He is still *releasing the captives and setting at liberty the oppressed.*

Lord Jesus, please help me to never lose the ability to be amazed and liberated by Your accomplishment at Calvary.

86

A CLEAN HEART

If we confess our sins, he is faithful and just, and will forgive our sins and cleanse us from all unrighteousness [1Jn 1:9].

It can be so incredibly tiresome fighting inwardly against our demons—and the fear that they might be exposed.

What is *your* struggle? What thoughts torment or alarm you? What is it about you that you dare not let anyone know? What is it that alternatively stimulates and then shames you? Sexual fantasies? Desire to be with someone other than your spouse? Hatred of a family member? Addictions? Fears? Dread? Remorse? Emptiness? Apathy?

God knows all about you. And He is willing to accept you—warts and snot and all! But you have to be willing to let Him clean you up—or rather, perhaps, clean you out. Confession is tremendously liberating. It releases all that fruitless inner conflict. It puts the problem where it belongs: out in the Light and in God's hands. He can do in you that which you will never be able to do alone. He will teach you the glorious pathway of Love.

Lord, thank You for your willingness to accept me right where I am. And thank You for loving me too much to leave me here.

87

KEEP FIRST THINGS FIRST

But seek first the kingdom of God and his righteousness; and all these other things shall be added to you--Jesus [Mt 6:33].

Congratulations! You are doing something important!

Stephen Covey, in his wonderful book, *The Seven Habits of Highly Effective People*, reminds us that things that are *urgent* are not always things that are *important* and vice versa. If we are not careful, we can allow our daily schedule to be full of activities that are not taking us in the direction that we really want our life to go. Exercise and spiritual growth are activities that are important but not urgent. Watching the evening news, making more money, attending meetings, and answering phone calls may be urgent but not necessarily important. Some of the most important activities of life do not scream for our daily attention. But if we do not attend to them, the time will come that we will regret neglecting them.

As a Christian counselor, each week I see Christians that have neglected their spiritual growth. They believe in God, and if pressed will admit that prayer, fellowship with other believers, Bible reading, Jesus and His teachings, and seeking God in spirit and truth are the most important priorities of life. But they will also admit neglect in these areas to the point that some major crisis has blind-sided them with what hopefully will be a wake-up call from God. We always have an accumulation of negative energy if our priorities are out of balance. Conscious spiritual growth keeps us clear of the negative energy that can build up to a critical point—a spiritual earthquake.

I hope that you feel good about spending this time in devotional meditation. And I pray that God will help us be mindful of the important things—the things of the Kingdom, today.

Lord, thank You for helping us be mindful of what is important.

88

THOUGHTS AND ACTIONS

Finally, brethren, whatever is true, whatever is honorable, whatever is just, whatever is pure, whatever is lovely, whatever is gracious, if there is any excellence, if there is anything worthy of praise, think about these things [Phil 4:8].

...take every thought captive to obey Christ [2Cor 10:5b].

If you know these things, happy are you if you do them [Jesus, John 13:17].

    A client recently returned from an out-of-state hospitalization for chronic depression. It was expensive—$30,000—and he said he primarily learned two things: the difference between "mentalization" and "excrement-alization," and that it was important to "take agency," that is, be proactive and do healthy things even if he did not feel like it. Thoughts and actions. Cognitive Behavioral Therapy has repeatedly been determined to be an effective therapeutic intervention. Cognitive: having to do with thoughts, and Behavioral: having to do with actions. The 12-step programs have long recognized the existence of "stinking thinking," and that it leads to deterioration. If we change our way of thinking, and some of the things we do, we move away from pathology, toward health. We move toward a higher quality of life.

    The above verses indicate that this knowledge is not new. The Bible promises blessings [a happier life] if we set our heart on certain things, think about certain things, do certain things, and abstain from doing certain things. If we are blessed, we are waking up to the Reality of God's Truth—the Eternal Reality that has been expressed in so many ways, languages, cultures, and ages; and for Christians, most perfectly in the life of Christ, Who washed His disciples' feet, teaching them to have a servant's heart. He then said "If you know these things, you will be happy if you DO them." He is clear in this statement that one must first *know* the Truth; but knowing is not enough. One must *do* the good that he has come to know. We are waking up to the Reality that we are free to think and do whatever we choose because God has created us in His image with a free will. But we are realizing that not every way of thinking and being is good for us. Some of our ways of thinking and being lead us to spiritual defeat, despair, regret, and remorse.

It is very important for us to pay attention to our thoughts and actions. When we do, we discover that many of our thoughts do not produce spiritual growth. Sometimes our thoughts are critical of someone, sowing seeds of anger and frustration within us. Some of our thoughts create desire that cannot healthily be fulfilled. Sometimes we have self-deprecating thoughts, creating feelings of inferiority and inadequacy. Some thoughts create feelings of suspicion and jealousy in us. And, we discover that there is always room for improvement in DOING more of the good that we have already come to know. And when we do, we discover again that Jesus was telling the Truth. We really are happier.

Lord, today please help me be aware of my thought life. I will bring every thought captive to You. And please help me to do the things that are befitting a child of God.

89

CHOOSING GRATITUDE

And do not get drunk with wine, for that is debauchery; but be filled with the Spirit, addressing one another in psalms and hymns and spiritual songs, singing and making melody to the Lord with all your heart always, and in every situation give thanks in the name of our Lord Jesus Christ to God the Father [Eph 5:18-20].

Here is an amazing thought: The God of creation wants us to be *thankful*. The all-knowing, ever-present, all-powerful Creator of the universe wants us to be thankful *in all situations*. This is a *choice* that we can make. And to make this choice on an ongoing basis is a direct and simple way to progressively raise the baseline level of our happiness. In our marriages and family relationships, we have an extra bonus: If we are thankful for our mate and family members, it not only increases *our* level of happiness, but also *theirs*. It feels good to know that someone appreciates you and is glad to have you in his/her life. Our mate is a person who has chosen to spend his/her life with us, support, encourage, work for us in various ways, and to be there for us. Our children are gifts from God. They teach us so much about God's love and enhance our lives in countless ways. How amazing that we tend to feel so little gratitude for the wonderful gift of these people! Our sad tendency is to complain about the problems they bring into our lives and to focus on their faults. God calls us to overcome this discouraging tendency, and to move into the light of gratitude.

Lord, please forgive me for complaining about life and my loved ones. Help me to be thankful in all situations and especially for the wonderful people You have brought into my life.

90

SALVATION IS NOT AUTOMATIC

Jesus answered him, "Truly, truly, I say to you, unless one is born anew, he cannot see the kingdom of God.... That which is born of the flesh is flesh, and that which is born of the Spirit is spirit. "[John 3:3,6].

Sometime in the early 90's, in a personal conversation with M. Scott Peck, author of the phenomenal book, *The Road Less Traveled*, I asked his opinion about the "New Age Movement." I had read his book and deeply respected him as a clear thinker and honest man, and I was overjoyed to learn that he had become a Christian. He saw two problems with the movement: first, it did not rely enough on scientific verification, and second, it did not take a sufficient account of the reality of evil. One of the characteristics of the movement was a sort of "all is light," "all is wonderful and free" mentality. Nothing in the spiritual realm posed any threat, and it adhered to a sort of universal salvation philosophy. Jesus, on the other hand, confronts and exposes evil, rebukes Satan, casts out demons, and even declares that one of His own disciples is a "devil" [John 6:70]. He talks about hell and spiritual blindness. He says that in order to even *see* the Kingdom of God one must be *born again* of the Spirit. This is a conscious decision that each accountable human must make. It is a submission to the Lordship of Christ, as the Messiah—the One Whom God has sent to show us the Way of abundant and eternal life. The Bible does not teach that all people are automatically ushered into the Kingdom of God. It teaches that if we *believe* in Christ, we will have life [John 20:31], and if we do not believe in Him, we will die in our sins [John 8:24]. In his book, *Rebel With a Cause*, Franklin Graham relates that, at some point in his early adulthood, while he was still floundering in rebellion and running from God, his dad, Billy Graham, told him that he would always love him, no matter what, but he must make a decision to either follow Christ or not. This was a turning-point conversation for Franklin. Submitting to the lordship of Christ is a seed that takes root in us and grows deeper and deeper, transforming the very core of our personalities. In Christ we begin to see our own sinful nature, confess it, and allow the Holy Spirit to cast it out, or transform it. We realize that we have strongholds of evil tendencies in us that we are not able to overcome in the flesh. Flesh dies. Only the Spirit is eternal. And only the Spirit is powerful enough to overcome some aspects of our sinful nature. Otherwise, over time, our personalities will be overcome by these sinful-nature manifestations like cancer cells overcome the physical body. Christ is, among other wonderful things, a very healthy spiritual immune system for us. He perpetually delivers us *from* deceitful and destructive invasions of evil, and *into* the freedom, peace and life of the Kingdom of God.

Lord Jesus, thank You for pressing us into the decision to submit into faith or be lost in the darkness. Thank You for making it very clear.

91

*DO YOU **FEEL** FREE?*

For freedom Christ has set us free; stand fast therefore, and do not submit again to a yoke of slavery...
For you were called to freedom, brethren; only do not use your freedom as an opportunity for the flesh, but through love be servants of one another [Gal 5:1,13].

Evil, taking opportunity through our weakness and blindness, enslaves. Christ sets us free with the only true freedom that exists for the human soul: the freedom to serve God and the human family joyfully. This movement from enslavement into the freedom of Christ is a process. It is an aspect of our ongoing sanctification. We are progressively waking up from our nightmarish delusions into the Truth that is called the "Gospel" or "Good News." The good news is that we are free. We are already free and have been from the moment we bowed to the Lordship of Christ. And since He loves us, He wants us to FEEL free. What good is freedom if one cannot feel free? Frequently, even though we are in Christ, we do not feel free. We allow desire and the worries and cares of the world to choke out the fruit of the Spirit [Mk 4:19]. This is a failure of growth—a failure of understanding—a failure in the sanctification process. The more mature we are in Christ, the more we *feel* free. We pay attention to the specific ways that we feel oppressed, and we bring the Truth of Christ to focus on it until it evaporates in the Light of His freedom. There is no oppressive force that is greater than the freedom of Christ. If we are in prison, we are free. If we are sick, we are free. If we are on our deathbed, we are freer than ever. If people misunderstand us and treat us badly, we are free. We are even [perhaps especially] free from legalistic religion—one of the most oppressive delusions on earth! We are free from our selfish little egos. There is no form of oppression that you can name that Christ did not capture and take hostage at the Cross [Eph 4:8]. If Christ did not set us free, then He failed in His mission. But if He did not fail in His mission, why do we so often feel oppressed?

Lord thank You for setting us at liberty. Please forgive us for being so slow to enter the Promised Land that You have already claimed for us. Please help us to feel free. Deliver us from our oppressive delusions.

92

THE DARK SIDE OF CHRISTMAS

Then Herod summoned the wise men secretly and ascertained from them what time the star appeared; and he sent them to Bethlehem, saying, "Go and search diligently for the child, and when you have found him bring me word, that I too may come and worship him." And being warned in a dream not to return to Herod, they [the wise men] departed to their own country by another way. Then Herod, when he saw that he had been tricked by the wise men, was in a furious rage, and he sent and killed all the male children in Bethlehem and in all that region who were two years old or under, according to the time which he had ascertained from the wise men [Mt 2:7-8,12,16]

From the very beginning, Satan was on the prowl, seeking [in this case, through Herod the king] to snuff out this Light that was coming into the world. We sing about the angels and the "heavenly host" associated with the birth of Christ, and it is very good that we do. His birth is the most wonderful event in history. But the demons were converging also. All this was not going unnoticed in the dark realm. Herod, entrenched in power, clinging to it like an owl clinging to a dead rat, coiled up like a snake when he heard from the wise men that a star had proclaimed the birth of the King of the Jews [Mt 2:2]. And with an evil pretense of reverence, asked them to let him know the location of this child when they discovered him, so that he could come and "worship him." Worship was the last thing on his mind. He only worshipped his power. So in the darkness of his soul, Satan could use him to stalk, and hopefully destroy the Christ child. But the heavenly host, working with those on earth who loved the Truth and had reverence for God, had other plans: namely, the salvation of the human family from the darkness of spiritual blindness. The unspeakable love of God was being born into the world in human form.

Always, there has been this resistance to the goodness, truth, freedom, peace, and joy that Jesus Christ was born to bring into our world. It has taken on many faces. Currently, there is resistance to calling this season "Christmas." Two of my Christian friends on this very day have commented to me about the discomfort and pressure they feel to replace the word "Christmas" with the word "Holidays." What is secularization if it is not the dimming of the light of Christ—the very light that He commanded us to shine into the world? Why is there so much pressure to abstain from speaking the very name of Jesus in so many sectors of our culture? If we give in to this pressure, we create dark space for all manner of evil to take root. Herod is still trying to destroy the Christ-child in you and me. But the angels will protect us—if we keep our hearts open to God and courageously seek the good. And the victory has been secured for us in Christ our Lord, whose birth let us proclaim, like the heavenly host, with a loud voice, and bright, loving hearts.

Lord God, thank You for protecting Christ in us from the evils of this world, so that Christ may continue doing His redemptive work through us, His earthly body. May we forever proclaim Your glory, and may Your Light forever shine in us, brighter and brighter, until the full Light of Day.

93

LOVING OR IMPRESSING PEOPLE

Let your light shine before men, that they may see your good deeds and praise your Father in heaven [Jesus, Mt. 5:16].

A man named Simon had practiced sorcery in the city and amazed all the people of Samaria. He boasted that he was someone great, and all the people, both high and low, gave him their attention and exclaimed, "This man is the divine power known as the Great Power." They followed him because he had amazed them for a long time with his magic [Acts 8: 9-11].

The ego dies a long, hard, slow death. We are all born purely selfish. When we are infants, we want comfort. If we are hungry, we do not care that our mother has to get up at three AM to feed us. We do not thank her. At two years of age, we do not like to share our toys, and we don't like it if a sibling seems to be getting more attention. As a teen, we may smile and congratulate our peers for their accomplishments, but we feel diminished and jealous inwardly. All this continues into adulthood, and is only overcome by the power of the Holy Spirit of Christ in us. In myself I am frequently confronted with my tendencies to *impress* people rather than love them, or even to impress them with how *much* I love them—how "spiritual" or "godly" I am. This always sickens me, and sends me [thankfully] to God for forgiveness.

Jesus was not working, serving, teaching, and healing for Himself. He did not come to earth as a man to impress people. He came to redeem them and to set them free. He came and worked and suffered the temptations and tribulations of humanity for OUR sake—not for His. He taught His disciples to let their light shine among men, "so they may see your good deeds and praise [*you?*]." Heavens no! So they will praise or give glory to "your Father in heaven." True disciples of Christ must never seek glory for the self. But if we are honest, we will recognize that, in our weakness, we all have at times. The praise of man is addictive. It feels so good to be applauded. Some people work their whole lives to receive the praise of man. How sad that it all dies when they die. The glory of the flesh is like the flower of the grass, the Bible says. Looks great in the morning, but by midday, it's withered [1Pet 1:24]. When we enter into the Glory of God through faith in Christ, we enter into eternal Life, freedom, peace, and ever-increasing joy. Our joy is in seeing the Kingdom of God advancing on the earth—the Love of God growing in the hearts of more and more people. This is the true joy of Christianity.

Lord, please continue to deliver me from ego-centeredness. Help me to understand, ever more deeply, that it's not about me. As John the Baptist, I also say, "I must decrease, and You [in me] must increase."

94

YOU CAN CHANGE YOUR LIFE

"This I command you..."
[Spoken by God or Jesus 13 times in the Bible.]

The fact that God commanded us to do and not do certain things presupposes a wonderful and frequently ignored reality. We have a free will! We can choose option A or B. We can continue doing things as we have done them. We are free to do so. We can also change the way we are doing certain things. If our way of being in the world is not working very well for us, we can change our way of being. This morning I woke up somewhat depressed. I had had some bad dreams and was having one of my "inadequacy attacks." I didn't feel very energetic. I haven't been getting much exercise. I forced myself to go for a brisk walk. While out, I encountered a neighbor whose husband has brain cancer and discovered that she could use some help—someone to stay with him while she made her early morning school bus run. <u>I volunteered</u>. <u>Already I'm feeling better</u>! <u>As I continued the walk, a few endorphins kicked in and I began thinking the thoughts that led to this devotion</u>. Writing devotions energizes and fulfills me because I believe they are helping others. Obviously I could have made different decisions that would have created a different morning experience for me. I could have given in to my tiredness and slept longer. Think what a difference that would have made. I don't know how many people will read this devotion in the years to come, and be encouraged by it. And it came by a simple decision to get up and going, even though I did not feel like it.

    I want us to be mindful of the wonderful opportunity that we have in every moment to make decisions, and the impact they have on our lives as well as the lives of others. I want us to make them prayerfully.

*"Lord, what is best for me and my loved ones today? Of my current options, which is best in Your sight? Help me not to give in to my weaknesses. Help me to see and do the **best**, which is Your will for me."*

95

HOUSETOP LIVING

Nothing is covered up that will not be revealed, or hidden that will not be known. Therefore whatever you have said in the dark shall be heard in the light, and what you have whispered in private rooms shall be proclaimed upon the housetops [Lk 12:2-3].

Jesus answered him, "I have spoken openly to the world; I have always taught in synagogues and in the temple, where all Jews come together; I have said nothing secretly [John 18:20].

One of the greatest challenges of the Christian life is simply living honestly and openly, having nothing to hide, no secrets to be discovered. This is also an incredibly liberating way to live. We have all gone through our personal versions of the Fall. Adam and Eve were innocent and free. They had nothing to hide and nothing of which to be ashamed—until they were deceived and partook of the forbidden fruit. Then they lost something that, theretofore, they didn't even know that they possessed: their freedom from fear, guilt, and shame. They had to go into hiding. They had a shameful secret. They feared being discovered. They went from living openly, in the light, nakedness, to the darkness of hiding in secretiveness and shame. All of us have betrayed, deceived, or made mistakes that we felt compelled to keep hidden. When we did, we became divided within ourselves. Some part of us we were presenting to the world; another part we were keeping hidden in the darkness of our own secret awareness. This always takes a toll on our soul because it was designed to flourish in the light of openness, like a flower in the sun. It takes energy to remain hidden. That is why those who confess a long-denied crime often report a deep sense of relief even if they must spend some time in jail. The truth sets us free. And if we have lived very long in the darkness of denial, we never want to lose that freedom again. We want to live always out in the light of truth with nothing to hide, no secrets to be discovered. We don't want to live in the closet; we want to live on the housetop, having everything confessed, not having to worry that our secrets will be discovered. This is the beauty of confession and the forgiveness of Christ. We re-enter the innocence of Eden before the Fall.

Lord, I don't want to live in hiding. I want to live in the freedom of Truth, having everything confessed and out in the Light. I don't want to worry, ever again, about being found out, discovered, "busted." Please, Lord, keep me honest.

No Matter what you do Ask God to Forgive you in Honesty in your Heart AND He will.

96

IT'S NOT GOOD TO COMPLAIN

And the whole congregation of the people of Israel murmured against Moses and Aaron in the wilderness, and said to them, "Would that we had died by the hand of the LORD in the land of Egypt, when we sat by the fleshpots and ate bread to the full; for you have brought us out into this wilderness to kill this whole assembly with hunger."

..."And in the morning you shall see the glory of the LORD, because he has heard your murmurings against the LORD. For what are we, that you murmur against us?" And Moses said, "When the LORD gives you in the evening flesh to eat and in the morning bread to the full, because the LORD has heard your murmurings which you murmur against him--what are we? Your murmurings are not against us but against the LORD." [Ex 16:2-3,7-8]

God had delivered them from slavery in Egypt with great miracles: The plagues, the parting of the sea, pillar of smoke by day, fire at night to guide them. But life was still difficult, and they were looking back into their slavery [or their idealized version of it] longingly. Stress can cause regression. But stress, as we have come to know, is an *internal response* to external stimuli. It's not about the stimulus; it's about the response. And God's children were responding by complaining. They thought they were complaining to Aaron and Moses, but as Moses revealed to them, they were complaining against the Lord.

When we are infants and children, we are relatively helpless and dependent on the bigger, older people around us to relieve our discomfort. At first, all we can do is cry, and when we do, we usually get some relief—Mom comes and changes the diaper or feeds us. Later, as adults, we have to *unlearn* this, because crying out to people, in the form of complaining, doesn't make the difficulties go away. In fact, they are all dealing with *their* difficulties that are as bad or worse than ours. As spiritually maturing adults, we begin to understand that *all* our complaining—our inner grumbling and murmurings—is, at root, a whining and complaining against God. It's like saying in a whiney voice, "God, You're not getting it right. This is not the way it's supposed to *be*. Why are You making it so *hard* on me?" Etc. This is a faithless attitude based on the belief that God either doesn't love us or just doesn't know quite what is the right way to handle things. If He would just listen to our complaints, He would change things and make it easier for us, and we know better than He that this is exactly what should happen.

Jesus, in His marvelous and concise way of saying things, went right to the heart of this delusion when He told us, "In the world you will have tribulation" [John 16:33]. Life is going to be difficult, no matter when, where, how or with whom you live it. And you don't get to choose the specific tribulations that you will encounter. But He also said, "Nevertheless, be of good cheer. I have overcome the world." [same verse]. When we find ourselves complaining, perhaps we can meditate on what Jesus meant by this saying.

Lord, no matter what, teach me to be of good cheer. And as always, to love.

97

YOU DON'T HAVE TO BE RELIGIOUS TO PLEASE JESUS

Now a centurion had a slave who was dear to him, who was sick and at the point of death. When he heard of Jesus, he sent to him elders of the Jews, asking him to come and heal his slave. And when they came to Jesus, they besought him earnestly, saying, "He is worthy to have you do this for him, for he loves our nation, and he built us our synagogue." And Jesus went with them. When he was not far from the house, the centurion sent friends to him, saying to him, "Lord, do not trouble yourself, for I am not worthy to have you come under my roof; therefore I did not presume to come to you. But say the word, and let my servant be healed. For I am a man set under authority, with soldiers under me: and I say to one, 'Go,' and he goes; and to another, 'Come,' and he comes; and to my slave, 'Do this,' and he does it." When Jesus heard this he marveled at him, and turned and said to the multitude that followed him, "I tell you, not even in Israel have I found such faith [Lk 7:2-9].

Here is a rather incredible story. Centurions were Roman officers in charge of a hundred men. They are spoken of positively throughout the New Testament. Cornelius, the first recorded Gentile convert, was a centurion [Acts 10]. And a centurion who watched the crucifixion, and the wonders attending it, proclaimed "Truly, this was the Son of God." [Mt 27]. They were chosen on merit and leadership ability and so were remarkable in terms of discipline and strength of mind as well as courage. The centurion in the above story was not a Jew. He was not one of God's chosen. He did not attend the synagogue, and unless he studied privately under personal motivation, would not have known the scriptures. And yet he had respect for the Jewish faith, having helped them build a synagogue. And they considered him "worthy" of anything Jesus might do to help him. This Roman officer exemplified great humility and respect for Jesus and a deep understanding of Jesus' authority in the spiritual realm. As the centurion had authority over men, and could bid them come and go, he realized that Jesus had authority over demons and angels and spirits of sickness and health. The centurion knew that Jesus did not have to "come under [his] roof" [something he did not consider himself worthy of] in order to heal his beloved servant. Jesus commended the centurion's faith as greater than any He had found in Israel. The centurion, as far as we know, was not a religious man. But he was a man of sincere, deep faith in Jesus. He apparently loved his servant, and he helped the Jews. And Jesus was pleased with him, and healed his servant. We see today the disconcerting truth that some people outside the religious life seem to have more of the Spirit of Christ in them than others who practice religious disciplines. Our religious life is only helpful to the degree that it helps us have more of the faith exemplified by this un-religious centurion.

Lord, please deliver me from meaningless religious practice. May everything I do be a simple and pure act of faith in You. May I have the humility, love and faith of this centurion.

98

PEOPLE NEED THE LORD

When he saw the crowds, he had compassion for them, because they were harassed and helpless, like sheep without a shepherd. Then he said to his disciples, "The harvest is plentiful, but the laborers are few; pray therefore the Lord of the harvest to send out laborers into his harvest" [Mt 9:36-38].

The Greek words rendered above as "harassed and helpless" convey the meanings: tired, weary, weak, despondent, cast aside [as one uncared for], thrown down, and abandoned. Jesus had compassion for these people, and He encouraged His disciples to pray for help in ministering to them. In our world today there are countless thousands of people who, spiritually speaking, don't know their right hand from their left. Just today I witnessed a distraught young mother smoking a cigarette with her toddler on her hip while she pumped gasoline into her car. In the schools I have repeatedly seen parents verbally attack teachers *in front of their children* when the children get into trouble. The child has no way of knowing that his parent is reacting wrongly, and feels empowered against his teacher—fertile soil for future problems for the child. Spouses blindly vent their frustrations on each other and their children. People make themselves sick worrying about everything under the sun. Young people believe that an education is primarily a means to make money and that money makes people happy, or that life is primarily about finding someone to love you. We repeatedly see random or domestic acts of violence. All these ways-of-being lead ultimately to or issue out of feelings of "harassment and helplessness," despondency and fatigue—to some sense of failure. And Jesus has compassion for these people, and wants His disciples to help them come to know the Truth that sets them free. Many of us who are in Christ are still suffering unnecessarily because of unsanctified areas of our own personality. We must allow Christ to enlighten us in these areas. We must hear, very deeply, what He is saying to us. And we must be obedient to Him, so that we can be progressively freer from the oppressive forces of evil. And as we are discovering this freedom, we must hear Him say to us, "I want you to pray and ask the Father to send laborers out into these fields. I want you to give My love to those who will receive it. I want you to teach them what I have taught you. Gather and feed My sheep. And I am with you always."

Lord Jesus, thank You for having compassion for me in my blindness and sending someone to share with me the Truth that continues to heal my inner being and liberate my soul. Please forgive me for ignoring and sometimes criticizing so many of your lost sheep. Give me Your sincere and deep compassion for them.

99

DON'T GET SIDETRACKED

Then the disciples came to him and asked, "Do you realize you offended the Pharisees by what you just said?" Jesus replied, "Every plant not planted by my heavenly Father will be rooted up, so ignore them. They are blind guides leading the blind, and if one blind person guides another, they will both fall into a ditch" [Mt 15:12-14 NLT].

Let your eyes look directly forward, and your gaze be straight before you. Do not swerve to the right or to the left; turn your foot away from evil [Prv 4:25,27].

Anything that you *need* from any human can ensnare you. Many hurting souls are ensnared by the need for approval, understanding, love, security, respect, affection, affirmation, etc., from some human. When we need something from someone, and we see that their lack of spiritual maturity is preventing them from giving it to us, we can become ensnared in a mission to get them to "grow up." This can be a very miserable, frustrating mission. On the surface it can appear to be love—we are trying to help the other person understand Christ, become more mature, or overcome selfishness and blindness. But in reality it is based on our *need*—what we need from that person. We know that if we could just get them to see the Truth, they would be able to love us in the way we need to be loved. We are out of touch with Truth our*selves* when we are on this mission: The Truth of *"My God shall supply all your need, according to His riches in glory by Christ Jesus"* [Phil 4:19].

Jesus did not [and does not] need anything from any human [John 2:23-25]. He loves us and wants everything for us and was willing to give His life for us, but He does not *need* anything from any of us. He did not *need* for Judas to understand. He was not following Judas around, pleading with him to open his eyes. He was not arguing with him about his misguided theology. He did not *need* for Peter to be strong. He did not need for the Pharisees to understand, and He told the disciples to "IGNORE THEM." He did not want His disciples [and He does not want you or me] to go off on a wild goose chase of trying to get those who are militantly blind to see. He wants us to continue on peacefully, lovingly, and joyfully offering what He has given us to all who have the ears to hear and eyes to see. But if they do not receive it, He wants His peace to return to us [Mt 10:12]. He does not want us to "lose it" because others won't "receive it." His sheep know His voice [John 10:27]. They will respond to Him when you speak His Word and love them with His love. We are not responsible for those who will not or cannot hear. We cannot force them to wake up. We cannot force them to be free. And we must not get ensnared in the fruitless, obstinate effort. We must rely on the discernment of the Holy Spirit in knowing how to sow the seeds of the Kingdom. And this must always be a peaceful endeavor for us [Jam 3:18].

Lord Jesus, please help me to love, serve, and work for the best for all—for the expansion of Your Kingdom. But please keep me free from the need for anything from anyone but You.

100

FEELINGS DO NOT DETERMINE REALITY

Trust in the LORD with all your heart, and do not rely on your own insight. In all your ways acknowledge him, and he will make straight your paths. Be not wise in your own eyes [Prv 3:5-7a].

I've frequently heard people say, "That's just how I feel." Sometimes the message is, "This is how I feel, and I need to express it. I know that my feelings do not determine reality, and are subject to error, but this is how I feel in this moment. My feelings may be different tomorrow or within the hour." This is a fine and healthy way to express and understand feelings. Other times, however, the message is, "This is how I feel, and my feelings are the most important reality. They have to be worked around. If you don't want me to feel this way, you have to change, which is what you should do, because my feelings are the most important reality." In this case, feelings are interpreted as reality. This is a terrible mistake. People have all kinds of feelings for all kinds of reasons—many of them sub-conscious. The psychological phenomenon of *transference* is very real. I can have very negative feelings toward a very kind gentleman because his mannerisms remind me of my abusive uncle. I can severely distrust my faithful wife because my mom cheated on my dad. In both cases, my feelings are out of sync with reality. If I trust my feelings as adequate indicators of reality, I will be living dysfunctionally. It is very important for me to be aware of and acknowledge my feelings. But it is equally important for me not to rely on them as adequate determiners of reality. God has determined Reality. We did not create ourselves or the world in which we live. Reality was here before we were born. God reveals Reality in His Word and by His Spirit in us. And this reality is always in congruence with Christ, the Messiah, and His teachings and His life. But it is not always in congruence with how we feel. If I have feelings of hatred toward someone, that is OK. I can acknowledge those feelings. But if I believe that it is OK to act on this hatred, if I believe that I am entitled to this hatred, if I believe that this person is worthy of my hatred, then I am deluded, because Jesus has said, *"Love your enemies, bless those who curse you, do good to those who hate you..."* [Mt5:44]. Jesus determines Reality—not my feelings. God loves me and cares about my feelings just like I care about my son's feelings. As a father, I cared about my son's feelings but could not always act in a way that was determined by them or that immediately gratified them because there were other aspects of reality that took precedence over his feelings. I realize that the same is true in my relationship with our Heavenly Father. I also know that He has my absolute best interest at heart, and that His way leads ultimately to the best feelings that can be experienced—peace, gratitude, freedom of soul, contentment, and joy. **His** way. Not the way of my own feelings or my "own insight."

Lord, thank You for Your Holy Word that is the gold standard of Reality. Thank You that we are not left to wander in the darkness of our own understanding. Thank You for shining the Light of Truth into our world. Thank You for Jesus.

101

POWER AND CONTROL VS. SERVANT LEADERSHIP

But Jesus called them to him and said, "You know that the rulers of the Gentiles lord it over them, and their great men exercise authority over them...It shall not be so among you; but whoever would be great among you must be your servant,...even as the Son of Man came, not to be served, but to serve, and to give His life as a ransom for many" [Mt 20:25-26,28]

One of the greatest temptations that we face perpetually is the desire or need for power and control. I have seen, much too frequently, in the context of marriage counseling, this deep-seated need to control one's spouse. We read about it or see it in the News in its extreme forms. Recently, it was reported that a husband drove to another state, kidnapped his estranged wife, put her in the trunk of his car, and drove her back to his apartment where he held her hostage until the police intervened. It is common knowledge for those who try to help abused women that the most dangerous time for her is while she is breaking away from his death-grip. He would rather kill her and also himself than let her get free of the prison camp that he has held her in. He is addicted to controlling her, and lost in a deep darkness. This is essentially a failure of faith. It is driven by a deep insecurity and gnawing fear that "If I can't control the situation, I'm going to be hurt [again], or I'm going to lose out, miss the boat, be left behind, unloved or abandoned. And I absolutely refuse to allow that to happen." It is counter-productive in that it creates what is feared—that is, abandonment. "Love" that is demanded and controlled can never be true, and therefore never satisfies the soul. Power and control are an evil and destructive counterfeit for love and faith. Love liberates. Evil enslaves and attempts to control.

Regarding power and control, Jesus and Satan responded oppositely. Satan coveted the power and authority of God and tried to seize it. He rebelled and tried to take matters into his own hands. Jesus, who frankly stated, "all power in heaven and earth is given unto me,"[Mt 28:18], laid it aside and submitted Himself to the sufferings and difficulties of humanity. He became a servant and taught all who follow Him to do likewise. He knew that God was going to work it all out for good [Rom 8:28]. If you have ever gotten to know someone who was addicted to power and control, you realized that they were very unhappy, frustrated, and angry. They live on a very shaky foundation that is always in jeopardy and requires ongoing vigilance to maintain. People and situations are always getting out of hand or threatening to. The truth is; control is a delusion that takes energy to maintain. Jesus delivers us, if we allow Him, from this dreadful, destructive delusion. He delivers us into faith, and the freedom of joyful servanthood.

Lord, please deliver us from the need to control. Please bless and protect all who are living under the dreadful curse of their own or someone else's need to control

102

DEATH

"In the sweat of your face you shall eat bread till you return to the ground, for out of it you were taken; you are dust, and to dust you shall return" [Gn 3:19].

    Our dog died today. I buried him in the woods behind our house. His body, no longer animated by his spirit, was good for nothing more than to enrich the soil and provide some food for other organisms. The experience served to remind me of the destination of all flesh. As I placed Alf's body in the hole, I silently said to myself, "I will join you."
    The Bible, like these life experiences reminds us of the transience of life. It is very important that we not fear death, for our fear will cause us to expend unnecessary energy keeping the reality of it pushed away or denied, and we will be deprived of the great blessing that its awareness brings to us. Death gives great importance to life. Death gives life a peaceful urgency that causes us to move onward toward and into those activities that we most want to accomplish. Death awakens us to priorities and spurs us toward their fulfillment. Death causes us to examine our way of being in the world. It reminds us that we only have a limited time to love our loved ones—all of whom must face their death also. Perhaps most importantly, death reminds us to cultivate our life in Christ; our spiritual life, which is eternal and constantly being renewed, even as the body

slowly deteriorates [2 Cor 4:16]. We are essentially spiritual beings in physical bodies. Our bodies will return to the dust—and that's important to remember—but our souls are eternal.

Lord, thank You for reminding us that this life is transient. Please help us to live it well, in the light of all You have taught us, and are continuing to teach us.

103

GOD IS NOT "NICE"

Then Jeremiah came from Topheth, where the LORD had sent him to prophesy, and he stood in the court of the LORD's house, and said to all the people: "Thus says the LORD of hosts, the God of Israel, Behold, I am bringing upon this city and upon all its towns all the evil that I have pronounced against it, because they have stiffened their neck, refusing to hear my words [Jer 19:14-15].

Now Pashhur the priest, the son of Immer, who was chief officer in the house of the LORD, heard Jeremiah prophesying these things. Then Pashhur beat Jeremiah the prophet, and put him in the stocks that were in the upper Benjamin Gate of the house of the LORD [Jer 20:1-2].

God loves us, but He does not try to be "nice." When we live in prosperity, we tend to grow soft. We want everyone to be nice, and we want everything to be OK. But according to God's Word, everything is not OK just because we or someone we love believes it to be. We want to be tolerant of everything, and if someone believes something to be true, we want to be nice to them and make allowances for them to follow their beliefs—maybe we will even join them in their ceremonies. I was in New York at a time when homosexuality was being celebrated. On Main Street, the same street on which the Easter Parade is held, a homosexual "wedding" was taking place. A number of courageous Christians were preaching into the crowd. In some way they were like Jeremiah in his time. They [as he] were not well received. The people in Jeremiah's day, and in ours, want God's people to be "nice" and tolerant. In the time of Jeremiah, God's people had been very tolerant of many gods. And God had patiently tolerated this idolatry for a long time. But His patience is limited. There comes a time for wrath. So God called Jeremiah to "uproot," "tear down," "destroy," and "overthrow" [Jer 1:10]. This is a very harsh ministry, and Jeremiah was not well received by the elite of his day. His message was not "politically correct." But the message that Jeremiah delivered to the people of his time came into reality. Judah was taken into captivity.

There are either many gods or there is one God. If there is one God, then we must not pretend that there are many. Jesus is either the Messiah, or He is not. We must love all people. Jesus has commanded it. But loving people does not mean that we should pretend to agree with their beliefs or their way of being in the world. We must not use violence in opposing false doctrine. That is never the way of Christ. But we must not be so "nice" that we passively act as if God has not revealed the Truth to us in His Holy Word, and especially in the life of Christ. The proliferation of the worship of many gods, and the worship of what man had made with his own hands [in our time, that would be things like TV, computers, sports, etc.], were the precise reasons that God called Jeremiah to warn the people that judgment was imminent. The belief in many gods divides people. The belief in one God unites people. A God Who loves all with a supreme love, and commands us to love each other, and Who has demonstrated His love in the giving of His Son, Who said, "They will know that you are my disciples by the love that you have for each other" [John 13:35]; this is the hope of the world. And this is the reason that God will not tolerate what man in his blindness wants us to tolerate. This toleration leads ultimately to violence. And the intolerance of God leads ultimately to peace in the human family, which is what God commanded Jeremiah to "build" and "plant" [Jer 1:10]].

Lord, please forgive us for trying so hard to be "nice" that we ignore what You have revealed to us in Your Word and through Christ. If Your Word is true then it is what is best for all, no matter what we believe or desire.

104

THE LITTLE THINGS OF TODAY ARE IMPORTANT

Are not five sparrows sold for two pennies? And not one of them is forgotten before God. Why, even the hairs of your head are all numbered. Fear not; you are of more value than many sparrows [Jesus, Lk 12:6-7].

And he saw also a poor widow put in two copper coins. And [Jesus] said, "Truly I tell you, this poor widow has put in more than all of them [Lk 21:2-3].

We are sometimes tempted to think that our life is insignificant. We feel inferior and inadequate. Others seem to be doing great things for the Kingdom while we sit on the sidelines taking up space. Jesus apparently does not want us to think this way. He reminds us that what is "great" in the eyes of the world may be insignificant in the Kingdom, and what is small and insignificant in the world, may be heroic and wonderful in the Kingdom. The poor widow put in "more than all of them." But how many people in the synagogue that day [other than Jesus] would have considered it so? How many of them, I wonder, were envying the richer, more impressive members of the congregation?—and feeling inferior by comparison. Isn't it wonderful that Jesus helped prostitutes, tax collectors, fishermen, and Samaritans understand that God was aware of them—loved them—wanted them to be in His Kingdom! And we know that He cares for us too, even though we are weak and not very productive for the Kingdom. Jesus tells us that He knows the number of hairs on our head! Jesus tells us not to fear; God is not going to forget us. He's not going to leave us behind as long as we continue to love and serve people in His name—even if it's just a cup of water [Mk 9:41].

Lord Jesus, please help me to remember that my life is important to You, and that every day—today—gives me an opportunity to put in my two pennies or give someone a cup of water in Your name. Please help me not to pass up today's opportunity.

105

IDOLATRY LIVES

"You shall have no other gods before me" [Ex 20:3].

I think it is fair to say that the *primary* determiner of my inner being and activities—that with which I am *primarily* preoccupied, think about the most, and *primarily* determines how I feel—is my god. Some people are primarily determined by the need for a drug to which they are addicted. Their god is the drug. Some are determined by the desire for money, sex or human acclaim. The need for excitement or fun is the primary driving force of some. The desire for a mate, the fear of financial failure, a situation at work, children, a family situation, husband or wife—all these can be idols because they can all become the *primary* determiner of one's inner being. The Reality of God, as He has been revealed in the Bible and especially in Christ, gets left behind in the dust of my preoccupation with any of these idols. And without realizing it, I am violating His very first Commandment. I may be praying, but I am praying for God to attain for me the object of my true devotion and desire. God becomes a pawn, in this case, in my game of trying to get the "main thing" that I really desire—my idol. I am sure that in a time of desperation, a drug addict in dire need of his drug, has prayed "God, please let me score a hit tonight!" And I know that many desperate Christians have prayed for God to restore a broken, idolatrous relationship—a relationship that is more important to them than God Himself. Everything to which we allow our soul to become attached, other than God, is destined to crumble into ruins. "Not one stone will be left upon another" [Mt 24:2]. Every relationship, every substance, every activity, all our toys, everything that excites us and makes life worth living, and our work will fade into nothingness. Only the eternal Truth and Goodness of Christ—only His Spirit in us—will sustain us throughout life into eternity. In Him all things are perpetually new! [2Cor 5:17]. In Him death is a victory! [1Cor 15:54]. In Him, though the outer body is deteriorating, the inner man is continually renewed! [2Cor 4:16]. In Christ we are more than conquerors over every situation, failure, and betrayal [Rom 8:37]. No matter what we lose, no matter how people behave or misbehave, no matter the political or economic situation, in Christ we can say, along with Julian of Norwich, "All shall be well, and all shall be well, and all manner of things shall be well!" And with Horatio Spafford, "It is well, it is well with my soul." And we can say this because God and God alone is our God. We are not being *inwardly determined* by anything less than the Prince of Peace [Is 9:6].

Lord God, You and You alone are my God. Thank You for revealing Yourself in Christ as One Who is merciful, kind, gracious, and forgiving, and Who's will it is that all should come into the Kingdom of peace, love, and eternal life. May I abide with You in this wonderful Place forever. Deliver me from attachments to the things of this world.

106

JOY

These things I have spoken to you, that my joy may be in you, and that your joy may be full. This is my commandment, that you love one another as I have loved you [Jesus, John 15:11-12].

Isn't it amazing that the God of all creation became a man, and as a man related to us that He wants us to be full of joy? Understanding and abiding in the Truth that Jesus has spoken to us enables us to have the fullness of joy. And His primary commandment is that we love one another as He has loved us. We may be discovering the reality of this principle from the scientific perspective. I attended a seminar recently at which the speaker, a Harvard M.D., speaking on the topic of helping children deal with trauma, cited recent brain research indicating that the same area of the brain "lights up" during altruistic activity as during heroin use. In the aftermath of Hurricane Katrina, I was moved to tears repeatedly as I witnessed first hand the joy in the countenances of so many first-responders passing out food, water, ice, and gasoline to people in need of these basics for survival. There was something very deep and wonderful resonating between the giver and receiver. The best word I can think of to describe it is "joy." If we could have seen an image of my brain at those moments, and of those who were serving, I think it would have appeared that we were "high." People who have made so much money that they never need to be concerned with making any more of it seem to fall into one of two categories. Either they become bored or depressed, and begin to decline [Elvis], or they discover the joy of altruism [Bill Gates] and spend their lives and resources making the world a better place for others. Thankfully, we don't have to be independently wealthy to know the joy of loving. Remember, Jesus said the poor widow, who only gave two copper coins, gave the most of all [Lk 21:3]. Maybe she was also the most joyful.

Lord, thank You for revealing these wonderful secrets of life to us. Please help us to love each other more and better each day, so that we may experience the fullness of joy.

107

VARIATIONS ON A THEME

For in him the whole fullness of deity dwells bodily, and you have come to fullness of life in him, who is the head of all rule and authority [Col 2:9-10].

In many arenas of life we see the phenomenon of variations on a theme. Bass, Redfish, Speckled Trout and Brim are variations on the theme *fish*. Cattle Egrets, Great White Egrets and Snowy Egrets are variations on the theme of *egrets*, which are a variation on the larger theme, *birds*. Our most beautiful music has a repeated melody, with variations straying away, then coming back to the theme. You and I are variations on the theme *human*. I am thankful that God has made infinite variations possible on infinite themes in life. Without a main theme, however, life becomes random and meaningless—an endless series of variations, originating nowhere and returning to nowhere. The Bible teaches that there is a Main Theme for the human family; and this theme has been revealed in Christ. In the Kingdom of God, our lives become beautiful variations on the Theme of the Love of God revealed in Christ. Christ Himself is our Main Theme. If we stray too far from the Theme, the music of life becomes noise. If we do not "abide in the Vine" our lives will not be fruitful [John 15:4]. For a Christian, marriage, childrearing, work, recreation, education, and the daily functions of life are variations on the Theme of God's Love for us, in us, and through us. We are so thankful to be anchored, rooted, and grounded in Christ, in Whom we have abundant and eternal life, peace, and joy. We are so thankful that God has revealed Himself to us in Christ. Each day is a brand new variation on the Theme of Life in Christ!

Lord God, thank You for revealing the Main Theme of life to us in Christ. May our lives be beautiful variations on this beautiful Theme.

108

THE SOLUTION

I am the way and the truth and the life. No one comes to the Father except through me. Anyone who has seen me has seen the Father [Jesus, John 14:6,9].

These are very bold words. Think about what Jesus is saying here. He is *the Way* to the Father. The Father is the spiritual Being Who is the Creator of the universe. He is the One Who thought up/imagined all that is, and spoke it into existence—every plant, animal, bird, all universal phenomena, and everything our scientists have discovered and will yet discover about life and how things work. He is the author and creator of the human body, manhood, womanhood, and the process of conception and birth. The variety and colors of all things. the way the sun reflects off the scales of a Speckled Trout, and the means by which the human eye can detect those lights and colors is a gift from the Father. Jesus is one with Him [John 10:30]. And Jesus deeply and passionately implores us to trust Him, and to not be troubled or afraid [John 14:1]. He tells us that we are loved more than we can yet know—more than we love our own children. The miracles that came through Christ were God's way of calling our attention to the validity of His words. At the Transfiguration, God spoke in an audible voice, heard by those present, saying, "This is my beloved Son, in Whom I am well pleased. Hear what He has to say" [Mt 17:5]. God even raised Christ from the dead to confirm to us that He was not just a great man, prophet, or teacher. Jesus, and those who wrote about Him were either liars or lunatics, or Jesus is the

Messiah, at one with the Creator of this universe—the Giver and Sustainer of life. If He is the Lord and if His words are true—and we must all come to the place of either accepting or rejecting Him—then there will never be enough intelligence, power, education, social programs, military might, or political correctness to preserve what we value in life. Only one thing will do this: Submission to Christ, in Whom we have access to the power of God, the Holy Spirit, which is the only Force powerful enough to subdue the sinful nature of humankind. Every day we must submit to Him and stand in the power of His love for everyone; His sincere desire for the best for everyone; His stern resistance to evil; His joy and gratitude to God for life; His victory over the dark and oppressive forces of this world; His infinite freedom of soul. If we are not *growing* in Christ, we are contributing to the world's problems.

Lord Jesus, please forgive me for being so easily distracted by things that do not contribute to the Kingdom. Today, Lord, may I love someone with Your love.

109

KEEP FOLLOWING CHRIST. DON'T LOOK BACK.

To another he said, "Follow me." But he said, "Lord, let me first go and bury my father." But he said to him, "Leave the dead to bury their own dead; but as for you, go and proclaim the kingdom of God." Another said, "I will follow you, Lord; but let me first say farewell to those at my home." Jesus said to him, "No one who puts his hand to the plow and looks back is fit for the kingdom of God" [Lk 9:59-62].

Jesus is always inviting us onward and upward. No matter what we have accomplished, what experiences we have had, or how far we have come, Jesus has more for us—more life, more meaningful, important work. The Kingdom of God is a peaceful Kingdom, but it is an active Kingdom. Jesus is always leading us onward toward the fulfillment of our heart's desire [Ps 37:4], through the valley of the shadow of death [Ps 23], into eternal life [John 3:16]. There is rest in the Kingdom, but there is no stagnation, no leveling off, and no once-and-for-all arrival. We are always tempted to be distracted by activities that have no ultimate value. Jesus said that we will give account of every "idle word" in the day of judgment [Mt 12:36]. Every thing we do in Christ has eternal significance. But not all our activities are ordained by God—even those that are outwardly benign. God calls us to stay focused on the eternal in order to best perform the temporal [Col 3:2].

Are we going to simply be fishermen and undertakers; or fishers of men and channels of eternal life?

Lord Jesus, thank You for keeping me on the wonderful pathway of eternal and abundant life—the pathway of love for all. Today may I be very awake and aware of Your Holy Spirit in me.

110

BE PREPARED

And at that time Michael shall stand up, the great prince who stands for the children of your people: and there will be a time of trouble, such as there has never been, and at that time your people will be delivered, every one that is found written in the book [Dn 12:1].

Then he said to them, "Nation will rise against nation, and kingdom against kingdom; there will be great earthquakes, and in various places famines and pestilences; and there will be terrors and great signs from heaven [Lk 21:10-11].

The Bible teaches us to be prepared for tribulation: the normal, every day type, and the cataclysmic type. Jesus said, *"In the world you will have tribulation. Nevertheless, be of good cheer, I have overcome the world."* [John 16:33]. As recorded in Matthew 24 and Luke 21, He also spoke of the cataclysmic signs of the end of the age. We are aware that many things could happen to drastically impact our lives. In the last century, for the first time in history, man has the capacity to destroy the earth with weapons of mass destruction. We see the possibility of pandemic illnesses for which we have no cure. We see major changes in the earth's climate and are uncertain of the long-term effects. The Bible comforts us with warnings and admonitions regarding how we are to live to be delivered through these tribulations.

How, then, should we live, in order to be prepared?

- Abide in Christ. Know Him personally. Commune with Him in prayer. Know and live by His teachings. Believe in Him in your heart, and confess Him with your lips.
- Be on guard. Luke 21:34: *Be careful, or your hearts will be weighed down with dissipation, drunkenness and the anxieties of life....[36] Be always on the watch, and pray that you may be able to escape all that is about to happen, and that you may be able to stand before the Son of Man.*

- Love. Do the work of love. If we say we believe, and do not love, we deceive ourselves, and we will not be able to stand before Christ, who said, *"They will know you are my disciples by the love that you have for one another" [John 13:35].*
- Be self-controlled. Don't get caught up in the things of the world, for it is passing away, and you will leave it behind. Keep your mind set on things that can not be seen—the things of God, Jesus, love, the Kingdom. *Be diligent, that you might be found of him at peace, holy, and blameless* [2Pet 3:14].
- *Be joyful always; pray continually; give thanks in all circumstances, for this is God's will toward you in Christ Jesus. Do not quench the spirit. Do not treat the prophecies with contempt. Test everything. Hold on to the good. Avoid every kind of evil. May God Himself, the god of peace, sanctify you through and through. May your whole spirit, soul and body be kept blameless at the coming of our Lord Jesus Christ. The one who calls you is faithful and he will do it.* [1Thes 5:16-24].
- Stand firm through any persecution or testing of your faith.
- Be the Light of the world that Jesus has ordained us to be. Fulfill the Great Commission [Mt 28:18-20].

Lord Jesus, thank You for warning us of what is to come and for enabling us to be prepared. May we abide in the eternal security of Your Spirit and Love.

111

THE DANGEROUS "RATIONAL" MIND OF MAN

"This people honors me with their lips, but their heart is far from me; in vain do they worship me, teaching as doctrines the precepts of men" [Jesus, Mt 15:8-9].

Jesus was quoting Isaiah in the above statement regarding the fact that the Pharisees had managed to come up with a smooth-sounding doctrine that enabled them to avoid taking care of their elderly parents, even though God had specifically commanded them [and us] to do so. You don't have to delve very deeply into the human psyche before you run into the phenomenon of "rationalization," which is described as a process by which we "devise reasonable explanations for behaviors that are different from the true motivation." When faced with a difficult task or requirement, even a healthy and righteous one, we tend to rationalize our way around it. We thus use our magnificent brains to our own detriment. The Bible warns us not to "lean upon our own understanding," but rather to trust and acknowledge God in all our ways [Prv 3:5-6].

Not one of us has been perfectly obedient. All of us have rationalized ungodly behavior. But if we were paying attention, we realized that things got worse, not better. God loves us and always has our best interest at heart. He's the One Who gave us these incredible minds that can masterfully find ways to work around His righteousness. And He gives us the freedom to do so. But if we are wise, we come to realize that we can never have victory over Eternal Reality. We do not determine Truth. Truth was here before we were born, and will be here after we pass from this life. The wise thing for us to do is to seek with all our heart to know what the Truth is, and then diligently submit ourselves to it. And Jesus said, "I am the ...Truth..." [John 14:6].

Lord Jesus, please deliver me from my tendency to rationalize away difficult righteousness. I confess that, in my sinful nature, I want to be God, and I want life to be easy. But I know that I am not; and I know it never will be.

112

LIVING BEYOND EGO

And Jethro, Moses' father-in-law, came with his sons and his wife to Moses in the wilderness where he was encamped at the mountain of God. Moses went out to meet his father-in-law, and did obeisance and kissed him; and they asked each other of their welfare, and went into the tent. So Moses gave heed to the voice of his father-in-law and did all that he had said [Ex 18:5,7,24].

In the 18th chapter of Exodus, we are gifted with a beautiful story detailing a great relationship between a son-in-law and father-in-law. Jethro had heard of the wonderful things God had done in delivering the Hebrews from Egypt. He decided to visit Moses in the wilderness, bringing along Moses' sons and wife, Zipporah. Moses greeted him with great respect, and they spent some time talking about the great things God had done for them [verses 8-9]. They praised God and made sacrifices to Him [verses 10-12]. The next day, Jethro noticed how overwhelmed Moses was in his ministry as a judge, and suggested that he delegate some of the work. Moses listened and heeded, and everyone was better off for it. There is no hint of ego interference in these transactions. What if Jethro had been upset because Moses was neglecting his husbandly duties in his desert wanderings? Moses had sent his wife and sons back to Midian into Jethro's keeping, during the travails of the exodus. Maybe Zipporah was feeling neglected by Moses and had been nagging her father to do something about it. Perhaps Satan had tempted Jethro to wonder if Moses was trying to dodge his family responsibilities altogether. And couldn't Moses have been tempted to be a little annoyed that Jethro was barging in on him with the extra responsibilities of women and children, during his important work as God's deliverer? And who was this old man to be giving advice to the one to whom God Himself had appeared in the burning bush, and who had stood down the very powerful Pharaoh, and through whom God had destroyed the Egyptian army in the Red Sea? Moses had struck the rock, and water had come forth for the thirsty wanderers. Did he need someone to tell him how to do his judging?

No, we see none of this. And how refreshing it is! How clean and fresh and good it is when men don't let their little egos get in the way of getting on with praising God for all His goodness and grace, and working together for the common good.

Lord, thank You for delivering us from our small-minded ego concerns that generate so much unnecessary conflict and deter us from the important work of the Kingdom.

113

MYSTERIOUS BUT NOT SECRET

Jesus answered him, "I have spoken openly to the world; I have always taught in synagogues and in the temple, where all Jews come together; I have said nothing secretly [John 18:20].

To them God chose to make known how great among the Gentiles are the riches of the glory of this mystery, which is Christ in you, the hope of glory [Col 1:27].

The world of the spirit is indeed mysterious: The reality of goodness and evil; how God has brought all things, including us, into being; Jesus being with Him in the beginning; this unfolding revelation of Truth; spiritual blindness—how some hear, receive and are liberated, while others continue to be used of the evil one to wreak havoc in the world. Mysterious indeed is the fact that God's love involves His allowance of evil for a time; and the victory won for the human family by the sacrificial death and resurrection of His Son. These are great mysteries. But there is nothing secretive or deceptive about Christianity. There is no hidden agenda—no "bait and switch" manipulations. Jesus is right out front with Who He is, and what He desires. He is the Messiah—the Savior, and He desires the redemption of our souls. As Lord, He offers forgiveness, freedom, peace, joy, abundant and eternal life for all. He requires us to be honest with ourselves and others about our sins. And His primary command is that we love God and each other as He has loved us. He makes it clear that His way is not easy. We must take up a cross, die to self, be willing to suffer for righteousness sake, and be misunderstood and persecuted—even die—for His sake. But in these sufferings and in this death is the only true life and freedom that exists for the human soul. All else is ultimately meaningless. Jesus is out front with all this. And we are all divided—not only between ourselves, but *within* ourselves—in terms of our response. None of us have responded wholeheartedly, unreservedly, and without faltering. But when we take any step toward Christ—when we submit to anything He requires of us—we are always thankful. The Holy Spirit confirms, deep within us, that we are moving in the direction of Life. Like a plant moving toward the sun, or a child responding to his mother's open arms, we know we were created to respond to Christ. And since we have made the conscious decision to make Him Lord of our lives, He has been revealing to us the great Mystery of God's Love unfolding infinitely around and within us. He continues to set us free with a freedom that we desire for all.

Lord, thank You for what You have revealed to us about our God and Father. Thank You for being out front with us, even though it cost You dearly. Today may I be more alive in Your Love than ever before.

114

ABUNDANT LIFE AND JOY

And the crowds that went before him and that followed him shouted, "Hosanna to the Son of David! Blessed is he who comes in the name of the Lord! Hosanna in the highest!" But when the chief priests and the scribes saw the wonderful things that he did, and the children crying out in the temple, "Hosanna to the Son of David!" they were indignant; and they said to him, "Do you hear what these are saying?" And Jesus said to them, "Yes; have you never read, 'Out of the mouth of babes and sucklings thou hast brought perfect praise'?" [Mt 21:9,15-16]

I heard on public radio recently of a group of Muslim fundamentalists that physically attacked a group of young people who were singing and dancing in a public place. Police, standing nearby, did not intervene. According to the fundamentalists, these people were violating religious principles. I have seen Christians who were joyless and critical in this same manner. I am thankful beyond description that God is not like some religious extremists who have a fear and hatred of human and earthly pleasure. When we see flowers—countless species of them—that smell good, are beautiful to look at, some of which evolve into fruit that is succulent and sweet; when we see woman's incredible, soft responsiveness to man; when we see white clouds spun into the blue web of infinity; when we see colossal, windblown snowy mountain peaks; when we are mesmerized by the infinitely beautiful patterns and colors of light dancing on spider webs, ocean waves, and children's fine, soft hair; when we can almost feel the warmth of a full moon on a cold, crisp winter night; when we feel the ancient, awesome reverence of a redwood forest or the Grand Canyon; when we see vast fields of flowers dancing in the wind: how can we doubt God's desire for us to celebrate, dance, sing, and rejoice with everything within us? How can we not respond to His clear, powerful invitation to run, like children, dancing through those fields, arms flailing, silly with laughter; or to sit in the pure sweet joy of a smiling heart, feeling His love enveloping, embracing, and calling to us in a thousand voices?

God please forgive us for getting lost in our morbid fears, worries and cares. Help us to enjoy all the earthly pleasure that is not offensive to You or harmful to anyone. And deliver us from indignation or envy of those who are celebrating the innocent joys of earthly life.

115

GOD IN WHAT CAN BE SEEN

Ever since the creation of the world his invisible nature, namely, his eternal power and deity, has been clearly perceived in the things that have been made. So they are without excuse...[Rom 1:20].

When we look deeply into the world in which we live—life all around us, infinitely complex and interwoven; a protective atmosphere; a warm, nurturing earth, perfectly balanced and tilted on it's axis so that it sustains us with everything we need for life; manhood and womanhood; our incredible brains that enable us to contemplate the meaning of life; the very process of perceiving beauty—we realize that this is not a random accident emerging out of inorganic dust and gasses. We realize that we have been given an unspeakably awesome gift, and there has to be a Giver, to Whom we are forever grateful.

And what can we learn about the Creator from His creation? The infinitely complex nature of life—the physical and bio-chemical processes of cells, bacteria, viruses, organs, organisms, species, ecosystems, etc.—reveal to us that God is incredibly intelligent. There can be no doubt that He knows what He is doing. The fact that we are here, and we are free, and we are man and woman, and we are mobile, creative, playful, humorous, and contemplative; the feelings we have for our children; the fact that there is beauty all around us that delights our senses and sustains our souls; all these and much more reveal to us that God loves us. The awesome power of the sun—able to burn human skin and too bright to look at directly, even from 93 million miles away—and the fact that there are more of them [the stars] than we can count, for as far as we can see into the universe, reveal to us that God is not limited in power. God is revealed in the created world as: incredibly intelligent, the Author of all love, with unlimited power—wise, loving, and powerful. When we put that together with what has been revealed by Him through the prophets of old and most vividly in the teachings and life of Jesus Christ as set forth in the Holy Bible, we see a glorious congruence that sets us free. We realize that, in Christ, we have nothing to fear or dread; that all is well; that we will never be lost; that all of life, including its tribulations, is a gift, and that death is a doorway into new adventures and greater enlightenment. Our soul finds a place of infinite rest and indescribable joy. And we know that we are here to love each other with His love, which is growing in us day by day. We desire all people to live in this freedom, peace and love.

Lord God, Your creation speaks in a million languages of Your power and deity. And oh the untold beauty of the message of all these languages. We celebrate life! We bow in deep, eternal gratitude.

116

ARE YOU A MURMURER?

And when they saw it they all murmured, "He has gone in to be the guest of a man who is a sinner."..."For the Son of Man comes to seek and save the lost" [Lk 19:7,10].

One of the manifestations of the sinful nature is murmuring, which means to complain or grumble in a low or indistinct voice. It is a form of judgmentalism in that it looks at an act or person in a critical or condemning attitude. We see it in a refined form in junior high school girls, who are renowned for forming cliques and murmuring about other girls or cliques. It is an unconscious way of attempting to elevate one's self by belittling others. It is also a form of gossip. Somehow, it feels good, in an unhealthy way to talk down about someone else. It makes us feel that we are the "in crowd"—in the know—and "they" are still in the dark, socially awkward, or just inept ["Thank God!"]. This murmuring is in a "low and indistinct voice," indicating an unwillingness to come all the way out into the light of bold speaking. There is a hiddenness or secretiveness about this manner of speaking in collusion with one or more others who also want to remain in the semi-darkness. It is never the kind of talking one would do in a public pulpit. Evil or good can be the object of murmuring. In the above, Jesus' redemptive love for Zacchaeus was the object of murmuring scorn. But in other times Christians have murmured against legitimate evil. The problem in this case is the lack of courage to speak boldly, or the failure to speak with compassion. When Jesus spoke against evil, He did so boldly and with the best interest of others at heart. When evil speaks against good, it is always for selfish or self-aggrandizing purposes. Evil seeks to elevate or justify itself. Goodness seeks the common good and glorifies God. When we are speaking against something or someone, we should be prayerfully considerate of our motivations. Do we seek to justify or elevate our self, or are we working for the common good? Are we speaking against evil or against good [from the biblical perspective]? Are we speaking boldly, or are we "murmuring"? Jesus' motivation was to "seek and save the lost." What is our motivation?

Lord Jesus, thank You for enduring the blindness of the human family, and for continuing to Love. Thank You for not giving up on us. Give us discernment about what to speak against, and boldness and clarity to speak in ways that further Your Kingdom.

117

JESUS DOESN'T ANSWER ALL QUESTIONS

And [the chief priests, scribes and elders] said to him, "Tell us by what authority you do these things, or who it is that gave you this authority."

He answered them, "I also will ask you a question; now tell me, was the baptism of John from heaven or from men?"

And they discussed it with one another, saying, "If we say, 'From heaven,' he will say, 'Why did you not believe him?' But if we say, 'From men,' all the people will stone us; for they are convinced that John was a prophet." So they answered that they did not know whence it was. And Jesus said to them, "Neither will I tell you by what authority I do these things" [Lk 20:2-8].

Here was an intense moment in Christ's ministry. This was a powerful "committee." These were highly respected, intelligent men with much authority. They were the judges, lawyers, politicians, and priests combined. They likely had stern countenances and decorated robes. They had already collaborated regarding how to ensnare this trouble-making imposter that was stirring up so much enthusiasm among the ignorant commoners. You can almost see people stepping out of their way as they approached Jesus. The disciples' hearts burned. But Jesus stood [or perhaps sat] firm, calmly poised in the Spirit. He had no hidden agenda and nothing to defend. They laid out their question like an open pit. And just as He had walked on the water, He walked right over it. He knew they weren't seeking the Truth. They lacked the humility and wisdom to recognize that they did not already possess it. Their agenda was set like a stone, and Jesus didn't waste His time answering their question, knowing full well that any answer would simply bounce off the stone. They were not His sheep, and they would not hear His voice. His sheep had a different agenda. His sheep wanted healing, truth, light, life, freedom, and peace of soul. These lost souls wanted to defend their dark world from the encroachment of the Light that they, through spiritually blind eyes, could only see as darkness. Jesus responds only to those who approach Him in humility, reverence, and respect. He welcomes them into eternal life. All others, in their blindness, arrogance and pride, condemn themselves to the outer darkness, where there is "weeping and gnashing of teeth" [Mt 8:12].

Lord Jesus, have mercy on me, a sinner. Deliver me from arrogance, pride and high-minded blindness. Deliver me from the delusion of having it all figured out. Thank You for giving me the grace to hear Your voice. Abide with me always.

118

WHERE DO I GET MY NEEDS MET?

And my God will supply every need of yours according to his riches in glory in Christ Jesus [Phil 4:1]).

This is an incredible promise from the Bible, God's Holy Word. In my mind I underline "every" and put an exclamation point after it! One of the most common mistakes that I see in my counseling practice is people trying to get their needs met from people. God commands us to *love* people. Nowhere, from Genesis to Revelation, does He ever encourage us in any way to *need* people. When Jesus gave us His ordination to go out into the world, it was to love, serve, teach—"Baptizing them in the name of the Father, Son and Holy Spirit." He never said that we would or should *need* anything from anyone except God. And He promised to be with us "always, even to the end of the age." People are here for us to love. They are not here:

For us to need;
For us to make happy;
To make us happy;
For us to use;

For us to dominate or be dominated by;
For us to get lost in;
For us to please;
To become more important to us than God;
To become the primary determiners of our inner being [that is, idols];
To drain us;
To become our excuse for unhappiness.

There is a major and important shift that we must make in our transition from childhood into adulthood: the shift from needing people, to loving them. To whatever degree we fall short of this shift, we are very unhappy, because people cannot meet the primary depths of need in the human soul. Only God can. If you are disappointed with how people are loving you, wake up and smell the coffee. It's not their failure; it's your focus. God wasn't lying, exaggerating or delusional when He said He would supply ALL your need. Break your "people addiction." Get free in Christ and in His love for people.

Lord, thank You for leading me out of the frustrating world of need for people into the sunlight of Your all-sufficient Love for me and Your love in me for all.

119

IT'S ABOUT BECOMING

Brothers, I do not consider that I have attained, but one thing I do, forgetting what lies behind and pressing forward to what lies ahead, I move on toward the goal for the prize of the upward call of God in Christ Jesus [Phil 3:13-14].

My wife, Lynn, loves infants. She glowingly told me recently about holding a little girl. "You could tell she was trying to focus her eyes on me; and she smiled." We all start out helpless and unable to do even basic things like focusing our eyes. By age six we have appropriated volumes of information into our minds. We do so because, as toddlers we are incredibly curious and relentlessly explore our world—to the point that we keep our parents busy keeping us safe. We are born reaching out, trying to focus, tasting, touching, trying to understand, and comprehending our world with insatiable curiosity. Sadly, in adulthood many people lose their interest in life and stop growing. We are tempted to level off, start coasting, and live as if we have attained whatever we're here to attain. This is contrary to God's Word and to His desire for us. God wants us to continue our spiritual growth all the way through death. He wants us to continue to be interested in the world He has created and especially in becoming more of what He created us to become—joyful, loving and free, servants of God and man. And He will make it possible for us to do so if we "seek, ask and knock."

Lord, please keep me interested in life and growth and becoming more of what You created me to become. Deliver me from boredom and from the delusion of having attained. I embrace the adventure and opportunity of today!

120

"ABIDE IN CHRIST"

Abide in me, and I in you. As the branch cannot bear fruit by itself, unless it abides in the vine, neither can you, unless you abide in me. I am the vine; you are the branches. He who abides in me, and I in him, he it is that bears much fruit, for apart from me you can do nothing [John 15:4-5].

The Greek word rendered "abide" is pronounced "men'o," and means "to remain as one; not to become another or different; to continue to be present." When we received Christ, He entered our lives permanently and began His sanctifying work within us. Abiding in Him as He has commanded means maintaining mindfulness of His presence and responding to the urgings of His Spirit, moment by moment. It means living with an open heart toward God. It means living prayerfully, lovingly, joyfully, and thankfully in communion with the Creator of the universe through His Son, Jesus Christ, Whose Spirit is with us always as He promised [Mt 28:20]. Following is a *partial* listing of what it means to abide in Christ. When we abide in Christ, we:

Are fully justified and redeemed [Rom 3:24]; Are free from the law of sin and death [Rom8:2]; Are free from condemnation [Rom8:1]; Are inseparable from the love of God [Rom 8:39]; Are unified with all believers, in all lands, for all ages [Rom12:5]; Are sanctified [1Cor 1:12]; Are wise, strong and honorable [1Cor 4:10]; Are alive in the Spirit [1Cor 15:22]; Are triumphant [2Cor 2:14]; Are new creatures in a perpetually new life [2Cor 5:17]; Are reconciled to the Creator of the universe [2Cor 5:19]; Are delivered from the complexities of life [2Cor 11:3]; Are free from every form of bondage [Gal.2:4]; Are the children of God [Gal 3:26]; Have equal and compassionate fellowship with people who are very different from us [Gal 3:28, Eph 3:6]; Are blessed with all the spiritual blessings of heaven [Eph 1:3]; Are being gathered together in a heavenly unity [Eph 1:10, 2:6]; Are created for good works [Eph 2:10]; Discover our eternal purpose [Eph 3:11, Phil 3:14]; Have eternal life [1Thes 4:16]; Give thanks in every situation [1Thes 5:18]; Find exceedingly abundant grace, faith and love [1Tm 1:14]; And have salvation [2Tm 2:10, 3:15].

Colossians 2:9-10 summarizes it very well: **For in him the whole fullness of deity dwells bodily, and you have come to fullness of life in him, who is the head of all rule and authority.**
It is up to each of us to appropriate the eternal Reality of these words into our inner, *felt* experience—by *abiding in Christ.*

Lord, today I will abide in You. Thank You for promising to never leave or forsake me. Thank You for your patience with me. May I experience the reality of Your promises more deeply today than ever before.

121

THE GOLDEN RULE

And as you wish that men would do to you, do so to them [Jesus]. [Lk 6:31].

Here is the summation of the philosophical study of *ethics*. And here is the solution to the majority of the world's problems in a single statement of our Lord. The work that it takes to fulfill this commandment of our Lord is the work of love. It is the work of God. No matter how long we have lived in the Faith, we should not assume that we have mastered the treating of others in the way that we wish to be treated. All people suffer. And all people want to be happy. To try to alleviate our own suffering and make our selves happy is not enough. It will never work. It is like the story of the man who was allowed to visit hell and heaven. What he witnessed in hell was emaciated, starving, miserable people sitting at a banquet table set with all manner of beautifully prepared, luscious food. They were starving because the eating utensils had very long handles, and they could not get the food into their mouths. They were condemned to perpetual starvation in the presence of sumptuous food. In heaven, to his surprise, the setting was exactly the same, even the detail of the long-handled eating utensils. *But the people were feeding each other.* We create heaven here on earth when we feed each other. There is enough of everything we all need, not only materially, but for the soul, if we choose to cultivate the love of Christ for each other—if we feed each other in this way. We feed each other by choosing to care, choosing to be mindful of each others' needs and sufferings, and to have compassion for each other. We must overcome certain inner experiences in order to do this. We must overcome fear, anger, critical attitudes, suspicion, hatred of persons, powerful desires and needs, feelings of deprivation and entitlement. All these block love and compassion. They cause us to be absorbed in self, and prevent us from living the Golden Rule. We can not feed others if we are desperately trying to feed ourselves. We must look to God to meet our needs, and look to others with the eyes of love--the eyes of Christ, Who did not need anything from anyone, but gave to all, even His very life. The great paradox of the Christian faith is that only by feeding others do we become fulfilled.

Lord, thank You for teaching us the Truth that sets us free. Help us to **live** *according to Your teachings, today and every day.*

122

BE PROACTIVE SPIRITUALLY

Therefore do not be anxious, saying, 'What shall we eat?' or 'What shall we drink?' or 'What shall we wear?' For the Gentiles seek all these things; and your heavenly Father knows that you need them all. But seek first his kingdom and his righteousness, and all these things shall be yours as well [Jesus, Mt 6:31-33].

  My son recently completed a 28-day rehab program for opiate addiction. He learned a lot about the disease of addiction during that time, but he told me that the most important thing he learned was that he had had a "spiritual void" that made him vulnerable to the addiction. My heart rejoiced within me at the validity of that truth. I had been concerned for some time about what appeared to me to be a lack of spiritual motive on his part. I have learned from my own sad experiences that if we don't stay proactive spiritually we get blind-sided by some insidious attack from Satan that turns out to be either a wake-up call or a precursor of worse things to come. Some of the dreadful stories that were told by others in the recovery program, and their families, reminded me that there is no bottom to the pit of wayward living.

  Jesus, speaking with the very voice of God, our Creator, focuses us on that which is most important. "First" means number one, top priority, second to none, of utmost importance. Rather than worrying about what we will wear, eat or drink, or work-related issues, marriage, children, and physical health or finances, Jesus says, "Seek the kingdom." All of those issues are important, but they take us off track if they become top priority. Seeking the Kingdom keeps me focused peacefully on whatever is most important—moment by moment. Living in the Spirit keeps us from getting lost in the world. Without the Spirit, we are blind. We think we know what we are doing; but we are deceived, and Satan uses us to hurt others and ourselves. In Christ, we are focused on loving people, and that keeps us safe. When we love people, we don't want to hurt them, and we keep ourselves on a pathway that is good for them and us.

In Matthew 12:41-45, Jesus warns about the dangers of a "house [soul] empty" of repentance, and the desire for wisdom. That house becomes an open place [a "void"] for evil to reside. My son attended church this Sunday past. My prayer is that he, and all of us, will keep the void filled with the grace, goodness, love, joy and peace of Christ—now and always.

Lord Jesus, thank You for revealing the Truth that keeps us safe from the subtle evils of this world. May Kingdom-living [living in Your love for all people] always be our top priority.

123

WHOSE CHURCH IS IT?

And I tell you, you are Peter, and on this rock I will build my church, and the powers of death shall not prevail against it [Mt 16:18].

The Church is not a building, and it is not a denomination. It is more than a specific organization of priests, pastors, elders, or deacons. No person or group of people has ownership of the Church. When Jesus asked the disciples who they believed Him to be, Peter responded, "You are the Christ [Messiah], the Son of the Living God." This was a profound response. Peter was a faithful Jew. He knew the Old Testament prophesies that foretold the coming of the One who would usher in the Kingdom of God and set things straight in the world. The Jewish nation had looked for the Messiah for generations—since the time of Abraham. Peter had mysteriously come to know that Jesus was this One. And in response to Peter's profound proclamation, Jesus made an even more profound proclamation: "Upon the rock of this understanding—this faith in Me as the Messiah—I will build My Church; and the powers of death shall not prevail against it." This proclamation has withstood two thousand years of history. As someone has said, "The Church is an anvil that has worn out many hammers." Many atheistic movements have attempted to eradicate the Church, but it has only become stronger under the oppression of persecution. Any objective evaluation of the Church of Christ reveals that its roots are so deep and widespread, it will never disappear from the human family—just as Jesus stated. But throughout history many humans, in their spiritual blindness, have attempted [following Satan's pattern] to hijack the Church and bring it into the service of their own power-hungry egos. This brings into focus the importance of maintaining a clear understanding of whose Church it is. Jesus has answered the question for us once and for all. "Upon this rock I will build **MY** Church." The Church is the ongoing incarnation of Christ Himself, continuing His loving service and ministries on the earth. The Church can only do those things that Christ, in His infinite Love for the human family, ordains—the things He did and commanded while on the earth. If anyone uses the Bible, "church," or any religious accoutrements for selfish, hateful, or harmful purposes, he is no longer acting within the context of Christ's Church, though half the world follow after him in misguided praise. The Holy Spirit has departed from the endeavor. Safety in the religious world is guaranteed only by secure knowledge of Christ's teachings, and a personal relationship with the Lord Himself, Who has promised to abide within us, and commanded us to abide in Him [John 15:4]. No human has the power or authority to change anything that Jesus has ordained regarding HIS Church. Those who are most worthy in the Kingdom are those who consider themselves servants—not lords [Mt 23:11]. Servants of God and man.

Lord, thank You for abiding with us and protecting us from false doctrine and power-hungry religious leaders. Thank You for washing Your disciples' feet. What a profound and glorious lesson for us!

124

BE STILL AND KNOW

But I have calmed and quieted my soul, like a child quieted at its mother's breast; like a child that is quieted is my soul [Ps 131:2].

When our boys were infants, I delighted in watching Lynn nurse them. When they were hungry, it looked as if they were writhing in pain—faces contorted, crying out, arms and legs flailing. When she picked them up, they were tense with anticipation, instinctively aware of what was coming. As their little bellies filled with nourishment, they slowly relaxed until frequently, they would drift off to sleep in her arms, totally satisfied. Our souls are often like a hungry infant—writhing, grasping, and needing. Turning our hearts toward God, we begin to experience the quietness of fulfillment, contentment, and satisfaction described in the above psalm [and countless other places in the Scripture]. We begin to receive the soul-rest that Jesus promised to those who come to Him [Mt 11:28-29]. We take a *conscious* part in this soul-resting process. Notice how the psalmist worded it above: "*I* have calmed and quieted...." In another place we are commanded to *be still* and know that He is God [Ps 46:10]. It is not something that God does; it is something that we initiate, and He completes or empowers us to accomplish. God wants us to quiet our souls—to be still and know that He is God. If you take a moment just now and tune in to your soul, what do you detect going on there? Are you grasping for anything? Are you dissatisfied, anxious, fearful, needy? Are you dreading anything or complaining about anything? Are you angry, frustrated, or irritated? If you look deeply into your soul, you may realize that some part of your inner being has not been obedient to God's command to be still. You may have to speak sternly to that part of yourself to awaken it into the reality of faith and trust and peace. You may have to compassionately remind that unawakened, childish part of your soul that all is well, and that you have everything you will ever need in Christ. You may find great peace in simply letting go of something you are clinging to or grasping for, and resting in the more-than-enoughness of God's eternal Presence. If you have received Christ, and you are sincere in your walk with Him, then you are abiding in His Spirit, and He will complete the work He has begun in you [Phil 1:6]. He is loving people through you. You have complete victory over evil. You will never be lost. He will keep you in His peace, and He will keep you from being lazy. You don't have to worry. All is well. The Loving Power that created a billion stars is flowing through you as you rest like a baby at its mother's breast.

Lord please give me the strength and courage to calm and quiet my soul – to be still and know that You are God.

125

ON EAGLE'S WINGS?

You have seen what I did to the Egyptians, and how I bore you on eagles' wings and brought you to myself [Ex 19:4].

When we think of being borne on eagle's wings, we might not associate it with what the Israelites had experienced in getting out of Egypt. They experienced thirst, hunger and terror, thinking they were going to die in the desert. They perpetually murmured against Moses [and indirectly, God] for dragging them through tribulations that seemed at times to be worse than the slavery from which they had been delivered [Ex 14:11-12]. Nevertheless, God reminded them, as He was about to give them the gift of the Commandments that would become the world's most influential ethical system, that He had borne them on "eagle's wings…to [himself]." This brings to mind the very popular composition, framed and hung on countless walls in homes and businesses, entitled "Footprints in the Sand." It depicts a life-journey in which the author wonders, in looking back on his life, why he walked alone during the toughest times—there was only one set of footprints in the sand. What God revealed to him was that it was then that He was carrying him. We understand by virtue of the fact that he asked the question in the first place that he did not *feel* that he was being carried. He felt that he was walking alone. This is a very important and wonderful understanding. Even when we feel that we are alone, abandoned, or forsaken [as Christ on the Cross]; if we are walking in faith and obedience, things are unfolding just as planned. A loving God, the creator and sustainer of the universe, Who loves us enough to give His only Son, Who is willing to take us under His wing as a mother hen her chicks, is bearing us on eagle's wings into victory over all the dark forces of the world and into eternal life. We live by faith—not by sight. And not by feelings!

Lord. Please forgive me for murmuring and doubting. I trust You to bear me on eagle's wings into the Promised Land. Help me to do my part by obediently loving people with Your love.

126

EVEN THE "LONE RANGER" HAD TONTO

And they talked with each other about all these things that had happened. While they were talking and discussing together, Jesus himself drew near and went with them [Lk 24:14-15].

But if we walk in the light, as he is in the light, we have fellowship with one another, and the blood of Jesus his Son cleanses us from all sin [1Jn 1:7].

A friend and brother in Christ recently shared with me that he felt like the "Lone Ranger." We agreed that it is very easy to become isolated in our walk, and not spiritually healthy to do so. Our brother the Apostle Paul exhorted us to continue meeting together with others of the Faith [Heb 10:25]. We must go out into the world to be the Light that Christ wants us to be in the world. But without consistent fellowship with others who are sincere and growing in Christ, we are in danger of getting lost in the world. Fellowship—*koinonia*—keeps us safe. In my isolation I can rationalize almost any evil thing. But the moment I bring my evil thoughts into the light of a brother's hearing, I realize immediately how dangerous and unhealthy they are. Thus we are commanded to "confess your sins to each other, and pray for each other, and so be healed" [Jam 5:16]. Some of my most powerful and enlightening moments of communion with God have occurred in fellowship [*koinonia*] with others in Christ. Jesus said that where two or more were gathered in His name that He would be there, in their midst [Mt 18:12]. We know that He is omnipresent, that is, there is no place or time that He is not present. Yet He Himself has emphasized "two or more." True *koinonia* is unfortunately rare. My friend, in the same conversation above, while looking up a verse to share one of his recent devotional readings with me, said, "It is so good to open this Bible with someone and not have that person anxiously excuse himself from my presence." It felt good to him to share the love of the Word with another human. It felt good to me too. That good feeling was the Holy Spirit in each of us, confirming the importance of *koinonia*. We need it. And we must not allow ourselves to go too long without it.

Lord, thank You for providing wonderful brothers and sisters in the faith for us. May we meet regularly with them and share in the gifts of Your Spirit with them. Deliver us from the dangers of isolation.

127

THE IMPORTANCE OF CHRISTIAN FRIENDSHIP

And let us consider how to stir up one another to love and good works [Heb 10:24].

Addressing one another in psalms and hymns and spiritual songs, singing and making melody to the Lord with all your heart, always and for everything giving thanks in the name of our Lord Jesus Christ to God the Father [Eph 5:19–20].

A client friend who had been going through a rough time came in for a counseling session looking significantly brighter than the last time I'd seen her. She told me about a recent spiritual epiphany. In a cell group exercise, she and other respondents were asked to write a list of prayer needs. With furrowed brow, she wrote a long list of needs. Her friend watched with growing concern. Later, this friend came to her with a long list of blessings that she knew had been bestowed upon my client friend. She gently, compassionately confronted her: "Susie [not her real name] you should be thankful! Look at all that God has been doing for you lately!" This impacted Susie deeply. She recognized God's voice speaking to her through her courageous, compassionate friend. The words stayed with her throughout the next day, and she found herself singing praises to God as she worked. That night, this is how she described what happened: "From way down deep in my spirit [she made a gesture with clenched fist indicating the pit of her stomach, moving upward and outward] thankfulness came up within me, and I cried and cried tears of joy and thankfulness. Alone on my bed, I was praising God from the depths of my being for I don't know how long. It was like a baptism in the Spirit."

We who have received Christ have been given tremendous gifts of the Spirit to help, encourage, strengthen, and enlighten. God, in His Word, has encouraged us to use these gifts in each other's behalf. Who knows how long

Susie would have languished in her deprived and empty feelings if her friend had not spoken those words of encouragement to her. And I was reminded also [and now so have you] that we are to be mindful of our blessings and thankful in all situations for all things. We are happier if we maintain an attitude of gratitude.

Lord, thank You for our wonderful friends in Christ. Please help us to be encouragers. And from the depths of our being, thank You for life and all the blessings of life.

128

APPROACH GOD REVERENTLY

And be ready by the third day; for on the third day the LORD will come down upon Mount Sinai in the sight of all the people. And you shall set bounds for the people round about, saying, 'Take heed that you do not go up into the mountain or touch the border of it; whoever touches the mountain shall be put to death; no hand shall touch him, but he shall be stoned or shot; whether beast or man, he shall not live.' When the trumpet sounds a long blast, they shall come up to the mountain"
[Ex 19:11-13].

A near-retirement, well-respected junior high school teacher once told me about an incident of his childhood in which he walked casually up to his dad and another man who were conversing and interrupted them. "My dad knocked me on the ground," he said. Somewhat shocked, and putting the incident in the current context, I asked him if he felt "abused." "No!" he immediately replied. "And I never interrupted any adults in conversation again without saying 'Excuse me.' I learned something about respect."

I think it is fair to say that I have grown up—and my children even more so—in a culture that is drifting away from respect for authority and reverence for God. If we are serious about our walk in the Spirit, we must continually compare what God has revealed to us in His Word to our cultural zeitgeist (the spirit of our time). And we must make the necessary adjustments in our lives, becoming more "holy," a word rooted in the meaning "to be set apart or consecrated" [from or within our culture]. This is how we become the "leaven" that influences the whole culture like yeast in bread. [Mt 13:33].

In the above verses God was about to deliver the Ten Commandments to the world through the newly liberated, desert-wandering Hebrews. He gave Moses specific directives about how this was going to be done. And they were to be followed carefully at the risk of loss of life. *God determined how He could be approached.* Jesus has revealed to us that God is a loving Father. But He also commands respect. He is not our heavenly "pal" or Santa in the sky. Just as we have not determined how the earth and universe operate, we do not determine how things operate in the spiritual world. The primary difference between humanism and Christianity is that humanism asserts that man determines who God is, and Christianity asserts that God determines [and reveals] who He is. He also has determined that His Son, Jesus, is "the way, the truth and the life" and that no one approaches the Father but through Him [John14:6]. If this seems a little narrow-minded to us, we must determine who is in control here, the creatures or the Creator. Jesus' resurrection [combined with His glorious, liberating teachings] seals it for those who come to believe that it happened. And if it didn't, then Christianity is a sham, and we shouldn't pretend otherwise. But if it did, then the most important accomplishment for any human is to bow reverently before Christ and say, along with Thomas, "My Lord, and my God!"[Jn.20:28].

Lord God, Creator of all, I bow reverently before You in gratitude and praise. You did not have to give me life. You owe me nothing. And yet You have given me more than I can be mindful of or thankful for. May Your name be praised forever and ever.

129

UNDER GOD'S WINGS

But Bo'az answered her, "All that you have done for your mother-in-law since the death of your husband has been fully told me, and how you left your father and mother and your native land and came to a people that you did not know before. The LORD recompense you for what you have done, and a full reward be given you by the LORD, the God of Israel, under whose wings you have come to take refuge!" [Ru 2:11-12]

The book of Ruth is a beautiful story of family love and loyalty, and of the providential care of God. Ruth made the courageous and seemingly disadvantageous decision to leave her homeland of Moab and travel to Judah with her mother-in-law, Naomi. Both were widows and powerless in their patriarchal world. Something about Naomi caused Ruth to feel more secure with her than with her own countrymen. She saw something in Naomi that caused her to make the pledge, "...thy God shall be my God..." [1:16].

Boaz looked compassionately and respectfully upon her as she gleaned from his already-harvested field. Perhaps he felt a special connection since his own mother, Rahab, the harlot of Jericho, had also chosen to come under the wings of Israel's God. He instructed his workers to look after her in a manner that did not embarrass her. His statement, quoted above, was at their first encounter, and he acknowledged that she had taken refuge under the wings of the God of Israel. This turned out to be a very favorable place for her, as for all who have ever, in the history of the human family, come under His wings. The gods of any nation shape the character of its people. A nation's god is whatever its people set their heart upon above all else. It could be power, or it could be economic prosperity, or pleasure and excitement. The God of Boaz caused him to treat a powerless, vulnerable woman from a foreign country with utmost respect. Even in the process of taking her eventually for his wife, he went through the proper procedures, calling in the elders to witness and acknowledge the proceedings. When we allow God to take us under His wings, He transforms us into compassionate, honorable and hospitable people. We understand that He loves all people, even "foreigners" who do not know Him. And we know that He holds us accountable for how we treat them. Think of what the world would be like if all were under His loving, protective wings.

Lord God, thank You for how You shape the nations of those who submit to You. Thank You for teaching us how to live peacefully and harmoniously together. Thank You for holding us accountable for how we treat the powerless and vulnerable.

130

RIGHT UNDERSTANDING; COURAGEOUS LIVING

"Hear, O Israel: The LORD our God is one LORD; and you shall love the LORD your God with all your heart, and with all your soul, and with all your might. And these words which I command you this day shall be upon your heart; and you shall teach them diligently to your children, and shall talk of them when you sit in your house, and when you walk by the way, and when you lie down, and when you rise (Dt 6:4-7).

All mainstream Christians believe that God has revealed Himself [and continues to reveal Himself] through the Holy Bible. And He has revealed Himself as "one Lord," not many gods. People of faith understand that we [humans] do not determine who God is. He determines and reveals who He is. This is a very important understanding, always in danger of sinking down into the quagmire of our egotistical desires to *be* god, or *determine* him—and always in danger of being buried underneath our desire to be "nice" to people who have concocted their own ideas about God. We should be civil and kind, and never arrogant or condescending, but we have been commanded by God Himself to "*teach [His ways] diligently to your children, and talk of them when you sit in your house, and when you walk by the way....lie down....and rise.*" We must not allow the oppressive forces of evil, always evident in our world, to keep us from being the "light" that Christ has ordained and commanded us to be: "*Let your light so shine before men, that they may see your good works and give glory to your Father who is in heaven*" (Mt 5:16).

The early disciples faced powerful oppression from the religious and political leaders of their day. Their response rings as a clear and courageous clarion call through the ages: *"So they [the elders, priests, and scribes] called them and charged them not to speak or teach at all in the name of Jesus. But Peter and John answered them, "Whether it is right in the sight of God to listen to you rather than to God, you must judge; for we cannot but speak of what we have seen and heard"* (Acts 4:18-20).

And what they had seen and heard was Jesus miraculously healing, teaching about the Kingdom of God, and arising from the dead— as those who follow Him today are healed and raised from the spiritual death of meaningless, self-centered living. And we have the same inner compulsion to tell the good news about Christ and the freedom, peace, joy, and abundant life He offers. And we face the same evil forces of oppression. We must, as they, be submissive to and reliant upon the Holy Spirit in order to overcome. We must continue to be the light that Christ has ordained us to be; and to love, and live in the faith, hope, and freedom of soul that we desire for our children and all people.

Lord, thank You for Your never-failing Presence with us, always, "even to the end of the age." We realize that we cannot be victorious over the subtle, powerful forces of evil without You. Please give us courage to be the light that You have ordained us to be. May Your love be the guiding light of our lives today and always.

131

THE KINGDOM IN OUR MIDST

Nor will they say, 'Lo, here it is!' or 'There!' for behold, the kingdom of God is in the midst of you." And they will say to you, 'Lo, there!' or 'Lo, here!' Do not go, do not follow them...For as the lightning flashes and lights up the sky from one side to the other, so will the Son of man be in his day [Lk 17:21,23-24].

We are so thankful for Jesus' wonderful teachings. He helps us in all ways to understand and grow spiritually. He teaches us that the Kingdom of God is within us—in our "midst." We do not have to run around chasing after every "exciting" new congregation or preacher that crops up. He wants us to be in fellowship with each other, but this is not always an "exciting" or "on fire" type of experience. We should not need too much excitement. Sometimes excitement is an escape from more important responsibilities—the "good works" for which we were created [Eph 2:10]. It is certainly OK to be excited about the Kingdom of God. But it is not *necessary*, and we should not *need* excitement in order to feel that we are where we should be. Jesus was not always excited, but He continued to do the good that God wanted Him to do. If we need excitement, we will be following after exciting teachers and preachers—we will be going "here" and "there" seeking the Kingdom that Jesus said is within us and that we will not be able to miss if we simply abide in Him. The time of His coming will be as obvious as lightning in the night sky. In the mean time, we know what we are supposed to do. He has taught us to love God with all our heart, soul, mind, and strength, and to love each other as we love ourselves. This is our fulltime occupation, and the greatest adventure we could hope for. Everything we will ever need is with us always—"even to the end of the world" [Mt 28:20]. We must be very serious about abiding in Christ. He has given us some stern warnings about the subtle and destructive dangers of evil. Jesus was a "fire and brimstone" preacher [Lk 17:29-30] despite the fact that such teaching has come into disrepute today. God does not want us to fear evil—AFTER we have come into the safety of Christ and AS we continue to abide in Him. If we have not come into the place of salvation and if we are not abiding in His Holy Spirit, He says that we are like the people in Noah's day who were laughing, eating, and drinking while the rain clouds were forming; or like the people of Sodom and Gomorrah who were not delivered from the fiery deluge because they were not seeking God or walking in His way. But when we open our heart to Christ and His infinite love for us, He has promised that He will not turn us away [John 6:37]. He will come in and commune with us, and we with Him [Rev 3:20]. Then we are eternally safe. We have come Home. We are in the very center of our Creator's will. We are on the pathway of abundant and eternal life, peace, and joy, and most especially, love for everyone in the human family. We are free!

Lord Jesus, thank You for Your wonderful teachings. Thank You for Your presence, the Holy Spirit, with us always. Today may we walk in the Light of Your presence, peace, love and joy. Deliver us from the fear of evil, and from the fear that we might somehow miss You or be left behind.

132

BECAUSE OF JESUS

For God sent not his Son into the world to condemn the world; but that the world through him might be saved [John 3:17].

    Because of Jesus, millions of people all over the world are trying to love other people—even their enemies. Because of Jesus millions are facing their failures and shortcomings, and taking responsibility for them instead of blaming others [and without morbid guilt]. Because of Jesus thousands of hospitals have been built because He had compassion for and healed the sick while on earth. Because of Him millions of the hungry are being fed because He taught us to take care of the needy. Because of Jesus victims of horrific crimes forgive the perpetrator and even try to minister to them. Thousands of orphans and elderly have been cared for because of Christ. Countless marriages have been saved because people have come to believe that God "hates divorce" [Mal 2:16]. And the children of those marriages have been spared the incredible pain associated with divorce. Because of Jesus countless thousands of people who have been enraged by the inappropriate behavior of others have prayerfully disciplined themselves not to return evil for evil [1Pet 3:9], but have chosen to forgive, in obedience to their Lord. Because of Jesus people who have grown up in incredibly dysfunctional homes have come to know true love, grace, goodness, and peace. Addicts recover; criminals become good citizens; selfish and self-centered individuals learn to care for others because of Christ. People who had been guilt-ridden because of the suffering they caused others have come to know complete forgiveness and restoration in Christ. There have been countless untold incidences in which the temptation to steal or take advantage of someone has been resisted successfully because of a person's accountability to Christ. The world, in its blindness, looks accusingly and condescendingly at the failures of Christianity. But if we look objectively at the net effect of the Christian faith, we realize that the world is immeasurably better off because of it. Indeed, when we look at the dark potential of humankind, it is possible that the world would not have survived without it.

I am so thankful that I am a Christian. But even if I weren't, I would want others to be, so that my world would be safer and saner for my children and myself.

Jesus, thank You so much for what You have brought into the world. May Your Light continue to shine in our hearts. May Your will continue to be done in the human family.

133

WHAT DETERMINES YOU?

Do not be conformed to this world but be transformed by the renewal of your mind, that you may prove what is the will of God, what is good and acceptable and perfect [Rom 12:2].

Jesus says to us "...he that seeks, finds..."[Mt 7:8]. And through Paul, God reveals that we are beings in process, moving toward completion, going from milk to meat [Phil 1:6; 1Cor 3:1-2]. Jesus' statement has to do with our *will*—making a *choice* to seek the truth. This is not a passive but rather an *active* endeavor. One of the ways we grow is in self-awareness—knowing what motivates and determines us. Let me challenge you to ask yourself these questions: "What primarily determines me? How I feel? What I do?" I find that I am frequently determined by my wife's moods and behaviors. If she is not behaving properly, loving and respecting me up to par [by my standards], I have a hard time living in the "abundant life" Christ promised me. And I have a hard time loving her in obedience to Christ. I see this same dynamic in many of the couples I counsel also. Whatever is determining me at any given moment is my "master." And the Bible makes it clear Who that is supposed to be. Thankfully, with conscious effort and God's help, we can awaken from these delusions and move out into the sunlight of being determined by the One Who loves us more than we love anyone. I do not want to be "conformed" to the "world" [people, circumstances, etc.] around me. I want to be "transformed" by awakening into the Reality that God has revealed in His Word, His Son, and through His Spirit in me. In this wonderful, awakened place, I am *influenced* by the "world," but not *determined* by it. And I have the right kind of influence *in* the world. I become a part of the *solution* to the world's problems rather than contributing to them or being dragged down into them. I become the light, salt, and leaven that Jesus has ordained me to be [Mt 13:33; 5:13-14]. When I am determined by the Holy Spirit instead of my wife's moods and behaviors, I am able to love her in spite of them. And this gives her the best opportunity to evolve toward a better mood! Just as Jesus was not determined by Judas, Peter, the Pharisees, or Roman soldiers, neither must we be determined by our "world."

Other than things that we can't control—like genes—we are primarily determined by what we *choose* and what we *allow*. The Bible tells us to "guard" our hearts [Prv 4:23]. To guard means to stand at an entrance and determine what comes in and what doesn't. In Christ we have the final word on how much we allow ourselves to be influenced by the "world." This is a glorious truth! Let's appropriate it—and celebrate it!

Lord, I want to be determined inwardly by You above all. Please keep me from the evil of being primarily determined by anything or anyone else.

134

JESUS TEACHES US HOW TO BE HAPPY

And he opened his mouth and taught them, saying: "Blessed are the poor in spirit, for theirs is the kingdom of heaven" [Mt 5:2-3].

When you love someone, you want him or her to be happy. God loves us. He is the Author of all love. God wants us to be happy. Jesus, speaking with the very voice of God, teaches us how to be happy. The "Sermon on the Mount" is the greatest discourse on happiness ever written. Jesus says that the "poor in spirit" are happy ["blessed"]. He said that it is very hard for the rich to enter the Kingdom of Heaven [Mt 19:24]. The poor are more "in touch" with their dependence upon God. They cannot depend on their money, insurance policies, lawyers, servants, etc. Usually they are closer to the earth, plants, animals, etc. They don't have access to as much entertainment to escape into. They don't have as much of a materialistic "cushion" between them and the crises of life. They are more dependent on others in their family or support network. All these lead to greater happiness. I once heard a man speak about growing up with his missionary parents in a third world nation. When he came to the United States, he said he was struck with two major awarenesses: how much "stuff" we had access to, and how unhappy we were compared to the villagers he had grown up with. Material wealth tends to isolate and spoil us. We have to be very careful not to let our wealth become our master. With God's help we can maintain awareness of how blessed we are materially and still remain "poor in spirit." We can remain detached from our possessions and wealth, and thereby enjoy them and be more thankful for them. If material blessings made people happy, Americans would be the happiest people on earth. But only spiritual maturity leads to happiness. Only loving people with Christ's love releases joy within us. Then all the earth is a joy to us. We are truly happy when we surrender to God, recognize our dependence on Him, and love others in obedience to Him.

Lord Jesus, thank You for teaching us how to be happy. Help us to walk in the Light of Your teachings.

135

THE PROBLEM IS THEOLOGICAL

What causes wars, and what causes fightings among you? Is it not your passions that are at war in your members? You desire and do not have; so you kill. And you covet and cannot obtain; so you fight and wage war. You do not have, because you do not ask [Jam 4:1-2].

In 1998 my family visited the war memorial in Honolulu. Tears flowed from my eyes as I saw, depicted in stone, battle after battle in which thousands of soldiers died, while behind and flanking me stretched thousands of uniformly-marked graves of the dead. My wife's uncle was buried there. On the stone was etched these words that had a profound impact on me: "**The problem basically is theological and involves a spiritual recrudescence and improvement of human character.**" There, anonymously quoted, was a summary of the whole problem, not only of warfare, but of the human family. The problem is theological. It involves an improper understanding of God, who He is, and what He desires for the human family. It involves the need for spiritual "recrudescence," a word I have not seen before or since, that means "a breaking out afresh." A proper understanding of God—this spiritual renewal or awakening—will lead to "improvement of human character" to the point at which people will have no need or desire to kill each other for any reason. This is the message of God through Christ. We are to love each other—even our enemies. This understanding and the ability to live it out comes only through the Holy Spirit. Our most important work is to believe in Christ and live in the Reality that He has presented to the human family [John 6:29]. Then we are doing our part to bring peace to the world. This peace begins in our own heart when we know that through Christ we are forgiven and loved by God, and that we have eternal life and spiritual victory over the problems of the world. There is no longer any internal conflict—or if so, it is resolved through prayer and communion with God. We do not inflict others with our internal conflicts. Our heart begins to smile with the peace that we desire for all people. We become peacemakers.

Lord, thank You for bringing peace to my heart. I offer myself to You anew, to be used as a peacemaker in our world. Please help us to stop killing each other.

136

DYING TO LIVE

Then Jesus told his disciples, "If any man would come after me, let him deny himself and take up his cross and follow me. For whoever would save his life will lose it, and whoever loses his life for my sake will find it [Mat 16:24-25].

Looking to Jesus the pioneer and perfecter of our faith, who for the joy that was set before him endured the cross [Heb 12:2]

The Gospel is "good news," but it initially sounds "bad." The truth will set you free, but it will scare you or hurt you or make you mad first. Jesus is clear that His way will never be easy. The Bible teaches that we are all sinners in need of redemption, and that we have to confess our sins to each other, and that we have to take up a cross daily, die to ourselves, and detach ourselves from everything in this world that we hold in higher esteem than God. This is hard stuff. Many never choose to submit to it. Those who do, fall perpetually short of fulfilling it. But with all that, it is still called the "Good News." People write beautiful songs and poems about how they have been set free and found new life. Millions gather every week and praise God for His goodness. They drag their kids into church, against their will sometimes, because they want them to experience the freedom and abundant life that this hard and difficult way of God leads to. The same Jesus that commands us to take up a cross also promises us joy. The same Lord who says that we must be willing to suffer for righteousness sake also says that we will be happy ["blessed"]. The One who says "take my yoke upon you" also says that He will give us rest for our souls. The One who says we should be willing to suffer persecution for His sake also promises peace, freedom of soul and eternal life. There are certain things that God does not allow, yet they feel very good to us. All of us have been attached to one of Satan's offerings at one time or another. Drugs, elicit sex, pornography, laziness, selfishness, or angry outbursts can feel good or provide instant relief. And all can become a stronghold in our life. If we cling to them, or simply give in to them, they will drag us down over time. Jesus said *"If your right eye causes you to sin, pluck it out and throw it away; it is better that you lose one of your members than that your whole body be thrown into hell."* This is a wonderful teaching to help arouse and awaken us to the dangers of spiritual sloth. We must always remember that the result of this work, cross-bearing, dying, suffering, etc. is **love, joy, peace, abundant life, freedom of soul,** and **gratitude.** If these glorious fruits are not being borne in our lives then we must question our walk. God really does love us. He's not just trying to deprive or control us or make life difficult for us. The rewards of abiding in Christ drive away the regret of whatever sufferings He requires of us like the morning sun drives away the darkness of night, continuing to the full light of a beautiful day.

Lord please give us grace to be willing to suffer the difficulties of obedience and love, so that we may know the true joy of life. May that joy arise in our hearts today. Help us to be aware of the beauty all around us, and may we not miss an opportunity to love.

137

LOVE: THE MOOD STABILIZER

Then he said to them, "My soul is very sorrowful, even to death; remain here, and watch with me" [Mt 26:38].
These things I have spoken to you, that my joy may be in you, and that your joy may be full [John 15:11].
A new commandment I give to you, that you love one another; even as I have loved you, that you also love one another [John 13:34].

A characteristic of immaturity is vulnerability to feelings. An immature person acts as he feels. If he is angry, he blows up. If he is tired, he will not work. If he is upset, he pouts. If he desires something, he will violate the principles of righteousness to get it. A mature person is steadfast, unswerving, resolute, and unfaltering. He is not *un*feeling; in fact he is aware of his feelings and can express them appropriately, but he does not *act* on them if it is not beneficial to do so. You can rely on him to respond in a manner that promotes the common good, no matter the situation and no matter his mood. Jesus, as indicated by the above verses, experienced the full range of human emotion from lethal sorrow to rapturous joy. But His actions were not determined by His feelings. Rather, He acted always out of *love*. And He commands us to act always out of this same motive. Living by the principle of love stabilizes us. It gets us off the emotional roller coaster that makes life so difficult for our loved ones and ourselves. When we are depressed, we can love. When we are elated, we can love. If we are tired, upset, angry, frustrated, disheartened or fearful; we can love. The important thing in life is not how we feel. When we come before God in the Judgment, He will not decide our fate based on how happy or unhappy we have been. We will be judged on how well we have *loved*, regardless of how we have felt. In fact, the best feelings come as a by-product of choosing, over and over, to live in the love of Christ. This is the pathway to joy. On the other hand, the most miserable people you will meet are those who are living for and by their feelings. And they make life more difficult for others also.

Lord, please give me strength to live above my feelings. I am thankful that You allow me to feel however I feel. But I understand that it is not pleasing to You *[or good for me] to **act** out of my feelings. Please give me strength to act based on Your Holy Spirit of love–the love of Jesus my Lord.*

138

CHOOSE YOUR SUFFERING

And after you have suffered a little while, the God of all grace, who has called you to his eternal glory in Christ, will himself restore, establish, and strengthen you [1Pet 5:10].

"I have said this to you, that in me you may have peace. In the world you have tribulation; but be of good cheer, I have overcome the world" [John 16:33].

We do not have a choice about whether or not we will suffer in this life. Each of us must go through our share of suffering. We can, however, choose whether our suffering is productive or not. We can suffer the consequences of our sin, or we can suffer the difficulties of righteousness. We can suffer disciplined living, or we can suffer the consequences of laziness. We can suffer by depriving ourselves of spending the money that we deposit in a savings account, or we can suffer paying interest on the credit card account. We can suffer in our addictions, or we can suffer the difficulties of recovery. We can suffer with obesity and shortness of breath, or we can suffer exercise and diet control. We can suffer the "deprivations" of monogamy and faithfulness to our mate, or we can suffer guilt, conflict, sexually transmitted diseases, and divorce. We can suffer the restraint of self-control, or we can suffer alienation from our loved ones. We can suffer facing the difficult truth about ourselves, or we can suffer the ongoing, deleterious effects of blindness. We can suffer the difficulties of forgiving those who have harmed us, or we can carry the weight of resentment and bitterness around like a ball and chain. We can suffer the pain of responsibility, or the pain of feeling like a victim. We can suffer the difficulties of living a devoted life in Christ, or we can suffer spiritual defeat in the ongoing attacks of Satan. The Bible teaches that if we walk in righteousness, resisting the temptations of Satan and drawing perpetually near to God, then our sufferings will lead to peace and joy. Jesus teaches that if we are walking in His Way, we can "be of good cheer" in the midst of our sufferings because we know that they are limited. We will soon emerge from them into the light of eternal gratitude. Moreover, we are assured that, in Christ, our sufferings are never wasted and have eternal significance. We know that *this slight momentary affliction is preparing for us an eternal weight of glory beyond all comparison* (2Cor 4:17).

Lord please help me to choose righteous suffering; and to be of good cheer.

139

THE IMPORTANCE OF EVIL AND DEATH

We know that in everything God works for good with those who love him, who are called according to his purpose [Rom 8:28].

God is the Creator of the universe. There is nothing in the universe that is outside the realm of His beneficent domain. Whatever He has allowed, He has allowed in the same perfect wisdom with which He designed the aerodynamics and colors of a butterfly's wings. Nothing can happen in the realm of human activity that is outside His graceful permission. This is not to say that evil is God's will, but rather that God, in His perfect wisdom and love, has chosen to *allow* evil. It is perfect that God allows evil—otherwise we would not be free. We would be forced into righteousness if we did not have the option of committing evil. God in His perfect wisdom created us in His image—free beings. God desires and commands righteousness in the human family, but He does not force us to be righteous. He provides all that we need in Christ and His Holy Spirit to overcome evil—to be victorious over it. In Christ, evil and death become part of the "everything" in the above verse that God is working for the good. God works evil and death for good for those who are in Christ, and [being in Christ] called according to His loving, redemptive purpose for the human family. Death for the Christian is the final victory and the beginning of a new adventure in a transcendent realm. Without death we would be trapped in this life on this earth, and after a few thousand years at most, life would be meaningless. Physical death gives life on the earth a necessary and beneficial sense of urgency. It is appropriate and necessary to grieve the devastating and wasteful effects of evil and to value and preserve life. But it is more important to maintain a foundational awareness that everything is being lived out within the domain of a loving, beneficent, all-powerful Creator. That is why Jesus can say with full awareness of evil and death, "Peace I leave with you; my peace I give to you; not as the world gives do I give to you. Let not your hearts be troubled, neither let them be afraid" (*John 14:27*).

Lord God, thank You for giving us freedom and for making life both meaningful and safe in Christ.

140

WHO DETERMINES TRUTH?

Jesus said to him, "I am the way, and the truth, and the life; no one comes to the Father, but by me..." [John 14:6].

Then he will say to those at his left hand, 'Depart from me, you cursed, into the eternal fire prepared for the devil and his angels [Mt 25:41].

What is ultimate Truth? Who determines what the truth is? Maybe Hitler was right. Maybe the truth is that, in order to make a better world, we should eliminate all people who are inferior—the weak, disabled, genetically defective. Hitler and many others believed this to be the truth. Maybe the Ku Klux Klan had the right idea. African Americans are inferior to Anglo-Americans, and they should be kept in subservient roles. The races should not intermingle to prevent a toxic and impure effect on the white race. Maybe radical Muslim fundamentalists are in touch with the truth, and Americans are devils, the destruction of whom Allah rewards with virgins in heaven. Some believe this to be true to the extent that they sacrifice their lives based on it. Maybe David Koresh had discovered eternal reality, and those who criticized and attacked him and his followers are deluded and living in darkness. Maybe Jim Jones is basking in the sunlight of heavenly bliss for leading his followers into suicide to escape the exposure of the American press. Maybe the man who abuses his wife because she fails to live up to his standards is totally justified and living in the good graces of God. Maybe *you* determine the truth, and whatever you justify for yourself is justified in eternity. Maybe *my* desires are in accordance with eternal Reality, and I should be able to possess every attractive woman that I see, no matter the consequences. Maybe some of my clients have discovered the eternal truth that, since their mate has hurt them in the past, they are now justified in having an affair and abandoning their families. Maybe we can all basically live however we feel like living and this will somehow turn out to be ok. Or, maybe the Creator of this universe raised Jesus from the grave to confirm to us that He is what He said in the opening verse [above]. Maybe humans don't determine the truth. Maybe the Truth was here before we were, and perhaps we simply have the wonderful opportunity to *discover* and submit ourselves to it. And maybe we can make the world a better place and be truly happy by humbly bowing to Jesus as Lord, looking to Him to empower us to overcome our selfishness and blindness, and love people as He has commanded and given example. And maybe if we don't, we will regret it dreadfully.

Lord Jesus, some of Your teachings are very confronting and difficult to receive. And yet Your resurrection speaks powerfully to the validity of Your words. Please help me to come to terms with what You have presented to the human family. I accept that I do not determine the Truth. Your sacrificial love and Your selfless life and teachings cause me to believe that You are indeed "the Truth." I bow in reverent and thankful submission to You as my Lord and Savior. May I abide with You always.

141

THE JUDGEMENT SEAT

Judge not, and you will not be judged; condemn not, and you will not be condemned; forgive, and you will be forgiven [Lk 6:37].

But when the Pharisees heard it they said, "It is only by Be-el'zebul, the prince of demons, that this man [Jesus] casts out demons" [Mt 12:24].

The Bible teaches us not to judge or condemn each other. We are not qualified to judge each other because we do not know all the facts. One of my favorite stories illustrating this is about a man on a subway who is irritated because another man is allowing his children to run rampant on the train while he sits, oblivious, his head in his hands. His children are running around, talking loudly, fighting with each other, and bumping into passengers. The observer takes it as long as he can then angrily confronts the neglectful father, who responds: "Oh, I'm so sorry. You're right. I didn't notice. You see; we just came from the hospital. My wife died a few hours ago." We must be very careful in pronouncing judgment because we do not live inside other people's skin. The Pharisees accused Jesus of working in the realm of evil. They probably thought they were right. When we silently or loudly accuse our loved ones of being lazy, unloving or irresponsible, we think we are justified. *But we may be placing ourselves in condemnation of the Holy Spirit!* When our heart is hard toward someone; when we look upon him or her with scorn; maybe God is looking upon *us* with scorn. What if I died unexpectedly while having critical, condemning thoughts toward someone, and I was suddenly before Jesus. What would He say to me? We all see "through a glass darkly" [1Cor 13:12]. Jesus commands us to love our enemies [Mt 5:44]. Loving people in truth enables them to grow beyond their character defects much more expeditiously than criticizing them. When we think critical, condemning thoughts of someone, we tend to put a curse on them. They have to fight hard not to think of themselves the way we think of them. Maybe they will become defensive and critical of us. All this is unnecessary if we obey Christ and abstain from judgmental and critical thoughts of our fellow humans. If someone is lost in the darkness of evil, try to help them if you can; pray for them; compassionately confront them, but do not hate, criticize or condemn them.

Lord thank You for bringing the Light of Your Truth and goodness into our world. Help us overcome our tendency to judge, criticize and condemn each other. Deliver us from believing that we are what others think we are. Help us to see ourselves and others through Your loving eyes.

142

GOD UPHOLDS THE RIGHTEOUS

Their partiality witnesses against them; they proclaim their sin like Sodom, they do not hide it. Woe to them! For they have brought evil upon themselves [Is 3:9].

Now many nations are assembled against you, saying, "Let her be profaned, and let our eyes gaze upon Zion." But they do not know the thoughts of the LORD, they do not understand his plan, that he has gathered them as sheaves to the threshing floor. Arise and thresh, O daughter of Zion, for I will make your horn iron and your hoofs bronze; you shall beat in pieces many peoples, and shall devote their gain to the LORD, their wealth to the Lord of the whole earth [Mi 4:11-13].

God uses evil, godless nations to judge nations that have degenerated into hypocrisy. In Isaiah 10:5, God refers to Assyria, the nation that was about to conquer Judah, as "the rod of my anger in whose hand is the club of my wrath." God's people had lapsed into empty ritual, oppression of the poor, idolatry, materialism, superstitious divinations, drunkenness, and trust in man. Despite constant warnings through the prophets, they failed to reform. So the unthinkable occurred: God's chosen people were conquered and taken into captivity by a pagan nation. A remnant was preserved, and they repented and were ultimately restored. God is a loving Father Who takes care of His own, even in their chastisement. But sin is a very serious matter to Him. He's not "Santa in the sky."

On the other hand, God upholds and sustains nations that fight for justice and righteousness, as opposed to greed and power. God's people must make sure that their motives are pure and good. They must pray for their leaders, asking that those leaders seek God's will in all decisions, laws, and policy. The military must be an arm of the God who hates violence and oppression. Most importantly, the military must be in submission to God, Who loves all, and desires the best for all, and does not delight in the death of any. If our government and military are not in submission to God, if we make decisions to go to war based on selfish or ungodly principles, then our children die in vain and we bring judgment upon ourselves. We must not make decisions based upon revenge, greed, fear, or hatred of people. We must make decisions based on the love of God for all, which involves the hatred of evil, but never of people. And first and foremost, the primary evil that we hate is that which we find in our own hearts. As we allow God to cleanse our own hearts through contrition, confession, repentance, and forgiveness; we become His true and worthy emissaries for all that is good, worthy and true; and we are confident of His sustaining presence and victory.

Lord, always be our Guide and Sustainer. Keep us true to Your Way. Deliver us from arrogance, greed, fear, hatred of persons and vengefulness.

143

MORNING IN THE HEART

Let me hear in the morning of thy steadfast love, for in thee I put my trust. Teach me the way I should go, for to thee I lift up my soul. Teach me to do thy will, for thou art my God! Let thy good spirit lead me on a level path! [Ps 143:8,10]

I love the morning! The beginning of a brand new day full of adventure and opportunity. The sun—breaking the horizon, adorned in beautiful colors, heralded by the singing of birds, ending the night—is a daily reminder of the new life we have in Christ, the forgiveness of sins, and a fresh start.

Eleanor Farjeon's words [set to a traditional Gaelic melody in many hymnals] celebrate the symbolism of the morning:

> *Morning has broken, like the first morning*
> *Black bird has spoken, like the first bird.*
> *Praise for the singing! Praise for the morning!*
> *Praise for them springing fresh from the Word!*
> *Mine is the sunlight! Mine is morning*
> *Born of the one light Eden saw play.*
> *Praise with elation, praise every morning*
> *God's recreation of the new day!*

We awaken with renewed energy from the night's rest, and renewed hope in our Lord for a productive and joyful day. We pray for the guidance of His Holy Spirit that we might be aware of His presence and that we might walk in obedience to His Love for all whom we encounter in this day. We are thankful for His promise to be with us always even to the end of the age [Mt 28:20]. He is with us today! All is well. We launch out in gratitude for the adventure of this day!

Lord, today may I hear and see, with fresh ears and eyes, your steadfast love. May the beauty of this day remind me of Your love. I put my trust in You. I lift up my soul to You. May I live this day wonderfully, lovingly, thankfully, in all ways that are pleasing to You. May Your Spirit lead me on a good path today. May I live this day in such a way that, tonight, when I lie down to sleep, I will be thankful and have a clean conscience before You, my Lord.

144

THE ONGOING WARFARE

In order that the just requirement of the law might be fulfilled in us, who walk not according to the flesh but according to the Spirit. For those who live according to the flesh set their minds on the things of the flesh, but those who live according to the Spirit set their minds on the things of the Spirit [Rom 8:4-5].

In El Paso, Texas there is a beautiful mountain range in the Chihuahuan Desert, splitting the city in half, and split itself by the Transmountain Highway. This highway runs through Fusselman Canyon, named after Charles H Fusselman, a Texas Ranger killed in pursuit of cattle rustlers in April, 1890. For ten years afterward, lawmen pursued and finally apprehended Geronimo Parra, the leader of the outlaw gang, and hanged him legally in El Paso in 1900. Humans have a deep need for justice. For decades after wars, war criminals are hunted down and brought to justice. Parents and friends of murdered loved ones work, wait, and pray for decades—lifetimes—for the perpetrators to be brought to justice. Something in us feels relieved and vindicated when we see criminals punished appropriately. We all feel the need for just laws, and we applaud those who make good ones, and those who fairly enforce them. But it is also "us" who break them and try to find ways around them. It is "us" who have a smoldering resentment for "government" and feel a little intimidated by police officers. It is "us" who, like Geronimo Parra, want to have "stuff" without having to work much for it. Our laws and those who enforce them are a reality because there is something in us that must be subdued, thwarted, punished, and contained. We recognize, deep within us, that if we do not maintain just laws and mature police and military forces, the darkness in us could overtake the goodness in us. We all have within us a Charles Fusselman and a Geronimo Parra. If we do not personally and consciously try to develop and cultivate the goodness in us, through abiding in Christ and our wonderful spiritual disciplines, then the "Geronimo Parra" in us will make it necessary for us to be hunted down and hanged, so to speak, in this life or the next, according to the laws of man, the best of which have originated out of the laws of God. Our ancestors named that canyon Fusselman Canyon rather than Parra Canyon because of the godly wisdom in us that knows to uphold and foster good. This must always remain a *personal* endeavor.

Lord, I pray that today I might be aware of the spiritual warfare within and around me. And that I might contribute to the goodness and add nothing to the evil. In Christ's holy name.

145

THE POWER OF FELLOWSHIP

For where two or three are gathered in my name, there am I in the midst of them" [Mt 18:20]

Not neglecting to meet together, as is the habit of some, but encouraging one another, and all the more as you see the Day drawing near [Heb 10:25].

And though a man might prevail against one who is alone, two will withstand him. A threefold cord is not quickly broken [Eccl 4:12].

The Bible teaches that there is safety and power in friendship. We need friends in Christ who help us attain our spiritual goals and overcome our "besetting sins." There are some sinful nature manifestations that are addictive: alcoholism, drug addiction, certain sexual activities, pornography, emotion-relief shopping, eating disorders, rage addiction, gambling, etc. When we have fallen into one of these pits, we must recognize our need for fellowship in order to recover. And if we remain in honest fellowship, we can avoid falling into these pits. Truth is the lifeline out of addiction. The Bible teaches us to confess our sins, not only to God, but to each other [Jam 5:16]. For most believers it is, strangely enough, easier to confess to God than to a trusted friend in Christ. This difficulty in confessing to humans is indicative of its *value* to us in terms of healing and overcoming. A sheep that has strayed from the herd is in danger of being devoured by beasts of prey. The comforting "rod and staff" of Psalm 23 were used to keep the sheep within the flock, away from dangers. Satan, like beasts of prey, isolates and devours. That which we keep hidden from others within ourselves becomes the dark space for Satan to gain a potentially fatal foothold. We are creatures of light, and we flourish in transparency. It takes courage to be transparent. We face the fear of rejection, and we must break through our stubborn walls of pride that keep us imprisoned in pretentiousness. And discernment is necessary also, because we must open ourselves only to those who are spiritually mature enough to handle our vulnerability compassionately—those who are also willing to be vulnerable, and confess *their* faults. We are all fellow strugglers. Some are just more honest about their struggles than others. And they are the ones who are progressing.

Lord, please deliver me from the fear and pride that keep me isolated. Give me courage to be honest with trusted friends about my most difficult struggles and failures, so that I might be victorious over them in the power of fellowship with You and others.

146

YOU AND YOUR SHADOW

So then it is no longer I that do it, but sin which dwells within me. For I know that nothing good dwells within me, that is, in my flesh. I can will what is right, but I cannot do it. For I do not do the good I want, but the evil I do not want is what I do. Now if I do what I do not want, it is no longer I that do it, but sin which dwells within me [Rom 7:17-20].

Here is one of the most wonderful and liberating truths that God has revealed to us. And He revealed it, in His infinite wisdom, through the one who considered himself the "chief" of sinners [1Tm 1:15]. Paul, honest man that he was, admitted that no matter how hard he tried, he could not do right. In the 7th and 8th chapters of Romans, he sets forth what is perhaps the most superb treatise of the human condition ever recorded. We can all identify with not being able to do the good that we know we should, and not being able to abstain from the evil that we hate. But we must also identify with the mysterious and wonderful liberation from guilt and condemnation that God has made available to us in Christ; and that Paul illuminates for us in these verses. Let me state it this way: I have a hand, but I am not my hand. I have a foot, but I am not my foot. When I receive Christ as my Savior, I also continue to have a sinful nature. But—praise God!—I am NOT my sinful nature. *"It is no longer I that do it [sin], but sin that dwells within me."* The very act of receiving Christ is testimony to the fact that I [the true me] have come to believe that God is good, true, loves me, and offers eternal life, freedom, peace, and joy. All His commandments are good and designed to help me—not deprive me. If I violate them, I always hurt others and myself and never experience a net good effect. The true me has come to know that it is never advantageous to violate the principles of God. And yet, because of my sinful nature, I do. But the "me" that violates the principles of God is not the true me. It is the "it" that dwells within me. The great truth of these verses is that in Christ we dis-identify with our sinful nature even while we continue to be influenced by it. It is going to continue to fade farther and farther away as we abide in Christ. And it will not be with us in heaven. And because of Christ, God does not see me as my sinful nature. He sees me as a beloved son. And as I continue to submit to Him in the sanctification process, He invites me to see myself in that same way.

Lord, I am so thankful for what You have done for me, and for all who believe and receive. Thank You for saving me, even though I can not perfectly obey You. Thank You for Christ's atoning sacrifice, and for the presence of Your Holy Spirit, sanctifying me daily.

147

DYING DAILY

For he must reign until he has put all his enemies under his feet. The last enemy to be destroyed is death. "For God has put all things in subjection under his feet." But when it says, "All things are put in subjection under him," it is plain that he is excepted who put all things under him. When all things are subjected to him, then the Son himself will also be subjected to him who put all things under him, that God may be everything to every one. I protest, brethren, by my pride in you which I have in Christ Jesus our Lord, I die every day! [1Cor 15:25 –28,31].

In First Corinthians 15 Paul describes a scenario in which all who are being saved are being gathered up into subjection to Christ, who is Himself subjected to God, "that God may be everything to every one." From the individual standpoint, this is our sanctification process, and from the universal perspective, it is what might be called the psycho-spiritual evolution—the movement from "Alpha" to "Omega"—the blossoming forth of the Kingdom of God. Our personal part in this glorious process involves dying daily to everything that pulls us away from the pathway of Christ. A function of evil is to retard the psycho-spiritual evolution. Committing evil is like driving with the brakes on. As Christians, we are inevitably going into the fulfillment of all things, and we want to encourage and facilitate that movement by living according to the Love of Christ. Evil is contrary to that Love and drags down the forward movement of the Kingdom. We all recognize our sinful nature within us, and we have not yet overcome its tendencies. This is what we die daily to—these tendencies. This is a form of righteous suffering, like the suffering of the recovering addict in withdrawal. It is a dying that leads into greater life—the "abundant life" that Jesus promised His followers. We are dying to everything in us that is not respectable, life-enhancing, and good for all. We are dying to selfishness, weakness, feeling like victims, feeling deprived, guilt, fear, shame, attachments to things of this world, feelings of inadequacy, dysfunctional coping activities, delusions about life, apathy, critical spirits, desire for anything other than communion with God for ourselves and others, and everything that is oppressive. We are dying, like Christ on the Cross, into a joyful new life, eternal and free. We are dying into His freely-given Love for all.

Lord, today I die to all in me that is not fit for heaven.

148

FREEDOM

The Spirit of the Lord is upon me, because he has anointed me to preach good news to the poor. He has sent me to proclaim release to the captives and recovering of sight to the blind, to set at liberty those who are oppressed... [Lk 4:18].

I was online yesterday at "freedomhouse.org" and viewed a map of the world differentiating free nations from those in oppression. This morning, when I opened my Bible, it fell open to a world map depicting Christian and non-Christian nations. I was startled by the correspondence between those nations that were predominantly Christian, and those that were cited as "free" by the freedom house organization [a non-religious, independent organization]. But then it makes sense that nations populated predominantly by people who profess the lordship of the One who made the above statement [Lk 4:18] could not be brought under the bondage of dictatorial or theocratic oppression. God has made it abundantly clear He wants his people free to worship Him and to love and serve each other freely—not out of compulsion or fear. God sent plagues against the Egyptians until they set His people free. Jesus made it clear that He gave Himself freely. No one forced Him to Calvary [John 10:18].

Political freedom, as wonderful and important as it is, is not the core or foundation of freedom. Political freedom is the by-product of spiritual maturity. Freedom of soul is a gift of God and the fruit of spiritual growth. Only God can deliver us from enslavement to sin, fear, guilt, denial, compulsions, addictions, *and the desire to exercise power and control over others.* And this happens over the course of a lifetime. None of us is as free as we can be if we stay on the pathway of Christ and His love. And being on His pathway means we care about those who are still in oppression. This is why there are Christian missionaries all over the world. And we pray God's blessings upon them—for safety and clarity in delivering the message of the Gospel, so that many may come to know the freedom of Christ. And many who live in "free" nations are enslaved by passions and spiritual blindness. Jesus sets us free. In His love, our soul is boundless. The whole universe is our home. The Creator of all is our Father. All people are our family. And many of them—those who have been awakened by Christ—realize it.

Lord, thank You for setting us free. Please help us to be increasingly mindful of this freedom that You have bought for us, at such a great price. May Your Light shine through us that others may be liberated also. Please bless those whom You have called into evangelical and missionary vocations in oppressed nations. May Your light shine brightly through them. Today, may we celebrate our freedom with sincere gratitude and in joyful service to each other.

149

FROM GENERATION TO GENERATION

And his mercy is on those who fear him from generation to generation [Lk 1:50].

My mom loves sharing with me about her and Dad—their life experiences. And I love hearing her stories. Once she said, describing their life together, "We were in the groove." The phrase itself initially seemed somewhat quaint to me. I envisioned them doing the Charleston and wearing clothes that I wouldn't be caught dead in. Now that I am becoming a part of the "older generation," I realize that my life with Lynn [my wife] seems antiquated to my sons and grandchildren. But it doesn't seem antiquated to me at all! When I look at our high school pictures, I am struck with how much we and life have changed since that time. I know how my children perceive those old pictures of Lynn and I because I have looked at the old pictures of my mom and dad's early life. But my memories of those earlier days were that we were on the "cutting edge" of our generation. We were "in the groove." Each generation re-creates the "good life." The "good life" for one generation is not good enough for the next. There is a strong and healthy in-born need to move beyond, throw off the old, and discover something new and "better."

But the "good life" of the successive generations, though different from its predecessors', is not fundamentally better, because something is lost—something unique and irreplaceable—as well as gained in each generation. Our ancestors had life experiences that we will never know, except through their stories. And we will not be able to convey to our children some of what we have experienced, nor will we be able to know some of their experiences. God blesses each generation *uniquely,* but *equally.* Each generation has the wonderful opportunity to carry the Light of Christ a little farther than the previous one. His love is steadfast, age-to-age. But the wonderful ways that His love is manifested, and the specific evils to overcome, vary. We celebrate the evolving Kingdom of God, and we are thankful to all past generations—all our ancestors who have submitted themselves to Christ, fought their battles, overcome, gained wisdom, and loved us with His love. They are in the "cloud of witnesses" [Heb 12:1] that continues to inspire and encourage us. We are one with them in Christ.

Lord, thank You for Your steadfast love generation to generation. And thank You for giving each generation a unique blessing and opportunity to carry forth Your magnificent Kingdom. Thank You for all our spiritual ancestors who have fought the good fight of faith. We pray Your blessings upon them on earth and in heaven. May I do my part to carry the Light of Christ through my generation into the next, and become, in due time, a part of the "cloud of witnesses."

150

WALKING THE TALK

If you know these things, happy are you if you do them [John 13:17].

In a small south Texas town, I spoke with a retired teacher visiting her hometown to attend the funeral of her aunt. We quickly came to know that we were both Christians and she shared excitedly about a Bible study she had been attending. While we spoke, two children, a brother and sister, started cautiously interacting with the lady's two small dogs that she held on a leash. Neither of us took much notice of them until something happened to upset the little girl, and she started crying. After a brief interchange with the little girl, the lady assertively dismissed the children. "Well you just need to go to your momma. Go on to your momma." I felt convicted later when I realized that we were both more interested in our religious conversation than in the little children. These Mexican children, I discovered later, were temporarily living with their Mom and Dad in the motel while the dad was doing some work in this small town. I was able to assuage my conscience somewhat later that evening by treating the boy with some friendly kindness—I let him sit on my motorcycle and paid him fifty cents for wiping my windshield.

The lesson for me was clear: It is much easier to be religious than it is to love people. It is much easier for me to write these devotions than to practice the principles that they set forth—the principles that Jesus has spoken and lived. It was Jesus Who was displeased with His disciples when they tried to prevent the children from interfering with His "more important" [in their thinking] work of teaching and healing [of being religious]. And it was Jesus Who said, "Let the children come to me, for of such is the Kingdom of Heaven." [Mk 10:14]. All our religious activities [including the writing and reading of devotionals] that do not convert into loving people with the love of Christ are vain and wasted at best. At worst they become a façade behind which we hide from the ugly truth about our failure to be what Christ has commanded us to be.

God please deliver me from vain religion, into the glorious light of Your love for all.

151

SOME GET IT. SOME DON'T.

And he answered them, "To you it has been given to know the secrets of the kingdom of heaven, but to them it has not been given... But blessed are your eyes, for they see, and your ears, for they hear..." [Mt 13:11,16].

If you are a Christian, you should be eternally thankful. You have been given ears to hear and eyes to see. On a walk I recently encountered a friend and brother of mine who lives in my neighborhood. He shared with me about his failure to understand unbelievers. "How can they ignore Christ and His wonderful teachings? Why is the road narrow and so few enter into eternal life?" Some of my clients who are "unequally yoked" in marriage [2Cor6:14], say to me regarding their mate, "He/she just doesn't get it." There is no arrogance in this statement—only sadness and a sense of bewilderment. Before we receive Christ as our Lord, a miracle occurs within us. We are miraculously given the gift of seeing that He is the Messiah—God in the flesh—the salvation of the human family. Many people do not receive this gift. This is a great mystery to us. I replied to my friend's questions about the narrow road: " I don't understand it either. How can someone hear the words *'You have heard it said of old time that you should love your neighbor and hate your enemies. But I say to you, love your enemies, bless those who curse you, do good to those who hate you, and pray for those who despitefully use you and persecute you, that you may be the children of your Father Who is in heaven'* [Mt 5:44] and not fall on their knees and say "My Lord and my God."? It is amazing to me that some can hear the wonderful teachings of Jesus and say something like, "Oh, that's real nice religious stuff, but I'm just not into it. See ya' later. Gotta go to work." How can they not see that Christ has given us in that single statement the solution to all animosity, hatred, bitterness, and violence? In Christ we get it. We get it that life is not about being loved—it is about loving. It is not about impressing people—it is about loving them. It is not about how much we get—it is about how much we give. It is not about becoming physically beautiful—it is about cultivating a beautiful heart. It is not about being served—it is about serving. It is not about being understood—it is about understanding. It is not about "feathering our nest"—it is about providing a "nest" for those who have none. It is not about perpetually getting what we need—it is about meeting the needs of others. We get it that we are loved beyond our comprehension, and that God has taken care of everything outside the realm of our control; that there is nothing to worry about or fear; and that the most important thing is to love people as Christ has given us example in His life on this earth. We get it. And we want all people to get it. But if they don't, we accept it, and carry on. We still love them, and we will help them if we can. But deep inside us, the great mystery remains: How can they ignore the One Who said, "I am the way and the truth and the life; no one comes to the Father but by me" [John 14:6]?

Lord, it is amazing and incredible to us that You have given us eyes to see and ears to hear the eternal Truth of the universe—the Truth that You embodied on the earth, and that continues to live in us. From the depths of our being we say, "Thank You!" And we pray that many others will hear Your voice and find rest for their souls.

152

WHERE TO TURN

Wash me thoroughly from my iniquity, and cleanse me from my sin! For I know my transgressions, and my sin is ever before me. Against thee, thee only, have I sinned, and done that which is evil in thy sight, so that thou art justified in thy sentence and blameless in thy judgment...Behold, thou desirest truth in the inward being; therefore teach me wisdom in my secret heart. Hide thy face from my sins, and blot out all my iniquities. Create in me a clean heart, O God, and put a new and right spirit within me [Ps 51:2-4,6,9-10 KJV]

A young married couple drifted away from actively pursuing their faith and began experiencing some of the problems that are associated with spiritual blindness. He began using drugs to help him perform better in his vocation and became addicted. She succumbed to an inappropriate relationship with another man while her husband was lost in the drug-induced fog. He was confronted at his work and entered a recovery program, leading to a spiritual awakening. He became serious about his growth, looked honestly at himself, confessed his need for God, began attending Church and got connected with a recovery support network. He apologized to his wife and asked for forgiveness. She, on the other hand, was not willing to give up her relationship with the other man. She felt that her vows were not valid because "we got married for the wrong reasons." She was not "happy" and had fallen out of love with her husband. She was skeptical of the Church and of the recovery process and people involved in it. Fundamentally, she wanted out and was finding the needed rationales to justify divorce. In her spiritual blindness, she saw a better deal in her lover, who was farther up on the socio-economic scale. Nothing could change her mind. She was certain that she was justified, despite the obvious changes in her husband. She avoided friends who counseled her to reconcile and begin her own spiritual growth. She spent time with friends who were living outside the Faith. She ultimately filed for divorce and began her pursuit of the "happiness" she desired. He sadly conceded, acknowledging her adamant mindset. Because of his growth, this major setback did not precipitate a relapse, and he continued in his journey into wholeness with Christ.

    Spiritual victory or defeat is not determined by the mistakes that we make, no matter how grave. It is determined by the direction in which we turn when we make them. And whether we continue to the end.

God please help us to always turn to You – to avoid mistakes, and to recover from them.

153

THE FAITH FACTOR

And without faith it is impossible to please him. For whoever would draw near to God must believe that he exists and that he rewards those who seek him [Heb 11:6].

Therefore being justified by faith, we have peace with God through our Lord Jesus Christ [Rom 5:1].

    A divorced friend recently shared with me about her teenage son's ingratitude and spirit of entitlement. Her family had been through a great deal of turmoil, and she knew that the boy had been affected by it. Her job was uncertain, and her financial life hung by a thread. She hated being alone without a life companion. I didn't have any answers, and as she talked we both began sinking in a quagmire of sorrow. Suddenly, she brightened the whole room with a beautiful, from-the-heart smile and said with absolute conviction, "But God has always been there for me, and I know that whatever happens He will take care of me." My heart rejoiced with this affirmation of the only Truth that can lead to Peace in the face of uncertainty—FAITH! Thank God for faith! As I drove home from this encounter with this dear sister in Christ, I thought of my Dad. In his last months on this earth he rarely could recognize my Mom, his wife of sixty-four years. His conversations made only smatterings of sense. In our conversations I would pace him emotionally—when he showed lightheartedness, I would reflect lightheartedness. When he was concerned, I'd be concerned—though I didn't know what we were concerned about. Sometimes a worrisome spirit would overtake him. He knew something was gravely wrong, and in his demented way, he was expressing his deep concern. I would reflect this same grave concern. But always, at some point, he would say something like, "Oh well, It's all gonna work out. It'll be o.k. God's in control." When he was in the hospital in the final days of his life, unable to make much sense of anything, at one point, as I stood beside him, he looked at me full in the face with a smile and *winked at me*! In the core of his being, he still knew everything was ok. Even Alzheimer's could not rob him of his FAITH. In that wink he conferred a lifelong blessing upon me just as surely as Isaac when he laid his hands on Jacob.

God please help us live faithfully, and convey the blessing of faith to our children.

154

MY CAT DOESN'T NEED ME TOO MUCH

But my God shall supply all your need according to his riches in glory by Christ Jesus [Phil 4:19].

I like my cat. She doesn't need me too much. She likes to be petted, and she will jump up in my lap. But after a short time, she becomes interested in something moving in the shrubs or the flat surface of the Jacuzzi top looks good to her, and she's off. I rarely have time to get tired of petting her. She has many interests—not just me. I am not the primary source of her well-being—only one of them. Even if I forget to feed her, she will go off and catch a lizard or a mole. And she won't hold it against me. This suits me just fine. My son's dog, on the other hand, is very people-oriented. If I put him outside on a chain attached to a long line that gives him the run of most of the backyard, and come inside the house, he yelps and whines incessantly. He thinks I have abandoned him. He has an anxiety attack. This irritates me because I know full well that he is ok. He has eaten; he is safe, and he can relieve himself if he needs to. But he needs to be near me, in the house with me, to feel safe. Sometimes I let him yelp until he tires out, so that he can see that he is ok, then I go out and let him in. I want him to be free from excessive need—like my cat. And like me in Christ. I love my son's dog as much as my cat. But my cat is more satisfied because she seems to understand that everything is ok even if people aren't doing what they are "supposed to." When I realize that God will supply all my need, I am not so upset when people don't do what I think they should. I can still be at peace within myself. I can still love them. I am free from the need for them to be what I think they should be. I am very thankful that Jesus didn't need His disciples to be there for Him in order to complete His mission. He would have failed, and my sins would not be forgiven. He only needed God. And so do we.

Lord Jesus, thank You for Your willingness to depend on God and not man to complete Your wonderful mission for the human family. Help us to depend on God and not man to be everything we were created to be—joyful, loving and free, servants of God and man.

155

THE NATION'S IMMUNE SYSTEM

Blessed is the nation whose God is the LORD, the people whom he has chosen as his heritage! [Ps 33:12]

He told them another parable. "The kingdom of heaven is like leaven which a woman took and hid in three measures of flour, till it was all leavened" [Mt 13:33].

On two recent motorcycle trips, one to El Paso and the other to my hometown of Sylacauga, Alabama, I decided to avoid the interstates, take state and county roads instead, and get a feel for some parts of the rural South. On both occasions I was struck with the number of churches along the way—hundreds of them. Many of them had roadside signs with admonitions, encouraging statements or invitations: "Looking for a church family? Try us!" Or, "The man who is not ready to die is not ready to live." They had names that included certain qualities of the Faith—like, well, "Faith", and "Hope", "Grace" and "Abundant Life." Many of them were named "New" something or other: "New Life", "New Hope," or "New Beginnings." One was named "New Morning Star Missionary Baptist Church." Another was named "Mt. Nebo," the mountain from which Moses looked over into the Promised Land, and on which he died. One church that seemed to invite me to stop and take a nap under the shade of its live oaks [which I did] was [appropriately enough] named "Pilgrim's Rest Baptist Church." I rested well there.

I've heard people make disparaging or scornful statements about the "Bible Belt." I felt very encouraged by all those churches. I know that in them every Sunday, children are being taught to respect and obey their parents and elders. Husbands and wives are being taught to be faithful and kind to their mates. Parents are encouraged to care for their children. And all are being taught to live the "Golden Rule"—to treat others the way they want to be treated. Jesus said the Word of God is to the world like yeast is to dough: a little goes a long way to enhance the quality. All those people in all those churches hear the Word of God—the wonderful teachings of Jesus—then they go out into their communities with the Light of it shining in their hearts. They are not perfect of course, but how can they not be a little better, week after week—A little better at loving the people in their communities? When I stop and talk to some of these gentle, friendly people, I imagine that they—or perhaps their parents or neighbors—attend one of those churches. I feel comforted. I am at home. I am among my people. I am among God's family.

Lord, thank You for making us a true family. May Your body of Believers—the Church—continue to flourish and prosper, and protect our world from evil.

156

NEW BEGINNINGS

Therefore, if any one is in Christ, he is a new creation; the old has passed away, behold, the new has come [2Cor 5:17].

Morning by morning he wakens, he wakens my ear to hear as those who are taught [Is 50:4b].

Restore to me the joy of thy salvation, and uphold me with a willing spirit [Ps 51:12].

Returning from a visit to my home town, on a ten-hour motorcycle road trip, I had opportunity to become more mindful of my thoughts and the attending emotional responses. Some examples are: "While you were home, you didn't visit your sister." [Sense of inadequacy or failure.] "Your private practice has fallen off. The phone hasn't been ringing as much lately." [Sense of failure and anxiety.] "Riding a motorcycle is dangerous. You are 57 years old. Your reaction time is not what it used to be." [Anxiety. Feeling diminished and foolish.]

Every day—every moment!—offers us a new opportunity to be more awake, aware, and alive with the abundant life that Christ promises. In the power of the Holy Spirit, we can arise from and shake off the dark and oppressive mindsets that so easily encumber us [Heb 12:1]—the mindsets of regret, remorse, feelings of failure or inadequacy, dread of anything in the future, any fears or anxiety. All these are oppressive to Life—the Life that Jesus died for us to have.

All of us have made mistakes, hurt our loved ones, missed opportunities to love, etc. And we all have tribulation yet to come. Satan loves to condemn us for these mistakes, and to strike fear or dread into our hearts regarding the future. Jesus is not holding our failures against us if we have confessed them and turned away from them. And we must be careful not to hold them against ourselves or each other. And He has promised to be with us always, and to never forsake us through whatever tribulations lie ahead [Mt 28:20]. Regarding both the past and the future, therefore, Jesus has set us free, just as he said He came to do [Lk 4:18]. Our brother, the apostle Paul, came to understand with great joy that nothing in the universe could ever separate us from the love of God in Christ [Rom 8:38-9]. God loves us and does not want us to feel condemned, inadequate, or fearful. He wants us to be at peace, joyful, and thankful, within the context of His love for all.

I found that as I became mindful of my dark thoughts, I could turn them toward the Light of God's Truth. "My sister knows that I love her, and she is well pleased that I spent all my time with Mom. I'll call her later." "God has sustained me financially, and will continue to do so." "I will drive safely, and enjoy and be thankful for the beauty of God's world passing by me on this beautiful day. Oh look! There's a Giant Swallowtail Butterfly sailing across the road into a green pasture with peacefully grazing cattle! Oh God, how beautiful! Thank You! Thank You!"

Lord, please help us stay alive, awake and aware of Your liberating, joyful Presence and Love. Deliver us from dark thoughts.

157

THANK GOD FOR MOCKINGBIRDS

Enter his gates with thanksgiving, and his courts with praise! Give thanks to him; bless his name! [Ps 100:4]

I stepped outside into a rain-cleansed, cool, cloudy evening. The sun had set, but its mellow light still softly illumined the sky and trees. Two mockingbirds, flanking my house to the east and west, sang in beautiful alternating melody, their evening swansongs. I've grown up with mockingbirds—perhaps one of the commonest birds in suburban America. But I have never grown tired of their beautiful songs. I hope I never do. One of the gifts of spiritual growth is re-connection with and deeper gratitude for the common, profound experiences of life. Have you ever considered how diminished life would be without mockingbirds? Or honeysuckles? What if we didn't have chickens? What a wonderful source of food! Think of all the ways we enjoy chicken. And their eggs! What if we didn't have potatoes? Or bananas? It's sad to think of life without any of these or countless other common but wonderful blessings that God has built into our daily lives. I've recently started noticing butterflies. What a tremendous and largely unnoticed gift of God are these beautiful creatures, flitting around our yards and forests, drinking nectar from flowers; themselves appearing as living, flying flowers! So many colors, sounds, tastes, sights! We will never be able to see and experience all the beauty that God has placed in our world. I love this quote from Alice Walker: "*Listen, God loves everything you love—and a mess of stuff you don't. But more than anything else, God loves admiration....I think it [angers] God if you walk by the color purple in a field somewhere and don't notice it.*"

If we are awake and aware, we are thankful. God is so good to us. He has given us so much. We should never complain about anything. We can and should be deeply thankful every day, all the time. If we can stay awake in the Spirit, we are thankful in all situations. We realize that God's love is all around us all the time.

Lord please help me to stay awake and aware of how wonderful it is to be alive in Your Spirit.

158

CHRISTIANS ARE RESPONSIBLE SERVANTS

And whoever would be first among you must be slave of all. For the Son of man also came not to be served but to serve, and to give his life as a ransom for many" [Mk 10:44-45].

For we are his workmanship, created in Christ Jesus for good works, which God prepared beforehand, that we should walk in them [Eph 2:10].

When my sons were young, my wife and I took them with us on my business trips. We ate in the hotel restaurants where I did business. They became accustomed to restaurant service. On one occasion, at breakfast, Marty, who was four or five years old at the time, felt the syrup jar and said with obvious disgust, "Hmpff! This syrup's not even warm!" He had come to expect a rather high level of service. This sense of entitlement is one of the dangers of prosperity, and though it was cute in Marty's childish innocence, it becomes grotesque in adolescence and especially adulthood. When our parents love us and try to provide the best for us, we are tempted to develop an attitude of entitlement. This same attitude can be fostered by our democratic political system in which the leaders are elected by the people as servants of the people. We can become very critical and demanding if these *servants* of ours don't provide the service that we *expect* and feel *entitled to*. And in their efforts to get elected, they frequently make unrealistic promises to provide services that we come to expect, and we feel deprived and cheated if they are not forthcoming. How ironic that, even though we live in the most prosperous nation on earth—perhaps in history—instead of being thankful, we feel deprived and short-changed! Because we feel entitled.

Jesus teaches us not to expect to be served. He does not want us to feel entitled to better things, services, etc. He wants us to discover the joy of serving and working to make our homes and communities better. He wants us to be more focused on what we can be doing for others than on what they are failing to do for us. He also wants us to be thankful for all that others have done and are continuing to do for us. If you look deeply into all the things that you use and enjoy each day, you realize that others provided almost all of them. We did not build the cars we drive nor the roads we drive on. Others provide our water and electricity. Others built our houses. We are the beneficiaries of all the wisdom and cunning that has been discovered through trial and error in the entire course of human history. Jesus wants us to serve each other joyfully and to be thankful for the immeasurable gift of all that others have done for us—and to God for making it all possible.

Lord, please forgive me for feeling entitled to being served rather than following Your wonderful example as a servant. Please help me to be more mindful of and thankful for the blessings of life, not only in Your Kingdom, but also in a prosperous and free nation.

159

PEACE ON EARTH, GOOD WILL TO MEN

"I do not pray for these only, but also for those who believe in me through their word, that they may all be one; even as thou, Father, art in me, and I in thee, that they also may be in us, so that the world may believe that thou hast sent me" [Jesus, John 17:20-21 KJV].

As Jesus prayed for us when He was on the earth, so He continues to pray today. He prays through His current earthly body: those who believe in Him, and who have received Him as their Lord; those in whom His Spirit abides. He prays for peace and unity in the human family. When He was born, the heavenly host proclaimed, "Peace on earth, good will toward men" [Lk 2:14]. Jesus brings peace into our hearts and good will toward all members of the human family. All true Christians desire and work for peace for all people. Jesus does not allow us to hate any person, no matter how blind and consumed by evil they may be. He prayed for the forgiveness of His tormentors, persecutors, and executioners—those who falsely accused Him. We must also pray for those who are lost in the darkness of hatred, bitterness, envy, and fear. And we must also ask forgiveness for ourselves because, unlike Him, we have been perpetrators of evil as well as victims of it. Like the Pharisees and Judas, we have been blind also. And we have been weak like Peter. We have not always responded to evil with good, as God has commanded us [Rom 12:21]. When we pray for the forgiveness of those in darkness, we are not being patronizing. We are not more loved or valued than those for whom we pray. They are not beneath us. We must avoid the attitude of spiritual superiority exemplified by the Pharisee in Luke 18:11, who thanked God that he was not like those other common sinners but rather fasted, tithed, etc. This attitude turns many away from the Faith, and is a stumbling stone for those who are seeking. It is a stench in the nostrils of God. But the contrition of the Publican in the synagogue that day—the one who prayed, "God have mercy on me, a sinner"—was a sweet aroma to Him, and that Publican went home justified. Humility is a prerequisite for peace between people. The humility that is born out of our awareness that "all have sinned ... none is righteous" [Rom 3:10, 23]. And peace within our own hearts is also a prerequisite to peace between people. The peace that comes with the deep and secure knowledge that God has forgiven us in Christ, and that we are no longer in condemnation. We are free in God's grace; and He commands us to forgive all who have hurt us in any way. As we receive the unspeakable gifts of forgiveness and salvation, and as we obey God in forgiving and even loving our enemies, we enter into eternal peace, and we become peacemakers in our generation.

Lord, may Your peace flow through us like a healing river into the hearts of many—today.

160

ARE YOU AMONG THE "FEW"?

"Enter by the narrow gate; for the gate is wide and the way is easy, that leads to destruction, and those who enter by it are many. For the gate is narrow and the way is hard, that leads to life, and those who find it are few" [Jesus. Mt 7:13-14].

Those who keep up with population growth say that we have recently reached 300 million people in the U.S. I wonder how many of them are finding

Life in Christ. I wonder how many could honestly say that they are happy, have peace and joy in their hearts, are loving their families or mates, and believe that life is good and unfolding as it should. Jesus said that that number would be small in comparison to those who get lost in the "world." He reminds us that it is "easy" to be lost, and "hard" to enter into "life." This teaching of Christ has the effect of awakening us—confronting us—shaking us out of our lethargy, and causing us to question ourselves deeply about the condition of our souls. Are you willing to ask yourself, and answer honestly: "Am I walking the Pathway of eternal and abundant Life? Do I believe deeply that my life is being spent in the best possible manner? Am I being sincerely obedient to Jesus' command to love as He loves? Do I take Him seriously in His reminder that it is 'easy' to be lost, and that it is 'hard' to enter into 'life'?" There are so many snares. So many people become addicted to substances or behaviors that absorb precious life-energies fruitlessly. So many adults continue to exhibit adolescent selfishness, wounding their mates and children. So many fail to grow up into the maturity of Christ, Who said that He came to serve, not to be served; to love rather than try to be loved. The "narrow gate" is Christ Himself. If we cling to Him—pray to Him—know and heed His teachings, then we will be moving in the right direction. Otherwise, no matter how intelligent and impressive we are, no matter what church we belong to, we could be in the number of those who are on the wide and easy way that leads to destruction.

Lord Jesus, thank You for Your stern confrontations that help us stay awake and aware and in the safety of Your Holy Spirit of love for all. Please keep us on the Pathway of eternal Life, which is the Pathway of Truth and Love.

161

GODLY VERSUS WORLDLY SORROW

As it is, I rejoice, not because you were grieved, but because you were grieved into repenting; for you felt a godly grief, so that you suffered no loss through us. For godly grief produces a repentance that leads to salvation and brings no regret, but worldly grief produces death. For see what earnestness this godly grief has produced in you, what eagerness to clear yourselves, what indignation, what alarm, what longing, what zeal...[2Cor 7:9 –11a].

We are very thankful that God has differentiated godly from worldly sorrow. We see the reality of this difference in our human experience, and it is very important to understand it. There is a type of sorrow that leads to death rather than repentance, salvation, and peace. A person can be sorrowful [or show a semblance of sorrow] and remain in an inner state of rebellion against the Truth, with a sense of entitlement to continue the destructive, sinful behavior. The sorrow in this case involves a sense of being a victim of life's or God's tough rules that are "just too hard to live up to." It is more a sorrow for being caught, than for the deed itself. It may also involve a sense of entitlement due to past tough breaks or difficult life experiences. The inner attitude is: "God hasn't been so good to me, so why should I be expected to live up to His expectations." Another aspect of this attitude is: "You should feel sorry for me because I am hurting so much because of what I did wrong." Or it can simply be a deep, tough kernel of rebellion against any authority that tries to tell me that I can't have whatever it is from the dark side that makes me feel good. Worldly sorrow can be a front—a defense against deserved punishment. It can be a manipulative attempt to avoid the losses that naturally accrue to sinful behaviors.

Godly sorrow involves a deep and complete facing and acknowledgement of the ugliness and destructive consequences of one's sinful behaviors. The contrite heart is totally broken open to all the ugly truth about itself. There is a sense of hopelessness from the human standpoint; that is, I know, in godly sorrow, that I cannot redeem myself. I can't make life work without God. I will never be rich, smart, strong, or even "spiritual" enough.

[*True* spirituality leads to this knowledge.] In godly sorrow there is deep and sincere remorse and empathy for those we have hurt. We want them to be healed. And we are willing to take part in their healing—to become a channel of God's love, as we have been a channel of selfishness. Simultaneously, there is a blessed sense of relief—a deep and growing knowledge that God is pleased that we have been courageous enough to face the truth about ourselves. We feel His love sustaining us in our grief and sadness, even as He continues to reveal the truth that we need to hear. There is a deep sense of humility and reliance upon God for the ongoing process of healing and growth—repentance—that we are now aware must take place. We want to make things right. We want to be careful not to hurt our loved ones again. We know now how easy it is to lose our way without Christ. We begin a new journey on a new pathway that leads to deep inner peace, gratitude, freedom, and reconciliation with God and His family—our family.

Lord, please deliver us from the self-deception of insincere contrition. May all our sorrows lead to new, healthier behaviors, forgiveness, healing, reconciliation with our loved ones, and peace.

162

MOMMA [& JESUS] SAID THERE'D BE DAYS LIKE THIS

I have said this to you, that in me you may have peace. In the world you have tribulation; but be of good cheer, I have overcome the world" [John 16:33].

Jesus wants us to be prepared for tribulation. He has assured us that it will come. We should not be too shocked or surprised when it does. The worst forms of suffering are manifested as the refusal to accept suffering—to feel somehow entitled that it not be happening—in *this* time, or in *this* way. We do not get to choose all our suffering. When we accept suffering [and as we do what we can to alleviate it], we overcome it. The same Lord Who has assured us that we would have tribulation has told us to "be of good cheer" because He has "overcome the world." This is an incredible statement: "I have overcome the world"! It is another example that Jesus is not just a great "teacher" or "prophet." He is the Messiah. And He has also promised to be with us always, "even to the end of the age" [Mt 28:20]. And so we can be assured in the midst of our suffering that we have within us the Power that will not only sustain us through it, but also bring forth something valuable and worthy within us. We become more confident and settled through tribulation [1Pet 5:10]. We are comforted by God, and become more able ministers through tribulation [2Cor 1:3-4]. We identify with all the saints of all ages and Jesus Himself through tribulation [2Cor 1:5, Rev.1:9]. Tribulation drives us toward God in Whom we always find victory [2Cor 1:8-9]. We gain patience through tribulation [Rom 5:3]. Tribulation causes us to rely on God and thereby gain a greater confidence in His all-sustaining Grace [2Cor 12:9]. Therefore, when [not *if*] tribulation comes, instead of complaining or having a panic attack, we can begin immediately to look for grace, sustaining power, and the comfort and gifts that God is offering us through it.

Lord Jesus, thank You for revealing the truth about tribulation, and for overcoming the world, so that we can be of good cheer in the midst of our tribulations. Please help us to appropriate all the gifts that You offer us through life's difficulties. And help us to comfort others in their sufferings as You have comforted us.

163

LIVING FOR THE FUTURE

And he told them a parable, saying, "The land of a rich man brought forth plentifully; and he thought to himself, 'What shall I do, for I have nowhere to store my crops?' And he said, 'I will do this: I will pull down my barns, and build larger ones; and there I will store all my grain and my goods. And I will say to my soul, Soul, you have ample goods laid up for many years; take your ease, eat, drink, be merry.'

But God said to him, 'Fool! This night your soul is required of you; and the things you have prepared, whose will they be?' So is he who lays up treasure for himself, and is not rich toward God" [Lk 12:16-21].

One of the most common mistakes that we make is *to live for the future*. We put in all our hard hours, keep our shoulder to the grindstone, stay on the treadmill 'til we collapse into bed, and then get immediately back on it at sunrise. We have a goal, way out in the future—retirement—when we will be able to take our ease and fish or travel. Meanwhile, we resentfully accept our poor lot in life. The trip is miserable, but that is our lot in life until the train arrives at the station—until our ship finally comes in. This lifestyle, lived diligently, can generate a tremendous amount of resentment, depression, apathy, or numbness. *Hope deferred makes the heart sick...*[Prv 13:12].

Jesus warns us against this delusion. He reminds us to live each day: fully, completely, and immersed in the Love of God for all people—to be "rich toward God." He reminds us that we might die today or tomorrow. Then what will all that effort mean? *"This is the day which the Lord has made,"* the Psalmist reminds us. *"We will rejoice and be glad in it"* [Ps 118:24]. The *living-for-the-future* lifestyle is a materialistic lifestyle. The focus is security, ease, and comfort in this life. But we have seen repeatedly in many arenas of human experience that joy and peace do not grow in the arid soil of ease and comfort but rather in the fertile soil of faith, love, and service. Peace and contentment are either a present reality, or they are a fantasy—a carrot on the end of Satan's stick, to keep us straining forward until we die. Once we receive Christ and begin living in His love, we have all we will ever need for peace, joy, and contentment.

Our ship has come in, and our train has arrived at the station. We are on the right pathway, going in the right direction. All our tribulation is helping us; shaping us into more of what we truly desire to be, which is what God wants us to be. We are not waiting for anything. Our life is no longer on hold until the long-awaited fulfillment of our dreams and efforts. We are integrated, whole, centered, and focused on loving people with God's love. The future is now. We are living in eternity.

Lord thank You for awakening us from the dreadful nightmare of living for the future. Please help us to never waste another moment of our life waiting for the future—postponing joy until the illusory magic moment finally arrives. Keep us mindful that You and Your love are a here and now eternal reality.

164

MANHOOD AND WOMANHOOD

**Three things are too wonderful for me; four I do not understand:
the way of an eagle in the sky, the way of a serpent on a rock, the way of a ship on the high seas, and the way of a man with a maiden [Prv 30:18-19].**

Are you bound to a wife? Do not seek to be free. Are you free from a wife? Do not seek marriage [1Cor 7:27].

Manhood and womanhood, properly comprehended, lead us to a greater understanding of God's love for us. He has created us alike, yet different, with the capacity to live together as intimate friends. A man and woman join together in the mysterious and wonderful union of physical intimacy, and a whole new human being, unique among the entire human family, may result! And this life is part the man, part the woman, and yet all new! New love is born—and new potential! The dynamics of manhood and womanhood offer us an endless supply of stories, episodes of romance and tragedy, and some of the most powerful feelings available to humans. In fact if we are not careful, we can get lost in the dynamics of manhood and womanhood. Some of the feelings generated in the mysterious and powerful world of romantic love—of the man/woman dance—are addictive and all-consuming. The feelings of desire, pursuit, passion, forbiddenness, fulfillment, affection-hunger, jealousy, rejection, intimacy, etc.: This is powerful stuff! It is what makes soap operas and romance novels [for women] and pornography [for men] intensely interesting and potentially addictive. King David's desire for Bathsheba drove him to [indirectly] murder her husband, Uriah, a worthy soldier warring to protect David's kingdom [2 Sm 11]. Samson's obsession with Delilah took precedence over every other motive in his life, and blinded him long before the Philistines gouged out his eyes [Jgs 16]. Reuben lost his birthright for sleeping with one of his father's [Israel] wives [1Chr 5]. King Herod's infatuation with his stepdaughter led to his making a frankly stupid public vow [anything up to half his kingdom], leading to his having to be-head John the Baptist, against his own better judgment [Mt 14]. Infatuated adultery leads to public embarrassment, break up of families, the dreadful, long-term hurt of betrayal, and the loss of innocence and purity in marriage. Not to mention STD's. God's warning is to *keep it in perspective.* Romantic love must be kept under the ruling authority of *agape* [Christlike] love. I'm certain that Jesus, being a man, had the same feelings for womanhood that I have. Yet, because of the nature of His mission, and what a wife would have had to endure, He did not allow Himself to feel the goodness and comfort of a woman—for *her* sake. Marriage [manhood and womanhood] is certainly a wonderful gift. But it never has been the top priority. Our individual relationship with God—the Author of manhood and womanhood—has and will always be in that position. Only in the context of submission to God, Who loves all and desires none to be hurt or betrayed, is man-woman love safe.

Lord, please help us to keep our human love in perspective. And forgive us and heal the hurts that have resulted from our past failures to do so.

165

GOD SPEAKS THROUGH HIS CREATURES

Then the LORD opened the mouth of the ass, and she said to Balaam, "What have I done to you, that you have struck me these three times?" And Balaam said to the ass, "Because you have made sport of me. I wish I had a sword in my hand, for then I would kill you." And the ass said to Balaam, "Am I not your ass, upon which you have ridden all your life long to this day? Was I ever accustomed to do so to you?" And he said, "No." Then the LORD opened the eyes of Balaam, and he saw the angel of the LORD standing in the way, with his drawn sword in his hand; and he bowed his head, and fell on his face [Num 22:28-31].

God speaks through His creatures. My cat likes to be petted—but not too much. When she is tired, she finds a comfortable place and naps. When she is hungry, she lets me know that she wants to be fed. But if I don't feed her, she goes out and finds food for herself—she kills a lizard or mole. And she does not hold it against me that I "neglected" her. She forgives me quickly – automatically. When she makes a kill, she brings it to my door—she wants to share it with me. [This feline habit inspired the familiar statement: "Look what the cat drug up."] She is always interested in life. She is curious. She never seems to be bored. She looks in every nook and cranny for something of interest. Someone has said, "Curiosity killed the cat." I think curiosity kept the cat alive. My cat was very patient with my son's dog, which had a hard time overcoming his fear of her. He wanted to chase her, and was fearful of the way she defended herself with her claws. But she used only the minimum amount of "force" to protect herself, and she "snuggled" him—to his great surprise—until he "got it" that she was not a threat to him. She didn't let her fear of him dominate her—though she certainly did have some fear of him. I am very thankful for the way that God has put His Truth and wisdom in all His creation—all His creatures. If we seek Him in spirit and truth we see Him everywhere.

Lord, thank You for all Your beautiful creatures, and for speaking to us through them.

166

THE WISDOM OF COLLABORATION

Where there is no guidance, a people falls; but in an abundance of counselors there is safety [Prv 11:14].

    Tiffany, my son's girlfriend of almost six years was having some difficulty with a co-worker. The co-worker's car had failed, and she was depending on Tiffany to drive 40 miles out of her way to pick her up and drop her off after work. The co-worker was making only token gestures of appreciation for this ongoing, severe sacrifice that Tiffany was making—even on her days off—to provide transportation for an older woman who was treating her like an underling and acting as if she was entitled to the service. Tiffany wanted to be a friend, but she was feeling used. She asked everyone in the family what they would do in her situation. "How would you respond?" she asked. "What would you say to her?" Without realizing it, she was practicing a biblical principle. She was seeking the advice of an "abundance of counselors." She listened intently as everyone in the family gave their opinions and suggestions, and allowed herself to be shaped inwardly by these offerings. Women, generally speaking, are better at this than men, who have to overcome ego and pride issues in order to submit to collective wisdom. There is a familiar legend that depicts this reality: Men tend not to ask for directions when lost. They will deny that they are lost—even if they don't know where they are. One of my female clients recently shared with me that her husband didn't want to come into counseling, even though they were having very serious problems in their marriage. "He thinks we should be able to work it out on our own. You know how men are." Collaboration is a safe and wise way to do the complicated business of life. God calls us to face and overcome our foolish pride that keeps us in isolation and prevents us from some of the farther reaches of success in life. There is a world of wisdom in our friends and family in Christ. We only retard our growth by not availing ourselves of it.

Lord, thank You for creating us with a legitimate need for each other. Help us to benefit from the collective wisdom of our friends and family in Christ. Deliver us from the pride that makes it difficult for us to stop pretending that we know more than we actually do, so that we can become wiser and freer.

167

BE THANKFUL IN *ALL* SITUATIONS

Give thanks in all circumstances; for this is the will of God in Christ Jesus for you [1Thes 5:18].

If you are waiting for life to smooth out and ease up to be thankful, you will never be thankful. There will never be an end to things to complain about. Jesus said that we would always have tribulation in this world. But He commanded/invited/encouraged us to be of "good cheer" anyway, because He has "overcome the world"—and we are in Him. Therefore, as we grow in Christ, we have this wonderful understanding dawning in us, and shining brighter, like the rising sun: There will never be a problem, trial, or tribulation that will defeat us—that we will not be able to *prosper* through. There will always be a response that we can make in Christ that will lead us to a higher level of abundant life. We see this in the history of the human family. Humans have responded triumphantly to every tribulation imaginable. We have a legacy of spiritual ancestors who have demonstrated a victorious response to every tribulation encountered by man. We know therefore that, in Christ, it is possible to overcome everything. Everything! But we must CHOOSE to respond faithfully and prayerfuly. We have seen that humans can be miserable in prosperous situations also. We see that it is not the *situation* that determines our level of happiness, but rather the internal *response* to the situation. And God commands us to respond *thankfully* in *all* situations. God is not asking us to put on blinders, enter into denial, and pretend that our situation is good when it is terrible. He is asking us to stay anchored in Eternal Reality when we are swept away in a very difficult trial. What is this Eternal Reality? God is still working all things together for good for those who love Him and are called into His glorious, redemptive purpose [Rom 8:28]. Jesus said He would be with us always even to the end of the age, and that He would never forsake us [Mt 28:20]. God has promised to be a very present help in times of trouble [Ps 46:1]. Even though we have been taught this Eternal Reality as long as we have been involved in the Church, we see that we still have tendencies to fret and complain. Our ears have become dull, and our hearts are insensitive to the Truth that sets us free. We need to pray for fresh eyes and ears to see and hear anew—more deeply than ever. Our fears and frets and complaints can awaken us to our need for spiritual growth! If we are growing in Christ, we are disappointing Him less frequently with our faithlessness. We are more thankful in all situations. Our heart is smiling more than ever in the secret, wonderful, inner assurance of the Truth of Christ, our Lord and Friend. In the name of Christ, I invite and encourage you to be thankful in ALL situations. Respond to trials in faith and love. Look for a redemptive purpose. Choose gratitude! It's great for the heart!

Lord God, thank You for caring for my inner being and for desiring that I be thankful in all situations. And thank You for making it possible, through Your Holy Spirit, for me to be so. In obedience to You, I choose to be thankful – no matter what!

168

WE ARE NOT VICTIMS!

For this reason the Father loves me, because I lay down my life, that I may take it again. No one takes it from me, but I lay it down of my own accord [John 10:17-18].

The husband of a couple with whom I counseled was having a problem with anger. His wife was subdued and cautious as she brought up episodes of his abusive anger. As we explored his inner world, what emerged was a core belief system described as follows: He had been "forced" to make certain choices—because of family obligations—that led him into a high stress vocation. Much of his identity was derived from his work as a high-powered trouble-shooter, riding herd on employees to get companies out of trouble, and keeping production high. He resented the long hours his job required, but this was his lot in life because he had a family to support. He would prefer doing many other things that he did not have time for. He was basically living for retirement when he would at long last be able to fish and golf to his heart's content. Meanwhile, he was under the gun, and his family—the *reason* he was under the gun—would just have to cope with his occasional, well-deserved outbursts. It was their price to pay for the six-figure income he generated for them. He was genuinely sorry for the pain he was bringing to his wife, but his sorrow was not generating any changes in behavior because he essentially saw himself as a victim.

When we come into Christ we are delivered from the quagmire of victimhood. There are no victims in Christ—only victors! Jesus has *overcome the world* [John 16:33]. And we are *in Him* [John 14:20]. We must not allow ourselves to think or behave like victims. Jesus was not a victim of the Pharisees, Judas, the Roman soldiers, or Satan. "No one takes my life from me," He declared, "I lay it down of my own accord." We must not allow ourselves to feel *forced* or *controlled.* We are free to choose, no matter how much pressure is upon us. Even if someone threatens to kill you if you do not do something, *you still have a choice!* No one can take away your freedom to choose how to respond to the pressures and options of life. You cannot even give it away. Giving it away is a *choice.* It is essentially delusional to believe that we are being forced or controlled. Whoever controls me must stand in my place in the judgment, because God, in His fairness, would never hold someone accountable for something over which they had no control.

*Lord, please deliver us from victim-mindedness and from feeling forced or controlled. You have set us free. Grant that we be able to **feel** free. And may we always use our freedom to make loving and wise choices.*

169

SURPRISED BY GOD

And Peter opened his mouth and said: "Truly I perceive that God shows no partiality, but in every nation any one who fears him and does what is right is acceptable to him. You know the word which he sent to Israel, preaching good news of peace by Jesus Christ (he is Lord of all)...[Acts 10:34-36].

Peter was a good Jew. He'd never eaten any unclean thing. God gave him a vision in which a sheet was let down from heaven upon which was a number of unclean animals, reptiles, and birds. [Acts 10:12-14]. He was told to "kill and eat." God used this vision to help Peter and others understand that God loved and blessed all people in every nation who feared and obeyed Him. This was a radical new concept for Peter, who had been taught his whole life that the Jews were the chosen ones of God, and only the circumcised could receive His blessings. This was such an ingrained doctrine that Peter was criticized by his fellow Jewish Christians for associating with the uncircumcised Gentiles [Acts 11:3]. He had a hard time convincing them that the Holy Spirit had actually come upon the Gentiles. This act of God was contrary to their beliefs, doctrine, and traditions. And yet they were convinced because of the evidence of the Holy Spirit. When we receive the Holy Spirit, we receive the Spirit of Christ Himself, even if we do not yet know Christ. Cornelius was a faithful and good man, so God honored him with His Spirit. And because God's Spirit was in him, he was able to receive the Gospel of Jesus with joy and without reservation. His Spirit in us is able to discern His Spirit in others, so Peter was able to believe that Cornelius [the uncircumcised Gentile] had actually been welcomed into God's family, even though it contradicted Peter's lifelong belief system. The evidence of the Holy Spirit, more than one's doctrine, sect, denomination, nationality, race, or creed, determines the validity of his or her place in the Kingdom of God. But as evidenced also by this wonderful story in Acts, if one has the gift of God's Spirit, he is able to receive the Gospel of Christ, which is the message that Peter was sent to share with Cornelius. There is of course, absolutely nothing in the life and teachings of Jesus Christ that is offensive or contrary to the Holy Spirit. Anything in us that is offended by or resistant to Christ is not of God—it is evil. [Which of His teachings is offensive?] Because Jesus' teachings are pure, we can receive them [and Him] without fear or reservation. Only goodness can come from Christ. He always leads us toward the fulfillment of every good thing in us. He delivers us from darkness, oppression, blindness, and death, into freedom, light, life, peace, and joy. And especially into love for all the human family—even those who are different from us in any way.

Lord, please help me to be willing to be surprised by Your magnanimous grace, goodness, and love for all. And deliver me from being offended or fearful of anything Jesus is offering or teaching.

170

SORROW AND JOY

"O Jerusalem, Jerusalem, killing the prophets and stoning those who are sent to you! How often would I have gathered your children together as a hen gathers her brood under her wings, but you would not" (Mt 23:37)!
These things have I spoken unto you, that my joy might remain in you, and that your joy might be full [John 15:11].

Jesus was deeply aware of the imperfections and failures of the human family. And it grieved Him. We who follow in His Way are also painfully and sorrowfully aware of the unnecessary suffering we bring upon ourselves by failing to heed what God has revealed to us through the prophets, and especially through Christ. We see how difficult it is to love one another. We see how disposed we are to selfishness, greed, lust, apathy, blame, and denial. We see our family members divided against each other because of [in the eternal perspective] trivialities. We recognize that our spiritual blindness has caused us much unnecessary suffering. We see animosity between spouses, brothers, neighbors, co-workers, and nations. Within our own hearts we see how we tend to condemn, judge, and hate. And yet we continue to stone the prophets—or, worse, ignore them. It is good and right that we should recognize and grieve this terrible loss of heavenly peace and harmony available to us here on earth. We must see all of Reality as it is. The Christian faith is not a blind faith.

But we are neither defeated nor excessively oppressed by our failures. We continue to allow the failures of the human family to inspire us to be progressively more successful at that which is most important—at loving. Our grief and sadness become fuel for more mature and productively-focused love. The more clearly we see the destructiveness and futility of spiritual blindness and selfishness, the more we are determined to bring our lives into the wonderful and eternally significant service of the Love of Christ. Like Him, we do not allow the evil and blindness of humanity to prevent us from working in the redemptive service of His Kingdom—our only and sufficient hope. And as our lives become more focused in His love, we experience the inner blossoming of the joy that He promised—the joy of knowing that we are fulfilling our eternally-ordained mission in our brief stay upon this earth. And that the Love of Christ will without fail be victorious over every form of darkness in us—and in the world!

Lord Jesus, we can never express adequately in words the wonder of Your goodness and Truth, and how grateful we are to have been welcomed into Your Family and Kingdom. May Your Love be the Light of our lives today and forever.

171

OUR LIFE'S WORK

If we say we have no sin, we deceive ourselves and the truth is not in us [1Jn 1:8].

All people are bringing some mixture of darkness and light into the world. Some people are bringing more darkness than light; others more light than darkness. As we draw ever nearer to God (the "Consuming Fire") the darkness is burned away (the "wood, stubble and hay"), and we become brighter manifestations of the Light, which is Christ in us. We do not, however, become God. We continue to have a sinful nature, and it is particular to us. Just as I have a particular personality, gifts, and physical features; I have a particular sinful nature. My combination of weaknesses and temptations are particular to me. Evil spirits can manifest through me, just as they did through Peter, to whom Jesus said, "Get thee behind me,

Satan." I have been born into a fallen world, full of untold manifestations of darkness or evil. My parents had sinful natures through which darkness was manifested toward and into me from the day I was born. These evil spirits that were in my family of origin are the spirits that are hardest for me to recognize because they have always been around or within me. They are familiar to me. I am acclimated to them. I am unaware of some of the ways that evil manifests through me. God will, however, if I cooperate with Him, reveal them to me through the process of my sanctification—my psycho-spiritual growth—a life-long process—the most important work on the planet—my life's work. My tendency to be blind to my sinful nature manifestations underscores the importance of my relationships. My family and friends with whom I share in the deep communion of everyday life will serve me by holding up a mirror that reveals (among other things) my sinful nature to me. I am truly blessed as I become desensitized and non-defensive to this process. As I learn the hard but wonderful lessons of love in daily life, I am being sanctified. My sinful nature is being exposed and burned away. As I carefully and prayerfully analyze my vanity, selfishness, anger, frustrations, denials, sexual perversions, fantasies, tendencies toward unhealthy isolation, addictions, abuses, judgments, critical attitudes, incivilities, laziness, envy, fear, guilt, hatred, materialism, apathy, etc., I will learn how I am bringing unnecessary suffering into the world. And as I cooperate with the God of truth and love-for-all in exposing these evil spirits to His Light, I fulfill my God-ordained destiny in the facilitation of the spiritual evolution—in the ongoing expansion of the Kingdom of God. We draw near to God (cast out the evil spirits; burn away the sinful nature) through the spiritual disciplines—through living a devoted life in Christ. In this way we become the true beings that we are created to be, and we facilitate the spiritual evolution of this world. Nothing is meaningful without this priority. This is a pathway of growing peace and joy.

Lord, thank You for revealing these wonderful mysteries to us. Thank You for revealing our sinful nature to us and for showing us how to overcome—and for forgiveness. Today, more than ever before, may we abide in You, and You in us.

172

FOR GOD'S SAKE DON'T STOP LOVING!

And because wickedness is multiplied, most men's love will grow cold. But he who endures to the end will be saved [Mt 24:12 –13].

Jesus told His disciples that as beautiful and revered as the Temple was, not a single stone would be left upon another [Mt 24:12]. [Nothing of this earth nor anything in the material world is permanent. Jesus wants us to understand that it will all come to an end.] And they asked Him when these things would come to be—when would He return and the age come to a close. Jesus replied by describing some of the signs that would herald that time: false prophets, imposters pretending to be Christ, wars and rumors of wars, earthquakes in diverse places, hatred and betrayal, persecution of believers, etc. And He said, *"Because wickedness is multiplied, most men's love will grow cold."* We are so thankful for Jesus' profound teachings that help us so much. Here He reminds us that wickedness or evil tends to diminish love. Have you noticed that when many things are going wrong in your life—when you are "under attack"—when Satan uses the people around you to hurt or criticize you—when you have a series of setbacks—it is very difficult to love? When we see our loved ones making bad decisions or being used or abused; when we see our young people being killed in senseless wars; when we see families falling apart and children neglected and abused, there is the temptation to sink into apathy and hopelessness. And have you seen how those who have been the victims of severe forms of evil—childhood abuse, violent crimes, war—tend to grow bitter or cold? When we have been hurt deeply by our fellow man, our spirit can be diminished. When it seems that no one else cares, it is hard to keep caring. When everyone else seems sold out, it's hard to hold on to your values. When others are throwing in the towel, it's hard to endure. But that is precisely what Jesus commands and encourages us to do. **Endure!** We know we are losing the spiritual battle when we stop caring and loving. We must never let that happen. Even if we have no feelings to sustain us, we always have a **will**. We can always *choose* to love no matter what else is going on in the universe. And if we keep making that choice, we can know that we know that we know that God is with us, and we will be "saved"! That is the promise of Jesus. And He has never lied or been mistaken.

Lord Jesus, thank You that You never stopped loving. Please help me to endure through whatever happens in this world, and to never stop loving.

173

JESUS IS IN YOU

In that day you will know that I am in my Father, and you in me, and I in you...Jesus answered him, "If a man loves me, he will keep my word, and my Father will love him, and we will come to him and make our home with him..." [John 14:20,23].

Here is a profound reality that can be for us an inexhaustible source of strength and inspiration: Jesus is *in us*. He has promised that if we love Him, He and our Father will make their "home" with us. In Christ we have communion with the Creator of the universe—the One Who thought up everything from aardvarks to zebras, and spoke them into existence. We are one with Him in Christ and in His love. Jesus—Who slept through the storm, calmed the stormy sea, walked on the water, courageously faced those who plotted against Him, healed the sick, raised the dead, prayed for the forgiveness of His brutal enemies, and arose from the dead—this Jesus abides within us. Try this: Put your hand on your chest—perhaps over your heart—and say "Jesus is in me." Try to feel the reality of His promise to abide in you. You are in Christ, and Christ is in you. Let this become a palpable, inwardly felt reality for you. In Christ we inherit His victory over the world [John 16:33]. In Him we are "more than conquerors" [Rom 8:37]. In any and all of life's chaotic, confusing or devastating experiences, we have the unspeakable opportunity to draw up into Christ-in-us, and respond with infinite wisdom, compassion, and strength. If life becomes for us a fiery furnace, in Christ, we, like Shadrach, Meshach, and Abednego, will emerge unhurt [Dn 3:25]. In Christ we are able to love even our enemies in spirit and truth. In Christ we do not take persecution, maltreatment, or betrayal personally. In Christ we are totally free within the context of love and a sincere desire for the good of all. Jesus, Who is in us, is all we will ever need for peace. In Him we embrace the difficulties of life with a peaceful heart. We know that we will always overcome as He has overcome. In Christ we have nothing to fear and nothing to dread. In Him we embrace death as our final victory [1Cor 15:26]. In Him our lives come into a laser light focus of love for God and man. In Him every day has an eternally significant purpose and meaning. We are so thankful that Jesus has made His home in us! We welcome Him and celebrate His presence every day! We live with open and free hearts.

Lord Jesus, my heart is Your eternal home. I am so thankful for Your presence. Abide with me forever.

174

THANK GOD FOR RUBY BRIDGES

Do not return evil for evil or reviling for reviling; but on the contrary bless, for to this you have been called, that you may obtain a blessing....But even if you do suffer for righteousness' sake, you will be blessed. Have no fear of them, nor be troubled... [1Pet 3:9,14].

But I say unto you, Love your enemies, bless them that curse you, do good to them that hate you, and pray for them which despitefully use you, and persecute you...[Jesus, Mt 5:44].

These principles of our Christian faith have no doubt saved us untold bloodshed in the process of overcoming racial prejudice. Hatred is fed by hatred, but it is destroyed, broken down, and disintegrated by Love. Ruby Bridges was six years old when in 1960 she was ordered by a judge to attend all white William Franz Elementary School. President Dwight Eisenhower ordered federal marshals to escort her into and out of the school, at which times large mobs of angry white adults gathered and shouted hateful comments and threats of violence toward her. Her mother, a devoted Christian, had taught Ruby to pray and hold her head up. Robert Coles, who was at this time a Harvard doctoral candidate and in the field studying the phenomenon of *character*, witnessed these events from the perspective of psychiatry, and wrote about it in his *Field Notes on the Nature of Character*.

In my own working life the question of "character" came up in the early 1960's when my wife and I were getting to know the black children who were initiating desegregation in the South, often against high odds—mob violence, even—and the young men and women who made up the non-violent sit-in movement. I remember the clinical appraisals, psychological histories, and socioeconomic comments I wrote then....One day, as I mumbled some statements suffused with the words of psychiatric theory to "explain" a given child's behavior, my wife said, "You are making her sound as if she ought to be on her way to a child guidance clinic, but she is walking into a school building—and no matter the threats, she is holding her head up high, even smiling at her obscene hecklers. Last night she even prayed for them!" It was my wife's judgment that Ruby Bridges, aged six, was demonstrating to all the world **character.**

As Christians we understand at the level of the *heart* that character is something that is wrought within us by the Holy Spirit in the process of our sanctification. It is a goodness that does not originate in man but can grow in him as he keeps his heart open to God. And we see the tremendous good that is brought into any culture by God's children, faithfully living in Christ. We bow in reverent gratitude to God for His enormous Grace in loving us in this way—in doing this wonderful work within and through us.

Ruby's mother looked back on this time as an answer to her simple prayers: "Our Ruby taught us all a lot. She became someone who helped change the country. She was a part of history, just like generals and presidents are part of history. They are leaders, and so was Ruby. She led us away from hate, and she led us nearer to knowing each other, the white folks and the black folks."

Ruby's Prayer:
Please God, try to forgive these people. Because even if they say those bad things, they don't know what they're doing. So You could forgive them just like You did those folks a long time ago when they said terrible things about You.

175

TRUE RELIGION

Then they led Jesus from the house of Ca'iaphas to the praetorium. It was early. They themselves did not enter the praetorium, so that they might not be defiled, but might eat the passover [John 18:28].

It is always important for us to remain mindful that religion—the performance of religious activities—does not deliver us from blindness. In fact some of the bleakest forms of blindness are lived out within the context of religion. The above verse represents a stark example. Here we see these Jews—perhaps the most religious people on earth at the time—refusing to enter a Gentile domain because it was the day before Passover, and they did not want to "defile" themselves, which would have precluded them from partaking of the Passover. Meanwhile, full of contempt and hatred, they were dragging around the bound Messiah, the Prince of Peace, the very Son of the God that had delivered them from bondage in Egypt—the event signified by the Passover. Jesus speaks to this issue in the "Good Samaritan" parable in Luke 10, and He addresses it in His encounter with Mary and Martha in the verses immediately following. It is not the "role" that we fulfill in life that matters—the priest and Levite both passed by on the other side of the road. Rather it is whether or not we show mercy to the needy. It is not how busy we are doing good things—as Martha. It is whether we are in communion with the Lord—as Mary, who sat at Jesus feet and heard His words. Closer to home, it is not the role that we fulfill in the Church that matters. We can be deacons, Sunday school teachers, pastors, priests, lay leaders, counselors or devotion-writers, and still continually do our versions of walking by on the other side of the road. We can be very busy doing religious things and even receive a lot of praise for what we do, and still be missing communion with Jesus, Who alone can give meaning, focus and priority to our busy-ness. We cannot have communion with Him if we do not know His teachings. I think there are many people who call themselves Christians who would be hard-pressed to cite three major sayings or teachings of Christ. We are deceiving ourselves if we say we are Christians and do not have personal communion with Jesus. God performed compassionate miracles through Jesus and raised Him from the grave to call our attention to Him. Jesus commanded us to abide in Him [John 15:4-7], and by so doing we would be delivered from the darkness [John 12:46]. God tells us very plainly that being religious will not deliver us from blindness. Only Jesus Himself can do that. And He is always ready and willing to enter our heart with every good gift of life—forgiveness, wisdom, peace, and love.

Lord Jesus, it is so easy for us to drift away from You into the activities of life— even religious activities. Please give us grace to abide in You personally; to have communion with You;, to speak with You and hear Your still small voice, confirming to us Your earthly teachings that lead us toward heaven and give our lives eternal significance.

176

SHIELD OF FAITH

Every word of God is pure: he is a shield unto them that put their trust in him [Prv 30:5 KJV].

Above all, taking the shield of faith, wherewith ye shall be able to quench all the fiery darts of the wicked [Eph 6:16 KJV].

My sister told me that on the night the state troopers came to her house and told her that her husband had been killed in an auto accident, when she laid down in her bed, she felt a "shield begin at my feet and move all way the up, covering my head, and I was able to sleep that night." Wave upon wave of grief would come over her in the following months, but she felt supernaturally protected by God that first night from the overwhelming power of the initial grief. Later, she would peacefully face her death, her body ravaged by cancer, protected by this same shield. Faith in God is described in the Bible as a "shield." Those who have put their trust in Him know from their own inner experience what this means. We have felt the fiery darts of Satan. And we have felt protected by the shield of faith in a loving, all-powerful God. We have felt the fiery dart of temptation, and we have seen it quenched by our faith in God's promise to never let us be tempted above our ability to withstand [1Cor 10:13].

We have felt the fiery dart of condemnation for our weaknesses and sins, and we have seen it quenched by our faith in a God Who, through Christ, forgives and imparts grace rather than punishment [Rom 8:1]. We have felt the fiery darts of the worries and cares of the world, and we have felt them quenched by our faith in God, Who has promised to be a very present help in times of trouble [Ps 46:1], and by Christ Who has promised to be with us always, even to the end of the world [Mt 28:20]. We have felt the fiery dart of overwhelming responsibilities, and seen it quenched by our faith in Him Who said, "My yoke is easy and my burden light" [Mt 11:30]. We have felt the fiery darts of betrayal, abuse, abandonment; and overcome them all in the power of His Holy Spirit, sustained by His promises. We have felt the fiery dart of the fear of being abandoned or left behind by God, and we have seen it quenched by His compassionate and fervent promises to never leave or forsake us [Heb 13:5]. We have felt the fiery dart of the fear of our own and our loved ones' death, and we have seen it quenched by our faith in Christ's words: "Let not your heart be troubled... In my Father's house are many mansions." [John 14]. For every fiery dart of Satan, there is a corresponding word of Truth that sets us free. God is our refuge, sanctuary, fortress, place of rest, and security. We are eternally safe in His love—the love He has manifested in Christ, His Son, our Lord, in Whom we "live and move and have our being" [Acts 17:28].

Lord, You are my Shield and Protector. You are my only security. I put my total and complete trust in You. Please keep me and my loved ones from evil, and from fear and the worries of this world. Keep us in Your perfect peace.

177

YOUR WORD IS YOUR BOND

When a man vows a vow to the LORD, or swears an oath to bind himself by a pledge, he shall not break his word; he shall do according to all that proceeds out of his mouth [Nm 30:2].

But above all, my brethren, do not swear, either by heaven or by earth or with any other oath, but let your yes be yes and your no be no, that you may not fall under condemnation [Jam 5:12].

The above verses demonstrate one of the progressions from the Old to the New Testament. This progression is symbolic of our collective and individual spiritual growth. Before Christ moved us more deeply into the very heart of God, the Law structured us from the *outside*. Jesus, moving into our hearts through the Holy Spirit, became the Law of Love *within* us. In Numbers God instructed Moses to require the fulfillment of words that were sworn or bound in a pledge. In Christ, as recorded in the Book of James [see also Matthew 5:36-7], we are brought to the understanding that our word *is* an oath and a bond. The old understanding is, if I say I will do something, I may or may not do it. But if I "swear" or make an "oath," then I will surely do it. Jesus leads us beyond this to an understanding that our word *is* an oath and a bond. To swear or make an oath is therefore [or should be] superfluous.

One of the very important aspects of our spiritual maturity is that we become better at speaking the truth and living up to our word. If we are honest with ourselves, we realize that we have all lied or presented things to be true that weren't, and we have all made pledges or promises that we did not keep. We must realize this to be sin. It tears at the fabric of healthy human connectedness. We desperately need to be able to trust each other. And trust is a by-product of truth—of living up to our word.

What this means on a practical level is, if I say to my wife "I'll be home at six," I should be diligent to be home at or very near that time; or call her and let her know otherwise. If I say to my son, "I'll take you fishing on Friday," I have made an oath to him that I should by all reasonable means fulfill. If I say, "I will call you the first of the week," I shouldn't wait until Thursday. If I borrow, I am *pledged* to return or pay back, and I should live up to that pledge diligently and on a timely basis. People notice when we don't fulfill our word. This is especially true of our family members and closest associates. And it determines their perception of us, though they may never verbalize it. And if we are Christians, the failure to fulfill our word is a poor testimony to the One Who has redeemed us and set us free. I am so thankful that when Jesus said, "I come to set the captives free"[Lk 4:18], He didn't forget, procrastinate, change His mind, or wimp out on His word, even though it led Him through Calvary.

Lord, please forgive me for not living up to my word. Please give me grace to be diligent to make sure that my "yes" is yes, and my "no," no.

178

THE CREATOR HAS SPOKEN

But as for you, continue in what you have learned and have firmly believed, knowing from whom you learned it and how from childhood you have been acquainted with the sacred writings which are able to instruct you for salvation through faith in Christ Jesus. All scripture is inspired by God and profitable for teaching, for reproof, for correction, and for training in righteousness, that the man of God may be complete, equipped for every good work [2Tm 3:14-17].

In many and various ways God spoke of old to our fathers by the prophets; but in these last days he has spoken to us by a Son, whom he appointed the heir of all things, through whom also he created the world [Heb 1:1-2].

The Bible is not just a book written by a number of men who had some idle time and figured they would write something from their imagination. It is inspired by the Creator of the universe—the One Who created everything, including us. The phrase, "Thus saith the Lord" appears 413 times in the Bible. We understand that *God is speaking to us*, giving us the Truth of the universe—the Truth that sets us free; revealing eternal Reality to us. The One Who imagined and spoke into existence everything from microbes to whales, and Who created us in His image, giving us the ability to imagine and create also—He has communicated the Truth to us. And this Truth culminates in Jesus Christ, Who said, "*I am the...Truth*" [John 14:6]. All Christians understand that the Old Testament points to Jesus, the Messiah. And the New Testament reveals His life and teachings—the fulfillment of that which is alluded to in the Old Testament. Christ is understood to be God in the flesh—the Living Word that was "in the beginning" [John 1]. There is no other prophet, priest, or king that is His equal. God spoke audibly from heaven [Mt 17:5, Mk 9:7, Lk 9:35] and raised Christ from the grave to confirm His special place in the human family. His life and teachings confirm His Messiahship. When asked what is the most important commandment, Jesus responded by reminding us that there is only one God and that we are to love Him with all our heart, soul, mind, and strength, and that we are to love each other unselfishly [Mk 12:28-31]. When we look deeply into this teaching, we realize that it is the solution to all the problems in the human family. This confirms to us that it is the Truth of God, our Creator, Who loves us and wants us to be free from hatred, fear, envy, and strife. The love of Jesus is the answer to the problems of the human family. This is very plain if we simply take the time to look deeply into His teachings and His life. God has spoken to us through Jesus. Some have received Him; others have rejected or ignored Him. The Bible, God's Holy Word, teaches that the spiritual "continental divide" for all of us is what we do with Jesus [John 3:18]. In Jesus we find completion and discover the true meaning of life. Without Him we are adrift in a sea of chaos and meaninglessness.

Lord God, You have created us and the world in which we live. And You have spoken the Truth to us through Jesus our Lord. We are very thankful for the life You have given, and for the Truth that sets us free.

179

COMING INTO FOCUS

So as to live for the rest of the time in the flesh no longer by human passions but by the will of God [1Pet 4:2].

We all begin our life in this world living by "human passions." When we are hungry, we cry [passionately] until we are fed. If we are in pain, we cry until we are made comfortable. We want to be the most favored of our siblings, and we are envious of the attention that our parents give them. We want to play and have fun, and we resist responsibilities and duties. Or we work too hard, hungry for the praise of our parents. Later, we become obsessed with obtaining a mate. More than anything, we want to be attractive. When we marry, we passionately pursue the making and spending of money. We want to have many pleasant experiences, dine out, and see many of the beautiful places of the world. If we are blessed with children, we are forced, maybe for the first time in our lives, into an unselfish mode of living. We have to spend massive amounts of energy taking care of little humans who are totally dependent on us for their existence, and who can give nothing in return. Our children are a great blessing to us in this way. They teach us to "suffer in the flesh." Yet we may find ourselves [perhaps secretly] resenting or despairing over the responsibility of our children. One woman was in the news a few years ago because she killed her own children to make way for a relationship with a man who did not want to be bothered with them. This is an extreme example of the selfishness that we all suffer from to some degree. And God is calling us to progressively overcome it. Our sanctification process is like coming into focus. When we first take Christ seriously as the Messiah, we are like floodlights, bright perhaps, in our zealous honeymoon phase with Jesus, but very broad and diffuse. We are still contaminated with much selfishness and "human passion." His love is shining through us, but it is not very focused. We are not wise. If we are willing to grow and apply ourselves, the Holy Spirit brings us into focus like a floodlight becoming a spotlight. Ultimately, we want to be like a laser, able to bring the love of Christ into a single, very effective beam of healing, ministry, service, and truth. We move farther and farther away from "human passions" and more and more into the will and love of God. We realize that our time on this earth is limited, and our primary desire is to be more effective for the Kingdom of God. We understand and recognize the perpetual battle between human passions and the will of God. Jesus bestows this great blessing upon us. He enables us to harness our human passions to the glorious and unselfish service of our Creator. In this service we discover boundless joy! This is the fulfillment of the promise of Christ [John 15:11].

Lord God, in the name of Jesus I ask You to please help me continue to overcome my selfish tendencies to be motivated by the desire for pleasant experiences. My deepest desire is to be motivated only by Your love for the human family. Please bring me into focus. May I know the joy of Jesus, Who was willing to suffer for the sake of others.

180

THE LIGHT OF THE WORLD

You are the light of the world. A city set on a hill cannot be hid [Mt 5:14].

  If you are a Christian, and you are sincerely living the Faith—abiding in Christ—then you are the Light of this world. You may not feel like the Light of this world, but the Lord has spoken and ordained that you are. We do not take pride in being the Light of this world; we consider it an awesome responsibility and opportunity. And we know that we are only able to truly *be* the Light of the world as and to the degree that we *abide in Christ*. He, then, has promised to abide in us [John 15:4, 14:20], and He is the True Light of this world [John 8:12, 9:5].

  Light is an amazing phenomenon. We cannot entirely define it; it transcends our understanding. We do know that without it we cannot see. Everything that we see, we see because light has illumined it. Without light there is only darkness. Because of light, we see beauty. And because of it we see that which is toxic and dangerous. Because of light we can discern that which is good for us from that which is harmful. It is dangerous to eat in the dark; we might take something into our body that is spoiled or contaminated. And it is dangerous to live in spiritual darkness. Light makes visual discernment possible. The Light of Christ makes discernment of Truth—goodness and evil—possible. Light is the only substance/matter that does not co-mingle with that with which it comes into contact. Water and air can become contaminated. Light cannot. Light can shine on the most toxic, stinking substance imaginable; and it will remain pure. Jesus was encompassed by the most toxic personalities of His day—evil religious leaders, power hungry political leaders, demoniacs, blood lusty soldiers, and Satan himself—but He remained pure, peaceful, and loving. He stayed the course of His mission even though all hell was released against Him. He was [and is] Who He was, despite His relational environment. And Who He was was [and is] Love incarnate. And we, now, who abide in Him are this Light and this Love in our world. We expose Truth. We love all, but we do not agree or join with all. And we are kept from evil [John 17:15], and we are unspotted from the world [Jam 1:27]. We can be around toxic personalities without being contaminated by their spiritual toxicity, which is their spiritual blindness. We bring the Light of Christ's Love and Truth to them, but we are not responsible for what they do with Him. We are here to shine and shine and shine like the sun on everything and everyone. And we are perpetually free in this Light—free to be what Christ has ordained us to be. Nothing outside our own will can ever change this!

Lord, thank You for ordaining and empowering us to be the Light of the world. Abide in us always.

181

MARTHA AND MARY

Now as they went on their way, he entered a village; and a woman named Martha received him into her house. And she had a sister called Mary, who sat at the Lord's feet and listened to his teaching. But Martha was distracted with much serving; and she went to him and said, "Lord, do you not care that my sister has left me to serve alone? Tell her then to help me." But the Lord answered her, "Martha, Martha, you are anxious and troubled about many things; one thing is needful. Mary has chosen the good portion, which shall not be taken away from her" [Lk 10:38-42].

There was much to be done, and Martha felt compelled to do it. Food to be cooked and served and guests to attend. Meanwhile, her "lazy" sister Mary sat and listened to Jesus. Resentment began to build up in Martha, and she could no longer contain it. "My sister has left me alone to serve. Tell her to help me!"

In all of us are the seeds of Martha and Mary. As Martha, we recognize that much needs to be done in our world: so many unmet needs; the fields are ripe and the laborers few [Lk 10:2]. We must keep our shoulder to the load and our mind to the task. If we stop or slow down, we will be left behind in the onward march; trampled in the rat race.

As Mary we recognize that "one thing is needful." We must stop the mad rush of the world long enough to sit quietly at the feet of Jesus and listen to the words of eternal life. Then our work takes on eternal significance and becomes focused, productive, meaningful, and peaceful.

If we cannot be like Mary, we will be a resentful, "distracted" Martha.

Lord, thank You for encouraging the Mary in us, and for not condemning the Martha in us. Help us to do the good works for which we were created while maintaining the peace that blossoms in us when we sit in Your presence.

182

BEYOND SALVATION

...He has granted to us his precious and very great promises, that through these you may escape from the corruption that is in the world because of passion, and become partakers of the divine nature. For this very reason make every effort to supplement your faith with virtue, and virtue with knowledge, and knowledge with self-control, and self-control with steadfastness, and steadfastness with godliness, and godliness with brotherly affection, and brotherly affection with love [2Pet 1:4-7].

Let your light so shine before men [Jesus, Mt 5:16].

Once we come into Christ, the great adventure begins. We become peaceful warriors for all that is good for the human family. And we come to realize that the enemy is both without and *within*, and we cannot overcome the enemy outside us unless and until we become engaged in eradicating him from our own lives. This is the wonderful process of our sanctification—our psycho-spiritual growth. It is a process that is Holy Spirit inspired and empowered, but it must become a *conscious* process. We must be *proactive* in becoming what God created us to become. Humans do not mature naturally or passively. Thus, the Scriptures admonish us to "make every effort" or "give all diligence" to cultivate certain virtues. This is every Christian's responsibility. We understand that we are not "saved" by our good works or virtues [Eph 2:8-9]. God's grace, imparted to us through faith in Jesus as the Messiah, secures our salvation. But we are created for good works [Eph 2:10], and genuine faith produces an inner desire to *be* good for the world and *do* good in the world. James reminds us that "faith without works is dead" [2:20]. And the above verses remind us that there is *inner* work to be done—the cultivation of certain personality traits: virtue [goodness], knowledge [of God's Word, Christ's teachings], self-control [not being driven by passions], steadfastness [persistence, determination, trustworthiness], godliness [emulation of the life of Jesus], brotherly affection [familial love, genuine friendship], and love [*agape*; the sacrificial love of Jesus; the crowning and defining characteristic of the Christian life]. And we are mindful that our life in Christ activates the inner, *felt experience* of the fulfillment of His promises to us: peace [John 14:27], joy [John 15:11], abundant and eternal life [John 10:10, 3:16], healing, deliverance, and freedom of soul! [Lk 4:18]. This is the testimony of every true Christian who stays the course [Lk 9:62].

Lord, today I will practice my faith by being good, showing compassion, practicing mindfulness of Your love in me for all people, practicing self-control, being a friend to all and opening my heart to Your gifts of joy and peace.

183

THE FRUIT OF OUR FAITH

For God sent the Son into the world, not to condemn the world, but that the world might be saved through him [John 3:17].

How do you usually feel after Sunday services [or other encounters with God or His people]? I hope you feel cleansed, renewed, loved, refocused, inspired, encouraged, and forgiven. I have experienced and have heard from others that we do not always feel this way. One of the great challenges of our Faith is to always remember that God loves us. It is not His desire to make us feel guilty, condemned, hopeless, afraid, ashamed, inferior, inadequate, evil, or disappointed—at least not for very long. When you love someone, you want him to feel good about life. You want her to have joy and peace. And Jesus promised these to us. Jesus lived a perfect life, and Christians are perpetually holding themselves in comparison to Him and striving to be more like Him. This provides Satan an opportunity to make us feel very bad about ourselves because we can never [in our earthly existence] be perfect as He is and was. This makes it very important for us to have discernment in preaching, teaching, and hearing the Word of God because it can have the effect of making us feel perpetually sad about how far short we fall of the righteousness of God. Or, it causes some to refuse to continue to subject themselves to this manner of preaching and teaching, and they turn away from the Faith. People don't like to feel perpetually inadequate and disappointed. And obviously, based on the fact that He gave His Son to be the atonement of our sins so that we could know that we are forgiven and free from condemnation, God does not want us to perpetually feel this way. The Holy Word of God—the "Good News"—can and has been used to beat and abuse people and even to control them with fear. When God's Word is used in these ways [or when it is perpetually heard in these ways] it is no longer the true Word of God. God knows better than anyone that we will not attain perfection in this lifetime. Yet He has still offered us peace and joy through Jesus our Lord. If we must be perfect to experience peace and joy, then we never will in this life. And Jesus has made it plain that He wants us to receive these gifts. So God imparts the righteousness of Christ, His Son, to those who receive Him as Lord and Savior. This in no way gets us "off the hook" of the ongoing, necessary work that we must continue in our sanctification process. God rightly expects us to be growing diligently in all the graces and fruits of our Faith—love, obedience, wisdom, knowledge, goodness, kindness, patience, forgiveness, and the righteousness of Christ. It is our *desire* to grow in these ways—in His way. But once we have faced the truth about our sinful nature and our need for redemption, we have peace and joy all along the Way because we are forgiven and free in Christ. We confess our sins, and God removes them from us as far as the East is from the West [Ps 103:12], remembers them no more [Heb 8:12], and cleanses us from all unrighteousness [1Jn 1:9]. We hold our heads up—not in denial or arrogant pride, but in joyful gratitude for what God, through Jesus, has done for us. And we are very careful to walk in His love for all people as He has commanded.

Lord, thank You for the "Good News" of my forgiveness and freedom because of Your sacrifice. Please deliver us from abusive and enslaving distortions of Your Truth.

184

UNFLAPPABLE

So when [Jesus] heard that [Lazarus] was ill, he stayed two days longer in the place where he was [John 11:6].

And a great storm of wind arose, and the waves beat into the boat, so that the boat was already filling. But he was in the stern, asleep on the cushion; and they woke him and said to him, "Teacher, do you not care if we perish?" And he awoke and rebuked the wind, and said to the sea, "Peace! Be still!" And the wind ceased, and there was a great calm [Mk 4:37-39].

On a talk show, I heard a highly acclaimed NBA point guard describing his mindset during games. He stated that he needed to maintain a broad perspective, being mindful of all players. Who has a possible play? How can he break open a play? And, in order to do this he tries to remain "unflappable." The term means, "not easily excited or upset, even in a crisis; calm."

The above verses relate crisis episodes in Jesus' and the disciples' lives: the fatal illness of a friend, and a potentially fatal storm at sea. In the first instance, you might imagine the messengers running up to Jesus and breathlessly relating the grim news about Lazarus' critical condition. Jesus, rather than hastily gathering everyone together and hurrying off to heal Lazarus before he died; calmly waited two days longer. In the second, you can see the fear in Peter's rain-drenched face as he shakes Jesus awake and shouts to be heard over the wind and waves, "Don't you care that we are about to die?!" I can imagine a tired look of disappointment in Jesus' eyes. *"Why are you so afraid? Where is your faith?" [Mk 4:40]*

Death is not a crisis to our Lord. And neither are the storms of life. And as we grow in Him, neither are they to us. We become unflappable, inwardly calm, and secure in the peace of God's eternal presence and care. No matter the apparent severity of temporary crisis, all is well, and ever shall be, in Christ.

Lord, please help us to become more unflappable in the crises of life. Help us to grow in faith, and the resultant peace. Help us to know, with inward felt experience, our eternal security in You.

185

REALITY

Heaven and earth shall pass away, but my words shall not pass away [Jesus, Mt 24:35].

The heart [is] deceitful above all [things], and desperately wicked: who can know it? [Jer 17:9]

And with all wicked deception for those who are to perish, because they refused to love the truth and so be saved. Therefore God sends upon them a strong delusion, to make them believe what is false [2Thes 2:10-11].

Within the human personality there seems to be at least two levels of "reality." There is the "reality" of the mind: thoughts, beliefs, and cognition. And there is emotional "reality": feelings and intuition. I can *think* or *believe* something to be true and not *feel* it to be. And I can *feel* something to be true but not be able to make sense of it with my mind. I have recently seen a client who *feels* that her husband is abusive. She *feels* victimized by him. When she brings up an "abusive" issue, he explains his motives and actions in a rational and believable manner; and they sound non-abusive in nature. While she does not disagree with his account [she doesn't accuse him of lying], she continues to *feel* victimized, even by events five years past. Each time she tries to bring up specific events, they evaporate in the light of either his prior confession and repentance [years ago], or his explanations of motives that differ from her judgments of him. So she repeatedly comes back to general statements of "truth" based solely on her feelings. [This is not to say that abuse doesn't happen. And typically abusers try to justify and minimize their actions. Their victims {who frequently *feel* or *believe* that they are at fault} need support and encouragement to protect themselves.]

One of our greatest challenges in our spiritual growth is the process of bringing our *emotional* and *cognitive* "realities" into alignment with Eternal Reality: the Truth of Christ. The Bible teaches us not to rely on our own understanding, but in all ways to acknowledge the truth that God has revealed to us in His Word and through the Holy Spirit of Christ [Prv 3:5]. Our feelings and our thoughts do not determine objective reality. And if we do not carefully, prayerfully, and diligently love and pursue the Truth [and submit ourselves to it], we will be victims of our delusions and the deceptions of the evil one. This happens not only in the unbelieving world, but also *within* religious contexts.

Lord Jesus, You are the Truth. Your way-of-being in the world, Your teachings, and Your Holy Spirit are my only refuge from delusions and deception. Please keep me from evil. Give me grace to remain safe in Your love for all.

186

JESUS OFFERS US A WONDERFUL OPPORTUNITY

These things I have spoken unto you, that in me ye might have peace. In the world ye shall have tribulation: but be of good cheer; I have overcome the world [John 16:33 KJV].

I love the little poem by A. A. Milne entitled *Happiness*:

John had great big waterproof boots on
John had a great big waterproof hat
John had a great big waterproof mackintosh
And that [said John] is that!

If you think of the *rain* as everything that falls within the category of *tribulation*: every problem, trial, difficulty, everything that you would ever complain about or be frustrated about; Jesus is our waterproof boots, waterproof hat, and waterproof mackintosh. When Jesus said that He had "overcome the world," He was speaking of every difficulty that we would ever confront in this world, including death. If there is a difficulty that Jesus did not overcome, then He is not the Messiah. And He also stated that He is "in us" and we are "in Him" [John 14:20]. If He is in us, and we are in Him, and He has overcome the world, then we also have overcome the world. There is nothing that we will ever face in this world that Christ [in us] has not overcome. Therefore we do not have to fear or dread anything! We only have to abide in Christ, and in His love for the human family. Jesus has given us the wonderful opportunity to experience a sincere, deep peace in the midst of a world that has fallen from grace. We are not of this world [John 17:14]! If we are *of* the world, the world can beat and torment us. But if our life is hidden with Christ [Col 3:3], who sits at the right hand of God, then we are like John in the pouring rain. We can play and splash in the puddles. Our Heavenly Father loves us, and we are eternally secure.

Lord Jesus, thank You for overcoming the world, and for promising to be with us always. Thank You God for a beautiful world. Thank You for commanding us to love each other, and for empowering us with Your Holy Spirit, so that we can be successful at it.

187

ASHES AND DUST

For no other foundation can any one lay than that which is laid, which is Jesus Christ. Now if any one builds on the foundation with gold, silver, precious stones, wood, hay, straw-- each man's work will become manifest; for the Day will disclose it, because it will be revealed with fire, and the fire will test what sort of work each one has done [1Cor 3:11-13].

Take a moment to think about your day today [if this is evening] or yesterday [if you're reading this in the morning.] What are you doing with your life-energy? Each of us has a limited number of days on this earth. At the end of that time, our body will go back into the earth from which it came, and our spirit will return to the God who gave it [Eccl 12:7]. The Bible teaches that our work [the results of our life-energy] falls into one of two categories that will be "revealed with fire." Gold, silver, and precious stones are *refined* by fire. Wood, hay, and straw are *reduced to ashes* in it. Some of what I do in my limited time on this earth is going to count for absolutely nothing. Vain works, idle conversations, selfish endeavors, entertainment, trying to impress people, feathering my nest, wandering around in shopping malls, fantasies, etc.—all dust and ashes! Some of my activities are going to increase the love of God in the hearts of some people. Some people are going to draw nearer to Christ because of my influence. When I have compassion for people—when I try to help them or encourage them in all that is good—I am being the Light in their lives that Christ has ordained me to be. Their lives and the lives that are influenced by them down through the ages will be enhanced because of this holy influence. The world will be a better place because these people will be trying to love others, as Jesus has commanded us. On the "Day" of judgment, I will be so thankful for the efforts I have invested in building on the "foundation" of Jesus Christ and His love for everyone. I will know that I have invested in eternal Life—the Life of Christ Himself. I pray that there will not be too much dust and ashes when we pass through the fire of testing.

Lord, today may I invest my life-energy in that which is pleasing to You. May I love people with Your love. May I encourage them in all that is good, and may I bring harm to no one.

188

GLORIOUS, LIBERATING DETACHMENT

But I say to you, Love your enemies, bless those who curse you, do good to those who hate you, and pray for those who despitefully use you, and persecute you; That you may be the children of your Father in heaven: for he makes his sun to rise on the evil and on the good, and sends rain on the just and on the unjust [Jesus, Mt 5:44-5].

Jesus not only spoke these wonderful words, He also lived the Reality of them. From the Cross, He prayed for the forgiveness of those who betrayed, falsely accused, and tortured Him. For me personally, these have been the most powerfully liberating words that Jesus spoke. I see in this teaching the solution to the relationship problems of the human family. These words of Christ should be on bulletin boards, newspaper headings, included in every book, in every language of the world! Herein lies freedom from some of Satan's most prevalent and destructive deceptions: The lies that "My behavior is justified or determined by your behavior. My happiness and/or freedom and/or peace are determined by whether or not others do what they are supposed to. I can only love people when they act right, treat me fairly, kindly and respectfully." We must not dismiss this commandment of our Lord because it is difficult to obey. If we do not learn to live the Reality of these words, we will be victims of other peoples' behaviors and attitudes. We will be determined by them, rather than by the Holy Spirit of God's love in us. These words reveal to us that God does not want us to be determined by each other; He wants us to be determined by His love and goodness. This is how we become free. This love of Jesus is the most powerful force in the universe. It is the Power by which the universe came into existence. The Bible says that "God *is* love" [1John 1:9]. We must let this Love be the determining and motivating force of our daily lives. **This Love *liberates* us from being determined by other peoples' sinful nature manifestations.** If we learn to *live* this teaching of Christ, we get ourselves emotionally and behaviorally *detached* from all that is not yet sanctified in others. We are not determined by their attitudes, moods, behaviors, failures, meanness, insensitivities, etc. We are only determined by God's love for them and for us. God does not want us to take other peoples' sinful nature manifestations personally—*even if they are directed at us*! This is the example He has given us in Christ, Who came to set the captives free [Lk 4:18].

Lord Jesus, thank You so much for teaching and living the Truth. And thank You for showing us how to be free, and for empowering us with Your Holy Spirit that we might love—even our enemies.

189

RAINBOW PERSPECTIVE

I establish my covenant with you, that never again shall all flesh be cut off by the waters of a flood, and never again shall there be a flood to destroy the earth." And God said, "This is the sign of the covenant which I make between me and you and every living creature that is with you, for all future generations:I set my bow in the cloud, and it shall be a sign of the covenant between me and the earth [Gen 9:11-13].

In 1979 I moved my young family from a sprawling suburb of clean, family-oriented Orlando, to the relative squalor of New Orleans [the "City that Care Forgot"] to attend seminary. We moved from a four-bedroom home to an on-campus, two-bedroom, quadplex apartment. I was frequently assailed with doubts about this "calling," based on what I was exposing my family to in the "Big Easy." One day my then-youngest son Brad and I were returning from somewhere, and I parked my Volks 411 at the curb in front of our apartment. As I was walking toward the apartment, I noticed that some oil or gasoline-contaminated water was pooled alongside the curb. As I stepped widely over it, my thoughts turned toward the pollution of this city that I had moved my family into. The cancer rate in New Orleans was higher than the national average. People were speculating that the drinking water, taken from the Mississippi River, was the culprit, being contaminated with up-river industrial waste. We had moved a few times, and this was the dirtiest city in which we had lived. Additionally, the crime rate was high—a form of "social pollution" to which I was exposing my little ones. As these troubling thoughts assailed my mind, I heard Brad's voice behind me: "Daddy!" I turned and saw him squatted over the "cesspool" with a look of awe and wonder. "Look! There's a *rainbow* on this water!"

I was struck with the vast difference in our perspectives. And it began to dawn on me; *his* perspective evoked the eternal Reality of God's Covenant and promises that take precedence over all the tribulations of the human family. God is greater than all our mistakes. And He has always taken care of His children whatever the circumstances. God was speaking clearly to me, comforting me through the voice of my three-year-old, reminding me of His promises, His compassion, and watchful care.

God, thank You for Your promise to be our Savior, Sustainer, Protector and Friend. Help us to maintain a "Rainbow Perspective." And thank You so much for what You teach us through our children.

190

ALIENATION

Remember that you were at that time separated from Christ, alienated from the commonwealth of Israel, and strangers to the covenants of promise, having no hope and without God in the world. But now in Christ Jesus you who once were far off have been brought near in the blood of Christ. For he is our peace, who has made us both one, and has broken down the dividing wall of hostility, by abolishing in his flesh the law of commandments and ordinances, that he might create in himself one new man in place of the two, so making peace, and might reconcile us both to God in one body through the cross, thereby bringing the hostility to an end [Eph 2:12-16].

And because iniquity shall abound, the love of many shall wax cold [Mt 24:12].

I have had dreams in which I was separated from my loved ones, wondering around in a strange land among people that I did not know. In these dreams I felt *alienated*. It is a terrible feeling. I think there are people who feel this way in their waking life—people who have been betrayed by their mates, unloved by their parents, or are not practicing the Love of Christ for others. If you look deeply into the Christian faith, you see that it unifies people in the Love of Christ. Jesus prayed for His followers to be "one," even as He and the Father were "one" [John 17]. Everything that is contrary to the Love of Jesus alienates people: selfishness, betrayal, apathy, hatred, unforgiveness, fear, etc. All who live in His Love are family. In Christ we really do care for each other. We are safe for each other. We become friends in the truest sense of the word. My wife and I were recently re-united with a couple that we had not seen in 33 years. Since we were all Christians, it was as if our friendship had never been interrupted by time or miles. We spent hours in joyful, sometimes tearful, companionship.

If Jesus is my Lord, I can never betray or hurt anyone. I must extend His Love to everyone—even my enemies! Christ's Love enables us to understand, and inwardly *feel*, the reality of "family". As long as there are Christians on the earth, I will have a family. I will never be alone. And as Elijah discovered in his time of alienation and despair, God will never allow me to become the only true follower of Christ left in my culture. Elijah thought he was the only one left who had not sold out to a foreign god, but God revealed to him that He had seven thousand loyal devotees who had not bowed the knee to Baal [1 Kgs 19]. But even if I am allowed to temporarily be in a setting bereft of true disciples of my Lord, I will never be alone because He has promised to be with me always, "even to the end of the world" [Mt 28:20]. Just as Our Father did not leave Him alone, [John 16:32], He will never abandon us. We will never be alienated!

Lord, please continue to help us be a true family. Thank You for all who have come into Your Kingdom—for all my brothers and sisters. I pray for those who feel alienated. May they come to know the joy of Your family. May I be prepared today to extend Your Love to an alienated soul.

191

CLEAR THINKING; SOFT HEART

And the word of the L ORD *came again to Zechariah: "This is what the* L ORD *Almighty says: 'Administer true justice; show mercy and compassion to one another. Do not oppress the widow or the fatherless, the alien or the poor. In your hearts do not think evil of each other.' But they refused to pay attention; stubbornly they turned their backs and stopped up their ears. They made their hearts as hard as flint and would not listen to the law or to the words that the* L ORD *Almighty had sent by his Spirit through the earlier prophets. So the* L ORD *Almighty was very angry"* [Zec 7:8 -12 NIV]

Here is the setting: God has delivered His people from exile and commanded them to rebuild the Temple. He is speaking through Zechariah, reminding them of their ancestors' violations that had brought God's wrath and the resulting captivity. Among other things, God had commanded them not to "think evil of each other in their hearts." "But they [those who had been taken away into captivity] refused to pay attention." God released His wrath against His people because [among other violations] in their hearts, they thought evil of each other, and they hardened their hearts against His commands to the contrary.

A few years ago, Lynn [my wife] and I attended a Family Life Conference—a wonderful conference designed to help couples mature in Christ. During the conference, the Holy Spirit revealed to me that I had a "critical spirit" against Lynn. Some part of my heart was almost perpetually hardened against her and judgmental and critical of her behaviors, moods, and attitudes. When I confessed this, it was as if a wet blanket of oppression was lifted off us. I am so thankful that God revealed this sin to me, so now, when the critical spirit tries to return, as it frequently does, I recognize it quickly [usually] and keep a soft heart toward my wife. I realize that I have never, nor would I ever in a thousand years, made her a better person by being critical and hard-hearted toward her. But by taking responsibility for my critical, hard heart, I set her free from the need to defend herself, giving her renewed energy to become what God wants her to become, which, of course, is what I always have needed and desired her to be. But the process of her growth is between her and the Lord—it's none of my business. My business is to be obedient to God by loving her "as Christ loves the Church," regardless of her moods, behaviors, etc. This is a wonderful pathway!

It is very important for us to pay attention to what is in our mind and heart toward others. When we focus on loving each other and keeping our hearts soft and open toward each other, rather than being critical and judgmental of each other, we are walking in the Light of God's will.

Lord, please forgive us for being critical, judgmental and hard-hearted toward each other. Give us grace to have compassionate hearts toward all people.

192

HELP MY UNBELIEF!

"[The unclean spirit] has often cast him into the fire and into the water, to destroy him; but if you can do anything, have pity on us and help us." And Jesus said to him, "If you can! All things are possible to him who believes." Immediately the father of the child cried out and said, "I believe; help my unbelief!" [Mk 9:22-24].

Here is some comfort for us. The father of the possessed son had some love and a little faith. He wanted his son whole, and he believed that *maybe* Jesus could heal him. Some of the disciples had not been able to help the young man. Now Jesus was here, and the father said, *"If you can do anything, have pity on us and help us."* Jesus repeated his phrase, *"If you can!"* perhaps underscoring his doubt, and shifting some of the responsibility for the healing work onto the father—the work of believing. The man did the best he could perhaps. He was at least honest. He wasn't a bulwark of faith. He had some doubt mixed in. But he asked Jesus to help him with that also. *"Help my unbelief!"* And it was enough! The young man was delivered!

If we have faith the size of a mustard seed [a very small seed], Jesus says we can move mountains [Mt 17:20]. A small kernel of faith in Jesus—built upon, nourished—can move mountains of fear, selfishness, guilt, and despair.

And do you doubt? Pray the simple prayer of the loving father: "Help my unbelief."

Lord Jesus, please help us to overcome our doubt in You and all that You have promised.

193

ARE YOU GETTING YOUR NEEDS MET?

**Meanwhile the disciples besought him, saying, "Rabbi, eat."
But he said to them, "I have food to eat of which you do not know."
So the disciples said to one another, "Has any one brought him food?"
Jesus said to them, "My food is to do the will of him who sent me, and to accomplish his work...." [John 4:31-34]**

In my counseling practice, I am frequently dismayed with how some clients are focused—sometimes fixated—on getting their needs met. They complain to me, in a critical manner, of how their spouse isn't affectionate enough, frugal enough, family-oriented enough, kind enough, attentive enough, sensitive enough, etc., etc., etc. One man recently said, regarding his wife and marriage, "I just don't think it's going to work. She's just not affectionate. She'll probably be a good wife for somebody, but not for me." When I met with her, I realized that she was trying, but felt she could never get it right for him. She had committed no major outward violations of their marriage covenant: she was faithful, etc. But she wasn't meeting his *needs*.

Focusing on my *needs* creates a pull inward, toward the center of my self. I *need* something to make me feel whole, loved, and content. I am working, trying to get the *need* met. I am trying to change the world [people, their behaviors, personality, etc.] outside myself to get them to conform to what I *need*. I feel entitled to getting this *need* met. I feel my mate is obligated. If she will not conform, I see her as a failure, and begin to criticize her, emotionally punish her, or look elsewhere to get my *needs* met. How does this way-of-being compare to Christ's Way? In the above verses, Jesus was probably hungry [a basic need]. It was noon, and the disciples had gone into the village for food. When they returned with the food, they were surprised that Jesus didn't eat. He was not focused on His need, even for food. He was focused on the needs of the Samaritan woman. He was focused on fulfilling the mission assigned to Him by His Father, namely, to open our eyes to the Kingdom of God, in which we all come to understand that we are to **love** each other—not try to get our **needs** met through each other. Loving people is not the same as *needing* them. Instead of a pull inward toward the center of my self, loving people consists of goodness, kindness, compassion, and grace going *out toward them*. If my spouse [or anyone in my social network] is failing at loving me properly, Jesus does not want me to be critical of her, withdraw my love from her, and emotionally punish her [all based on my *need*]. He wants me to encourage, forgive, and be patient [based on His Love in me]. The Scripture teaches us to look to God for *all* our needs [Phil 4:19]; and to look to each other only in the love of Christ. From the human standpoint, Jesus did not get His needs met on the earth: He was misunderstood, falsely accused, rejected, abandoned, and betrayed. But He did not allow this to keep Him from loving each of us enough to sacrifice His life for our salvation. And this is the same love to which He calls each of us. Awakening into and being transformed by His love is the only way to get our needs met. What we really *need* is not to be loved, but to love. And we only have imperfect people to love. But thankfully, we have a perfect Spirit abiding in us [if we have received Christ] meeting all our needs and helping us to be successful at loving [vs. needing] people.

Lord Jesus, thank You for not letting Your personal [unmet] needs keep You from Loving me. I ask You to help me to become mature in this way also.

194

FRIENDSHIP IS VERY IMPORTANT

You are my friends if you do what I command you. No longer do I call you servants, for the servant does not know what his master is doing; but I have called you friends, for all that I have heard from my Father I have made known to you [John 15:14 -15].

And let us consider how to stir up one another to love and good works, not neglecting to meet together, as is the habit of some, but encouraging one another, and all the more as you see the Day drawing near [Heb 10:24-25].

Jesus called Himself our "friend." This is most amazing! Jesus, Who is the Word incarnate, the Son of God, Who claimed to possess "all power in heaven and earth" [Mt 28:18], regarding Whom God spoke in an audible voice from heaven saying "This is My beloved Son; hear Him" [Mt 17:5]; Who arose from the dead; Who said "I have overcome the world" [John 16:33]—this Jesus has called Himself our Friend! We are the friends of Jesus! And He teaches us how to be friends to each other. In His love, we are truly good for each other. We help and encourage each other. And we have been commanded not to neglect this endeavor of being a friend to our friends in Christ. I think God wants us to enjoy each other and to have fun together. I think He wants us to enjoy the wonderful personalities of our friends in Christ. Isn't it amazing that we are all wonderfully different! We have different perspectives and ways of responding to life's circumstances. We have different aspects of Truth to offer to each situation. Have you noticed how refreshed we are when we get together and enjoy each other? We have to be careful not to let our "religion" keep us from being authentic and enjoying life with each other. I think that is one of the mistakes the Pharisees made, and why Jesus said our righteousness must exceed theirs [Mt 5:20]. Jesus wants us to be free to enjoy the "abundant life" that He died for us to have. And He doesn't want "religion" to oppress this joy and freedom. True religion must have the effect of *enhancing* our joy and freedom. Jesus wants us to love each other, and within the context of this love, to enjoy life and enjoy each other. Otherwise, why would He have made us so diverse and interesting to each other? One of the peaceful commitments we must maintain as the friends of Jesus is to be good friends to each other. Our Lord calls us to be mindful of each other; compassionate and kind to each other; to enjoy each other; and to encourage each other in all that is good. He does not want us to be isolated or lonely. He wants us to get together and celebrate the life He has given us, and to encourage and take care of each other. What a wonderful opportunity!

Lord Jesus, thank You for being such a wonderful friend to us, and for commanding us to be friends to each other in the same manner. Help us to enjoy each other in Your love. Deliver us from pretentious religious roles. Help us to be "real."

195

ANGER

And he said to them, "Is it lawful on the Sabbath to do good or to do harm, to save life or to kill?" But they were silent. And he looked around at them with anger, grieved at their hardness of heart... [Mk 3:4-5].

In the temple he found those who were selling oxen and sheep and pigeons, and the money-changers at their business. And making a whip of cords, he drove them all, with the sheep and oxen, out of the temple; and he poured out the coins of the money-changers and overturned their tables. And he told those who sold the pigeons, "Take these things away; you shall not make my Father's house a house of trade" [John 2:14-16].

Be angry but do not sin; do not let the sun go down on your anger... [Eph 4:26].

There is a tremendous amount of unnecessary human suffering because of undisciplined anger. One of the highest marks of Christian maturity is the ability to exercise self-control when angry. We must be very careful to understand what God is saying to us about anger. He says that anger, per se, is not sinful. Jesus was angry at times in His earthly ministry. He was angry because of the hypocrisy of the Pharisees, who refused to come out into the light of truth about their hidden agendas. He was angry because of the hardness of their hearts. He was angry because they had allowed religious rules to take precedence over compassion for human suffering; and moreover, they refused to acknowledge it. They refused to look honestly at themselves. Denial angers Jesus.

Jesus was also very angry because of greed in the religious context. The "money-changers" were profiting from worshipers coming into the temple to make their sacrifices. Anytime people in religious roles or functions allow greed to take precedence over the God-human connection, Jesus is angry, and those who practice in this way place themselves in jeopardy. Greed in the religious context turns many people away from the Faith—people who might otherwise find freedom, peace, and joy in Christ. This is a very serious offense that engenders the righteous wrath of God and all His people.

Jesus' anger in both these instances was focused on dynamics that prevented people from discovering the Truth of the Kingdom. Jesus was not angry because of something someone had done to hurt Him. His anger was due to hypocrisy, denial, and the fact that the people that God loved were being blocked or misled regarding their spiritual growth. Most human anger, by contrast, has to do with a reaction to ego-injury. Like two-year-olds, we tend to strike back in anger at any one who keeps us from getting what we want, or who mistreats us in any way. We tend to take offenses personally; something Jesus did *not* do.

God allows us to be angry. There are times when it is the most appropriate emotion. But He does not allow us to sin in our anger as we are sorely tempted to do. And He requires us to get through or beyond it quickly [over night]. He does not want us to nurse it or ruminate on it, which will cause us to languish in it. He does not allow us to abuse anyone in any way. He does not allow us to be critical or hard-hearted. He wants us to speak the truth in love, get it out of our craw, forgive, and get on with the abundant, joyful, peaceful life that Christ died for us to have. He expects us to follow Christ's example by not taking offences personally; by loving our enemies; and by channeling our anger into behaviors that benefit the human family. This is a high calling, but we have His Spirit in us to make it possible.

Lord, thank you for teaching us about the difficult emotion of anger. Please help us to be angry without sinning, and to not let it smolder within us. Give us the gift of self-control, especially in our anger.

196

JOYFUL CONVICTION

And they read from the book, from the law of God, clearly; and they gave the sense, so that the people understood the reading. And Nehemi'ah, who was the governor, and Ezra the priest and scribe, and the Levites who taught the people said to all the people, "This day is holy to the LORD your God; do not mourn or weep." For all the people wept when they heard the words of the law.

Then he said to them, "Go your way, eat the fat and drink sweet wine and send portions to him for whom nothing is prepared; for this day is holy to our Lord; and do not be grieved, for the joy of the LORD is your strength"[Neh 8:8-10].

God's people had served their time in captivity to the Babylonians. The Persians had overcome the Babylonians, and Artaxerxes, the Persian king, had compassion for his Jewish servant Nehemiah, and commissioned him to return to Jerusalem to rebuild the city. At the completion of the rebuilding of the wall, the people gathered together and ceremoniously and reverently read the Law of Moses. They were convicted and began to weep and mourn, seeing how far they and their ancestors had drifted from the way of life that God had revealed to them. But Nehemiah, Ezra, and the Levites interrupted the mourning and grief. "This day is holy to the Lord your God; do not mourn or weep…for the joy of the Lord is your strength."

Whenever we allow the Holy Spirit to convict us of our sins; whenever we grieve and suffer contrition because of our selfishness and blindness, there is rejoicing in heaven, and it is a Holy and joyful day to our Lord. This is the joy of the father at the return of his prodigal son. This is the mourning that Jesus said in the Sermon on the Mount is blessed, for we shall be comforted in it. And interwoven in this mourning and sadness is a clear and strong current of joy like fresh, cleansing waters from a deep underground spring. And underneath it is a firm foundation of faith in His loving forgiveness and restorative grace. There is celebration in heaven and in all God's children on earth whenever anyone repents of his sins. And the repentant sinner is very soon brought into the light of this joyful celebration—even before his tears have dried.

Lord thank you for Your willingness to forgive me in Christ and to restore me to peace with You and with all Your people—my family. And especially thank You for the joy that blossoms in the midst of repentance.

197

THE SOLUTION CAN BECOME THE PROBLEM

And the servants of the householder came and said to him, "Sir, did you not sow good seed in your field? How then has it weeds?"
He said to them, "An enemy has done this."
The servants said to him, "Then do you want us to go and gather them?"
But he said, "No; lest in gathering the weeds you root up the wheat along with the weeds" [Mt 13:27-29].

Jesus gave us this parable, as well as many others, to help us understand life in the Kingdom—successful and peaceful life. Ripping up the weeds seemed to be a logical solution to the problem. But the master of the house [symbolic of God or godly wisdom] realized that if the servants did so, they would do more harm than good. They had to let the evil seeds grow, intertwined with the good, for a while. They had to wait until the harvest. Then the matter would be resolved.

In my counseling practice I have frequently seen misery caused by an obsessive need to right some wrong, get someone to "be honest," show appreciation, or "love me better"—generally speaking, to change some uncontrollable situation or relationship dynamic. They are trying to rip up the weeds. Their rationale is logical on a shallow level: "The situation is evil! It should not be happening! God would not want it to be this way! Those weeds should not be growing with the wheat! The householder did not plant them, and he does not want them there. I have to rip them up! I am entitled to the truth! My mate should be more loving!" Etc. And, of course, on the superficial level, they are correct. But from the wisdom standpoint, they are dead wrong, and their misery is the evidence of it. There are some wrongs that can be righted, and they should be. There are injustices that can be brought to justice, and they should be. But there are some crevices that evil can creep into and operate from that are not yet accessible to human effort, like cancer cells that have invaded critical organs, making surgery impossible. In these cases we have to take a different approach, maintain peace, wait upon the Lord, trust that justice and truth are eventually unavoidable, refocus our efforts in more fruitful directions, and get ourselves free from the compulsive need for immediate results.

Lord, thank You so much for revealing these truths to us, and for the freedom and peace they bring to us

198

WHAT IS TRUTH?

Pilate said to him, "So you are a king?" Jesus answered, "You say that I am a king. For this I was born, and for this I have come into the world, to bear witness to the truth. Everyone who is of the truth hears my voice."
Pilate said to him, "What is truth?" [John 18:37-38a].

This is perhaps the greatest question posed by humans. Philosophy seeks the answer in the world of thoughts, concepts, and ideologies. Science seeks it in the material, measurable, observable world. Psychology seeks truth in the context of the mind, behavior, and emotions. Theology seeks to accurately determine the truth that God has revealed to us in revelation to the prophets through the ages. It is wise to seek the truth. We have come to know that we can get lost in the world; we can become entangled and bogged down in all manner of meaninglessness.

One of my favorite comic series is Gary Larson's *The Far Side*. In one cartoon he depicts a herd of lemmings rushing off into the ocean. One of them, near the rear of the herd, has an inner tube around him. *That* lemming took time to *seek the truth*.

One of the many bold statements Jesus made to help us understand that He is the Messiah is: "I am the... truth" [Jn14:6]. Those of us who have received Him have increasingly come to believe and know that He is. But what does it mean that Jesus is *the truth*? There are many ways we could attempt to answer that question; in fact the living out of our daily lives in Christ is perhaps the most significant answer. Those of us who abide in Christ abide in Truth. He commands us to love all people, even our enemies. His Spirit sustains us through all life's difficulties, reminding us to "be of cheer" because He has "overcome the world" [Jn 16:33]. We know that we are not perfect, but He died for our freedom from guilt. We are perpetually forgiven, and we perpetually forgive those who hurt or mistreat us in any way. We do not fear man or what he can do to us, but we love him, and work for the best for him. We are willing to confront evil and injustice [as He did], but we do not allow ourselves [He does not allow us] to become bitter or hopeless. And we do not return evil for evil [1Th 5:15], but overcome evil with good [Rm 12:21]. We do not harbor grudges. We confess our sins, admit our mistakes, take responsibility for them, and seek His help in overcoming them. We gratefully receive the gift of the peace He perpetually offers us [Jn 14:27]. No matter how many times we fall or fail, He helps us up and forgives us. We do not presume upon His grace, but do the best we can to get better, day-by-day, at being honest, compassionate, and responsible servants of God and man. We do not expect life to be easy—He told us it would not be—but we know that the Big Picture is very good: that's why it's called the "Gospel," which means *"good* news." We realize that we are being healed and delivered from the wounds and effects of the evil in which we have been immersed in this world. We understand, as never before, that we are not "of this world," as He is not [Jn17:14]. And perhaps most amazingly, without putting on blinders to anything from the dark side, we are surprised, over and over, by joy springing up inside us, as from an internal artesian well. Within the context of what Jesus has revealed to us—living in Him—we discover that the world is a beautiful, temporary home, infiltrated by evil, which we overcome in Him as we practice, imperfectly, but increasingly better, the principles that He lived and taught. God is good. All is well. This is the Truth.

Lord Jesus, it is most amazing to us what you have revealed and are continuing to reveal to us. Thank you for bringing the Truth to the human family. Help us to live according to this glorious, liberating Truth, better today than ever before.

199

BE GENEROUS

Then the King will say to those at his right hand, "Come, O blessed of my Father, inherit the kingdom prepared for you from the foundation of the world; for I was hungry and you gave me food, I was thirsty and you gave me drink, I was a stranger and you welcomed me, I was naked and you clothed me, I was sick and you visited me, I was in prison and you came to me."

Then the righteous will answer him, "Lord, when did we see thee hungry and feed thee, or thirsty and give thee drink? And when did we see thee a stranger and welcome thee, or naked and clothe thee? And when did we see thee sick or in prison and visit thee?"

And the King will answer them, "Truly, I say to you, as you did it to one of the least of these my brethren, you did it to me" [Mt 25:34 -40].

In the story from which these verses were taken, Jesus reveals that we will be judged according to how generous we have been with our fellow humans who are in need. Psalm 41:1 reads *"Blessed is he who considers the poor; the Lord will deliver him in time of trouble."* And Jesus teaches that it is *"more blessed to give than to receive"* [Acts 20:35]. God is indescribably generous.

The earth that He created is bountiful enough to provide for everyone upon it, even at our current population. Jesus gave His life for our salvation. We cannot say that we are Christians and be tightfisted with our material blessings and miserly of heart. Fear and greed motivate hoarding of wealth. Christ's love compels us to consider the needs of others in our world, and to discover the joy and freedom of generosity. Everything that we hoard and store up becomes a responsibility to us or to those who inherit it—to be a good steward of it. It can become a source of worry for us if we are attached to it. If we give our children a material inheritance and do not teach them to be generous, the inheritance will not be a true blessing to them. It can become a means for them to deteriorate spiritually. Everything that we give becomes treasure in heaven that will never be lost. A good gift, rightly given to one in true need, is a great joy to the giver and receiver. It is hard to imagine a better investment than this type of investment in the human family. As Christians, we have the God-ordained obligation to think carefully about how we manage our material blessings and whether we are being generous and helpful to others in need. We must pray and ask God for prudence and wisdom, so that our giving most efficiently serves the needy and glorifies His Kingdom. It is important to cultivate a generous heart so that we are *always* giving the gifts of kindness, compassion, grace, forgiveness, and encouragement in our daily living, for even if we do not have material needs, we are all in need of these gifts of the heart.

Lord thank You for Your unspeakable generosity toward us. Please forgive us for not being generous to each other, and help us to be more so. May the bounty of this earth be shared fairly with all its inhabitants. And may we be generous of heart to all whom we encounter today.

200

LIVING THE FAITH

For as the body without the spirit is dead, so faith without works is dead also [Jam 2:2].

If you know these things, happy are you if you do them [Jesus, John 13:17].

None of us live the Christian faith perfectly; and we should be dancing every day because Christ died so that we don't have to feel guilty or scared because of it. But we are deceiving ourselves and missing out on the abundant life that Jesus promised if we are not *living differently* because of our faith in God through Christ. What we truly believe affects how we live. If I believe that Jesus is the Messiah, then I not only hear, but also *heed* His teachings. James said that even the devils also *believe* in one God, and tremble in fear because of Him [Jam 2:19]. But they don't *act* according to their belief—they do not submit to His lordship and apply themselves to His teachings. The Christian faith, in order to be real, must be practiced daily. The teachings [the *Spirit*] of our Lord must permeate every cell in our body and penetrate to the bones of our soul if we are going to experience peace, joy, freedom, and abundant life. We have the opportunity to move more deeply into the Reality of the Gospel [the *Good* News] every day. Every day we can emerge, like a butterfly from its cocoon, shaking off the worries and cares of the world, faithfully facing our fears, choosing to take on the challenge of loving people, guarding our hearts from the penetrating darts of the evil one, holding on to hope and the knowledge that our lives in Christ have eternal significance. Every moment we have the opportunity to awaken to how blessed we are; to be thankful for food, clothing, and shelter, and to be content with these blessings. Every day offers more beauty than we can perceive, and it is a gift from our Creator—a constant reminder of His love for us. No day is without some opportunity to push back the darkness of evil in some arena; to brighten up the world with more of Jesus' Light and Love. Every day offers the marvelous gift of another opportunity to be a joyful servant of God and man in our corner of the world.

There is something that you can do today—perhaps right now—that will be a wonderful manifestation of God's love to someone [a touch of the hand, a kind word, a gift to a worthy charity, an encouragement to forgive, a refusal to enter into gossip, a card to someone, some patient attention, etc.]. May the Lord bless us to peacefully *practice* our faith in Him, and to experience the joy He promised.

Lord, thank You for Your glorious Truth. Help us to live and move and breathe in Your Holy Spirit today. Help us to live in accordance with Your teachings, and to do some good for the advancement of Your Kingdom today.

201

LIVING PEACEFULLY

And the effect of righteousness will be peace and the result of righteousness, quietness and trust forever. My people will abide in a peaceful habitation, in secure dwellings, and in quiet resting places [Isa 32:17-18].

    I have grown up in what might turn out to be the "Golden Age" of America. My childhood in central Alabama in the 50's and 60's was ideal, peaceful, secure, nurturing, and free. I know this is attributable primarily to growing up in a country, and more specifically, family and community that had been shaped [not perfected] by Judeo-Christian ideals. Everyone in my community was a Christian, or had respect for the Christian faith. The concept of atheism was unheard of in my world. If you had doubts about God, you weren't public about it. Everyone that I knew seemed to have respect for God and the Christian faith—even non-church-goers. Anti-social acts were shameful, and caused one to be excluded from the good graces of the community—something to be avoided like the plague. Of course evil was lurking, as always, in the darkness, but there was pressure to keep it there—under cover in the darkness. Meanwhile people felt compelled to be kind and to keep their shameful demons out of the light. They confessed their sins in church on Sunday, and did the best they could to avoid them during the rest of the week. This created an atmosphere of peace—a good place to grow up.

    I fear what might happen to America if we become uprooted from our Christian heritage and principles. We have seen dreadful examples, all throughout history, of what humans can do to each other in blind, atheistic philosophies, and fanatic religiosity. Christianity is safe because it is bound to One Who commands His followers to love their enemies, and teaches us that our battles are not against flesh and blood, but against our own sinful tendencies toward selfishness, cruelty, meanness, lust and greed. Christ causes parents to teach their children to be fair and kind to their peers, rather than to compete against them for human praise and material reward. Christianity, properly lived out, causes boys to become men who are faithful to their wives and good to their children; and women to be graceful, nurturing, and kind. Jesus helps us understand that God loves all people and holds us accountable for how we treat them. Christ helps all who know Him to realize that they have a sinful nature to overcome, and that they need God's help in doing it. When the majority of people in any community are sincerely trying to live according to the Truth that Jesus revealed about God and His Kingdom, they ***abide in a peaceful habitation, in secure dwellings, and in quiet resting places.***

God, please help us hear and heed what You have revealed to us through Your Son, the Messiah, Jesus Christ—that we might have peace.

202

OUR DIVIDED WORLD

For whoever is ashamed of me and of my words in this adulterous and sinful generation, of him will the Son of man also be ashamed, when he comes in the glory of his Father with the holy angels [Mk 8:38].

For I am not ashamed of the gospel: it is the power of God for salvation to everyone who has faith, to the Jew first and also to the Greek [Rom 1:16].

Because of secularism unprecedented in the history of this nation and a misunderstanding and mis-application of the doctrine of "separation of church and state," there is a conspicuous split in ourselves and our culture between our inner faith and our way of being in the world. I am among the 80 plus percent of Americans who believe in God, Christ, heaven, and hell. Yet when my son walks out the door to do his socializing, I say "Have fun" or "Be careful," rather than "Go with God," or "Remember who you are in Christ." The latter statements would be more true to my heart, but much less socially acceptable, much more likely to make me feel "preachy"—like an old religious fogy. It is somehow very uncool to be religious. Our television stations are a visible example of the split between religion and secularism. Programming is either 100% secular (with only critical or demeaning references to religion) or 100% religious (to the point of overdosing the audience in short order) with minimal blending of the two. And in the world of movies, one is much more likely to see a movie derived from literature that is covertly anti-Christian [currently *Beowulf* and The *Golden Compass*] than from a pro-Christian perspective [*Amazing Grace*]. I found a copy of my 1967 high school graduation program. It included prayers, hymns, and other Christian references that would be a violation of current interpretations of separation of church and state. And yet I can say, definitely, that that yeast of Christianity mixed into my public education has been immeasurably valuable to my inner sense of well-being, gratitude, and personal balance in life and of my ability to do less harm and more good for my fellow man. I thank God for it, and I lament my sons' loss of it in these more religiously suppressed times. Our Christian faith tends to be pushed into a quiet corner by the secular powers of our times. We can easily enough be Christians at church on Sunday, but God forbid that we should utter a word about Christ in a business meeting or at a football game. [What has He to do with those endeavors?] Or even in our own living rooms! We are ashamed to do so! It would feel like trying to force a square peg into a round hole. In the core of our beings, we believe that God created this world, in whatever way our scientists discover that it has evolved and is unfolding, yet our outward manifestations are as secular as an unbeliever. Jesus is a little embarrassing for us. He makes people feel uncomfortable. So we carry on as if we were atheists—except for our Sunday gatherings. Jesus warned us that judgment looms over our shame of Him and our cowardice to be who we truly are in Him.

Lord Jesus, please forgive us for keeping a low profile to avoid embarrassment. Help us to remember that this world desperately needs Your love, truth, peace, joy, salvation, and eternal life. Grant us the courage and faith to let Your light shine brightly; to heal the split within ourselves and our world.

203

IS IT ABOUT YOU, OR IS IT ABOUT US?

Then Jesus told his disciples, "If any man would come after me, let him deny himself and take up his cross and follow me. For whoever would save his life will lose it, and whoever loses his life for my sake will find it [Mt 16:24].

...The second [commandment] is this, "You shall love your neighbor as yourself." [Jesus, Mk 12:31].

The first sentence in Rick Warren's phenomenal book, The Purpose-Driven Life, is, "It's not about you." This is a very important biblical truth that we must all come to understand. One of the greatest spiritual battles that we must be seriously engaged in if we want to be free in Christ is the battle against ego or self-centeredness. This is a gargantuan struggle that continues as long as we live on this earth. We all start out primarily concerned with our *self*—our needs, desire for comfort and praise, etc. We want to be first in line, first to be picked in team sports, the class favorite, most popular, captain of the team, head cheerleader, etc. We compete against our own brothers and sisters for the attention and praise of our parents. Just like James's and John's mother, we want our children to be honored above other peoples' children [Mt.20:20]. All this is egocentric—me and mine over you and yours. Obeying Christ's second great commandment involves us in the process of overcoming this natural but counter-productive tendency. In Christ we begin to understand that life doesn't work if we compete from the egocentric standpoint. I cannot be just for me. I have to be for you also—and those whom you love, as well those I love. My circle of concern must expand beyond myself and those who are close and similar to me. It must embrace the whole family of humankind. God loves me and is deeply concerned for me, but He is equally concerned for those who are very different from me and difficult for me to understand and identify with. He loves those who have different political and even religious views. He did not want the Ninevites to perish, and sent a reluctant and apathetic Jonah to preach to them and give them the opportunity to live. Jonah, like us, was more concerned with his personal comfort and self-image than with the lives of the Ninevites. He avoided the difficult task of caring for others, and ended up in the belly of a fish. He lamented the loss of his little vine, providing shade from the sun, and he was indignant toward God for not punishing the Ninevites, even though they had repented, because God's willingness to forgive contradicted Jonah's fire and brimstone preaching. [How dare God?!] Jesus forbids me to allow my desire for good things for myself to take precedence over the legitimate needs of others in our world. He continually reminds me that I am not the center of His universe. I am loved by Him, and He provides for me beyond my ability to comprehend and be thankful enough for. But He has equal love for others and requires me to perpetually rise above selfish concerns into the joyful and deeply gratifying atmosphere of love for them. We are so thankful that God has required us to love each other, and given us His Spirit to empower us to overcome our deeply-ingrained selfishness.

Lord Jesus, thank You so much for delivering us from the prison cell of self-centeredness into the glorious light and freedom of Your love-for-all. Please help me remember that life is not about me, but about us.

204

THE GIFT OF PEACE: [A CHRISTMAS DEVOTIONAL]

Peace I leave with you; my peace I give to you; not as the world gives do I give to you. Let not your hearts be troubled, neither let them be afraid [Jesus, John 14:27].

Glory to God in the highest, and on earth peace, good will toward men [Lk 2:14].

  Jesus gives us great gifts—unspeakably wonderful gifts! He is Himself a gift from God to us, and we are eternally thankful to God for the gift of His Son and to Jesus for His willingness to become the gift of abundant and eternal life to us. This is why we give gifts at Christmas, the time set aside by our ancestors to celebrate Jesus' birth. We do not know exactly the time of year that Jesus was actually born, but it doesn't matter. How wonderful that *this* time of year was chosen—the darkest and coldest season—to celebrate His birth. Because of Christ we light up our world in the darkest month, and we warm our hearts in His love in the coldest season of the year. The love of Jesus lights up our world and warms our hearts. We will always be receiving gifts from the infinite storehouse of God's love, manifested to us through Christ, our Lord. As we mature, we are able to see more deeply into God's goodness and love, and we already know there is no end to these, just as there is no end to the universe He spoke into existence. Our heart is surprised, awakened, and renewed over and over again with the goodness of God. We are like children waking up on Christmas morning to many gifts under the tree. Even if we grew up poor or in unloving homes, in Christ we have become rich, and we have love lavished upon us from all directions. The whole world and life itself, even with all its problems, is a multi-media, never-ending message of God's love to us: the incredible beauty of nature, manhood and womanhood, children, our amazing bodies, our senses, consciousness, our family in Christ, our victory in Him over all the dark forces of evil and even death itself which is our final victory!

  Because of the gift of Christ, we have peace in our hearts. We are no longer conflicted within ourselves. We know that we have a sinful nature, and it is not good, and we cannot do all the good that we wish that we could. And we do certain things that we know are not good. We cannot be perfect, no matter how hard we try. But Jesus has died for our sins! Our faith in Him sets us free. As recorded in Romans 5:1, *Therefore being justified by faith, we have peace with God through our Lord Jesus Christ.* And because of our devotion to Jesus, even though we are not perfect, we see that we are getting better. Day by day His Holy Spirit in us encourages the good, convicts regarding the bad, forgives, reminds us to love, and keeps us on a heavenly path. Jesus wants us to have peace. He gave us *His* peace [John 14:27 (above)]. When He was born the Heavenly Host proclaimed *"peace on earth, good will toward man."* We do not have to worry anymore. We are realizing that in Christ, there is nothing to worry about. He reminds us to *"let not your heart be troubled,"* about *anything*! He helps us love each other better and better, day by day, and we know that this is our purpose for being here. Jesus enables us to have peace with God. Peace with God enables us to be at peace within ourselves. Peace with self enables us to have peace with others. Our sincere desire is to abide deeply—ever more deeply—in this peace and love of Christ, and that it will continue to spread throughout our world. This is the Kingdom of God. This is what we celebrate at Christmas.

May the peace of God, which passes all understanding, keep your hearts and minds through Jesus Christ our Lord. May His love and joy fill your heart as never before this Christmas, and increase, in you and in our world, throughout the coming year.

205

COME AND SEE!

Philip found Nathan'a-el, and said to him, "We have found him of whom Moses in the law and also the prophets wrote, Jesus of Nazareth, the son of Joseph."

Nathan'a-el said to him, "Can anything good come out of Nazareth?" Philip said to him, "Come and see" [John 1:45-46].

Jesus' first two followers were previous disciples of John the Baptist, who sent them to Him. One of them was Andrew, who brought his brother, Simon Peter, to Jesus. Jesus Himself invited Philip to follow Him, and Philip told his reluctant friend Nathanael [probably the same as Bartholomew] to "come and see" this One of Whom Moses and the prophets had written—this Jesus of Nazareth. Nathanael was promptly convinced that Jesus was indeed the "Son of God" and the "King of Israel" [John1:49]. The very fact that Andrew was John's disciple reveals that he was seeking the truth. Jesus draws those to Him who are seeking the truth. What is it about Jesus that caused these men of diverse personalities and vocations to not only drop everything and follow Him, but also actively seek to introduce their friends and relatives to him? How did they come to know that He was the Messiah? What caused Simon Peter to come to know that Jesus had the "words of eternal life"? [John 6:68]. If you have become a disciple of Christ yourself, you have the inward, indescribable answer to this question. It is the same mysterious Spirit that has drawn us all to Christ, and that causes us to continue to invite others to, "Come and see!" Jesus calls the world to Himself through those whom He has given freedom, peace, and joy. We see in Jesus the answer to the world's questions and the solution to the world's problems. We feel deeply, as we sit in His presence and hear His teachings, that God—the God of this universe—is speaking words of eternal life to us. This feeling grows into an ever-deepening conviction within us that has a life of its own—that we do not have to strain to maintain—that becomes in us a "well of water, springing up to eternal life," just as He said [John 4:14]. Like the first disciples, we go to our brothers and friends. Like the Samaritan woman at the well, we run into the village and say "Come and see! Come and see this Jesus of Nazareth! Could it be that He is the One spoken of by Moses and the prophets? Could He be the Messiah? Come and see, and judge for yourself!" And those who are sincerely interested in eternal Truth—who are not so caught up in transient, vain, and ultimately futile pursuits—will take the time to come and check out the One Who made the incredible assertion "I am the...Truth" [John 14:6]. And if they are blessed, they will feel what we have felt in His presence: unspeakable Love. And they will hear what we have heard in His words: the voice of God. They will discover what we have discovered in Him: abundant life, peace, and joy. And they will see Him Whom we have seen: the Messiah!

Come and see! Come and see!

Lord, please give us a sincere love for those whom You would call to Yourself through us. Teach us to be worthy and proficient in inviting all to "come and see." And may they see You as You are

206

OVERCOMING

For I do not do the good I want, but the evil I do not want is what I do. Now if I do what I do not want, it is no longer I that do it, but sin which dwells within me [Rom 7:19-20].

We have a sinful nature. It is very important for us to always remember this. Unless a miracle happens, we will never be rid of our sinful nature. If an angel appears and tells you that God has eliminated your sinful nature and you are now perfected in Christ, look carefully and prayerfully and deeply into that angel, and I think you will see Satan. Christ died because you and I have a sinful nature that we cannot overcome. I cannot overcome my sinful nature. Only Christ, in me, is capable of overcoming my sinful nature. Without Christ, some aspect of my sinful nature will eventually overcome me, and Satan will use the doorway of my sinful nature to hurt me and my loved ones. Seven years into my marriage, I committed adultery because I have a sinful nature. I was a Christian at the time, but I was not strong in the Lord, and Satan used my sinful nature to hurt me, my wife, my children, and the woman with whom I committed adultery—all for a few minutes of pleasure. Satan hates love, commitment, goodness, and everything that leads to joy and peace. And he operates, in his stealing, killing, and destroying missions, through the sinful natures of humans. It is my responsibility to make sure that I am abiding in Christ so that Satan cannot use my sinful nature [my weakness and blindness] to steal, kill, and destroy the peace, joy, and abundant life that Christ died for us all to enjoy. If I am abiding in Christ, I am perpetually mindful that God loves me and everyone with whom I have to do. Jesus will not let me do anything to hurt, deceive, or betray anyone. We are infinitely thankful to Him for this wonderful service that He renders to us. He enables us to be safe for our loved ones. He teaches us how to genuinely love all people—even our enemies. As I maintain communion with Jesus, the greatest Friend of the human family, He gives me the gift of His love for all people. In this love, and only in this love, I am safe from Satan's deceptions. Satan cannot use me for his sinister purposes. Everything that humans do to hurt, use, or deceive others, is evidence of the reality of Satan and of our sinful nature. The daily news is resplendent with evidence of evil. In Christ our sincere desire is to be agents of good rather than evil. He ordains and empowers us to be light in the world—not darkness. And as we continue to abide in Him, we bring more and more of His goodness into the world and less and less of Satan's ruin. This is the great joy of our lives. This is our purpose for being in the world. Everything comes into its proper perspective as we allow Christ to bring our lives into the Kingdom of His love for all. He has overcome the world of evil [John 16:33]. And we are in Him [John 14:20]. In Him we have overcome, and we are overcoming, the world. We are overcoming our selfish and blind usefulness to the prince of this world—the enemy of our souls. We are perpetually offering ourselves as joyful, living sacrifices to God in the service of His Kingdom of love for all.

Lord Jesus, we can never fully express our gratitude to You for what You have done, and are continuing to do, for each of us and for the human family. May Your name be praised forever and ever! Please continue to keep us from evil.

207

THE END

...men fainting with fear and with foreboding of what is coming on the world; for the powers of the heavens will be shaken. And then they will see the Son of man coming in a cloud with power and great glory. Now when these things begin to take place, look up and raise your heads, because your redemption is drawing near [Jesus, Lk 21:26-28].

"First the elms will die. Then the maples. Then the fish will go belly up in poison waters. The strawberries will no longer bear fruit, and then our world will be close to dying." Tom Porter, a Bear Clan Chief and spiritual leader of the Mohawks.

People of all cultures and religions realize the earth will perish. Science tells us the sun will wax hotter and burn up the earth. This concurs with what is written in 2 Peter 3:10: *and the elements shall melt with fervent heat, the earth also and the works that are therein shall be burned up.* Everything in the universe is in a state of flux and change. Every living organism dies. Cataclysmic events have occurred in the history of the earth, and more will occur. Scientists have presented a number of scenarios depicting how they might: an airborne virus; nuclear war, ozone depletion, depletion of earth's resources due to over-population, collision with a comet, etc. A time will come when the earth and everything on it will be no more. God apparently wants us to be aware of this reality. He has placed it in His Word for the human family. Awareness of the transient nature of the earth and all physical existence helps us to be mindful of the awesome beauty and goodness of life—the unspeakable gift of simply being here. The barrenness of space also helps us appreciate what God has given us here on the earth. Our newly acquired ability to destroy it can awaken us to how precious and vulnerable the earth is; how marvelously adapted it is to provide everything we need for life and beauty. The atmosphere of the earth is like a nurturing womb, protecting us from the lethal forces impinging on its boundaries. And yet it will perish, despite our best efforts to preserve it. [And we should certainly make these efforts, with all diligence. God forbid that humans should be the cause of the demise of the earth.]

How are we to respond to the knowledge that the "powers of the heavens will be shaken" and "the earth and everything in it shall be burned up"? Jesus said that many will faint with fear and foreboding. But He commanded His friends, those who have received Him, when that time comes, to "look up, for your redemption draws near!" This is a most amazing and comforting teaching for us! We may die before a cataclysmic event or the end of the world happens. Or we may be called by God to endure or witness it. In either case, it is important for us to teach our children the truth about these possibilities, so that they and their children will benefit from the awareness, and so they will not be afraid. Jesus wants us to be prepared for anything that might happen. And He does not want us to fear. He is with us always. We are eternally safe in Christ, no matter what happens. We want future generations to know this. One of them will have to endure "the end." At that time we want them to "look up" and embrace their new beginning with those of us who have already crossed over into the heavenly adventure!

Lord, grant us grace to live in peaceful, perpetual preparedness for anything that might happen to us personally, to the human family, or to this beautiful earth You have given for a temporary home. You are our eternal security. We neither have nor need any other.

208

NEW YEAR; NEW LIFE

Therefore, if anyone is in Christ, he is a new creation; old things have passed away; behold, all things have become new [2Cor 5:17].

There is something fresh and inspirational about newness. Newborn infants delight us. New toys brighten up our children's lives. [And we adults like our new "toys" also.] Our senses are awakened when we try new culinary dishes, or visit places we've never seen, meet new friends, or have new experiences. We bring in the New Year with fireworks and celebration and with hope of prosperity in all facets of life. There is something in us that strains against routine, sameness—the "old" ways. Each generation wants to bring some newness into the culture and does so by dressing differently, decorating their bodies differently, and cultivating new idiosyncrasies. [The previous generation usually labels some of them "idiot-sincrazies".] Obviously, there are good and evil ways to introduce newness into life. There are certain principles that are eternal, and anything "new" that violates them depreciates the culture. This is one of the reasons that Christ, our faith, and some religious traditions are so important to us. They keep us anchored in all that is good, true, meaningful, and healthy for the human family. Jesus keeps us from drifting in treacherous directions, as we have seen happen countless times in human history and in our own lives. The word "religion" derives from Latin words meaning *"to bind back."* True religion is liberating *because* it *binds* us to eternal Truth and *constrains* us from deceptive evil that ultimately enslaves and destroys life.

    We must be very careful, however, to *balance* the "binding," "constraining," and traditional nature of our Faith with a deepening understanding of God's appreciation of *newness.* Our Creator knows that we need newness, freshness, novelty, adventure, and innovation; and He has provided more of it than we will ever be able to experience within the context of our life in Christ. In fact, outside of Christ, everything eventually loses its luster, dries up, and ceases to refresh. But, as our brother the apostle Paul came to understand [and experience] in Christ *everything is new!* In the same sense that you can never put your foot in the same river twice, life, like a river, is constantly changing. Jesus awakens us to the eternal freshness of life, and He reminds us that there are ever-new opportunities and means of loving people. We will never be without an opportunity to love. And love is always as fresh as the first light of dawn! In Christ we are perpetually new! His Spirit in us is like an artesian well, springing up to eternal life [John 4:14]. Our inner self is being renewed day by day [2 Cor 4:16]. May we enter this New Year with a deep awareness of the ever-newness of Life in Christ, and with a sincere commitment to avoid dullness and boredom, and to stay alive with the abundant life of Christ, in Whom life is always interesting, challenging, and meaningful.

Lord thank You for providing for all the needs of our soul, especially the need for newness. Please deliver us from the delusions of boredom and dullness, into the Light of Your ever-fresh, cutting-edge love for all people.

209

DON'T WORRY. BE HAPPY.

And [the other seeds] are the ones sown among thorns; they are those who hear the word, but the cares of the world, and the delight in riches, and the desire for other things, enter in and choke the word, and it proves unfruitful [Jesus, Mk 4:18-19].

These things I have spoken unto you, that in me ye might have peace. In the world ye shall have tribulation: but be of good cheer; I have overcome the world [Jesus, John 16:33].

It seems that the more we have, the more potential we have for worry. Perhaps it's because we have more to lose from the worldly standpoint. I once counseled a man who had attained his goal of early retirement. He had accumulated a fortune by investing in the stock market. When I saw him, the economy was in a severe downturn, and he was one of the most miserable men I have ever met. I feared he might commit suicide. His wife was threatening to leave him because he was making her miserable also with his compulsive worrying about how much he was losing each day and of the prospect of having to return to work after so many years of retirement. I was struck by the irony of the fact that he brushed shoulders every day with scores of people who had never dreamed of owning as much money as he still had in his accounts, and yet they were ecstatically happy by comparison. Any of them would have gladly exchanged financial positions with him. I think that, in a prosperous culture such as ours, one of the primary spiritual battles Christians must fight is the battle alluded to by Jesus above—the battle against the worries and cares of the world and the desire for or attachment to riches. At this writing, our economy is in a downswing. There's talk of recession. And I can imagine millions of people fearfully eyeing their retirement accounts. I certainly have. And even though there's not much to worry about there, I still discern within myself this gravitational pull into an oppressed, worried heart. We worry about healthcare, living arrangements, our ability to be independent when we can no longer work, etc. Thankfully, the Holy Spirit, activated by the Word, prayer, and meditation, reminds us of the futility and weakness of worry. Jesus, who did not own a single significant earthly possession, said that He would give us *His Joy* and *Peace*! [John. 15:11; 14:27] God has promised to supply *all* our need [Philippians 4:19]. The aspects of our personality that are still attached to material possessions for security are constantly in jeopardy of worry, for there is never quite enough security in that realm. We always need just a little more, or there is always the threat of loss that can never be completely shut out. Jesus is our *only* security. There is no other security but Jesus. Paul sums it up nicely for us in 1Tim 6:6-11:

There is great gain in godliness with contentment; for we brought nothing into the world, and we cannot take anything out of the world, but if we have food and clothing, with these we shall be content. But those who desire to be rich fall into temptation, into a snare, into many senseless and hurtful desires that plunge men into ruin and destruction. For the love of money is the root of all evils; it is through this craving that some have wandered away from the faith and pierced their hearts with many pangs. But as for you, man of God, shun all this; aim at righteousness, godliness, faith, love, steadfastness, gentleness.

May this be our aim. And may the peace of Christ attend us every step of the way, no matter what happens to the economy.

Lord, thank You for Your teachings and example regarding materialism and possessions. May we abide always in Your eternal security, peace, and love.

210

GET A LIFE!

For you have died, and your life is hid with Christ in God. When Christ who is our life appears, then you also will appear with him in glory [Col 3:3-4].

As we grow in the Spirit, we begin to understand more and more clearly [as did our brother Paul] that *Christ* **is** *our life*. Can you affirm that truth deeply to yourself? Can you say, and really mean it, "Jesus *is* my life. I have no other life than Jesus. Jesus is all in all, and everything that I will ever need."?

One aspect of our sanctification is the drawing up of all our life-energies into Christ. If we look carefully at our lives, we see that we are scattered among many endeavors: Buying and selling, paying bills, working, entertainment and pleasure, fantasies and sexuality, worries or concerns about finances, retirement, or health, relationship concerns or difficulties, etc. These concerns, though not necessarily evil in themselves, may or may not have anything to do with Christ. It depends on our mindfulness [or perhaps better stated, *heartfulness*]. Are we bringing His Presence into our daily activities? When we shop, are we careful to express God's love to the cashier? At restaurants, are we sending out His love to the waiter/ress? Do we express thanks to Him for our food, being mindful that many in the world are hungry? And are we doing anything to help those hungry ones? Do we seek to abide in His Spirit in our parenting endeavors, or simply survive the day? Do we pray about how to use our daily energies most lovingly, joyfully, and peacefully? Do we respond to His spirit as we converse with others, or do we get lost in our egoistic concerns about what they will think of us? Generally, are we mindful of Christ's Presence with us as we go about the business of daily living? Does His love motivate us, or are we motivated by something less: Fear of loss, desire for more possessions, worldly acclaim or the praise of men? Perhaps we are simply going through the motions of a routine to which we have become habituated, without much vitality or eternal significance. Jesus constantly awakens us [if we turn toward Him] from meaningless routines and from the lower motivations of life. He awakens us into His vibrant Love, which is always on the cutting edge of life; a here and now Reality that perpetually challenges and enlivens us, and empowers us to enhance the lives of those around us—to bring Light into whatever forms of darkness they may be experiencing, awakening joy within us—the joy of servanthood. The business of Christ is the business of our life. More and more, we should be able to honestly say, "Christ is my life."

Lord Jesus, You are my life; all else is passing away. My life is hidden within Your eternal goodness, grace, love, joy, and peace. Please continue to deliver me from the various ways that I tend to get lost in this world. Please keep awakening me into all that is truly alive, free, meaningful, and eternal. May Your Light shine brightly through me today.

211

SATAN'S HATRED

If the world hates you, know that it has hated me before it hated you. If you were of the world, the world would love its own; but because you are not of the world, but I chose you out of the world, therefore the world hates you...If I had not done among them the works which no one else did, they would not have sin; but now they have seen and hated both me and my Father. It is to fulfill the word that is written in their law, "They hated me without a cause" [Jesus, John 15:18-19,24-25].

They are like children sitting in the marketplace, and calling one to another, and saying, we have piped to you, and you have not danced; we have mourned to you, and you have not wept [Jesus, Lk 7:32].

Evil manifests as hatred toward anyone who genuinely gets himself—by God's grace—free from the psycho-spiritual entanglements and attachments of the world. Satan hates, condemns, and tries to destroy what he cannot control, use, or intimidate. He hates freedom. At its lower levels, we see this as envy of anyone who seems to be doing better than us. If a brother or sister is being praised or gifted by our parent, our sinful nature tends to feel belittled, deprived, and smolders in resentment [perhaps behind a smiling face.] If someone is trying to live righteously, he or she may be mockingly labeled a "goody two-shoes," "Pollyanna," or accused of having a "holier-than-thou attitude." Christians are frequently labeled "intolerant" because they are trying to live by the Scriptures. This is the same hatred that caused Cain to murder his brother Able [Genesis 4]. It is the same evil hatred that convulsed in Haman's soul when Mordecai did not show him reverence, compelling him to try to eradicate, not only Mordecai, but all the Jews [Esther 3]. It is the hatred of the Pharisees and of Herodias for any religious expression that did not bow to their authority, driving them to behead John the Baptist, and crucify Christ. It was Satan's hatred working through the blindness of Hitler's atheistic philosophy. This hatred is blind in that it sees godliness as evil, like the Pharisees accusing Jesus of using the power of Satan to exorcise demons [Matthew 12:24]. This hatred may be manifested as disdain for or a condescending view of the Christian lifestyle [something frequently depicted in movies and television programs]. On a late night Christian television program, I once heard a taped message of the dialogue between a radio broadcaster and a Christian who had called in during a live broadcast at a gay festival somewhere in Colorado. [The television host warned, prior to the message, that youngsters should be excluded from hearing it.] The caller politely expressed his biblical viewpoint of sexuality, which, of course, was exclusively heterosexual. The broadcaster's response was a vicious, hateful, obscene attack. It was if he was possessed. He was so out of control that the broadcaster, as reported by the television host, subsequently was fired. At the end of his tirade, he said something like, "You see! We're out here trying to celebrate life a little in a peaceful manner, and you call up and ruin it." He said this despite the fact that the Christian caller never lost his temper and never said anything unkind or inappropriate, even in response to the broadcaster's vicious verbal attack. He had simply stated what most Christians believe to be biblical truth on a program that was open to all callers and all opinions. The broadcaster lost it and then blamed the caller for the fact that he lost it. We must recognize this evil hatred; Jesus has called it to our attention. But we must not fear it, and we must not react to it. We must continue to live in the freedom and truth of Christ, and in His love—

even for our enemies. If we begin to hate in response to this hatred, we are being ensnared by the evil one.

Jesus, thank You for overcoming the world on our behalf. Thank You for not returning evil for evil. Thank You for empowering us to not return hatred for hatred.

212

TO GET CLEAN, COME CLEAN

And there was a woman who had had a flow of blood for twelve years, and who had suffered much under many physicians, and had spent all that she had, and was no better but rather grew worse. She had heard the reports about Jesus, and came up behind him in the crowd and touched his garment.

For she said, "If I touch even his garments, I shall be made well." And immediately the hemorrhage ceased; and she felt in her body that she was healed of her disease. And Jesus, perceiving in himself that power had gone forth from him, immediately turned about in the crowd, and said, "Who touched my garments?"

And his disciples said to him, "You see the crowd pressing around you, and yet you say, 'Who touched me?'" And he looked around to see who had done it. But the woman, knowing what had been done to her, came in fear and trembling and fell down before him, and told him the whole truth.

And he said to her, "Daughter, your faith has made you well; go in peace, and be healed of your disease"[Mk 5:25-34].

This woman had a twelve-year bleeding problem. She had tried everything available to her and spent all her resources trying to be healed but had only gotten worse. According to the Levitical laws, she was considered "unclean" [Leviticus 15:25f] like a leper and should not have been in a crowd or near anyone since anyone who touched her [or anything she lay or sat upon] would also be declared "unclean" for a time. For twelve years she had been considered "unclean" and was, to some degree therefore, alienated. She bore the shame of being "unclean." Perhaps she had not let it become widely known, making it possible for her to enter the crowd that thronged Jesus without public condemnation. Perhaps only a few close friends and family members knew her shame but tried to keep her secret. In a close community, it would have been difficult to keep the secret for twelve years, and she probably suspected that many knew, and politely said nothing but looked upon her with pity, or perhaps some fear of contagion. Jesus was her final hope of being delivered from this sickness, shame, and alienation. So she made her way with trembling heart and faithful anticipation, through the multitude and in faith touched his garment. Jesus felt her faith in a way that distinguished her touch from all the others who had brushed or bumped him in the crowd. and he stopped. And, the flow of the crowd stopped with him. He turned and said, "Who touched my garment?" Those close by wondered how he could distinguish one touch from another in the mass and curiously sought the faces of the crowd for some reaction. The woman now faced exposure—all her shame coming out in the open. Her bloody uncleanness, her violation of the law, her brazen approach to this Holy One, and putting her unclean hand upon his garment, unbidden, uninvited. She must have felt a compulsion to run away in fear and shame. Jesus appeared to have not known who the culprit was. Maybe no one would notice if she simply melted away in the crowd. Instead, for whatever reason, she "fell down before him" in complete submission and humility in total brokenness in "fear and trembling" underneath which there must have certainly been a budding sense of relief and joy straining toward the surface of her emotions. [Could it be that she had really been healed?] And she told him the "whole truth." Everything. Her shameful secret of uncleanness. Her twelve-year fruitless struggle for healing. Her deteriorating health. She confessed it all, rendering herself totally vulnerable. How would he respond? How would the crowd respond? Would her shameful, secretive, illegal means of procuring this healing cause it to be negated or taken away? *"Daughter, your faith has made you well; go in peace, and be healed of your illness."* With this statement, the tension in her and in the crowd is released. The budding joy in her heart, and in those friends and family members, begins to burst forth into full bloom.

There is a clear sense in this story, however, that the healing was not complete until she came forth and openly responded to Jesus' question, "Who touched my garment?" She had to come clean. She had to tell the "whole truth." She had to come out of the shadows of secrecy about her shame and uncleanness. She had to courageously face Jesus and the crowd with her truth. Only then did Jesus make her healing official by proclaiming *"your faith has made you well."*

Lord Jesus, thank You for calling us forth out of our shameful secrecy into the light of truth, freedom, healing, peace and joy. Help us to have the faith and courage of this woman.

213

AMAZING GRACE

For I do not do the good I want, but the evil I do not want is what I do [Rom 7:19].

Wretched man that I am! Who will deliver me from this body of death? [Rom 7:24].

...even the righteousness of God, through faith in Jesus Christ, to all and on all who believe. For there is no difference; for all have sinned and fall short of the glory of God, being justified freely by His grace through the redemption that is in Christ Jesus, whom God set forth as a propitiation by His blood, through faith, to demonstrate His righteousness, because in His forbearance God had passed over the sins that were previously committed, to demonstrate at the present time His righteousness, that He might be just and the justifier of the one who has faith in Jesus [Rom 3:22-26 NKJ].

In this life, we never attain perfection. [It is somehow perfect that we do not.] No matter how far down the road of sanctification we are able to progress, we still see the need for further growth. At the time of our death, some area of our lives will still not be what we know it should it be. There will be some sinful nature manifestation that we will not be able to eradicate from our personality. There are three basic ways to deal with this reality of our imperfection: 1. Denial [the way of the world], 2. Ongoing guilt and remorse [the way of the defeated Christian and spiritually sensitive], or 3. Receiving the Grace of God, the forgiveness of sins, and the righteousness of Christ. This third way is, of course, God's desire for us. We understand that Jesus was able to walk a perfect walk, *who in every respect has been tempted as we are, yet without sin* [Hebrews 4:15]. He was tempted to use His power selfishly [to feed Himself when very hungry] [Matthew 4:3], to use it frivolously or to impress people and make a name for Himself [Matthew 4:6], to gain power and control the whole world [Matthew 4:8-9], and to avoid the Cross of Calvary and live a normal, long life on the earth, perhaps taking a wife and having children [Matthew 16:21-23]. He was falsely accused, betrayed, abandoned, denied, tortured, mocked, beaten and crucified, and He continued to love and forgive. He did not succumb to hatred or self-pity. He prayed, not for revenge, but for the forgiveness of His tormentors. He thus became the only perfect life that lived upon this earth; and the only suitable sacrifice for the sins of the human family. The Bible teaches clearly that God imparts the righteousness of Christ to imperfect sinners who put their faith

in Him, receive Him as their Lord, and allow His Holy Spirit to begin the wonderful work of sanctification in them. [See Romans 3:22, 5:17, 8:10, 10:4, Gal 2:21, 1Cr 1:30, Phl 1:11, and elsewhere.] For those, there is no longer condemnation [Romans 8:1]. There is freedom, peace, and joy! It is as if God is saying to us, "I know you cannot be perfect, no matter how hard you try. I have given you my Son. He has lived as a man, as a human. He has been tempted in all ways as you are, yet without sin. He has become for you a perfect sacrifice. Put your faith in Him. Let His Spirit abide in you, and I will no longer see you as a sinner. I will see you as a righteous, beloved child of God—a friend of Mine. And His Spirit, which is My Spirit, will help you become all that you were created to become and all that you *can* become as a human in a fallen world. And We will deliver you from this world, even as you continue to live in it. And you will be free. And I will give you peace, and the desires of your heart."
And our response is unbounded gratitude expressed as joy and the desire to love God and man better than ever.

Amazing Grace, how sweet the sound, that saved a wretch like me. I once was lost but now am found, was blind but now I see. [John Newton]

Lord, today may I live in Your love for all.

214

LIFE IS DIFFICULT

Then Jesus told his disciples, "If any man would come after me, let him deny himself and take up his cross and follow me [Mt 16:24].

We are afflicted in every way, but not crushed; perplexed, but not driven to despair...[Paul, 2Cor 4:8].

In the world you will have tribulation [Jesus, John 16:33b].

Any way you cut it, dice it, dress it up, or live it, life is difficult, and it does not get easier when we become a Christian. Jesus wants us to know this, and Satan does not. Satan would have us believe that when we come into Christ everything becomes smooth and easy. We have the answer to all the questions, the dawn breaks, and it all makes sense, and we can see how everything is working together for good. We enter into the wonderful family of God in which everyone is loving, helping, and serving each other with smiling faces and gracious hearts. We always feel like doing good and we never speak a grouchy or complaining word. [Like all those people we see in church on Sunday morning!] The reason Satan wants us to believe this is because it won't take long for us to become disillusioned about the Christian life. We will discover in very short order that salvation does not deliver us from our [and our loved ones'] sinful nature. And, it does not deliver us from a fallen world in which people don't do what they ought. Accidents still happen. We are still maltreated and misunderstood. Our mate does not become more gracious overnight. And we still struggle with selfishness and whatever character defects we had before we came into Christ. This reality is particularly difficult for first-generation Christians who haven't had the opportunity to grow up in Christian homes or hang out with Christian friends who, of course, are not perfect, happy, self-controlled, or peaceful all the time. Coming from outside to inside the Faith, it is easy to have misconceptions about what it will be like, and we may become disappointed when the bubble bursts.

But the bursting of that bubble can and should be the beginning of the greatest adventure of life—the truth about what the Christian life *can* be. As Christians we follow Christ, Who died a horrific death after being falsely accused, betrayed, denied, abandoned, mocked, and tortured. Why should we think this should be an easy life? Partly, because we live in a culture that oozes and schmoozes comfort, pleasure, and entitlement. And no matter how "Christian" we are, that toxicity gets into us. It's in the cultural air we breathe and water we drink. It's no surprise that American Christianity would absorb some of that toxic philosophy. Some brands of "Christianity" become totally consumed in it: "God wants you to prosper! Sow some seed-faith money into my ministry, and see if He doesn't pour down a blessing upon you!" etc. Jesus has long since departed from such garbage. He is leading those who have clearer eyes focused on a much nobler goal than the carrion around which those vultures have gathered. The true followers are finding joy in trying not to complain about the difficulties of loving imperfect people with Christ's love—in spirit and in truth. They are discovering a clean gratitude for breaking free of the bonds of the flesh that drag down the spirit. They do not expect life to be easy. But they feel the difficulties of the cross fading away as they draw ever-nearer the All-Consuming Fire in which there is eternal peace, freedom, and the same "joy that was set before Him" [Heb 12:2].

Lord Jesus, thank You for telling it like it is. Help me to accept the difficulties of living in obedience to You. Deliver me from unrealistic expectations about life in this fallen world. But please allow me to experience all the joy You promised Your followers.

215

DON'T LOSE THE BLESSING

If you forsake the LORD and serve strange gods, then he will turn and do you hurt, and consume you, even though he has done you so much good [Jos 24:20].

    It is common sense to assert that, either there is *no* god, there are *many* gods, or there is *one* God. If there is no god [or if you believe so] then you should look elsewhere for guidance because I don't know how to order life from the atheistic viewpoint—I don't know what meaning can be derived therefrom. If there are many gods we might ask how they decided to divide things up—Which created what? To which do we pay homage for the blessing of food? Manhood and womanhood? Which god do we turn to in time of need? Do they all get along with each other, or is there competition in the heavenly realm [as in Greek mythology]?

    The Bible plainly asserts that there is in reality only one God, and that everything else that man has promoted into His place is an idol that has no power to bless its worshipper. The reason God is a "jealous" God [something that has turned at least one popular TV personality away from Him] is because He does not want His children wasting their precious life-energy in vain pursuits. He wants us to be blessed. But He, being a God of Truth, can only bless Truth—not falsehood or vanity. And so the Bible repeatedly encourages the pursuit and love of Truth [the word itself occurs 235 times in the Bible]. And, the Bible decries idolatry as the supreme and most destructive form of falsehood or delusion.

    In the last chapters of the book of Joshua, we read of his final warnings to the Israelites. He is old. He had experienced the desert wanderings, the faithless fear that kept them from an earlier entry into the Promised Land, and finally the conquest and occupation of the land flowing with milk and honey. He had personally witnessed, and called to their remembrance *that not one thing hath failed of all the good things which the LORD your God spoke concerning you; all are come to pass unto you, [and] not one thing hath failed thereof [23:14]*. Now he warned them that if they allowed the subtle creeping in of false gods, the blessings would end and curses begin.

    America has been a blessed nation. It's Constitution and Founding Fathers were deeply influenced and formed by the Christian faith. Churches, proclaiming the Truth of the one God of Israel, and the Messiah Jesus Christ, dot its landscape from shore to shore. Within these churches, children have been taught to honor and obey their parents and treat others as they wish to be treated. Men and women have been taught to honor the marriage covenant, and to grow in their love for each other. All have been commanded to love the unlovable, weak, and powerless, those in prison or poverty, to overcome selfishness and greed, to be generous and compassionate, humble and contrite, to make sacrifices, when necessary, for righteousness sake.

But other "gods" [now as in the days of Joshua] vie for the attention of God's people—gods of pleasure, power, wealth, entertainment, materialism, comfort, and ease. We are tempted to become absorbed in romantic relationships, work, hobbies or family. None of these may be evil in and of itself, but all become evil [idolatrous] if placed at the apex of one's motivation, desire, or adoration. We do well to hear the words of Joshua, that brave and faithful old soul, knowing that he was soon to depart from the earth, having nothing to lose, needing to impress no one, caring deeply for his people: ***If you forsake the LORD, and serve strange gods, then he will turn and do you hurt, and consume you, even though he has done you so much good.***

God, please continue to bless America. We know that You can only do so to the degree that we draw near to You, in spirit and truth, and as we continue to live in obedience to Your commands and in the Light and Love of Jesus Christ our Lord. Please forgive us for being distracted and drawn astray by the false "gods" of this world that appeal so alluringly to our flesh, which is passing away.

216

ARE YOU HAVING TRIBULATION?

I have said this to you, that "in me you may have peace. In the world you have tribulation; but be of good cheer, I have overcome the world" [John 16:33].

No, in all these things we are more than conquerors through him who loved us [Rom 8:37].

This teaching of Jesus has helped me more than I can say. As a counselor, I see many people who are having severe tribulation. Because of the lies of the evil one, some of them believe that their tribulation can defeat them. They believe, because of the lies propagated in our culture, that they should not have tribulation, or that their tribulation should not be so severe, and that they are victims of this tribulation. Jesus teaches us very clearly we will have these problems and difficulties in our life, and we should not be surprised by them, and, most importantly, WE ARE NOT OVERCOME BY THEM.

My eighty-five year old mother has a sixth-grade education. Her mother died when she was two years old. She was a "pillar to post" child. She lost her husband of 64 years to Alzheimer's disease. She lost her oldest daughter to cancer. Now, she has cancer herself in her breast and bones. She has experienced some tribulation. But if you talk to her, you will learn very quickly that she is not a victim to any of these tribulations. She knows that God is good. She is prepared for her death and looks forward to seeing her loved ones again. She continues to give, love, and serve. She has faith that, as long as God leaves her here on the earth, she has a mission. She is not perfect, and she will admit it. But she is thankful in the midst of her grief. And she is still faithful and hopeful amid the crazy things she sees going on in the world. She continues to pray for her children and to do the best she can to encourage them to live good lives in Christ. She is more than a conqueror in Christ. She is a living example that nothing [absolutely nothing] can defeat a child of God.

Whatever tribulation you may be facing, I hope that you will have the faith of my mother—the same faith that has sustained countless followers of Christ who have endured even greater tribulation than she. Please remember that Jesus descended into the darkest depths possible for humans to endure: He allowed Himself to feel forsaken by God [Mt.27:46]. And yet He arose on the third day. Whatever tribulation you are facing, if you abide in Christ, I promise you, based on the eternal Truth of the Scriptures, you will arise! However you feel, remember: You are more than a conqueror in Christ. This is a truth that has stood the test of two thousand years of history.

Lord Jesus, thank You for teaching us all we need to know to overcome all the tribulations of this world. Thank You that we are not only conquerors, but MORE than conquerors in Your Holy Spirit.

217

RELATIONAL RESPONSIBILITY

"Judge not, that you be not judged. For with the judgment you pronounce you will be judged, and the measure you give will be the measure you get. Why do you see the speck that is in your brother's eye, but do not notice the log that is in your own eye? Or how can you say to your brother, 'Let me take the speck out of your eye,' when there is the log in your own eye? You hypocrite, first take the log out of your own eye, and then you will see clearly to take the speck out of your brother's eye" [Jesus, Mt 7:1-5].

Healthy relationships are grounded upon honesty, sincerity, and responsibility. This involves a willingness to be introspective and non-defensive. We must be very careful to work on our own issues. This is much easier to talk, read, or think about than it is to do. Our mate's issues are out in front of us, and they grate our nerves and test our patience. Our own issues, though no less toxic, don't really bother us that much. We've had a lifetime to adjust to them. Perhaps our parents had the same issues, and we're therefore blind to them, since they seem normal to us. Additionally, we are very aware of every ounce of strife and sacrifice that we endure for the sake of the relationship, because we *feel* them—they exist inside our own skin. We do not, however *feel* our mate's sacrifices and strivings toward health and responsibility; therefore we cannot possibly be aware of all of them, as we aware of our own. We simply see our mate doing what they are *supposed* to do—what we *expect* them to do. The temptation is, therefore, to feel like we are doing most of the hard work to make the relationship work, while our mate is lolly-gagging along, frisking and frolicking, not even thankful for all the hard work we're doing. The seeds of resentment can grow in this fertile soil.

For example, our mate, because of anything from hormones to a bad night's sleep, may be doing everything in his/her power to simply be civil. Because we don't live in their skin and are not aware of this effort, we could be harboring a critical, hard heart toward them for not being warm and affectionate. As we grow spiritually, our effort becomes to focus more on our own issues that come to light *because* of our mate's issues, rather than being critical of our mate's issues. The criticism in our own heart is the problem—not what we are criticizing in our mate. A succinct statement describing this is, "When you have a critical finger pointed at someone, you have three pointed back at yourself." You should always direct your attention in the direction of the three [at least initially and most searchingly.]

Lord, please forgive me for my tendency to be judgmental and critical of others. I realize that I have blind spots and character defects that I need to be aware of and working on rather than wasting my energy in this critical manner. Give me grace to practice the "beam and speck" principle diligently.

218

YOU ARE RESPONSIBLE FOR YOU

Now while he was in Jerusalem at the Passover Feast, many people saw the miraculous signs he was doing and believed in his name. But Jesus would not entrust himself to them, for he knew all men. [John 2:23 -24].

    The above phrase in verse 24 is incredibly enlightening. Jesus did not entrust Himself to those who were believing in Him. This exemplifies Christ's incredible wisdom. The word "entrust" is translated from the Greek word *pisteuo,* which means: *to believe; to be persuaded of; to place confidence in; to trust or rely upon; to trust in, as being able to aid in either obtaining or in doing something: saving faith.* Jesus knew all men too well to place His faith in them. And we must be guided by this same wisdom. We are called to love all men; but *not* to put our faith in them. When we put our faith in any human or group of humans, we place the responsibility for our emotional well-being in their hands. We place our self in a position of *need* [we *need* something from them, in order to be OK within our self]. This is always a dreadful mistake from the spiritual standpoint. It is an eternal impossibility for me to place the responsibility for my life in someone else's hands. If I could do so, that person would have to stand in judgment in my place because he [not I] would be responsible for me. And we all know, at our deepest level, that no one other than our self will stand in judgment for us. Therefore, no one is responsible for me but me. I am responsible for myself—not my parents, children, spouse, friends, co-workers, enemies, etc., only me. And only you are responsible for you. Whenever you feel like a victim, or whenever you are blaming someone for your negative life experiences, you are out of touch with this reality. We are not responsible for everything that happens to us in this life, and we are not responsible for how people treat us. But we are one hundred percent responsible for how we *respond* to all experiences and treatment. Jesus commands us to love our enemies [Mt 5:44], and God commands us not to return evil for evil, nor to be overcome by evil, but to overcome evil with good [Rm 12:17-21]. Clearly, God does not want us to be inwardly or outwardly determined by negative life experiences, nor by people—especially their sinful nature manifestations or failures. He wants us to be determined only by His Holy Spirit residing in us through Christ. Regardless of life experiences, regardless of how others have treated us, we are not victims! We are victors—more than conquerors—in Christ! Jesus does not withhold any of His promises from us because of past life experiences or the way others have failed to love us. We begin to see that an important aspect of our sanctification process [if we desire to be free] is to withdraw our trust in [need for] people or in the safety of this world, and deposit it wholly and completely in Jesus, as He relied solely on God [even when things were going well for Him!]. God commands us to *love* people but not to *entrust* ourselves to them. People are just people. They always fail at some point. Only God is worthy of our faith. As we look to Him to supply ALL our need [Phil 4:19, Mt 6:32, Lk 12:30] we discover the freedom necessary to love people, for it is impossible to adequately love people when we are looking to them to supply our need.

Lord Jesus, thank You for giving us such a wonderful example of freedom from vulnerability to the failures of humans. Deliver us from the mistake of entrusting ourselves to men. But please, Lord, empower us, through Your Holy Spirit, to love them in spirit and truth.

219

KNOW YOUR ENEMY

For we are not contending against flesh and blood, but against the principalities, against the powers, against the world rulers of this present darkness, against the spiritual hosts of wickedness in the heavenly places [Eph 6:12].

One of the great truths of Scripture [evident from Genesis to Revelation, addressed specifically by Jesus, presumed or elaborated in practically every book of the Bible] is that there is a fallen angel who has rebelled against the God of love Who created everything. This fallen angel [Satan] is the epitome of evil and is a dominant power in the world in which we live. In fact he is called the "prince of this world" [John 12:31, 14:30, Eph 2:2]. He is a cunning deceiver who works to destroy or oppress all that is good: Life, freedom, peace, joy, and especially love. Jesus called him a "murderer" and the "father of lies" [John 8:44]. Either Jesus was delusional, or we have a personal, cunning deceiver who exists in the spiritual realm, and who has dominion over "the world rulers of this present darkness [and] the spiritual hosts of wickedness in heavenly places." As clear as this teaching is in the Scripture, it is frequently overlooked, and even denied within the Faith, and, of course, it is dismissed as "Medieval superstition" by intellectual worldlings [unbelievers].

The result of this denial and ignorance is our increased vulnerability to his deceptions. Because we do not recognize our true enemy, we see each other as the enemy. We war against flesh and blood. We see the terrorists as the enemy, or the liberals, or conservatives, or our wives, husbands, in-laws, illegal aliens, neighbors, bosses, employees, etc. Any of these humans can only be an enemy to the degree that they have been deceived by the same evil power that each of us must do battle with daily. And Jesus has made it clear for all people and all time that the first line of battle is and will always be within our own hearts [Mt 7:3-5]. This is not to say that wars between humans are not necessary. They are necessary because whole nations or cultures of humans have fallen into major destructive deceptions of the evil one. The military will always be necessary until the missionaries' work is done. As Christians, we recognize that evangelization is the work of curing the disease that warfare is the feverish symptom of. Fighting against flesh and blood [like taking an aspirin for fever] will continue to be necessary until all men are filled with the Spirit of Jesus Christ, and therefore able to recognize that they are brothers who have a common enemy. Until that time the fever will continue to break out in one place after another. But we must always remember that those humans against whom we fight in the flesh are not our true enemy. If we are fighting for the Right, it simply means that they have been more deceived by Satan than we have. But that man who thinks that he has not in any way been deceived has fallen into the darkest form of deception.

Lord Jesus, please deliver us from evil. We cannot deliver ourselves from it.

220

ALL WE HAVE IS JESUS

But we have this treasure in earthen vessels, to show that the transcendent power belongs to God and not to us. We are afflicted in every way, but not crushed; perplexed, but not driven to despair; persecuted, but not forsaken; struck down, but not destroyed [2Cor 4:7-9].

As for these things which you see, the days will come when there shall not be left here one stone upon another that will not be thrown down [Jesus, Lk 21:6].

One of my recent clients told me this story. His mother died when he was very young, and his dad worked nights, having to sleep during the day. As he put it, "Me and my siblings pretty much raised ourselves." He described the New Orleans area neighborhood in which he grew up as "pretty bad. Lots of fighting and crime. I have friends who are in jail for life, and some who are dead." Someone shared Christ with him in his early adulthood, and he began the sanctification process—his deliverance. He married a godly woman and they worked in the church, teaching couples in Sunday school classes in the Chalmette, LA area. A few years prior to his coming to see me, he needed two back surgeries, and then discovered that he had esophageal cancer. He took it in stride. "I was prepared for my death," he said. What he was *not* prepared for was his wife's being diagnosed with cancer a few months before Hurricane Katrina wiped out his life as he knew it. His church, his job, his community, were all blown or washed away. Then, within a few months after Katrina, his wife died. [Are you thinking of Job?] Two of his children were already launched from the nest, and the one remaining at home may have given him the only reason that he could get in touch with to live. He began a downward slide into depression and the old lifestyle. His sister was alarmed to the point that she persuaded him to contact me, and God blessed us with a mutually edifying journey together.

What came to bold relief for me in this journey with him is that everything can be taken away—*Everything*. There is no security except Jesus, Who said "I am with you always, even to the end of the world" [Mt 28:20]. Unless God has sent an angel to assure you otherwise, at any time you could lose your mate, your children, your parent/s, your health, your financial standing, your job, or anything else that has ever provided any security or comfort to you. When Jesus said, "In the world, you will have tribulation," this is what He was talking about. There are no limits to the tribulation that humans have endured, except what God, in His mercy, has set upon them. But Jesus has promised to be with us through it all, and He therefore can rightly assure us to "nevertheless, be of good cheer" because he has "overcome the world" [John 16:33]. Security, hope, or faith in anything or anyone other than Jesus is futile, vain, and foolish. Jesus is all we have. And He is all we will ever need. And like my friend, we may be surprised at how much faith we have put in some other relationship or aspects of life when we begin to suffer the loss of some of it, as we most assuredly will sooner or later. Jesus wants us to be prepared.

Lord Jesus, please help me be prepared to lose anything or everything in my world. You are all I have ever needed. Thank You for assuring me that You will never leave or forsake me.

221

SORROW

And taking with him Peter and the two sons of Zeb'edee, he began to be sorrowful and troubled. Then he said to them, "My soul is very sorrowful, even to death; remain here, and watch with me" [Mt 26:37-38]

Jesus experienced deep sorrow. He was in Gethsemane when He spoke these words. The world was closing in on Him. He knew that He had been betrayed. Judas was at that moment leading the sword and club-bearing vigilantes to Him. The most agonizing leg of His earthly journey was beginning, leading to the Cross, which was looming on the near horizon like the evil grinning face of Satan. He needed prayer warriors, but they couldn't stay awake. Except for the Father, He was alone. And in a short while, He would cry out an utterance that revealed that He felt "forsaken," even by the Father [Mt 27:46]. His soul was sorrowful, "even unto death."

By entering into this sorrow, Jesus blessed us very deeply. He made sorrow Holy for all the human family. We live in the same fallen world that rejected Jesus, lorded over by the same evil prince who continues to deceive so many and to inflict immense devastation in so many lives. And even though now, thanks to Jesus, he is a "lame duck," defeated prince, he can still muster attacks against God's children that make us feel, at times, like Christ in Gethsemane. Sometimes like Him, we too cry out in anguish, "My God, why have You forsaken me." Sometimes we feel desperately, relentlessly alone. Sometimes Satan leads his band of demons in all-out attacks from all directions, and the world closes in on us as it did Him. One of the lies of Satan is that Christians should never feel alone, forsaken, or sorrowful. Well, that would mean that Jesus was not a very good Christian! Thank God, we, like Jesus, can feel however we feel. We don't have to feel good, excited, thankful, joyful, and free all the time [even though we know, beyond any shadow of doubt, that God is on the throne and all is well]. What we must do, also like Him, is continue on through whatever feelings we have, toward the completion of our mission to be the "light of the world" [Mt 5:14]. We must continue to love with His love.

Jesus didn't wallow around in the sorrow. After this time [or perhaps *during* this time] of desperate sorrow expressed in the Garden of Gethsemane, He did a few things: He faced down the vigilantes, kept the disciple from giving way to violence, faced the hatred and indignation of the priests and elders, endured the fabricated lies of His accusers, watched compassionately as Peter collapsed in weakness and fear, suffered horrific physical torture, and responded by praying for their forgiveness. He was not defeated by hatred, fear, or sorrow.

And as we abide in Him, neither will we. We too, like Him, will say, at some point, "Rise, let us be going..." [Mt 26:46].

Lord, words can never express how good You have been to us, nor describe the grandeur of the victory You have won for us. Please help us to be adequately thankful to You. And may we always know Your presence [felt or not] in our deepest sorrows. And especially may we not falter from our mission, no matter how we feel.

222

CONVICTION AND ENCOURAGEMENT

"...I am with you always, even to the close of the age"[Jesus, Mt 28:20].

"Let not your hearts be troubled; believe in God, believe also in Me [Jesus, John 14:1].

"Peace I leave with you, my peace I give to you: not as the world gives, give I unto you. Let not your heart be troubled, neither let it be afraid" [Jesus, John 14:27].

The Holy Spirit convicts us. This is a manifestation of God's love. He does not allow us to be selfish, lazy, or unconcerned about our spiritual growth. When we look deeply and honestly into the life and teachings of Jesus, we realize that we have not attained perfection. We still have steps to take. But it is clear that God does not want us to be too hard on ourselves because of our imperfections. Jesus was speaking to sinners like us [in fact He was talking to *us*] when He said "Peace I give to you...." I think that all of us sometimes, and some of us *most* of the time, are somewhat compulsive and fearful about our growth and imperfections. This keeps us from experiencing the peace that Christ offers to all us imperfect sinners on the road to "New Jerusalem." Jesus clearly wants us to not only be convicted, but also *encouraged*. He does not want us to be in a perpetual state of conviction, feeling inferior, sullied, degraded, or anxious about our standing with God. I think when we hear people complain about "hell-fire and brimstone" preaching, what some of them are saying is that they do not want to feel perpetually afraid or inferior. [What others of them are saying is that they do not want to suffer *any* conviction or the facing of their imperfections, and this is a much more sinister problem]. We must certainly face the reality of hell and our own sinful nature, but we must also receive God's grace and forgiveness through Christ and rest peacefully as He carries us down the road of our sanctification.

As John Newton penned, "**Twas grace that taught my heart to fear, and grace my fears relieved.**" Some people never get to the fear: They are in too much denial to realize that they are accountable to a perfect and holy God. Others, however, never get to the "relief" from fear. They stay in a perpetual state of high or low-grade fear because they are keenly aware of their sinful nature. Maybe they are still in denial about some aspect of their sinful nature in which case relief will come with confession and repentance. But I have seen Christians who seem to have all their sins on the table, and are doing the best they can, yet are still living in sullied fear or feelings of condemnation. The voice they need to hear is, "Let not your heart be troubled...I am with you always. I do not condemn you. You are justified."

Lord Jesus, thank You so much for encouraging me. I do not want to presume upon Your grace, but I certainly want to receive it, and the peace You bring to us sinners who have received You as our Lord.

223

THE DISCIPLINE OF POWER

And behold, one of those who were with Jesus stretched out his hand and drew his sword, and struck the slave of the high priest, and cut off his ear. Then Jesus said to him, "Put your sword back into its place; for all who take the sword will perish by the sword. Do you think that I cannot appeal to my Father, and he will at once send me more than twelve legions of angels?" [Mt 26:51-53].

And Jesus came and spoke to them, saying, "All power is given to me in heaven and in earth" [Mt 28:18].

"... I am gentle and lowly in heart, and you will find rest for your souls. For my yoke is easy, and my burden is light" [Mt 11:29b-30].

In a recent counseling session, I sat with a married couple who were having problems with the seventeen year old son of the husband [step-son of the wife]. The father was an ex-Marine; and still very much respected and strove to live by the Marine code of "honor, integrity, respect, valor, and courage." He told me repeatedly of the things he had said to his son about his lying and disrespect and betrayal of his girlfriend. A number of times, his wife started to speak, but he talked right over her. Each time, she slumped a little lower in her seat. Everything he was saying was very good. I agreed with every intervention that he said he had made with his son. But the more he talked, the more exasperated I felt, and I detected that his wife did also. At last I interrupted him and respectfully said, "You know, you have a very powerful personality. It's as if you fill up this whole room. ...Sometimes, the most effective thing we can do is *discipline* our power and hold back a little and make space for others to come into the circle of influence." At this statement, his wife perked up like a wilted flower in a summer rain. She smiled and nodded her head in agreement. He was a good man, he was not a "controller" [though I suspect his wife feels him to be.] He simply had never considered that he was overbearing with his power.

Jesus, being the Messiah, was one hundred percent *correct* in His doctrine, love, and wisdom. What He was bringing to the human family, and what He continues to offer us, is the ultimate Truth that sets us free—the very voice of the Creator of the universe. Additionally, Jesus had the *power* to call from God for twelve legions of angels. [A legion was a unit of Roman soldiers consisting of between 4200 and 6000 men.] He frankly stated that *all power in heaven and earth had been given to Him.* Jesus teaches us that, even when we are *right*, and even when we have the *power* to force righteousness, there are times when we must discipline or withhold our power.

Like all the lessons of Jesus, this is a very important one. And like many of them, it is a difficult one, especially for men. We tend to be like Peter, or like the zealots in Christ's time. We want to take up the sword make things right. We know we are right, just as Peter knew that Jesus was right. And we believe we have the power to force the "right" into existence. But sometimes, that is not God's way.

Lord give us grace to know when to discipline or withhold our power. Help us not to overpower and exasperate our loved ones. Help us to trust that You are working through them also and to be willing to listen more than to speak.

224

THREE HEALTHY RESPONSES

I dwell in the high and holy [place], with him also [that is] of a contrite and humble spirit...[Isa 57:15].

But if ye forgive not men their trespasses, neither will your Father forgive your trespasses [Mt 6:15].

And let the peace of God rule in your hearts, to the which also ye are called in one body; and be ye thankful [Col 3:15 KJV].

    Here is a concise method to help you know if you are growing in Christ. There are at least three basic responses to life in the Kingdom that every mature person must experience: Contrition, forgiveness, and gratitude.

    The Bible teaches that all have sinned and fallen short of the glory of God [Rom 3:23]. All sin hurts people. There is no sin that does not have some hurtful or oppressive effect to some human. Since we all have sinned, and in our imperfection, *continue* to sin, we must be willing to experience *contrition*. If I overlook or downplay the fact that I have hurt people in my life, I delay my own growth and alienate myself from God's grace. God says that He dwells with him who is of a "contrite and humble spirit." God does not dwell in denial and pride. It is a good practice to be mindful of those whom we have hurt or wrongfully neglected, and to offer up the gift of contrition.

    Others have hurt us also, since they, like us, have been blind and imperfect. We have all been both *perpetrators* and *victims* of evil. Jesus taught us in the "beam and speck" illustration to consider our own sins first and with the greatest concern. Then we would be able to help others in their failures. [Mt 7:3-5]. In addition to contrition, we must seek and give *forgiveness*. Of all the beautiful points that Jesus made in the prayer that He taught us to pray – the Lord's Prayer – He elaborated afterwards on the theme of forgiveness. He indicated that if we did not forgive, we would not be forgiven. This is a very clear and stern command that our Lord has given to us. *We must forgive!* And we must seek forgiveness of those we have hurt. We should frequently examine our hearts to know if we are harboring any anger, resentment, or ill will toward anyone, and we should let it go. Otherwise, our hearts can become quite hard over time, and we may not even notice that it is happening. [But others probably will!]

    Finally, no matter how much we give, we realize that we can never give as much as we have been given. How can we repay God and our parents for the gift of our lives? Everything that we experience each day is a gift, and the result of other peoples' work and effort: The food we eat, clothes we wear, vehicles we drive, all the technology at our disposal, our wonderful physical bodies that enable us to sense and experience the beauty of the world around us—all gifts! In Christ, all our sins are forgiven and God is holding nothing against us, even though we have hurt and neglected so many. The only rational response is *gratitude*—deep, abiding, and growing thankfulness.

Lord please forgive me for hurting and neglecting so many in my life. I forgive anyone who has ever hurt or neglected me in any way, and I ask You to forgive them. And I am so thankful for the gifts of life, salvation, freedom, and the wonderful people You have given to me. Thank You for Your eternal Presence and Love.

225

GOD AND POLITICS

Put not your trust in princes, nor in the son of man, in whom there is no help [Ps 146:3].

Pilate therefore said to him, "You will not speak to me? Do you not know that I have power to release you, and power to crucify you?" Jesus answered him, "You would have no power over me unless it had been given you from above..." [John 19:10 -11].

Throughout the history of the human family there have been good rulers, kings, and governors, and evil kings, rulers, and governors. Nations have risen and fallen, based on their faithfulness to or deviance from God's will. But God's will has steadfastly continued through all the ups and downs of the roller coaster of human endeavor. Evil nations have been used of God to chastise His wayward children. When they repented, they were restored. Those who were not faithful were left behind. Those who trusted God, even in the face of seemingly insurmountable odds, were rewarded with success. In this sense, nothing has changed in the history of the human family. Herod was king of the Jews when Jesus was born. Augustus reputedly stated that it was safer to be one of Herod's pigs than one of his children, since he had a number of them executed to protect his power. He was exceedingly evil. And it was during his reign that the Savior of the world was born. And Herod's best efforts to destroy this newborn King were futile because the God of this universe supernaturally protected Him.

Evil kings and governors have never, and will never thwart the will of God and the onward march of His Kingdom. Therefore, the children of God need never fear evil rulers or governors. We only need to continue to abide in Christ and in His love for the human family, and in His trust in our Heavenly Father, Who is continuing to work **all things** together for good for those who love Him and are called to His glorious purpose [Rms. 8:28]. It is important to remember that God uses the blindness of evil, as well as the obedience of His chosen ones to bring about His good will. We can rightly say, therefore, along with David, "I will fear no evil, for Thou art with me…"[Ps. 23] Christians should be good citizens, vote prayerfully, and pray for the leaders of their nations. But they should always remember that the ways of this world fluctuate between good and evil like the swinging of the pendulum. Sometimes the prince of this world seems to have the upper hand, but he never does! As the old, uneducated [but very wise] black shoe-shine man stated when asked what he understood about the complicated book of Revelation: "God is gonna win in the end!" And as Jesus reminded us: We are in this world, but we are not *of* this world. [Jn15:19]. Thank God, we are not of this world! We exist in the Heavenly Kingdom reigned over by Christ our Lord Who has defeated the prince of this world, and in Him we have abundant and eternal life that is independent of any earthly kingdoms, nations, or rulers. If a nation follows in the Way of Christ, it prospers. Otherwise it deteriorates. But God's faithful ones always persevere, no matter what.

Lord Jesus, thank You for reminding us that we have nothing to fear as we abide in You. Thank You for reminding us that all earthly power is under the authority of our loving heavenly Father. Thank You that You did not fear the political or religious leaders of Your day, but rather went about doing our Father's will. May we follow diligently in Your steps in this regard. May we fear no evil. And may Your will be done on earth as in heaven.

226

STAYING ACTIVE

I pray that you will be active in sharing your faith so that you will have a full understanding of every good thing we have in Christ [Phm 6].

There is a witticism that I heard frequently growing up: "Idle hands are the devil's workshop." I have found it to be very true. When I "drift," I don't drift in a good direction. Another way this has been expressed is, "Nature abhors a vacuum." Where there is nothing, something wants to be. If you clear a section of land, it will not stay cleared for long. Something will grow there. It may be thorns, briars and poison oak, but something will grow. We are concerned about our loved ones when they become inactive—and rightly so. Inactivity is associated with depression. And becoming active is one way to help overcome depression. The happiest people you will encounter are actively engaged in something they believe in—something that is good for them and their loved ones.

Of all things for us to be actively engaged in, the sharing of our faith is most advantageous, and brings us the most joy. This is true because we know that the sharing of our faith expands the Kingdom of God in which people love each other and grow in peace and joy. We also realize that sowing seeds of faith has positive implications that extend beyond our death into eternity. Being active by exercising my body and making money is helpful, but not deeply satisfying because it can be selfish. It is what I do with my body and my money that can bring deep satisfaction—if I use my energy and resources to bring light into the world. Jesus says that we are the light of the world, and that we are to let this light shine into world [Mt 5:14-16]. When we receive Christ, we receive every good gift for the soul—everything that brings us joy and peace. We come to realize that we are here to practice the love of Christ for everyone in the human family. We become light. But darkness works to overcome the light [though it never has and never will]. Jesus warned us that the "worries and cares of the world and the deceitfulness of riches" [Mk 4:19] would diminish the fruitfulness of our lives—dim the light in us. Being active in sharing our faith keeps us moving forward and brings us more deeply into the heart of the abundant life Jesus promised [John 10:10]. All of us have been involved in futile efforts. We have all experienced the disappointment of rigorously climbing a ladder, only to find it was leaning against the wrong wall. Living in the love of Christ and sharing our faith never disappoints us. We always have a deep satisfaction when we sow seeds of faith and love in others. That is why I get up at 2 a.m., like I did this morning, to write this devotional. And that is why I will be able to go back to bed now and sleep very well with a prayer in my heart that someone will be deeply blessed with the joy that comes when we share our faith.

Lord, thank You for sharing with us. Thank You for being very proactive in loving us. Help us to follow You in this way. Deliver us from complacency and futile effort. May we be fruitful for Your wonderful Kingdom, into which You have so graciously and at such great sacrifice, invited us.

227

E PLURIBUS UNUM

"I do not pray for these only, but also for those who believe in me through their word, that they may all be one; even as thou, Father, art in me, and I in thee, that they also may be in us, so that the world may believe that thou hast sent me. The glory which thou hast given me I have given to them, that they may be one even as we are one, I in them and thou in me, that they may become perfectly one, so that the world may know that thou hast sent me and hast loved them even as thou hast loved me..." [Jesus, John 17:20 -23].

For he is our peace, who has made us both one, and has broken down the dividing wall of hostility... [Eph 2:14].

    Lynn and I had the tremendous blessing of celebrating Christmas and the New Year with our family in the Washington, D.C. area. We visited the Capitol, White House, Pentagon, and Mount Vernon, among other outings. [I highly recommend visiting this area as a pilgrimage of our nation's history.] A primary theme of our nation, inscribed on all denominations of our coins, and very evident in our Capitol, is "E Pluribus Unum;" Latin for "out of many, one." This is a wonderful concept, of which we can all be proud and thankful. America has been called a "melting pot," and more recently a "salad bowl" because of this concept of welcoming all cultures and nationalities to share in the unity of democracy. As the above verses indicate, this was a Christian concept before it was an American concept. Perhaps it is an American concept *because* it was [and is] a Christian concept. Jesus prayed, as recorded in John 17, for the unity of the human family. Paul, as indicated in his letter to the Ephesians, recognized that Christ breaks down the dividing walls of hostility that have prevailed for so long between different cultures and nations. Anyone who receives Christ as his or her Lord becomes a brother or sister to everyone in the human family. Jesus causes us to realize that there is only one God of this universe, and that He created and loves all, desires the best for all, and requires us to love each other.

    Whatever our differences, we become one in Christ—and without losing our unique cultural and individual identities! In Christ, rather than a source of conflict and division, our differences become various gifts that we offer to each other and to the human family. Jesus teaches us to love our "enemies" [Mt 5:44]; and God has commanded us to be hospitable to strangers and foreigners [Lev 19:33-34]. When I was younger, growing up in Alabama, I had a narrow concept of what an "American" and a "Christian" were. Americans were white Anglo-Saxon Protestants; and Christians were basically Baptists with a few Methodists and Presbyterians. All others, even "Yankees" with their strange accent, were weird and suspicious intruders. I am thankful that, just as God helped Peter expand his concept of the family of God by bringing Cornelius into his life [Acts 10], He has brought some wonderful people into my life who, though very different from my narrow definition of an American Christian, nevertheless radiate clear evidence of the Holy Spirit, and contribute to the American ideal. I am thankful that God unifies us in His love. I am thankful for the diverse cultures, languages, and physical characteristics of the people of this earth. May we learn to love each other as Jesus has commanded us, and thereby fulfill, in the truest sense, that phrase on all our coins: E Pluribus Unum.

Lord, we join with You in praying that we might all be one, as You and our Father are one.

228

STAYING FRESH

Therefore, if anyone is in Christ, he is a new creation; the old has passed away, behold, the new has come [2Cor5:17].

This is one of my favorite verses in the Bible. Our Lord reminds us in this verse that life is always new and fresh. Even if we do not feel that life is new and fresh, it is. And we can grow spiritually to the place that we actually *experience* life in this way. A statement that emphasizes this truth is: *You can never put your foot in the same river twice.* Life and the physical world are constantly changing. Every morning you wake up to a brand new world! Each day, every moment, is composed of variations of reality that have never been and will never be again. Boredom, in this context, is a delusion, and unnecessary. If we simply open our eyes, we will see that everything is in a state of fluidity. Life, like a river, is flowing, changing, and evolving. Even if you repeat the routine of your daily responsibilities, there is newness in your environment. People are changing, growing, becoming. The sky and weather are always exceptional.

Most importantly, we can love better and better as we grow in Christ. And this is the greatest adventure of all! Each day there are people within our sphere of influence. Jesus has commanded us to love them. Love is always fresh and new. Yesterday's love can never be good enough for today. When we encounter each other in Christ's spirit, we are on the cutting edge of reality with each other. We are not bound to anything in the past. We become like children, seeing each other for the first time. We are enthralled by the wonder of the present moment. We are very alive and open to the potential that we have to encourage and uplift. We listen deeply to our friends. We prayerfully seek ways to intervene in their lives compassionately. We pay attention to our way of being because we want to have a positive influence. We notice the beauty of the earth. All around us are incredible manifestations of God's love: birds, butterflies, flowers, trees swaying in the wind, the little creatures of the earth, children, smiling faces, people helping people, manhood and womanhood, and a constantly changing sky. My prayer is that we will be more alive today, [this very moment!] than we have ever been. That we will be more at peace in our faith in the God of this universe Who has made His love abundantly clear to us through Christ. And that we will stay very awake to the ever-newness of His love in our hearts for all the people within our sphere of influence. In this way we will experience a growing awareness of what it means to be a new creature in Christ.

> Morning has broken, like the first morning;
>   Blackbird has spoken like the first bird.
> Praise for the singing, praise for morning,
>   Praise for them springing fresh from the Word.
> Fresh the rains new fall sunlit from heaven,
>   Like the first dew fall on the first grass.
> Praise for the sweetness of the wet garden
>   Sprung in completeness where His feet pass.
> Mine is the sunlight; mine is the morning;
>   born of the one light Eden saw play.
> Praise with elation, praise every morning,
>   God's recreation of the new day!
>   Eleanor Farjeon

Lord thank You for making my life new. Please deliver me from the delusion of boredom. Please keep me fresh in Your love for all with whom I have to do. Keep me aware that I am always on the cutting edge of Reality.

229

REBUILDING

Then I said to them, "You see the trouble we are in: Jerusalem lies in ruins, and its gates have been burned with fire. Come, let us rebuild the wall of Jerusalem, and we will no longer be in disgrace." I also told them about the gracious hand of my God upon me...They replied, "Let us start rebuilding." So they began this good work [Neh2:17-18].

At various points in our life we have the challenge of rebuilding. Sometimes major losses or setbacks beset us, and we must decide how we will respond. Divorce, death, personal failure, or catastrophic loss presents us with a tremendous opportunity for transcendence and growth; or spiritual defeat. The story of Israel's failure, captivity, and restoration offer us a blueprint for successful rebuilding. Israel had failed to walk in the light of God's commands and precepts, though given gracious and ample opportunity to do so through the prophets sent to them. So they were taken away into captivity. They lost their land, autonomy, and integrity. But they never lost the love of their Creator. And in due time, there arose courageous souls who knew it was time to be restored and to rebuild. Under the Holy Spirit inspired leadership of Ezra, the Temple had been rebuilt. Nehemiah then recognized the need for the restoration of the wall around the city. The principles of his leadership are inspirational for all who would rebuild major constructs of their lives. If you read through the book of Nehemiah, you will clearly see these principles enacted. Nehemiah first demonstrated a **compassionate recognition of the need.** He wept and mourned when he saw the great trouble and disgrace of his people. He immediately **prayed and fasted**, seeking the grace and empowerment of God [1:3-4]. He took **personal responsibility,** confessing his own sins and acknowledging the sins of his ancestors, even though it had been at least a hundred years since his people had been taken into captivity [1:6-7]. He **faced and overcame his fears**, approaching King Artaxerxes with a request to return to Jerusalem [2:2-3]. He spent time in **careful preparation** [2:7-9]. He carefully **evaluated the situation and assessed the need** [2:11-16]. He **collaborated and engaged the cooperation of the people** [2:17-3:32]. He **prayerfully and persistently overcame the opposition** [Ch. 4]. He did not allow the work of rebuilding the wall to take precedence over the **care and concern for all people involved** [Ch. 5]. He led the people to officially and clearly acknowledge that it was their own and their ancestors' sin that had led to the destruction of their way of life. They **took responsibility and did not blame anyone for what they had lost. And they praised God and thanked Him for the successful restoration** [Ch. 9]. Finally, they **joyfully dedicated the fruit of their labor to God, and carefully**

renewed their commitment to walk in His way [12:27-13:30]. Every step of the way, Nehemiah acknowledged the "gracious hand of God" upon him.

Lord please forgive us for our foolish and blind transgressions. You have always acted justly and fairly, but we have presumed upon Your grace and expected that to which we were not entitled. Help us to rebuild the broken aspects of our lives, just as You helped the people in Nehemiah's time. And give us grace to walk always in gratitude and obedience to You and Your steadfast love for all. May we abide always in Your Love, Peace, and Joy.

230

RIVERS OF LIVING WATER

He who believes in me, as the scripture has said, 'Out of his heart shall flow rivers of living water'[John 7:38].

A friend recently told me about some of the problems he had in his relationship with his father, who had fallen far short in some significant aspects of his parenting. As he grew into adulthood, and as a Christian, he began to learn about his dad's history as a Viet Nam vet, and how confused and conflicted Americans were about the war; and how, as a result, we did not welcome our veterans home with as much compassion and gratitude as they deserved, and how this added to their psychological trauma. He read about Post Traumatic Stress Syndrome. He began to understand some of his dad's behaviors. At one point he said to his dad, "You don't even have to apologize. It's OK. I understand." Can you imagine the healing that must have flowed into that father's heart with that statement?

When we walk in the Spirit of Christ's love, we are blessed with a tremendous potential for healing. Love enables us to understand people and their behaviors more deeply. Jesus heals our heart of the wounds inflicted upon us through our imperfect caretakers and loved ones. Instead of being critical of them, we forgive and have compassion for them. This compassion has the potential of touching their hearts in a healing and liberating manner. This is another way of describing what Jesus spoke about in the above verse. It represents the expansion of the Kingdom of God. And, it is happening in countless homes, workplaces, and relationships today and every day. We can be very thankful for this "river of living water." We can all bathe in its refreshing, clean, pure and healing flow.

Lord, may the river of living water flow through me, healing my wounded heart, and washing away all my selfishness and apathy and self-righteous indignation.

Dedicated to L.P.

231

THE EVIDENCE OF GOD

By this all men will know that you are my disciples, if you have love for one another [Jesus, John 13:35].

He answered, "Whether he is a sinner, I do not know; one thing I know, that though I was blind, now I see" [John 9:25].

    Some years ago, in my hometown of Sylacauga, Alabama, I went into a fast food restaurant with my dad, who was moderately advanced in Alzheimer's. We met a man who obviously knew Dad, and who Dad obviously did not recognize; but, as he had learned to do, acted politely as if he did. When Dad asked how he was doing, he smiled broadly, and in a pleasant southern accent replied, "Ah man, I'm doin' fine! Mindin' my wife! Catchin' a lot o' fish!" I was struck by the fact that he considered "minding my wife," an aspect of "doing fine," and when we sat down together, I asked him about it. With tears welling up in his eyes, he told me that he used to drink and "beat" his wife. "But that was before the Lord came into my life," he said. "Now I realize what a good woman the Lord gave me. Everything she ever tried to get me to do was good. But before, I was too blind to see it." As a counselor, I have seen the kind of blind animosity that can cause a man to abuse his wife. I have seen women who've been spiritually beaten down by constant criticism and intimidated by fear. I was struck again, even more deeply, by the incredible contrast between the evil of that patronizing, abusing, domination, and the level of enlightenment and freedom that would enable a man to brag on the fact that he 'minded his wife." Tears welled up in my eyes also. Tears of deep gratitude for what God can do in a man's life, and for the tremendous difference that that change makes in so many lives.

    If you want to see the evidence of the reality of God, there it is! Take a long hard look at this friend of Dad's—and countless others like him. Look at their lives before Christ. Look at the selfishness, self-centeredness, blindness, meanness, betrayal, apathy, callousness, and numbness to the beauty and goodness of life. Look at how they are unable to see their beautiful children as anything but an encumbrance, or as a reflection of themselves. See how they feel trapped in their marriages, and deprived by their spouses, who are only trying to love them. See how they are consumed with the need for pleasure, and wrecking their health in the pursuit of it. Look at how they are consumed with fear or feelings of deprivation and meaninglessness. See how they invest vast amounts of energy to impress people, and will not lift a finger to love them. Then take another look at them after their conversion—after Christ comes in and transforms them. Look at how they now can genuinely care for another human being! Look at the humility! Look at the compassion and generosity! See how they take responsibility for what they have generated in life! Look at the unforced kindness! See how they can encourage and uplift with a word! Notice how, now, they can say, "I'm sorry," without blaming anyone for their mistake! Now they are at peace and even experience joy. As my Mom said to me [in gratitude and deep respect for Dad], "You're dad became a man when he joined the church."

I personally need nothing more than this measurable and enduring transformation—this metamorphosis, this psycho-spiritual evolution, this spiral of growth that is evoked by receiving Christ as Lord—to convince me of the reality of God in Christ. I need no other confirming miracle than the one I have experienced within myself, and that I see in countless others. One thing I know: I once was blind, but now I see!

Lord Jesus, we bow in deep gratitude for what You have done for us. You have taught us the Way of Life. And You are always with us, empowering us to walk in this glorious Way. You are transforming us into what God created us to become.

232

PEOPLE WHO LOVE PEOPLE

But my God shall supply all your need according to his riches in glory by Christ Jesus [Phil 4:19].

This is my commandment, That you love one another, as I have loved you [Jesus, John 15:12].

Some years ago Barbra Streisand sang a song declaring, "*People who need people are the luckiest people in the world.*" As a counselor, I see repeatedly that people who need people are some of the most miserable people in the world. One of the commonest mistakes that humans make is to fixate on some person in an effort to get his/her needs met. Biblically speaking, this is heretical. The Bible teaches plainly that we are to look to God for our needs, and focus on *loving,* [not needing] other people. People who *love* people are the luckiest [most blessed and happy] people in the world. When we need people, we attach ourselves to the roller coaster of their performance. If they are doing a good job of meeting our needs, we are happy; if they are not, we are unhappy. Our love for them is dependent upon how well they are doing at meeting our needs. We are perpetually in the judgment seat, evaluating their performance; and, people being people, they are usually not doing very well. We feel disappointed, deprived, and frustrated because our needs are not being met. We may become very critical of this person for not meeting our needs. If we are married to him/her, we may begin to think we have made a mistake because this person is not meeting our needs. We begin to believe that someone else would do a better job of it. People who need people frequently feel that they "give and give and give, and get little or nothing in return." These are giving out of their need. They are giving to receive. We are called by God to grow spiritually to the point that we are able to receive our fulfillment in communion with Him and in the joy of serving. Then our giving will be from the overflow of our heart rather than from our need.

It is certainly true that people need people. God made us this way. As a counselor, I need clients in order to provide for my family. I need my family and friends. I need mechanics to repair my car. I need farmers, grocers, doctors, dentists, construction workers, cashiers, soldiers, and politicians, to name a few. We all need each other. But this is not the focus of our attention and efforts. Jesus did not ordain His disciples to *need* people: He ordained them [and us] to *love* people. When we love people, we focus on *their* needs—not *ours.* Whatever I need from people, God will see that I receive as I continue to focus on loving people as He has commanded me. My needs are God's business, not mine. Jesus causes us to realize that our primary need, above all needs, is to love people with His love. When we love people in this way, we are the luckiest, happiest, and most blessed people in the world!

Lord, thank You for delivering us from the dreadful misery of needing people, into the glorious light of loving them.

233

POUTING

In everything give thanks: for this is the will of God in Christ Jesus concerning you [1Thes 5:18].

And we know that all things work together for good to them that love God, to them who are the called according to his purpose [Rm 8:28].

    Pouting is an interesting phenomenon. It's defined as: "To thrust out the lips, especially in ill humor. To be sullen; sulk." Sullen is defined as: "Obstinately and gloomily ill-humored; morose; glum; melancholy." Sulky is "doggedly or resentfully ill-humored." My two-year-old grandson does it very well. When his dad or mom refuses to grant a desire, his pouting demeanor is so cute I have to turn aside so he doesn't see me smiling. As I recall, his dad and uncles were pretty good at it too. In fact, it is a common, instinctive childhood response expressing displeasure at not getting what one wants. "Poor me! You shouldn't treat me so badly! You're mean! I don't love you anymore!" It is low-grade or passive anger, arising out of ego-injury or perceived deprivation of what one feels entitled to.
    Remnants of this, as we all know, linger into adulthood, at which stage of life it is no longer cute at all. It takes a little longer to overcome than diaper soiling, and it stinks just as much—in fact, progressively more so with age. In adulthood, the negative energy of pouting is usually directed toward one's spouse, or toward God, or just life in general (which is also, indirectly, God). As the above verses clearly indicate, it has no place in the personality of a child of God. A pouting, sulky, sullen attitude is a stench in the nostrils of God, and is as alien in His Kingdom as a fish in the desert. As we progress in the Kingdom, we evolve into joyful servants who (contemporary television commercials notwithstanding) do not think about what we are entitled to or deserve (except with gratitude that because of God's grace, we do *not* get it). We are not injured by others' failures in loving us, and we do not try to emotionally punish them by pouting. Because we are so keenly aware of our own selfish struggles and our need for grace, we give it to others when they fail. We do not hold grudges nor sit in the judgment seat over others' failures. Like the psalmist, we recognize that *the LORD [is] on my side;... what can man do unto me?[Ps 118:6]* We know, in our deepest core, that even when we are not getting what we want, we are getting what we need. Because we have responded to God's love with love for Him and all His creatures—because we have received Christ to be our Lord—we know with growing certainty that He is working *all* things together for good for us;

even the things that we used to pout about! And we are thankful in *"every thing"*!

Lord, please help me to never pout again—about anything! Amen.

234

LIFE IS NOT WHAT WE WANT IT TO BE

These things I have spoken unto you, that in me ye might have peace. In the world ye shall have tribulation: but be of good cheer; I have overcome the world [Jesus, John 16:33].

...do not let the sun go down on your anger [Eph 4:26].

I have been angry at God. The "voice" of my anger was something like: "This is *hard*, and it doesn't seem fair or right. Why do You allow things to be this way? I don't feel that You are good to allow things to be so difficult and hurtful. I don't have any choice but to submit to it—after all, You are God—but I don't have to like it, and I *don't!*"

I am very thankful that I did not get stuck for too long in that anger. Jesus' statement about having tribulation in this world helped me greatly with letting go of my anger. I am writing this because I have recently seen another unfortunate example of someone who is stuck in that anger; and that person is very unhappy. Those who fall into this pit are caught up in a vicious cycle that spirals downward. They are smoldering in rebellion against their only hope. Some who are caught in this vicious cycle have fallen into some sinful, destructive life patterns and may feel they cannot overcome them. Shame and hopelessness may then multiply the alienation. Though they are unhappy, and becoming progressively more so, when they hear the words of life that could set them free, instead of contrition and submission, they harden their hearts and turn away. But as we have learned [usually the hard way] life outside the Kingdom just doesn't work. Peter was absolutely right in his response to Christ's question, *"Will you also turn away from me?"* Peter replied, *"Lord, to whom shall we go? You have the words of eternal life."* [Jhn 6:67-8]. In this hurt, anger, and rebellion, obedience can look like a steep and rough climb to nowhere—an obstacle course that we have run before, and that didn't pay off. It feels like we are letting God [or somebody] off the hook; and He or they don't deserve to be let off. And, of course, Satan is right there on the left shoulder breathing lies, nursing hurts, feeding hopelessness and entitlement to something better or easier than this unfair pathway that God has laid out for us, reminding us that we are a victim. We become like a child who's been sent to his room to do his homework but is angry because he can't stay outside and play. He refuses to do his homework, and when Mom comes to the door to offer some encouragement, he sulks and pouts in the corner, refusing to look at her. He condemns himself to a whole evening in his room, when an hour's worth of homework would have gotten him outside playing again. God, like that healthy mom, cannot give in to our temper tantrums because it feeds something in us that will ultimately destroy us if we do not allow His Spirit to cast it out of us. Nothing can be gained in the Kingdom of God by angry entitlement, nor by sulking or pouting. We alienate ourselves from God and all sustaining help when we languish in these. He compassionately and sadly waits, like the father of the prodigal son, for us to come to ourselves and come home with contrite hearts at which time He will joyfully kill the fatted calf and celebrate our return from death into life, restoring us to our rightful place as a full-fledged child of the King [Lk 15:11-24].

*Lord, please deliver me from smoldering anger and rebellion, and from feeling entitled to something better than I have received. I accept, deeply and thankfully, that even though life is not what I want it to be, it is exactly what I **need** it to be. I ask for grace to keep a cheerful heart through all of life's tribulations. I know that You are good beyond measure, and that this life You have given me is a blessing—not a curse.*

235

GREED

I took counsel with myself, and I brought charges against the nobles and the officials. I said to them, "You are exacting interest, each from his brother." And I held a great assembly against them,... So I said, "The thing that you are doing is not good" [Neh 5:7,9].

Greed is one of the seven deadly sins. Deadly means fatal: it will destroy a nation. Democracy makes way for much personal and corporate freedom. If the primary driving force behind that freedom is the making of money, then there will never be enough of it. The needs of the soul will be neglected, and the culture will begin to wilt toward death. The soul flourishes in an atmosphere of generosity. Humans don't do well when they view each other as competitors for space, goods, or dollars. Yet, as we know from the concept of "sibling rivalry," we are born with this tendency. The childish ego wants to be the most attended to, loved, praised, and showered with toys. This tendency does not simply evaporate in adulthood. Our toys just become more expensive. The childhood desire for the approval of parents evolves into the desire for the approval of our peers, and this may involve impressing them with what we own or can afford. Men learn that wealth attracts beautiful women and affords prestige, the promise of security, and pleasure. The desire for these attributes is not necessarily evil, but we see that if it becomes the primary driving force of the personality, that personality is unbalanced and distorted. Jesus moves us in a different direction. He says that we are happier [more blessed] if we *give* than if we receive or acquire. Desire, need, and greed, like gravity, are forces that generate a pull inward toward the center of the personality. Love, generosity, and good will, like light, are forces that radiate outward toward others. One of the great paradoxes of human experience is that we can never be fulfilled by pulling inward but only by radiating outward. Jesus describes His followers as "light"—not gravity. [Mt 5:14] The joyful life is not one that is flooded with possessions and capital, but one that is compassionate and generous. We see clearly that those who have acquired much wealth are only happy if they are using it philanthropically—to make the world better for others. Those who continue to use their wealth for selfish pleasure tend to die young—or old and bitter. Wealth is ruinous for those who do not evolve spiritually—who do not mature into generosity and detachment from materialism. And thankfully, one does not have to be rich to be generous. Jesus said that the widow who gave only a few pennies into the treasury gave the most of all because she gave out of her need. [Mk 12:41-44] Perhaps she was also the most joyful and free.

Lord, thank You for Your glorious generosity toward us. Please help us to be generous toward each other. Deliver us from the prison cell of greed and selfishness, into the glorious light of compassion and good will.

236

WE HAVE ALL FAILED

For all have sinned and fall short of the glory of God [Rom 3:23].

If we say, "We have no sin," we are deceiving ourselves, and the truth is not in us [1John1:8].

> *"For if you forgive people their wrongdoing, your heavenly Father will forgive you as well. But if you don't forgive people, your Father will not forgive your wrongdoing [Jesus, Mt 6:14-15].*

One of the hallmarks of mature faith is awareness and acknowledgement of our sinful nature and all its manifestations. The world sees this as a morbid pathway to guilt and feelings of inferiority; but as Christians, we have come to discover it as the *only* honest pathway into freedom and peace.

Even though we realize this, it is still difficult for us to exercise the wonderful discipline of awareness of our failures and confession. We are reluctant to suffer the painful feelings associated with failure. Pride blocks us. We see others' failures more clearly than we see our own and tend to focus on the "speck" in their eye rather than the "beam" in our own [Mt 7:3f].

There seems to be a direct link between our unwillingness to look honestly at our own character defects and our critical and judgmental attitudes toward others. This failure causes much enmity between people. We have a tendency to see our self as a victim and the other as the perpetrator. We live with the delusion that "life would be fine if only s/he would look honestly at him/herself and make the necessary changes." But we are loath to put those shoes on our own feet.

When we do, however, exercise this wonderful discipline of our faith, we are blessed with forgiveness and humility. We know that God is smiling upon us, for we have been obedient to Him. We are able to forgive others for their failures. We recognize our own need for grace, so we are no longer reluctant to give it to others. We become more *graceful*. We are kinder and less critical. We are not blind to the failures of others, but we see those failures through the eyes of grace. We are no longer critical and punitive. We can encourage and help much more effectively when we do not feel victimized by our loved ones. The changes that they need to make are much more likely to happen in an atmosphere of grace and humility than one of criticism and prideful hurt. As Jesus said, when we get the beam out of our own eye, we can help others get the speck out of theirs [but only if they want the help!]. We are amazed to discover that, when we confess our own sins and do the spiritual-growth work that God wants us to do, we no longer feel victimized by others, *even if they do not grow in that same way!* We discover that what we really needed was not for them to change, but to grow our selves. God really is fair! He did not create us to be victims of the failures of others. He created us to be free, peaceful, and responsible. But we must look honestly and deeply at our own failures, confess them to God and those we have hurt, seeking and receiving forgiveness. And we must completely and deeply forgive everyone through whom we have been hurt in any way if we are to experience this great freedom and peace. Just because we are Christians and attend church regularly, we should not assume that we are being successful at this. We should ask God for help in becoming mature enough to examine our self honestly in gaining awareness of our sinful nature manifestations, confession, and giving and receiving forgiveness, leading to grace and peace.

Lord, please forgive me for my failures and weaknesses. I also forgive everyone through whom I have been hurt or wounded. I release myself from all grudges or hardness of heart toward anyone. I sincerely desire the best for all people, even my "enemies." I receive the gift of Your loving heart of forgiveness and grace toward me, and through me toward all. Help me to love better.

237

GOOD FRIDAY

And about the ninth hour Jesus cried with a loud voice, saying, "Eli, Eli, lama sabachthani? that is to say, My God, my God, why hast thou forsaken me?" [Mt 27:46].

Good Friday was truly good for the human family; but it was far from good [from the worldly standpoint] for Jesus. He was betrayed, denied, and abandoned by His own disciples. He was falsely accused by His own people. He was mocked and reviled. It is very difficult to read the events in Matthew 27 and Mark 15 reflectively, and especially to contemplate Jesus being "scourged." The International Standard Bible Encyclopedia describes the instrument by which it was administered: *A Roman implement for severe bodily punishment. ...It consisted of a handle, to which several cords or leather thongs were affixed, which were weighted with jagged pieces of bone or metal, to make the blow more painful and effective.... The victim was tied to a post (Acts 22:25) and the blows were applied to the back and loins, sometimes even, in the wanton cruelty of the executioner, to the face and the bowels... So hideous was the punishment that the victim usually fainted and many times died under it.*

And then He was nailed to the cross and allowed to slowly die. These events, and Jesus Himself, are amazingly and accurately described in Isaiah 53, written prophetically seven hundred years earlier. There we read, *"But he was wounded for our transgressions, he was bruised for our iniquities: the chastisement of our peace was upon him; and with his stripes we are healed. [vs.5].* One of the wonderful and important disciplines of the Christian faith is to maintain a growing awareness of the price that was paid for our salvation. Like spoiled children, we are constantly tempted to take it for granted—to presume upon God's grace and mercy toward us, and fail to be adequately thankful that we are no longer in condemnation. We are free from guilt, shame, and fear because Christ entered into the farthest depths of the pit of human experience. Most amazingly, and perhaps most painfully, He either was, or at least felt, FORSAKEN BY GOD! Theologians have many comments to make about this statement and what it means. But at the very least, in those moments, Jesus, the Lord of Love and Prince of Peace, the perfect Lamb of God, felt *forsaken* by His heavenly Father Whom He had so obediently served. I cannot imagine a deeper psychological pit of despair and hopelessness than to be God forsaken. And Jesus went there on my behalf. He not only had to suffer the worst imaginable physical trauma, but He also had to go as low as the human soul could possibly go in order to be our Messiah. Lest we sink into excessive despair in contemplating this, we are reminded by Paul in Hebrews 12 that *"it was for the joy that was set before Him"* that He endured the cross. His joy was in accomplishing His earthshaking mission to deliver the human family from the death grip of the prince of this world. Whatever we suffer, physically or psychologically in this brief time on earth, Jesus can always say to us, "I know how that feels. Hang on. Don't worry. Sunday's coming!"

Lord Jesus, may I never forget what You have done for me. And, by Your grace, may I live a life worthy of Your sacrifice.

238

THE POWER OF THE RESURRECTION

Act 4:33 And with great power gave the apostles witness of the resurrection of the Lord Jesus: and great grace was upon them all.

In Christ we are not focused on *power*; we are focused on Love, as our Lord has commanded us. But we find that this Love is the most powerful force in the universe, delivering us from all evil forces. After Jesus' resurrection He told His disciples that *"All power in heaven and on earth is given to me...And I am with you always, even to the end of the age"* [Mt. 28:18]. And this power was to be used to teach all people about the Kingdom that He had established—a Kingdom of Love, Peace and Joy, existing in a Spirit of familihood—the Spirit of Christ Himself. In Christ we find all that we need. We discover the liberating Truth of His words and His promises. He said, *"I have overcome the world"* [Jn. 16:33] and in Him we also overcome the world [1Jn. 4:4]. Millions of Christians

throughout two thousand years of history have discovered the truth of Christ, and the power of His Spirit to live lives characterized by faith, hope and love; and to face death with courage and hope. And this has happened despite four periods of major persecution in the first one hundred, fifty years of its beginnings, and the fact that it was considered heretical by the religions existing at its onset. Any Christian can tell you, from a personal perspective, that a major reason for the success of Christianity is the Love that they feel emanating through Christ and His teachings. Something about Him resonates deeply within us. It's interesting [and enlightening] that even the people and religious groups that discount Christianity have great difficulty finding anything negative to say about Christ Himself. The one teaching that many seem to balk at is His statement about being "the way, the truth and the light" and that *"no one comes to the Father but by me"* [Jn14:6] . It seems that, even though they agree that His teachings are excellent, and the world would be immensely better off if we heeded them, they cannot accept Him as the doorway to the Father—or Creator. The Resurrection speaks to this, and it crowns the perfection of Christ's mission. The Resurrection is more verifiable historically than anything that happened that long ago. There are more copies of Greek New Testaments than any other manuscript of its age; and all four Gospels and the Epistles speak of the Resurrection. Many intelligent men, including historians have studied the events surrounding the Resurrection— some with the intent of disproving it—and have come up with no viable disputation of its validity. Many unbelievers converted to the Faith in this process. Every theory of how such a story could have been falsely propagated and yet found such deep and wide acceptance by so many in such a brief span of time falls ultimately in the ash heap of unreason. Those who lived with Him— His disciples—died because they believed the truth of His resurrection, and refused to recant. The Gospel writers wrote from first-hand experience. Paul, whose writings began within twenty-five years of Christ's crucifixion, speaks of those who were still living at the time of his writings who had witnessed the Resurrection [1Cor.15:4-6]. Anyone reading his epistle would have had the opportunity to speak to those who witnessed it, to disprove or confirm it. Paul was putting his credibility, moreover his *life*, on the line regarding the Resurrection of Christ, which, I repeat, had occurred only *twenty-five years earlier*. The credibility of the Resurrection empowered many early Christians to persevere through the persecutions, and, bolstered by Jesus' commandments regarding love, emboldened them to minister to people with contagious fatal illnesses who had been abandoned by those without faith. This courageous love attracted many to Faith in Christ, and, coupled with the joy we see in those who have been set free in Him, continues to bring many into the Kingdom.
It makes sense that a loving God would not want His children, created in His image and given foreknowledge of death, to live in fear of it. Jesus' teachings are so pure and selfless, His birth so unpretentious, His life so beautifully lived in

the dark arena of human suffering; how can we not trust Him and those He discipled to be honest about life after death? And how perfect of our heavenly Father to confirm it all by raising Him from the dead as a testimony to the human family of His place as Savior and Friend. If you have doubts about the Resurrection, I encourage you to do an intellectually sound in-depth study of it. Our Faith is founded upon it.

Lord, I sometimes have doubts about Your resurrection. But there is so much evidence, and Your teachings resonate such Truth for the human family, how could I think You or Your devoted followers would be deceptive about anything? Please help me resolve my doubts and come down firmly and finally on the peaceful and secure foundation that frees me from the fear of death. Thank You for not leaving us in the darkness about death. Today please empower me to be a joyful, peaceful servant to the glory of Your Kingdom.

239

TRUE SUCCESS

A dispute also arose among [his disciples], which of them was to be regarded as the greatest. And Jesus said to them, "The kings of the Gentiles exercise lordship over them; and those in authority over them are called benefactors. But not so with you; rather let the greatest among you become as the youngest, and the leader as one who serves [Lk 22:24-26].

Beloved, let us love one another: for love is of God; and every one that loves is born of God, and knows God [1John 4:7].

By this all men will know that you are my disciples, if you have love for one another [Jesus, John 13:35].

There are many ideas about success afloat in our culture: Good marriage, job, money, travel, prestige, acclaim, and authority to name a few. On the lower end of the scale, I recently heard of a medical doctor who stated to a friend that his primary goal was to impregnate as many women in his community as possible. It is sobering to think that we could spend our whole lives strenuously climbing a ladder, only to discover that it is leaning against the wrong wall! At this moment there are countless elderly persons in nursing homes or on deathbeds who cannot bear to look honestly back upon their lives because they have been spent in vanity and selfishness. When we come before

Christ, we will have to face the truth about how we lived our lives. There will be no denial, no place to hide, no rationalizations, no excuses. The same Truth that will be heaven for those who have loved, pursued, and submitted to it, will be hell for those who have hated, resisted, and denied it.

Jesus, in His life and teachings, brought *success* into a laser beam focus for us. Whoever loves and serves the best is the greatest—the most successful. This is our pathway and goal. But if we are honest, we recognize within ourselves many [not necessarily evil] motivations competing with this pure love and servant-orientation. We do want to have much good sex. It feels great to be applauded by people and to deposit a big check in the bank account. We want to lie on the beach and eat in restaurants—and we expect good *service*! We are indignant toward ignorant or inept people who cause us delays. We don't want to be bothered too much with the "needy." We are easily offended if we are not respected, and we pout if we are not appreciated. We are frustrated when life doesn't work to our advantage. We still have much useless ego in us to be overcome. We need the help of the Holy Spirit to maintain forward movement toward success as Jesus defined it. The pleasures and distractions of the world are powerful and consuming—but they are empty and void of satisfaction at the end of the day. Loving people with Christ's love and keeping a servant's heart opens up an infinite universe in our souls for joy and makes life an endless feast and the greatest of all adventures.

Lord, today may I fulfill Your desire by being a gracious, kind, compassionate, and joyful servant to everyone in my sphere of influence. May I bring some of Your Light into someone's life. Please deliver me from useless or selfish endeavors that provide no satisfaction. Help me to use my life energy wisely and compassionately.

240

WHAT DO YOU EXPECT?

These things I have spoken to you, that in me you might have peace. In the world you will have tribulation: but be of good cheer; I have overcome the world [Jesus, John 16:33].

Now when he was in Jerusalem at the Passover feast, many believed in his name when they saw the signs which he did; but Jesus did not trust

himself to them, because he knew all men and needed no one to bear witness of man; for he himself knew what was in man [John 2:23-25].

What do you expect from the people in your life? What do you expect from life in general? These are important questions, worthy of some thoughtful consideration.

Someone has said, "An expectation is a resentment waiting to happen." Unfulfilled expectations provide fertile soil for the growth of frustration, anger, and resentment. Sometimes in subconscious, smoldering ways, and sometimes in flaming, overt ways, we expect people and life to be something other than they are. And to whatever degree this is going on inside us, we walk around with some level of disappointment, frustration, anger, or resentment, leading ultimately to bitterness. We may experience these unfulfilled expectations as a slightly depressed sense of "Oh well, it's not what I thought it was going to be. Guess I'll just have to make do with this second-rate lifestyle." Or we may experience them as a flaming, inner *demand* that it [or they] be different. What is anger if it is not a powerful inner demand that situations or persons be different than they are? And, much good has come from properly channeled, righteous anger at injustice or abuse. But much suffering comes from unrealistic expectations and excessive needs and dependencies on things and people.

Regarding expectations, the above verses impart wisdom to us from God's infinite storehouse. Jesus teaches us what to expect from *people* and from *life*. Regarding people, He did not entrust Himself to them "because He knew all men"—He "knew what was in man." He knew that all people have character defects, weaknesses, and potential for betrayal. No human can ever provide a reliable enough foundation for one's ultimate faith. No human can ever reach that place deep in our soul that longs for fulfillment. And what does Jesus teach us to expect from life? *Tribulation.* If you have not yet gotten to the place of acceptance and peaceful expectation of tribulation, you should expect to be shocked and disappointed. Tribulation is coming for you and everyone you love. And how does Jesus teach us to *respond* to these realistic expectations from people and life? He teaches us, by His words and His life, to love these imperfect and unreliable people who have hurt and betrayed us, to forgive them, to seek forgiveness for our failures in loving them adequately, and to look to Him to protect us from excessive emotional vulnerability to them. And regarding the tribulations of life, He teaches us to "be of good cheer" because He has "overcome the world." And we are *in* Him.

Lord, please deliver us from unrealistic expectations from people or life. We understand that we are to love people, even if they fail us. We understand that we have also failed. And we understand that we will have tribulation in this life. Teach us how to live with cheerful hearts, nevertheless.

241

BEYOND ROMANCE

Love is patient and kind; love is not jealous or boastful; it is not arrogant or rude. Love does not insist on its own way; it is not irritable or resentful; it does not rejoice at wrong, but rejoices in the right. Love bears all things, believes all things, hopes all things, endures all things. Love never ends [1Cr 13:4-8]
...So shun youthful passions and aim at righteousness, faith, love, and peace, along with those who call upon the Lord from a pure heart [2 Tm 2:22].

Romantic feelings are like a drug. We have incredibly powerful feelings when we are "in love." Recent research indicates that certain chemicals are active in the brain when a person is "in love" that cause him to behave as if he is under the influence of a drug. He/she does not exercise good judgment. One may break up his family, abandon his children, hurt those who have devoted themselves to him, suffer sleep deprivation, neglect long-term responsibilities, leave behind fortunes and kingdoms because he is "in love." This is true even though we now know that these chemical reactions in the brain are time-limited. They cannot endure. And when they fade, one is left with the same challenges and normal difficulties of life and relations that were there before the great "fall" [into "love"]. Only now, his life is complicated by the havoc that has been wreaked by the poor decisions he made while "under the influence"—divorce, vocational setbacks, debt, poor health, etc. And he discovers that when he moves in with his new girlfriend and lives with her for awhile, she is astoundingly less desirable than when she was the "forbidden fruit" that he could only access on the sly. One of the great lies of Satan is that these feelings can be maintained indefinitely. And there is a tremendous load of unnecessary suffering in our world because of this lie.

It is very important to differentiate between *love* and being *in love*. Being *in love* is something that a person truly can "fall" into. It takes no effort to fall. It happens automatically, and it feels very good. *Loving*, on the other hand, requires diligence, sacrifice, and on-going peaceful effort. And it does not always feel good. This is 2011 A.D. [anno Domini, "In the Year of Our Lord"] because the greatest act of Love in human history occurred [approximately] 2011 years ago. Jesus submitted Himself to the Cross and became the Savior and Deliverer of the human family. And it did not *feel good*. In fact He prayed to be delivered from it. We must not confuse this Love with romantic feelings. And we must be willing to let go of or sacrifice romantic feelings for the sake of this greater love that facilitates the psycho-spiritual evolution of the human family.

The same God Who gave us the capacity to "fall in love" calls us into the greater Love that is beyond romance. We do not have to feel deprived. In His Love for us, He calls us to greater heights and brighter vistas than any romantic movie or poem could possibly depict. He calls us into the Love that never fades away but rather is like an artesian well of living water—like a beautiful flower that never stops blooming—a love that becomes within us a never-ending source of fulfillment, joy, and peace. This is the Love that Jesus commands His followers to abide within—this Love for God and man that shines like the sun with compassion and good will toward all and refuses to hurt or betray others for the sake of better feelings. Instead of looking back longingly and mournfully on those romantic feelings of adolescence and early adulthood, we can look ahead faithfully to the greater love that breaks like rising sun on the new horizon. We can trust His Love and know that the best is yet to be—not only in heaven, but here on earth also as we abide in His Love and peacefully do the good for which we were created. We regress when we selfishly pursue romantic feelings, forsaking the Love of Christ, and we will live to regret it. We are moving toward the best feelings available to human beings when we are willing to sacrifice for the greater good of God.

Lord, please deliver us from our addiction to romantic feelings so that we can move onward and upward on the wings of Christ's Love into the greater joys of Your Kingdom.

242

CIVILITY

Let your speech always be gracious, seasoned with salt, so that you may know how you ought to answer every one [Col. 4:6].

And be kind one to another, tenderhearted, forgiving one another, even as God for Christ's sake has forgiven you [Eph 4:32].

For we all make many mistakes, and if any one makes no mistakes in what he says he is a perfect man, able to bridle the whole body also [Jam 3:2].

At this writing, in the news recently have been three glaring examples of incivility and offensive speech: a professional tennis player during a televised national competition, a musical entertainer on a national stage, and a congressman during a presidential speech. [All three subsequently apologized.] Additionally, between the political parties of our nation there has been an alarming amount of harsh, sometimes hateful rhetoric. If we see this lack of self control on national television exhibited by professionals in the national limelight, where there is social pressure to look good—how much more so must it be occurring in schools, workplaces and homes.

As a counselor, I have repeatedly seen the destructive effects of this lack of self-control in the context of marriage and family relations. Some of the hallmarks of maturity are civility, control of the tongue, and a fundamental attitude of politeness and kindness, even toward those with whom we disagree. This is not a manifestation of weakness, but rather a wonderful manifestation of strength: strength in the form of temperance or self-control [one of the fruits of the Holy Spirit {Gal 5:23}]. We can assertively hold forth for what we believe without being offensive or impolite. God commands us to do the best we can to be at peace with all people [Rom 12:18]. And Jesus has commanded us to love our enemies and do good to those who hate us [Mt 5:44]. We are admonished not to return evil for evil, but rather to overcome evil with good [Rom 12:17, 21]. The problem is that we frequently act or speak impulsively based on a powerful feeling. It is very important and helpful to cultivate a deeper awareness or mindfulness of our powerful feelings. Whenever we are overcome by a powerful emotion, we must learn to be very careful, very mindful, and take an equally powerful hold on our responsive behavior. We must *willfully* insert *thought* and *prayer* between impulse and action. Our desire as Christians is to be motivated by the Holy Spirit—not by powerful feelings. And the Holy Spirit loves those toward whom we are responding, even if they are in the wrong. The ground floor of behavior for Christians should be civility. No matter the situation, we should never go below civility in any arena of social discourse. And in order to accomplish this, we must be willing to be introspective, choose to care about how we come across to others, and put some prayerful thought into our own patterns of feelings and behaviors.

Lord, please help us to speak and behave gracefully. Please deliver us from knee-jerk reactions that hurt or offend others and discredit Your Kingdom. Please help us to always be respectful and civil, even if others are not being so.

243

REFUGE

The LORD also will be a refuge for the oppressed, a refuge in times of trouble [Ps 9:9].

...so that through two unchangeable things, in which it is impossible that God should prove false, we who have fled for refuge might have strong encouragement to seize the hope set before us. We have this as a sure and steadfast anchor of the soul, a hope that enters into the inner shrine behind the curtain...[Heb 6:18-19].

God is our refuge and strength, a very present help in trouble [Ps 46:1].

At that day you will know that I am in my Father, and you in me, and I in you [John 14:20].

God is our refuge! This is a wonderful and amazing reality that we can inwardly experience on an increasing basis. We have all experienced that the world can be extremely difficult and stressful. The world can become for us like the fiery furnace into which Shadrach, Meshach and Abednego were thrown. But as we read, since the "Son of God" was in there with them, they emerged safe and did not even have the smell of smoke on them [Dan 3]. Jesus teaches us that we are *in* the world but not *of* the world [John 17:16]. Since we are not *of* the world, we cannot be beaten or destroyed by the world. This is a spiritual reality that we must learn to inwardly experience. It is a wonderful practice to affirm periodically, "I am not of this world! Thank You God, that I am not of this world!" This actually *enhances* our ability to do the good works that help the world become a safer and saner place for the human family, because we need not fear anything that happens in the world—and fear blocks love. Christians care about the world [the people in the world], but they are not worried about anything because God commands us not to worry and reassures us that we really have nothing to worry about. Our souls are anchored in Christ Who sits at the right hand of God [Mk 16:19], and Who is simultaneously in us [John 15:4], and in Whom we live, move and have our being [Acts 17:28]. Death is our final victory [1Cor 15:54], and "to live is Christ, and to die is gain" [Phil 1:21]. As we live in ever-increasing mindfulness of these eternal truths, we discover deep peace, gratitude, and even joy rising up within us. Whatever happens in this world, we can know that we are safe in Christ Who has told us plainly that we will have tribulation in this world, but reminds us constantly that he has overcome the world, so we can keep cheerful hearts. His Truth and His Spirit in us is the only true refuge for the human soul. And it is a safe and eternal refuge. Our primary focus and goal is simply to be obedient to Christ Who has commanded us to trust God and love each other as He loves us. As we abide in His love for all people [even our enemies] we can know beyond doubt that all is well, and all is well, and all shall ever be well. No matter what happens politically, economically, geographically, relationally, or personally, God is a very present help, and we are safe in Christ. We can draw up into Christ-in-us, and we are as safe as Shadrach, Meshach, and Abednego in the fiery furnace. We will not even have the smell of the smoke of this world on us.

Lord, please help me always remember that I am in You, and You are in me, and that You are a safe refuge in times of fear or despair. Please keep me mindful of the eternal Truth that keeps me free from fear and despair.

244

HOW MUCH TRUTH DO YOU LOVE?

And then the lawless one will be revealed, and the Lord Jesus will slay him with the breath of his mouth and destroy him by his appearing and his coming. The coming of the lawless one by the activity of Satan will be with all power and with pretended signs and wonders, and with all wicked deception for those who are to perish, because they refused to love the truth and so be saved. [2 Thes 2:8-10]

Some see Truth as a friend, inviting them into the fulfillment of the desires of their heart. Others see Truth as a threat, depriving them of what they want and need, restraining them in their personal pursuits. Some Truth is easy for us to love; some of it confronts and discomfits us. No matter how we see Truth, it is what it is. We do not control or determine it. It was here before the first star was born, and will be the same ten billion years after the earth is no more. My beliefs do not alter eternal Truth. The same Truth that will be heaven for those who have trusted, diligently sought, and submitted to it, will be hell for those who have resisted, hated, and denied it.

Jesus claims to be "...the Truth..." and He offers Himself to you—to abide in and with you, forever. [John 14:6, 20]. Those who claim to be Christian fall within a broad spectrum in terms of love for Truth. Some are wolves in sheep's clothing. They do not love the Truth. They are hiding in the darkness. Judas was [superficially] a "disciple," but in reality he was Satan's emissary. I personally know of a "preacher" who sexually molested his own children. All of us have been horrified by the evil exposed in people who claimed to be Christians. They were using their religion as a mask for evil behaviors. These cause many to doubt the reality and goodness of the Faith, and their judgment will certainly be severe. Others are sincere in the faith, but weak, and fail in diligence and growth. They may have simply inherited their faith from their parents. They assume they have arrived. Their lives are not fruitful, and they are vulnerable to being deceived and ensnared by the evil one. As a young Christian, I committed adultery early in my marriage because I was weak and blind. My faith was sincere, but my desire for pleasure and adventure was greater than my love for and submission to the Truth. I did not understand that the love and pursuit of Truth is the greatest adventure of all. On a deep level, I did not trust that God's way was really the best for me, so I took matters into my own hands—I acted in the darkness. In doing so, I brought much unnecessary suffering into my own and my family's life. I allowed the evil one to rob me of some of the peace and joy of Christ. [I am so thankful that He has forgiven and restored me. And I am thankful to my wife for forgiving me also.] Those who profess to be Christian exist up and down a scale from malicious deceivers [who are themselves desperately deceived] to those whose deepest and most sincere desire is to bring as much of Christ's love into the world as they possibly can before they depart from the earth, and who, by God's grace, are being successful at it. We have the awesome opportunity and responsibility to determine where we are on this scale and to move a little farther in the right direction.

Lord, You are the Truth. And You Love us more than we can yet know. Please give us grace to love You more, and to trust You more deeply. Fill us more completely with Your Holy Spirit so that we will be bringing more of Your Light into the world, and so we can be truly free.

245

THANK GOD FOR GRACE!
[OUT OF THE MOUTHS OF BABES]

For I do not do the good I want, but the evil I do not want is what I do [Rom 7:19].

And Jesus said unto him, Why do you call me good? None is good, save one, that is, God [Lk 18:19].

...All have sinned and fall short of the glory of God, they are justified by his grace as a gift, through the redemption which is in Christ Jesus, whom God

put forward as an expiation by his blood, to be received by faith. This was to show God's righteousness, because in his divine forbearance he had passed over former sins; it was to prove at the present time that he himself is righteous and that he justifies him who has faith in Jesus [Rom 3:23-26].

We just spent a wonderful Thanksgiving with our family in northern Virginia. Lynn and I had the great pleasure of enjoying our sons, daughter-in-law, and three grandchildren, all together in one place at one time! In a conversation with my youngest grandson, Parker, we were talking about how God wants us to be good—to obey our parents, etc. He said, "I try to be good Paw Paw, but I don't know how." My soul delighted with this eternal, profound truth of the human condition spoken in the simple elegance of a three-year-old. An elaboration of my response is something like, "Me too, Parker. I try to be good, but I cannot always. That's why Jesus came into our world. He was perfectly good, and died for our sins so that God would not be mad at us when we can't be good. God just wants us to keep trying and keep getting better, as best we can. And He gives us His Holy Spirit to help us. And as long as we admit it when we do bad, He forgives us and even forgets all about it. So, because of Jesus, even though we are not always good, we can be happy."

We will never reach the end of the peace, joy, and gratitude available to us as we meditate on the fact that because of Jesus, God is smiling upon us, even as we stumble along on the pathway of righteousness. His mercy endures forever, and His grace is inexhaustible!

Lord Jesus, please help us not to regard our sins lightly. But may we grow in our inner experience of joy and gratitude for the forgiveness that You bought for us at such a dreadful price. And may we always be obedient to You by loving each other as You have commanded us.

246

DRIFTING INTO THE DARKNESS

But false prophets also arose among the people, just as there will be false teachers among you, who will secretly bring in destructive heresies, even denying the Master who bought them, bringing upon themselves swift destruction. And many will follow their licentiousness, and because of them the way of truth will be reviled [2Pet 2:1-2].

Recently a highly respected, world-renowned golfer, Tiger Woods was exposed as an adulterer. Since his exposure, some thirteen women have come forth publicly, claiming alliances with him. (Doubtless some of them are fabricating for public attention.) I do not condemn Mr. Woods or the women with whom he dallied. I committed adultery myself many years ago and consider it a stupid, weak, and selfish failure on my part. What alarms me more than the act itself is that one of the women, head held high, smiling, spoke into a camera for national television and stated that her sexual relationship with Mr. Woods was "sacred!" Meanwhile, Mr. Woods has publicly apologized for his "imperfections." Apparently, *he* does not consider his relations with the woman "sacred." I looked up the word "sacred." It has religious connotations. It means "hallowed; entitled to reverence or respect." On the one hand, it is amazing, even shocking, that any sensitive, fairly intelligent adult could use that word to describe adultery. [If her relationship with him was "sacred," then were his marriage vows profane? How could something be sacred that is forbidden by God, condemned in every civilized culture, embarrassing to Mr. Woods, excruciatingly hurtful to Mrs. Woods, and disruptive [perhaps destructive] to a family with young children? If a divorce ensues, will it be a "sacred" divorce? When the reason for the divorce is explained to the children, will it be described as a "sacred" event? Could I ever say to my daughter, if she related to me that her husband was in an illicit affair, "Oh, don't worry honey, I'm sure it's a sacred affair."? On the other hand, it falls right in line with what the Bible says about the insidious manipulation of Truth by the evil forces of this world. I can't help but wonder how many people—of the millions who heard that statement—are somehow gratified and relieved and quite ready and willing to believe that adultery can be a sacred act. First Corinthians 11:19 reveals: *For there must be also heresies among you that they which are approved may be made manifest among you.* From this we understand that those who are "approved" by God and saved for eternity, are "manifest"ed by being set apart from those who, through lack of devotion and submission to an Authority greater than themselves, fall prey to nice-sounding, but ultimately selfish and vain heresies. Our work in the Kingdom of God—the work for which we have been called out in Christ—is to help enlighten as many as possible of those souls who could fall into such deceptions as this. We do not hate or condemn them. We do, however, expose the foolishness and ultimate irrationality of their thinking. We teach our children through our words and actions that true success is manifested in faithfulness, honesty, integrity, and compassion. God forbid that we could be the products of a daughter [or a nation of them!] who could grow into an adult who believes that adultery is "sacred."

Lord, please keep the fire of Truth burning brightly in us, so that the dark and destructive demons of deception will be kept at bay.

247

AMERICA'S HOPE

Blessed is the man who walks not in the counsel of the wicked, nor stands in the way of sinners, nor sits in the seat of scoffers; but his delight is in the law of the LORD, and on his law he meditates day and night [Ps 1:1-2].

I delight to do thy will, O my God: yea, thy law is within my heart [Ps 40:8].

Our Republic is founded upon the radical hope that people can govern themselves with a minimum of external control. Our Founding Fathers knew full well that this could only happen if the populace was not only smart, but also wise and self-controlled. This is why they emphasized not only education [and why today we have free public education] but also religion. Because religion, when it works, fosters spiritual maturity, which is manifested as wisdom [not the same as intelligence], compassion, altruistic concern for others [the Golden Rule], and control of the passions. It is the absence of spiritual maturity more than the absence of intelligence that necessitates the police force and the other strong arms of government. That is precisely why the French historian and political scientist, Alexis de Tocqueville, made the following statements about America when he examined it in the 1800's: *"The Americans combine the notions of religion and liberty so intimately in their minds that it is impossible to make them conceive of one without the other. America is great because she is good. If America ceases to be good, America will cease to be great."*

He found the source of her goodness, above all other systems and processes, being proclaimed from the pulpits of her churches.

Another concise statement regarding the hope of our Republic comes from the pen of Edmund Burke: "*But what is liberty without wisdom and without virtue? It is the greatest of all possible evils, for it is folly, vice, and madness, without tuition or restraint.*"

This leads us to a deeper and more liberating understanding of what it means to "delight in the law of the LORD." All of the Law is designed for the well-being and prosperity of the human family. It all issues out of and is fulfilled in the Love of God for each human individual. When we look deeply into the Commandments and the teachings of Christ, we see that there is nothing with which to take issue—all we can say is that it is good, and we should follow in its Way. But, like Paul, we see another "law" warring within us, making it impossible for us live by the Law of God. This is our sinful nature, and we must subdue it with the aid of the Holy Spirit. Our tendency, however, is to give in to it and make a myriad of excuses for ourselves. When we do, we chip away at the foundation of our peace and prosperity. If enough of us give in to our baser nature, we will destroy our Republic in the same manner that cancer cells ultimately destroy their host organism and themselves in the process.

Lord, please give me the wisdom and fortitude to delight in Your Law. Please empower me to overcome my weak and selfish self. Forgive us for ignoring Your Truth and Your Way. I choose to love others as I love myself. I choose the Way of Christ my Lord.

248

POLITICS POWER AND PEACE

Scoffers set a city aflame, but the wise turn away wrath [Prov. 29:8].

The next day Moses came upon two Israelites who were fighting. He tried to reconcile them by saying, 'Men, you are brothers; why do you want to hurt each other?' [Acts 7:26].

Blessed are the peacemakers, for they will be called sons of God [Jesus, Mt 5:9].

There are two great powers at war with each other in our world: good and evil. One is manifested as sincere love and a desire to serve the human family, the other as selfish desire for power and pleasure. We see this battle being waged in our own hearts and in the world. One particular arena in which it comes into focus is the political arena in which the potential for service and the potential for power are great—perhaps greater than any other arena. Those who desire to serve and those who desire power are both drawn into the political arena. Both, of course, present themselves as servants, for obvious reasons. The desire for power and pleasure must be hidden beneath some other, more acceptable motivation. [Herod pretended that he wanted to worship the new King coming into Judaism; but his true desire was to murder Him, thereby defending his power. See Matthew 2]. The desire to serve and work for the common good is always in danger of being corroded by the desire for power and pleasure, and some who begin with good intentions are insidiously overcome by the trappings of power and public acclaim. Additionally, and perhaps more disheartening, those who desire power tend to be more competitive and aggressive than those who desire to serve. Good men weary of defending themselves and attacking others; power-hungry men thrive on those activities.

As clearly evidenced in the life of Jesus, and as it has always been, those who seek to serve the common good with pure motive become the target of those who are entrenched in power. And the energy for the good that could be done is drained off into defending against those who feel threatened in their pursuit of power. Those who do not wish to engage in these tactics are nonetheless thrust into it—they must defend themselves. And the great challenge of the citizen-voter in a democracy is to determine who the true servant is.

As Christians, we are called to do this peacefully. We are not to "sling mud" or fan the fires of alarmism. We must listen very carefully and look deeply and prayerfully into accusations before we get on board the "gossip" train. We must realize that there is much we don't know about a given situation; that there are those who slant the truth in both directions, and we must not be fearful or paranoid. We remain mindful that the line that separates good from evil passes through the heart of every individual. In Jesus' time, as now, there were good and evil Jews, good and evil Pharisees, good and evil Roman soldiers, and even good and evil "Christians" [Judas]. And all of them were in reality, a *mixture* of good and evil, with one ultimately predominating over the other. We must be careful about drawing lines. Especially we who abide in Christ, whose glorious love and victory for the human family were not thwarted by the most dedicated efforts of evil politics—nor will they ever be.

Lord Jesus, please keep us from evil. Keep us in Your perfect peace. Give us discernment to support all that is good, and deliver us from the fear of evil.

249

CHRIST AND THE LAW

For I say to you, except your righteousness shall exceed the righteousness of the scribes and Pharisees, you shall in no case enter into the kingdom of heaven [Jesus, Mt 5:20].

Wherefore, my brothers, you also were made dead to the law through the body of Christ [Paul, Rom 7:4].

Think not that I have come to destroy the law, or the prophets: I have not come to destroy, but to fulfill. [Jesus, Mt 5:17].

Therefore whatever you desire that others should do to you, do you even so to them: for this is the law and the prophets [Jesus, Mt 7:12].

The major theme in the human endeavor has been the struggle to know and do good versus evil. Laws are enacted to set forth what is determined to be good and evil. And society appoints officers with authority to enforce them because we have never been able to abide by them. Something in us rebels against restrictions and desires the forbidden, even to the detriment of our own and others' well being. And if something is pleasant or advantageous to us, we want it, even if it is "illegal." We recognize a need for a controlling force. Edmund Burke brought this into a concise focus: *"Society cannot exist unless a controlling power upon will and appetite be placed somewhere, and the less of it there is within, the more there is without. It is ordained in the eternal constitution of things that men of intemperate minds cannot be free. Their passions forge their fetters."* The Law is the *external* controlling power. The Spirit of Christ is the *internal*.

Before Christ, we are all in some way like adolescents who *have* to do good to prevent punishment, but who resent it and feel deprived and controlled. If we can "sneak around" and not get caught, we do. Our parents, and later, the "Law" keep us in check. But our opinion of their rules is usually negative: something to keep us from having fun and feeling free. If we mature properly, we begin to see the rationale for these rules and laws; but the adolescent seeds continue to grow in us. At the extreme level, some adults must be placed in jail cells [the epitome of external control] to prevent them from breaking the Law.

Jesus gloriously fulfills and transcends the Law. He delivers us into Divine Love, which becomes the Law by which we live. We joyfully submit to the constraints of God's Love in us for every human—even our enemies [Matthew 5:44]. We no longer need someone to police us. Our desire and our delight are in the Law of Love. We have a glorious internal control—our will is God's Will. We are free, and we want all people to be free in this Love.

In this light, the test of Democracy is the test of whether we can live the Christian Faith, for people who cannot overcome selfishness and licentiousness cannot govern themselves. There will have to be an *external controlling power*.

Lord, please empower us to live joyfully in Your Love for all, so that we can be free.

250

"I DON'T CARE"

For every man shall bear his own burden [Gal 6:5].

A TV documentary portrayed a young woman with an eating disorder [and obviously depression] who was feeling hopeless about her therapy and unwilling to continue it. To her mother, who was tearfully urging her to continue the therapy, she said, "You don't get it! I just don't care about my life anymore!" Her mother showed the strain and pain of carrying the weight of her daughter's uncared care.

That's how it happens: If I don't care about myself, those who love me must carry the weight of my uncared care. And it is a heavy load. And they begin to resent having to carry it—to carry *me*. But if they put it down or express their anger, they feel guilty. Not caring for myself is therefore one of the most selfish things I could do.

"But how do you care when you don't care?" one might ask. Like love, it is a *choice*—an act of the *will*. One can choose to do that which he does not feel like doing. And to choose to care when the feelings are not there is a great act of love. Caring, like loving, must become, as Jesus said, a "yoke that is easy, and a burden that is light." If caring is wearing me down, I am not caring in the way Jesus [Who loves me] wants me to care. But to stop caring at all can never be the solution.

One who doesn't care about himself is like a man who has a million dollars in a closet in a remote room of his house. The money is mystical in that, when the man dies, it disappears and cannot be used for any purpose. It is only valuable if the man digs it out himself. It is buried underneath decades of accumulated junk, most of it associated with painful memories the man has tried to forget. The man is living in poverty, barely able to pay his bills, his electricity being cut off for weeks at a time, and eating out of restaurant garbage bins. A friend says to him: "Why don't you dig out your money? You could live like a king! Or, you could invest it for your children, or give it to charity." "Oh, it's buried under all that junk. I tried to get it out once, but it was just too painful—too much trouble. It's easier just to watch TV and eat out of the garbage bins."

God has not given us the option of not caring for ourselves. The life He has given us is valuable above comprehension, and it is a terrible delusion to live as if it is a worthless burden. We are commanded to love others as we love ourselves. And if we don't love ourselves, not only will we not be loving others, we will be burdening them with the weight of our uncared care and unlived life.

God, thank You for my life. Please help me to always remember, no matter how I feel, that my life is a tremendous gift and opportunity. And help me be a good steward of my life energies, bringing much Light into the world.

251

SHINE HIS LIGHT. STAY SAFE.

Let your light so shine before men, that they may see your good works, and glorify your Father which is in heaven [Mt. 5:16].

The LORD is my rock, and my fortress, and my deliverer, my God, my rock, in whom I take refuge, my shield and the horn of my salvation, my stronghold and my refuge, my savior; He saves me from violence [2Sam 22:2-3].

I have witnessed two clear examples recently of how Jesus protects us when we abide in Him and let His Light shine through us: A friend of mine was at an out-of-town social gathering without his wife with whom he had been having some long-term problems. He was approached by a very attractive woman who, though not overtly flirtatious, was exuding an air of "possibility." My friend, due to the problems he'd been having with his wife, had already been struggling with straying thoughts. "You know what saved me?" He asked me. "This," he said, holding up his wrist on which was a bracelet with the words "Trust Jesus." He and his wife have two beautiful young children. His identification with Jesus, symbolized and communicated by this bracelet, likely saved him, by his own account from a mistake that could have had devastating effects on his family.

A young woman came to me seeking advice about her relationship with her fiancé. They were both raised in a religious family, but despite his assurances and church attendance, she was sensing that he was distant from Christ. She definitely wanted a marriage that was Christ-centered and was struggling with how to [or whether to] proceed in the engagement. I recommended that she, as powerfully and clearly as possible, assert to her fiancé that she wanted his covenant to her to be, above all other vows, that he would be a Christ-centered husband. When she courageously brought up the topic, as she expected based on prior conversations, he was frustrated and defensive, and finally admitted to her that he did not "get it about a personal relationship with Jesus" and that he "never would." When she politely said that she might not be able to proceed into marriage, she saw a side of him that had not manifested before. He went into what she described as a childish tirade, accusing her of abandoning him and pressuring her through emotional coercion to stay in the engagement. He was kicking things around in his apartment and smashed his phone. He refused her offering of counseling. He later called her in the throes of a panic attack and tearfully pleaded with her to talk to him to help him regain his composure. She prayed with him until he was calm. She now saw clearly that he was not mature enough to be the husband she needed and desired. Her courageous stand for truth prevented her from making what would have likely been a grave mistake with long-term implications. By not allowing her desire to be married or her attraction to her mate overshadow her spiritual discernment and love for Jesus, His Spirit in her exposed an aspect of her fiancé's personality that they both needed to see. And by not caving in to his desire to forge ahead toward marriage, she loved him in a much more powerful way, giving him an opportunity to look into his dependency needs for her that are rooted in his being unfounded in Christ, through Whom God supplies "all our need" [Phil 4:19].

One cannot help but wonder [and be amazed and thankful!] about how many of these episodes transpire daily in the Kingdom of God, and how much unnecessary suffering is avoided. If we abide in Him and let His Light shine, He will protect us.

Lord, thank You for providing a refuge for Your followers from the perils of evil. Please give us grace to abide in You and to let Your Light shine through us. Keep us from evil.

252

THE BIG PICTURE

And this is the condemnation, that light has come into the world, but men loved darkness rather than light, because their deeds were evil. For every one that does evil hates the light, neither comes to the light, lest his deeds should be exposed and reprimanded. But he that loves truth comes to the light, that his deeds may be made manifest, that they are formed by God [John 3:19-21].

Here is a concise description of what may be called "the big picture." The big picture is that there is good and evil—light and darkness. And they both reside in all of us. They are interwoven in the fabric of human personalities.

Jesus came, and is available to all, to deliver us from the darkness that is in us. Yet we have the inclination to cling to it. Every human must make the choice to submit to and work for the Light, or to allow himself to be absorbed in the darkness. Not to choose, is to choose lostness in the darkness. And it is a terrible lostness. It is blind to the fact that it is lost. When Jesus prayed from the Cross *"Father forgive them,"* He stated a profound truth: *"for they do not know what they are doing."* He told His disciples that there were blind people leading other blind people into the *"ditch"* of meaninglessness (Mt 15:14). They were unknowingly propagating evil in the world. They were Satan's pawns. We all have been Satan's pawns. Jesus was praying for each of us when He prayed *"they don't know what they are doing."*

What human, other than Jesus, has lived totally in the Light of Truth? We are all partly in the Light, partly in the dark. We *"see through a glass darkly"* (1Cor. 13:12). Each of us has the awesome responsibility of moving toward the Truth as a conscious endeavor. Jesus said *"I am the... truth..."* (John 14:16). We must *seek* and *ask* and *knock* (Mt 7:7) in order to become mature and free servants of God and the human family; otherwise we become a contributor to the problems in the world. This is the Great Adventure of life—to take a conscious part in the unfolding of the Kingdom of God by submitting to Christ, Who alone is powerful enough to overcome the darkness in us. As He said, *"I have overcome the world"* (John 16:33). Without Christ, we become a little god unto our self—and a human does not make a gracious god. And our god dies when we die. In Christ we have communion with the Eternal Creator, Who empowers us to overcome the dark Prince of this World, Satan. We have no hope outside of Christ. We need no other help than Him. *For in Him dwells all the fullness of the Godhead bodily* (Col 2:9). Without Christ we are vulnerable to the pitfalls of this world: selfishness, addictions, despair, fear, guilt, shame, denial, pride, meanness, sexual perversion, undisciplined anger, alienation, hatred, jealousy, suspicion, feelings of deprivation, ingratitude, etc. Who among us has not been burned by one of these fires? Without Christ we will be consumed in them! We see so many of our family and friends being consumed in them—and we lament it, as did Jesus (Mt 23:37, Mk 6:34). We have this supremely important work to do: becoming Light in the world (Mt 5:14). Let us pray that we will be less and less distracted by things of lesser importance.

Lord Jesus, thank You for bringing the light of truth to the human family. Thank You for overcoming the world; and for abiding in us, empowering us to overcome also. Thank You for exposing evil in and to us. May we abide always in the Light of Your love for God and our fellow man.

253

THE FOUNDATION

Therefore whosoever hears these sayings of mine, and does them, I will say he is like a wise man, who built his house upon a rock: And the rain descended, and the floods came, and the winds blew, and beat upon that house; but it did not fall: for it was founded upon a rock [Jesus, Mt 7:24-25].

We are troubled on every side, yet not distressed; we are perplexed, but not in despair; persecuted, but not forsaken; cast down, but not destroyed... [Paul, 2Cor 4:8-9].

Our best friends of 20-plus years just lost their forty year old son in a four-wheeler accident. He was a Christian man, married with three beautiful children. My friends' grief was and is devastating. As Lynn [my wife] and I walk with them through this dark valley, we try to offer words of condolence and encouragement that feel like dim candles in the vast darkness of their grief. In my spirit, however, I sense in them the same foundation that I sensed in my Mom when she lost her daughter, and then her husband and best friend of sixty-four years. With my friends, as with my Mom, even in the darkest depths of the grief, I know that they are going to be alright. For many years they have been growing in their faith in the God who loves them, loves their children, and is somehow working all things [even death] together for good for those who trust and love Him [Rom 8:28]. Through the years this faith has become an unshakable foundation underneath any conceivable tribulation that could befall them. It is the "rock" that Jesus spoke about in the above verses. The house built upon that rock can withstand even the hurricane-force winds and floods of the death of a child. Those winds and floods are indeed, as I stated above, *devastating*. My friends are not bracing up with a "stiff upper lip" and trying to pretend that they are stronger than they actually are. They are experiencing all the waves of emotional turmoil associated with the death of their beloved son and the aftermath of confusion and turmoil in trying to help their daughter-in-law and grandchildren pick up the pieces of their shattered lives.

This "rock," this secure foundation, is not a pretentious veneer covering a shattered inner core of the personality. It is not something that must be clung to with great valor and effort. It is instead a calm inner knowing that runs deeper than the tumult of the hurricane—like a depth in the ocean of one's soul that is not churned up by the violent storm on the surface. In Christ we are anchored in eternity; and eternity transcends birth and death. In Christ we can feel the full force of our grief without being swept away by it. On some level we know that some unnecessary baggage is being swept away in this storm. Priorities are being re-focused; something valuable is being wrought in us in this crucible of grief. After Katrina I noticed that the air was purer, cleaner, and fresher than I had ever experienced. Birds sing after the storm.

There are losses in life that ache in the soul in depths that we did not know existed. We grieve, even wail and lament. The powerful waves roll over us. But the "house" stands! We are not "destroyed"!

When darkness seems to hide his face, I rest on his unchanging grace;
In every high and stormy gale, my anchor holds within the veil.
On Christ the solid rock I stand, all other ground is sinking sand.
Edward Mote

Lord Jesus, thank you for your abiding presence with us, even when we cannot feel you—even when comfort seems far away. Thank you for this foundation—this solid rock that is eternally unshakable.

Note: Six months after the death of our friend's son, and after the second printing of this book, Lynn and I lost our son, Bradley [see "Rainbow Perspective" devotional # 189]. He was thirty-five. Bradley's death taught us, in the most personal way, the truth of this devotional. Even though we miss him intensely, we know now, more profoundly than ever, that no earthly loss can shake the foundation of Christ's peace.

254

JESUS RESOLVES DIVISION

Blessed are the peacemakers: for they shall be called the children of God. [Jesus, Mt 5:9].

For he is our peace, who has made us both one, and has broken down the dividing wall of hostility, by abolishing in his flesh the law of commandments and ordinances, that he might create in himself one new man in place of the two, so making peace, and might reconcile us both to God in one body through the cross, thereby bringing the hostility to an end [Eph 2:14-16].

At the Constitutional Convention in 1787, the Founding Fathers got heatedly entrenched on the issue of State's representation—an issue so controversial that it endangered the whole process. At some point, Dr. Ben Franklin made the wise suggestion that the members seek guidance from God. Below is an excerpt from his speech taken from a letter written by James Madison to Jared Sparks in 1831, containing Franklin's written speech:

> The small progress we have made after four or five weeks close attendance & continual reasonings with each other, our different sentiments on almost every question, several of the last producing as many noes as ays, is methinks a melancholy proof of the imperfection of the Human Understanding....In this situation of this Assembly, groping as it were in the dark to find political truth, and scarce able to distinguish it when presented to us, how has it happened, Sir, that we have not hitherto once thought of humbly applying to the Father of lights to illuminate our understandings?... I have lived, Sir, a long time, and the longer I live, the more convincing proofs I see of this truth- that God governs in the affairs of men. And if a sparrow cannot fall to the ground without His notice, is it probable that an empire can rise without His aid?... I therefore beg leave to move, that henceforth prayers imploring the assistance of Heaven, and its blessings on our deliberations, be held in this Assembly every morning before we proceed to business, and that one or more of the Clergy of the City be requested to officiate in that service.

This intercession broke the logjam, and paved the way for the forward progress of our wonderful Constitution.

The diverse beliefs of man are always in danger of becoming not only hindrances to the forward march of civility, but also passions fueling violent conflict. If we fail to exercise the wisdom of Dr. Franklin—if we fail to open our hearts to the God of creation who loves all and desires the best for all—our creeds and philosophies will become our idolatrous gods that lead us toward destruction. Jesus has commanded us to love our enemies [Mt 5:44]. In His Spirit we can never allow hatred to overwhelm us. Guided by His Spirit, we will always find common ground, even between the most diverse philosophies. No matter how diverse we are, Jesus reminds us that we are all in the family of mankind; we are all created in the image of God. In His Spirit, we realize that we can live together peacefully and harmoniously. All hateful division between humans comes from the dark prince of this world working through the darkness of our spiritual blindness. Jesus opens our eyes and elevates us to a new plateau of peace and compassion. We are delivered from egoistic selfishness, fear, and the addiction to power. Our effort to resolve our conflict then becomes a collaborative, peaceful pursuit of the Truth—the Truth that sets us free and enhances the lives of all—the Truth that originates in the heart and mind of God, and is imparted to us by Him as we "humbly implore" His assistance.

Lord, please give us wisdom to work together peacefully, becoming good stewards of this earth and all our energies, working for the Common Good. In Christ's name, Amen.

255

METAMORPHOSIS

And do not be conformed to this world: but be transformed by the renewing of your mind, that you may prove what is that good, and acceptable, and perfect, will of God [Rom 12:2].

Some say we can see the fingerprint of God in His creation; and I believe it to be true. He has placed in His creation a most amazing phenomenon that we call *metamorphosis*. It is a process by which one creature becomes a totally different one—so different that, if placed side by side, you would never guess that it was the same. A caterpillar looks absolutely nothing like a butterfly. The beetle that lives in the dark underground for years looks nothing like the cicada that emerges from its shell and flies its season in the sun. The Greek word translated in the above verse to "transformed" is *metamorphoo*, meaning *"to change into another form; to transform or transfigure"*. It is the same term used to describe what happened to Jesus on the mountain in Matthew 17:2, when *"His face shone like the sun and His raiment was white as light."* And it describes what happens to us when we receive the unspeakable gift of the new life that Christ becomes in us. *"Old things pass away. Everything becomes new"* [2Cor 5:17]. We leave behind the old shell of the person we used to be and launch out into a brand new life, feeding on the nectar of Truth, basking in the sunlight of His Love for us and in us for all people. We are no longer miserly little creatures, selfish and fearful, wandering around aimlessly in the darkness of meaninglessness. We are no longer the prey of the dark creatures of night. Now we are free to soar in the clear and bright atmosphere of freedom and peace. We know why we are here. And we know where we are going. We abide in our Great Lord and Friend Who has overcome the world [John 16:33]. The very core of our being, our heart, has been transformed. The motivating force of our actions is completely different. The worries and cares of the world that used to torment us, and even that great monster death that loomed so large and fearsome on the horizon, wither like a spider on a hot stove and blow away like dust in the wind.

Every day—every moment—we have the wonderful opportunity to respond to the invitation that God perpetually extends to us to be transformed—*metamorphosed*. Our life can become a series of metamorphoses. No matter how much of the freedom, peace, and joy of Christ we have received, there is more for us if we are willing to love with His Love, open our heart to Him anew, and wake up from the dark delusions that so easily beset us. In this new life, with our new eyes, we see through the fog more clearly the Reality that causes us to rejoice like Elisha's servant when his eyes were opened to the protective chariots of fire [2Kings 6:17]. We see that all God's promises that seem too good to be true really *are* true. Our heart smiles and we rest in that deep soul rest that Jesus promised those who receive the Truth that He offers [Mt 11:29]. We become peaceful agents of transformation—the Light of this world [Mt 5:14]. And if you put us beside the person we were before Jesus began this wonderful work in us, you would not even know that it was the same creature.

Lord Jesus, thank You for transforming us into Kingdom creatures: beloved, peaceful, joyful servants of God and of our fellow man.

256

Passion or Principle?

Hsa 7:6 Their hearts are like an oven; …. Their passion smolders all night; in the morning it blazes like a flaming fire.
Jam 1:14-15 but each person is tempted when they are dragged away by their own evil desire and enticed. Then, after desire has conceived, it gives birth to sin; and sin, when it is full-grown, gives birth to death.
Mat 4:4 Jesus answered, "It is written: 'Man shall not live on bread alone, but on every word that comes from the mouth of God.'"

One of the great blessings of being created in the image of God is emotions or feelings. But they become a curse if we do not master them or bring them under the authority of the principles that Christ has presented to us. Humans have a broad spectrum of feelings. We can feel safe and secure, or we can feel anxious. We can feel affectionate or cold. We may feel angry, frustrated, irritated, alienated, apathetic, humiliated [not to be confused with humility], embarrassed, lonely, depressed, fearful, peaceful, joyful, or content. Desire is a feeling, as well as hatred, hopefulness or hopelessness. And you can probably add to this list. There is much unnecessary suffering in our world because of our tendency to act out of our feelings. If a child feels angry, he may physically attack his adversary. If a woman feels angry, she may verbally lash out in an attempt to hurt her husband, who may respond by verbally or physically counter-attacking. Sarcasm is an expression of contempt or disdain. One of the important characteristics of Christian maturity is mastery of feelings. And it is a perpetual challenge for us. Humans have many powerful impulses fed by feelings that, if acted out, bring suffering into our lives and the lives of our loved ones. When we fail to control these impulses, we have to do remedial work—rebuilding trust or affection—in order to maintain healthy relationships. Jesus taught and lived principles that are contrary to many of our feelings. He taught us to love our enemies, bless those who curse us, do good to those who hate us, and pray for those who despitefully use us [Mt. 5:22]. The Bible teaches us not to return evil for evil, but rather to overcome evil with good [Rom. 12:21f]. These principles are counter to our impulses. But they are incredibly practical in that they bring resolution to human conflict rather than escalating it. We need the power of Christ's Spirit in us to overcome the acting out of these destructive impulses. We have a tendency to justify our actions that are based on feelings rather than the principles of Christ. "I'm sorry I said those things to you, but I was just so stressed out by my work." "I wouldn't have said those things if you had not been so disrespectful to me." "I wouldn't have had the affair if you had been loving me better." Etc. ad nauseum. These rationalizations or excuses are like saying, "I wouldn't have shot myself in the leg if....whatever" because each time we act inappropriately out of feelings we set ourselves back in the progress of our life and relationships. We diminish the quality of our own lives, and then we make excuses for doing it. Jesus chose to suffer because it fulfilled the principle of love for the human family--you and I. He did not *feel* like doing it. And God related to us through Paul that it was for *joy* that he made that choice [Heb. 12:2].

Paradoxically, when we live by our feelings, we create misery; but when we live by the principles of Christ, we discover true joy and peace--the greatest feelings of all.

Lord please help me bring every emotion, every desire, every thought into the realm of Your loving authority, that I might not sin against You and my fellow man, and that I might know joy and freedom of soul.

257

SNAKE BIT

Mat 23:28   Even so ye also outwardly appear righteous unto men, but within ye are full of hypocrisy and iniquity.

My little Jack Russell Terrier, Axel, got bit on the lip by a water moccasin three days ago. Despite an injection of antihistamine and antibiotics, the poison in his blood has made him a really sick little guy. He hasn't eaten a single bite of the morsels of "gourmet" food I have offered him; and he threw up some of the water he drank. He is very lethargic, sitting in one spot for hours, sometimes trembling, then moving to another spot, not comfortable anywhere. His urine had dark brownish red blood in it. Snake bites are nasty experiences.

When we look deeply into ourselves—into our hearts—we realize that, spiritually speaking, we have all been snake bit. When Adam and Eve were deceived by the serpent in the Garden of Eden, the human race was injected with poison. We see that humans, throughout all history, and to this day, inflict all manner of evil upon each other, because of this poison that is within us. If we are honest, we see hateful, mean, insensitive, selfish, or apathetic tendencies in ourselves and in all humans. *"None is righteous; no not one"* [Rm 3:10]. We see how difficult it is for a man and woman to live out a love relationship—even when they covenant with God before witnesses to do so, and even when they have children together whose lives are deeply impacted by their inability to love each other. We see selfishness and hypocrisy and terrible, hateful delusions being lived out in religious contexts. We see our tendency to sit in harsh judgment of others, while minimizing or denying our own character defects. [Mt. 7:4-5]. We see our tendency to complain, feel deprived, and blame others for our unhappiness. We see how we demand good service, and are unwilling to serve. We recognize our reluctance to fulfill our righteous responsibilities. We see that we tend to be absorbed in entertainment and activities that do not help anyone or make the world a better place. Truly, we are full of poison, like my little Axel.

The only medicine that we have to cleanse this poison out of our hearts is the blood of Christ. We cannot heal ourselves any more than we can pull ourselves up by our bootstraps. We cannot even know that we are dying of this poison until we allow Christ to open our eyes. We desperately need, above all other needs, the mercy, grace and forgiveness of God given to us through Jesus Christ, the compassionate and wonderful Healer of all souls who turn to Him in honest recognition of their depravity and lostness.

I saw on the internet that some dogs die from snake bites. I see in this world that people die from the poison of the sin that has been injected into our world by the evil one. Many die from this poison because they never even know they have been snake bit. I am so thankful [and I hope you are also] that God has revealed to us in Christ that we were dying of this poison of sin in our souls. When He opened my eyes, I was horrified at how devastating and lethal that poison is, and how much damage it had already done to my soul. Jesus cleansed me with forgiveness and grace, and continues to renew my inner life. He teaches and empowers me to love people with His love. I am sustained by His gracious promises to be with me always, cleanse me from all unrighteousness, and complete this wonderful work that He has begun in me. The poison is being perpetually cleansed from my soul.

I'm pretty sure Axel is going to be OK. And I know, beyond all doubt, that as I abide in Christ, I will too. I will be much more than OK.

Lord Jesus, You are the great healer of our souls. You enlighten us and set us free from all the oppressive forces of evil in this world, and in our hearts. You cleanse us from all unrighteousness, and forgive us our sins. We are eternally thankful to You. We will abide in You forever.

258

GUILT: GETTING FREE

If we confess our sins, he is faithful and just to forgive us our sins, and to cleanse us from all unrighteousness [1John 1:9].

There is therefore now no condemnation to those who are in Christ Jesus, who walk not after the flesh, but after the Spirit [Rom 8:1].

There are two forms of guilt: realistic guilt and false guilt. *Realistic guilt* stems from unconfessed sin. It oozes up through the cracks of denial. The solution: honest facing of the truth about one's self, and looking to God for the power to overcome. Some of our sinful behaviors are deep-rooted and habitual. They may be strongholds in our personality. We may know, deeply, that even if we confess the sin, the behavior is likely to recur. We must not let this keep us from bringing the sin into the light of God's love and grace toward us. We still must confess. Otherwise, the consciousness of the sinful behavior sinks deeper into our soul—further from the Light that is the only hope of deliverance. From that depth of denial, guilt oozes upward into our heart. The tendency then is to harden the wall of denial. But like the hardening of our arteries retards the flow of blood, the hardening of denial constricts the flow of love and grace. God forgives, in Christ, even our *besetting* sins, as long as we are honest and sincere with Him about them. He does not expect us to be perfect—but He does expect us to be honest and to be a little better today than yesterday. He is fair. And as our brother Paul came to understand, His grace is sufficient for us. [2Cor 12:19]

False guilt is a chronic habit of feeling guilty even though one has confessed her sin and is walking in forgiveness and grace. After years of living in denial, it may be difficult to learn how to feel totally forgiven. It may seem too good to be true, or we simply don't know how to feel free from the guilt that has permeated our personality for so long. I have heard some people say, "I know God has forgiven me, but I can't forgive myself." I encourage them to imagine themselves before Christ, with the scars on His body, mindful of the Cross experience, and to hear Him say, "You are forgiven because I paid the price of your sin." And then hear themselves say to Him, "I know, Jesus, and thanks a lot. But I just can't seem to forgive myself." Whose forgiveness is more important, God's or yours? Can you stand before God and say, "I am worthy of heaven because I have forgiven myself"? When we see it in this light, we begin to realize that our guilt is just another of Satan's oppressive lies. We realize that God loves us, and wants us to be free from guilt and shame, and everything else that oppresses us or diminishes the "abundant life" that Jesus died for us to have. If we are courageous enough to be honest with God, He blesses us with life and grace and peace beyond measure. Sometimes we must rise up into a warrior spirit to drive away Satan in his attempts to steal what God has given us. In His Spirit, we have more than enough Power to do so.

Whether our guilt is false or real, God offers us freedom from it. It's up to us to receive His wonderful offer. There is no need to live in guilt, and it is a waste of precious life to do so.

Lord Jesus, thank You so much for Your sacrifice that paid the price for my sin. Please help me to receive the gift of total and complete forgiveness. May the Light of Your Spirit drive away all darkness within me, especially the darkness of guilt, however deeply imbedded in my soul it may be. Search out every crack and crevice, eradicate it, and allow me to feel the full measure of the freedom, peace, joy and abundant life that You died for me to have. And with renewed energy, I will obey You by loving all people with Your Love.

259

THE PURPOSE OF PROBLEMS

These things I have spoken to you, that in me you might have peace. In the world you will have tribulation: but be of good cheer; I have overcome the world. Jn. 16:33

Consider it pure joy, my brothers and sisters, whenever you face trials of many kinds...
Jms.1:2

In order to help children learn math, their teachers give them math problems. God wants us to learn about life, so He allows us to have life problems. In some way that we begin to understand in Christ, it is perfect for us to have life problems. If you are having problems, you have a wonderful opportunity to grow toward the fullness of the potential that God has placed within you. When parents try to eliminate the problems that their children face in life, we see that it does not help them. We call these children "spoiled". We would all be useless if we had never faced and overcome problems; and we would not be happy, as we are tempted to think. If you are alive, you should congratulate yourself and be thankful to God. You have survived! You have already overcome many problems. And all of your ancestors, going all the way back to Adam and Eve, have also survived, bore children, kept them alive, so that you could be the repository of all the skills and strength that they employed to survive. We should continue our growth to the point that we no longer lament our problems. Our problems are growth knocking on the door—the breaking of the shell of our outdated understanding. When we take our problems to Christ—when we bring them into the Light of His teachings and principles—we always benefit, persevere, even prosper. I have frequently seen or heard this statement: "Jesus is the answer." Jesus will always offer us the solution to our problems. He will help us understand what we need to do; or show us that we need to do nothing—just accept. And He will empower us to do what we need to do, or to accept. And He will give us peace in the midst of the problems that He told us we would have. Life has never been easy. We should not expect life to be easy. Satan wants us to feel like victims. He wants us to believe that God is not fair. When we look deeply into the created world—the earth, all its creatures, the sky, the ocean, the sun, stars, moon, manhood and womanhood, childbirth, flowers, beauty, music, humor, etc.—we realize that God knows exactly what He is doing. And since we have been given the gift of life, we realize that He loves us. Since God knows what He is doing and loves us, we begin to realize that our problems are a very important part of the perfection of all things. Then we stop wasting our time complaining about them and feeling victimized, and start the wonderful process of learning from them, overcoming them, accepting them, or whatever it is God wants us to do with them that enhances rather than diminishes the life that Christ died for us to have. We realize that we can "be of good cheer." Our problems will never overcome us in Christ, Who has "overcome the world." Even death is a victory for us [1Cor. 15:54-55].

Lord Jesus, we are so thankful to You for overcoming the world and making Yourself available to us—even to the end of the age. Please forgive us for doubting the victory we have in You—for lapsing into complaints and fears. In obedience to You, we will be of good cheer, knowing that all our trials have purpose, and that they will soon be over. Meanwhile, please empower us to bear each other's burdens and celebrate the victorious Love You have brought into the world.

260

SERVANT LEADERSHIP

Mat 20:25-26,28
But Jesus called them to him and said, "You know that the rulers of the Gentiles lord it over them, and their great men exercise authority over them.
It shall not be so among you; but whoever would be great among you must be your servant,...even as the Son of Man came, not to be served, but to serve, and to give His life as a ransom for many"

One of the greatest temptations that we face perpetually is the desire or need for power and control. I have seen much too frequently, in the context of marriage counseling, this deep-seated need to control one's spouse. We read about it or see it in the News in its extreme forms. Recently it was reported that a husband drove to another state, kidnapped his estranged wife, put her in the trunk of his car and drove her back to his apartment where he held her hostage until the police intervened. It is common knowledge for those who try to help abused women that the most dangerous time for her is while she is breaking away from his death-grip. He would rather kill her, and also himself, than let her get free of the prison that he has held her in. He is addicted to controlling her, and lost in a deep darkness. This is essentially a failure of faith. It is driven by a deep insecurity and gnawing fear that "If I can't control the situation, I'm going to be hurt [again], or I'm going to lose out, miss the boat, be left behind, unloved or abandoned. And I absolutely refuse to allow that to happen." It is counter-productive in that it creates what is feared – that is abandonment. "Love" that is demanded and controlled can never be true, and therefore never satisfies the soul. Power and control are an evil and destructive counterfeit for love and faith. Love liberates. Evil enslaves and attempts to control.

Regarding power and control, Jesus and Satan responded oppositely. Satan coveted the power and authority of God, and tried to seize it. He rebelled and tried to take matters into his own hands. Jesus, who frankly stated that "all power in heaven and earth is given unto me,"[Mt.28:18] laid it aside and submitted himself to the sufferings and difficulties of humanity. He became a servant; and taught all who follow Him to do likewise. He knew that God was going to work it all out for good {Rmns.8:28}. If you have ever gotten to know someone who was addicted to power and control, you realized that they were very unhappy, frustrated and angry. They live on a very shaky foundation that is always in jeopardy, and requires ongoing vigilance to maintain. People and situations are always getting out of hand, or threatening to. The truth is, control is a delusion that takes energy to maintain. Jesus delivers us, if we allow Him, from this dreadful, destructive delusion. He delivers us into faith and joyful servanthood.

Lord, please deliver us from the need to control. Please bless and protect all who are living under the dreadful curse of their own or someone else's need to control.

261

THE JOY AND PENETRATING LIGHT OF CHRISTMAS

Lk. 2:13-14
And suddenly there was with the angel a multitude of heavenly host praising God and saying, "Glory to God in the highest, and on earth peace and good will among men with whom he is pleased!"
Lk. 2:34-5
And Simeon blessed them and said to Mary his mother, "Behold, this child is set for the fall and rising of many in Israel, and for a sign that is spoken against...that the thoughts of many hearts may be revealed."

It's Christmas morning and there is joy in countless households. Parents are delighting in the joy of their children as they discover that Santa was pleased with them this year; just as the shepherds and wise men, along with Mary and Joseph discovered that God was pleased with us, and was providing the gift of His son – our salvation. How wonderful that we celebrate the birth of our Lord by trying to replicate, as best we can, this great joy, especially for our children, but also for all the human family! We light up our world and give gifts. We surprise our children with lavish gifts. Each year the goodness, peace and joy of this celebration should penetrate our hearts and permeate our souls more deeply, and last throughout the year as we continue our devotional living. The joy of Christmas is infinite and everlasting! No one has discovered the depths of it. We all have a perpetual invitation from God Himself to move ever more deeply into the gift of Christmas! Evil, then as now, seeks to devour the gift. For many, Christmas is not a pleasant time. Removed from the spirit and maturity of Christ, it can be a hectic time of fighting traffic and spending too much money. For some it is a drunken brawl when all the unresolved family issues come loudly and painfully into focus. The light of Christmas is a penetrating and revealing light. Christ reveals us to ourselves, and then begins to deliver us from the worst that is within us. This is an ongoing process for which we are very thankful. The more we grow in Christ, the more we realize what we have been delivered from – all manner of potentially destructive blindness and sinful nature manifestations. The more we grow, the more clearly we see the ongoing battle of evil against good, and the tremendous victory that Jesus has won for us. And the more we are able to celebrate, very deeply, the joy of Christmas.

Lord Jesus, thank You for coming to us as a human and bringing the gift of salvation, so that we now have joy, peace and good will within the human family. Please continue to reveal us to ourselves and set us free from the enslavement of sin.

262

DO YOUR PART

Pro 6:6-9 Go to the ant, you sluggard; consider its ways and be wise!
It has no commander, no overseer or ruler,
yet it stores its provisions in summer and gathers its food at harvest.
How long will you lie there, you sluggard? When will you get up from your sleep?
Ecc 10:18 Through laziness, the rafters sag; because of idle hands, the house leaks.
Gal 6:5 For every man shall bear his own burden.

Life is difficult. All creatures of this earth must work to survive, gather—sometimes compete—for food, raise their young, protect themselves and their young from predators [in our case, evil]. In every life, family, and community, there is work to be done. The Bible teaches that we must be sure to do our part of that work. It even says that if a man will not work, he will not be given food! [2Thes. 3:10]. If I do not contribute fairly to the work that must be done in my family, job or community, then someone else must take up the slack. And this creates negative energy in my family or workplace. People resent being depended on unfairly or having to do more than their fair share of the work. And my soul languishes in laziness—it is not a happy pathway. The happiest people you will meet are productive people. They are involved in activities that are meaningful to them, and helpful to others. If we want our children to be happy, we must teach them to work. They need responsibilities so they can have the good feeling of contributing to their family and accomplishing meaningful tasks. Their souls will not flourish if they are too involved in pleasure-seeking, entertainment, games, computer, TV, etc. And we must help them avoid the pitfall of believing that work is primarily about making money, and that money [or what it buys] will make them happy. If they cannot be happy in their work, they will never make enough money to buy happiness.

Jesus said that the most important work that we do is the work of believing in Him [Jn 6:27-29]. If we do this work, all other work will come into its proper place because Jesus will not allow us to be lazy; nor will He allow us to become "workaholics". He will keep our lives in perfect balance. This is true because we know that He loves us; and He loves others as much as He loves us. He is responsible and compassionate, and He wants us to be also. In Christ we do our part [or a little more, since it is more blessed to give than to receive {Acts 20:35}], but we do not enable others in their weakness by doing for them what they should do for themselves [See Paul's teachings about caring for widows in 1 Tim. 5]. We are trying to bring our lives into a clear and healthy focus that is productive and not wasteful. The Bible teaches that the most productive work we can do—the work of God's people—is to promote and increase the Kingdom of God. This is the work of the Church [God's people]. No other work gets neglected in this work of the Kingdom. All work becomes holy when done in the Spirit of Christ, Who washed His disciples' feet. It is very important for all believers to contribute to the work of the Kingdom. I hope you will be prayerfully involved in supporting the work of the Kingdom through your resources, gifts and abilities. Please pray that God will help you be responsible and diligent in your work; and that He will give you discernment about how to help in propagating the Kingdom, which is the greatest gift that we can give to the world.

Lord please deliver me from laziness. Help me to work heartily and joyfully. Teach me how to use what You have given me to contribute to the growth of faith in Christ as the Messiah, so that others can find peace in the family of God.

263

THE FINAL WORD

"But you shall receive power when the Holy Spirit has come upon you; and you shall be my witnesses in Jerusalem and in all Judea and Samaria and to the end of the earth." And when he had said this, as they were looking on, he was lifted up, and a cloud took him out of their sight [Act 1:8-9].

    We who have received Jesus as the Messiah have come to know Him as the Way, the Truth, and the Life—the solution to the problems of the human family. We know that in Christ we are overcoming selfishness, greed, lust, pride, hatred, and violence. In Him we are understanding, more and more, God's love for all people, and His desire for their freedom from the oppressive forces of evil. He is our Lord. And we are very thankful that He is.

    When a loved one is going away for an extended time, there is generally a final word of goodbye; a final encouragement or admonition. We use our most important words in these times. Our Lord's final words before ascending into heaven were that we would be empowered by His Holy Spirit, and we were to be His "witnesses" in the entire world. The Holy Spirit is predominantly a spirit of love—Christ's love—for all people. It is not primarily an emotional experience. It is a gift, and it is a choice—a choice to love, trust, and obey God—based on a deep conviction of the Truth of Christ. In this spirit, we are Christ's witnesses in our world. We want our world to be safe. We want people to be free and happy. We have come to know that Jesus sets us free and blesses us with inner peace and joy. This is what we desire for all people. And this is what Jesus will give them. Evil works to oppress the effort of witnessing. We have all experienced the reality of this oppressive force. But the Holy Spirit in us is the greater force [1Jn 4:4]. All Christians must remember Jesus' final words to us. We must find a way to let the Holy Spirit speak through us, so that we will be witnesses to others regarding the truth and goodness of Christ. We must sow the seeds that bear the fruit of salvation, abundant life, peace and joy: everything Jesus promised, and is fulfilling in us, His witnesses.

Lord Jesus, today, may Your Holy Spirit empower me to be a witness of Your goodness, truth, and love in my corner of the world. Help me to remember that You love everyone I will meet today.

ALPHABETICAL INDEX

A Clean Heart	114
A Final Word	360
Abide In Christ	155
Abundant Life	109
Abundant Life and Joy	148
Alienation	246
Alive and Awake	68
All We Have Is Jesus	287
Alphabetical Index	366
Amazing Grace	278
America's Hope	324
"And Peter": God's Amazing Forgiveness	21
Anger	253
Approach God Reverently	165
Are You A Good Person?	92
Are You A Murmurer?	151
Are You Among the "Few"?	205
Are You Getting Your Needs Met?	250
Are You Having Tribulation?	282
Ashes and Dust	242
Asleep In the Storm	66
Avoiding the Obvious	26
Be Generous	258
Be Prepared	143
Be Proactive Spiritually	158
Be Still and Know	160
Be Thankful In All Situations	215
Because of Jesus	171
Becoming A Family	67
Beyond Romance	316
Beyond Salvation	235
Blaming the Sufferer	79
Boyhood, Manhood	17
Choose Your Suffering	178

Choosing Gratitude	117
Christ and the Law	326
Christianity for Dummies	44
Christians Are Responsible Servants	203
Civility	317
Clear Thinking; Soft Heart	248
Come and See!	266
Coming Into Focus	231
Contrition Or Condemnation	78
Conviction and Encouragement	290
Death	134
Decadence and Decay	35
Discernment and Setting Boundaries	60
Do You Feel Free?	119
Do Your Part	345
Don't Get Choked	49
Don't Get Sidetracked	130
Don't Lose the Blessing	281
Don't Worry. Be Happy.	272
Drawing Near To God	14
Drifting Into the Darkness	322
Dullness of Heart	102
Dying Daily	189
Dying To Live	175
E Pluribus Unum	297
Even the "Lone Ranger" Had Tonto	163
Feelings Do not Determine Reality	131
For God's Sake Don't Stop Loving!	222
Freedom	113
Freedom II	190
Freedom Together In Marriage	105
Friendship Is Very Important	252
From Generation to Generation	191
Full, Fat, and Forgetful	70
Get a Life!	273
Getting Free From Relationship Entanglements	72

Glorious Lucidity	52
Glorious Servanthood	74
Glorious, Liberating Detachment	243
God and Politics	294
God In what Can Be Seen	149
God Is Not "Nice"	135
God Sets Limits	76
God Speaks Through His Creatures	213
God Upholds The Righteous	183
Godly Versus Worldly Sorrow	207
Good Friday	310
"Good! Now You Know How It Feels!"	77
Greed	307
Guilt: Getting Free	339
Healing Dissension	80
Help My Unbelief!	249
His Holiness and Love	22
Housetop Living	124
How Alive Are You?	112
How Bad Can It Get?	56
How Much Truth Do You Love?	320
How To Do What We Do	108
I Don't Care	328
"I Rule Hammond"	55
I'm So Overwhelmed!	103
Idolatry Lives	138
Is It About You, or Is It About Us?	263
It's About Becoming	154
It's Not Good To Complain	126
It's Not That Bad	71
Jesus Doesn't Answer All Questions	152
Jesus Is In You	223
Jesus Knows Your Stuff	63
Jesus Teaches Us How To Be Happy	173
Jesus Offers us a Wonderful Opportunity	241
Jesus Resolves Division	333

Joy	139
Joy Embracing Sorrow	43
Joyful Conviction	255
Keep First Things First	115
Keep Following Christ. Don't Look Back.	142
Kingdom Suffering	19
Know Your Enemy	286
Letting Go	64
Life Changing Decision	41
Life Is Difficult	279
Life Is Not What We Want It to Be	306
Living Beyond Ego	146
Living For The Future	210
Living on Tips	83
Living Peacefully	261
Living the Faith	259
Love as Confrontation	96
Love Your Enemies	94
Love: The Mood Stabilizer	177
Loving Beyond the Comfort Zone	89
Loving or Impressing People	122
Manhood and Womanhood	211
Martha & Mary	234
Metamorphosis	335
Minding the Mind	32
Momma (& Jesus) Said There'd Be Days Like This	208
Morning In the Heart	184
My Cat Doesn't Need Me Too Much	198
My Son	84
Mysterious But Not Secret	147
New Beginnings	200
New Year; New Life	270
Obedience Leads To Healing	90
On Eagle's Wings?	162
Our Divided World	262
Our Life's Work	220

Overcoming	268
Passion or Principle	336
Peace On Earth, Good Will To Men	204
Peaceful Warriors	47
People Need The Lord	129
People Who Love People	303
Please Don't Take Jesus For Granted	87
Please Don't Take Your Life For Granted	82
Pleasure and Power	58
Politics, Power and Peace	325
Pouting	305
Power and Control vs. Servant Leadership	133
Rainbow Perspective	245
Reality	240
Rebuilding	300
Refuge	319
Relational Responsibility	283
Right Understanding; Courageous Living	168
Rivers of Living Water	301
Salvation Is Not Automatic	118
Satan's Hatred	274
Security In The Elder Years	59
Seeing More Clearly	106
Self-Control: Pathway To Fuller Life	104
Servant Leadership	342
Shield of Faith	227
Shine His Light. Stay Safe	329
Snake Bit	338
Some Get It. Some Don't.	194
Sorrow	289
Sorrow and Joy	219
Sowing Seeds of Life	23
Stay With Us	38
Staying Active	295
Staying Fresh	298
Surprised By God	218

Swallow The Frog	88
Take Warning	52
Thank God for Grace!	321
Thank God For Mockingbirds	201
Thank God For Ruby Bridges	224
The Big Picture	330
The Bleak Darkness of Evil	46
The Blessedness of Mourning	101
The Body of Christ	61
The Creator Has Spoken	230
The Daily Buffet	54
The Dangerous "Rational" Mind of Man	145
The Dark Side of Christmas	121
The Discipline of Power	291
The End	269
The Evidence of God	302
The Faith Factor	197
The Final Word	347
The Focus of Life	25
The Foundation	332
The Fruit of Our Faith	237
The Futility and Sadness of Envy	45
The Gift of Peace	265
The Golden Rule	157
The Hatred of Christianity	29
The Heresy of Jesus	24
The Importance of Christian Fellowship	164
The Importance of Evil and Death	179
The Importance of our Sanctification	33
The Joy and Light of Christmas	334
The Judgment Seat	181
The Kingdom In Our Midst	169
The Kingdom of Heaven	16
The Light of The World	233
The Little Things of Today Are Important	137
The Most Dreadful Words You Could Ever Hear	53

The Most Important Thing In The World	111
The Narrow Gate Into Eternal Life	100
The Nation's Immune System	199
The Need for Solitude	15
The Ongoing Warfare	185
The Power of Fellowship	186
The Power of the Resurrection	311
The Problem is Theological	174
The Purpose of Problems	331
The Solution	141
The Solution Can Become the Problem	256
The Source of Confidence	39
The Wisdom of Collaboration	214
The Wonderful Power of Jesus	85
They Caught Nothing	34
Thoughts & Actions	116
Three Healthy Responses	293
To Get Clean, Come Clean	276
True Freedom	18
True Religion	226
True Success	313
Trusting His Love	30
Under God's Wing	167
Unflappable	239
Variations On A Theme	140
Victorious Acceptance	36
Victory Beyond The Circumstances	107
Walking The Talk	193
We Are Not Victims!	216
We Are So Blessed	93
We Have All Failed	308
We Live What We Really Believe	31
What Determines You?	172
What Do You Expect?	314
What Does God Owe Us?	75
What Is Truth?	257

What We Have Inherited	27
What We Owe	40
Where do I Get My Needs Met	153
Where To Turn	195
Who Are You?	97
Who Determines Truth?	180
Who is Jesus?	50
Whose Church Is It?	159
You and Your Shadow	188
You are Responsible for You	285
You Are The "Righteousness of God"	99
You Can Change Your Life	123
You Can't Judge a Book By Its Cover	69
You Don't Have To Be Religious To Please Jesus	127
Your Word Is Your Bond	228

READERS' COMMENTS

I have had the opportunity of watching Mark Graham's ministry for more than 25 years. I have seen it up close and from a distance. He has been the example of caring concern and theological faithfulness. *The Blossoming of the Soul* is an excellent resource for understanding how the Word of God speaks to our needs. Mark takes the Scripture and applies it faithfully to the experiences we all face. These devotionals will draw you closer to God and will help you get to a more peaceful place in your own life.
Waylon Bailey, Th.D., President Louisiana Baptist Convention, Pastor First Baptist Church, Covington, LA

Mark, my friend, you may have just distributed your most powerful thoughts to date. This seems to get at the heart of nearly every difficulty we experience as human beings. At least for me this is one of my biggest struggles. Thanks for these thoughts. If this understanding could somehow penetrate the world cultures, it may be possible to experience a level of peace that otherwise seems impossible.
I thank God for you, Mark.
Clint Cheveallier President/CEO [R] Volunteers of America

I have been on a path of spiritual awareness for some time now. Over the last few months of reading Mark's inspirational words I have come to appreciate, accept and forgive MYSELF. His book has allowed me to free my conscious of many of my imperfections. I have purchased my fourth case of books, which I continue to pass along to friends and patients. ALL of the material is pertinent to our everyday lives. I can honestly say that I can feel peaceful and content as I walk with Him in my daily devotional.
Chuck Schof, DDS
Schofnsteen@charter.net

Mark

I found your devotional book to be most rewarding not only in my life, but my family's life. My wife and children and their spouses have all read your book. I can say after reading your book I think it has helped me become a better father, better husband, and better friend to my loved ones. As you know, I gave six of the books as Christmas gifts and I can say they were received quite well.
Wayne Johnson, Pelham, AL

Mark,

I have thoroughly enjoyed your devotionals and the practical applications that bring God's Word to life in everyday situations. They have allowed me to meditate on verses and store them in my heart for use as weapons of warfare or encouragement for the weary. Keep up the great work!
Your sister in Christ,
Kelley Gallagher-Cone
Wilmington, NC

Mark's insight and understanding combine to illuminate the reader's daily path and to help open hearts to the Spirit's leadership so that growth and peace can abound.
<u>The Blossoming of the Soul</u> is a must read for anyone who seeks peace, joy, love and personal growth……a very helpful resource to anyone who would lead.
J. Clint Cheveallier, President/CEO (R)
Volunteers of America, Inc.

I volunteer with St. Vincent de Paul (the charitable arm of the Catholic Church), visiting the poor of my inner-city church neighborhood. Often, a person's "need" goes beyond the "means" of our society, and I struggle for "ways" to help them. I guess *need means ways*, and Mark shows me THE way, guiding me to the "spiritual" reason for my feelings. Mark's devotionals encourage me to trust the Lord and help His people, as I am commanded. Sure enough, the gifts come, just as promised in scripture, and we are blessed by God to help others!
Carol Brill, Counselor
Shreveport, LA

The author's thoughts come from a transparent heart touched by grace and tried in the crucible of life. Within you will find the healing of hope and an increase in faith in the all-mighty presence of God.
These devotionals call for reflection that triggers growth, mercy, and forgiveness.
Tony DeVillier
Covington, LA

The devotionals in *The Blossoming of the Soul* keep me grounded & help me get closer to God. I've known Dr. Mark for a long time & he's the main reason that I AM a Christian. I especially like the use of Dr. Mark's real-life experiences & events to help reveal how a scripture from 2000 years ago can relate to us today; and how we can see God & see opportunities to share God in our everyday lives. I don't have the greatest attention span when it comes to reading, so short devotionals are great for me.
Joshua Boudreaux
Alma, AR

Mark Graham's book, *The Blossoming of the Soul*, has been a tremendous blessing to me. At times when I've needed it most, I've felt the Lord speak to me through this book and bring me hope, inspiration, as well as conviction. It is my strong belief that by reading this book, the reader will be touched and develop a stronger relationship with Christ.
Sincerely,
Kelly Strahan.
Slidell, LA

A Final Word:

I hope these devotionals have been helpful to you in your growth in Christ. If you have comments or feedback of any nature, please contact me via e-mail at:

Marlyn3@bellsouth.net.

My mailing address is:
25 Spruce Dr.
Covington, LA
70433

My website is:
Markgrahamlpc.webs.com

My blog site is marlyn249.blogspot.com

CPSIA information can be obtained at www.ICGtesting.com
Printed in the USA
LVOW05s0801290114

371433LV00002B/2/P